D0597822

CANADA
THE TWENTIETH CENTURY

Fred McFadden
Don Quinlan
Rick Life
Mary Jane Pickup

Fitzhenry & Whiteside

Contents

Canada The Twentieth Century

Revised Edition
© 1993, 1990, 1982 Fitzhenry & Whiteside Limited
Richmond Hill, Ontario

All rights reserved. No part of this publication may be reproduced in any form without permission in writing from the publisher.

Every reasonable effort has been made to find copyright holders of illustrations and quotations. The publishers would be pleased to have errors or omissions brought to their attention.

EDITOR-IN-CHIEF   Robert Read
EDITORS   Frank English, Ian Gillen, Steven Rauchman, Elizabeth Reid, Dorothy Salusbury, Rosalind Sharpe
DESIGNER   Susan Budd
CARTOGRAPHER   Susan Wilkinson

My contribution to this book is dedicated to my parents in gratitude for their inspiration and encouragement. D.Q.

Printed in Canada

Canadian Cataloguing in Publication Data

McFadden, Fred, 1928-
   Canada, the twentieth century

Rev. ed.
For use in schools.
Includes index.
ISBN 0-88902-535-5

1. Canada – History – 20th century.* I. Quinlan, Don, 1947-   . II. Life, Rick, 1953-   . III. Title.

FC600.M34 1989   971.06   C89-094335-4
F1034.2.M34 1989

Introduction

Students frequently ask, "Why do we have to study history?" The study of the history of a country has often been compared to the examination of an individual's memory. You could not make wise decisions today if you did not remember what had happened to you previously. In the same way, citizens cannot make wise decisions unless they know something of their nation's past.

Your study of Canadian history should increase your *knowledge* of some of the important developments in Canada's history. It should make you aware of some of the issues, tensions, questions, and problems that have emerged. You will see the gradual changes in our population, our society, our laws, and our way of life, that have contributed to our present-day Canadian society. You will also see the roles of the many leaders who have both shaped the events of the past, and been shaped by them.

An intelligent citizen needs not only knowledge of the past, but the *skills* to act upon that knowledge. Your course will provide you with the opportunities to develop your abilities to communicate — by writing, by discussing, and by making oral presentations. You will have opportunities to go beyond this text to develop your research skills. You will be required to think, to analyze, to compare, and to evaluate the ideas of the past. You will be asked to participate with your fellow students in cooperative learning activities, to solve problems and, to present solutions.

All of these skills are not only the necessary skills of a student, but also of the successful citizen as well.

We hope that your study of Canada in the twentieth century is interesting, useful, enjoyable, and challenging.

Skills for Studying History

The activities for acquiring these skills will be found on the following pages:

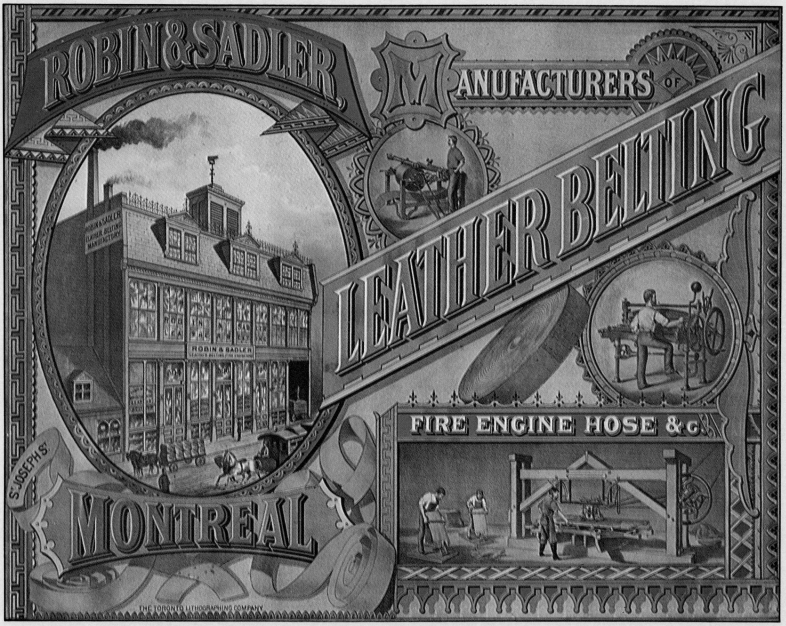

An advertising poster at the turn of the century. Fire hoses are now made of rubber and cotton. Before rubber and modern synthetics such as vinyl became common, leather was used for its strength and flexibility.

"October, a thousand shades of orange and yellow," by Clarence Gagnon. This is one of a series of illustrations that the artist painted between 1928 and 1933 for the famous French-Canadian novel *Maria Chapdelaine*. While ploughs like this were still used on small long-established farms, in the early years of the century machinery was making life easier for farmers all over Canada.

"New Canadians at Gonor, Manitoba," a woodcut by Valentine Fanshawe. Immigrants like this group of Ukrainian Orthodox churchgoers brought their ways of life and religious beliefs to their new country.

The cities grow. *Left:* the Union Bank building under construction at King and Bay Streets, Toronto, 1915, by Owen Staples.
Below: this was the scene a block east at the corner of King and Yonge Streets as seen by Dorothy Stevens in 1916.

The Canadian National Exhibition in the well-established East.

The Dominion Exhibition in the still-growing West.

The Second Battle of Ypres, 22 April to 25 May 1915, by Richard Jack. Canadian soldiers face the first poison gas attack.

"WHY DON'T THEY COME?"

WHY BE A MERE SPECTATOR HERE WHEN YOU SHOULD PLAY A MANS PART IN THE REAL GAME OVERSEAS?

OVERSEAS CANADA BATTALION
148
GRAND ESCVNT AVCTA LABORE

JOIN THE 148TH Battalion.
A.A.MAGEE, LT COL.
Headquarters
197, PEEL ST. MONTREAL.

AFFILIATED WITH McGILL UNIVERSITY CONTINGENT CANADIAN OFFICERS TRAINING CORPS.

J.J SIBBONS LIMITED, MONTREAL-TORONTO.

If You Gave Every Dollar You Own

how little would the sacrifice be compared to theirs. We are not asked to give. We are asked only to *lend*. To lend at good interest secured by the best collateral on earth.

Victory Bonds

THIS SPACE DONATED BY

FASHION CRAFT MFRS.
LIMITED
MONTREAL

If interested tear out this page and place with letters to be answered.

Above: an advertisement in *Men's Wear Review,* November, 1918. During the war, advertisers often gave up their space to promote the war effort.

Left: A World War I recruiting poster. By this time, hockey was already known as a "spectator sport."

"Launching the Seaplane," 1918, by Arthur Lismer. This plane was being launched from a United States naval air station at Eastern Passage, Nova Scotia. "Pusher" propellers were common in this period and are still used on some types of aircraft today.

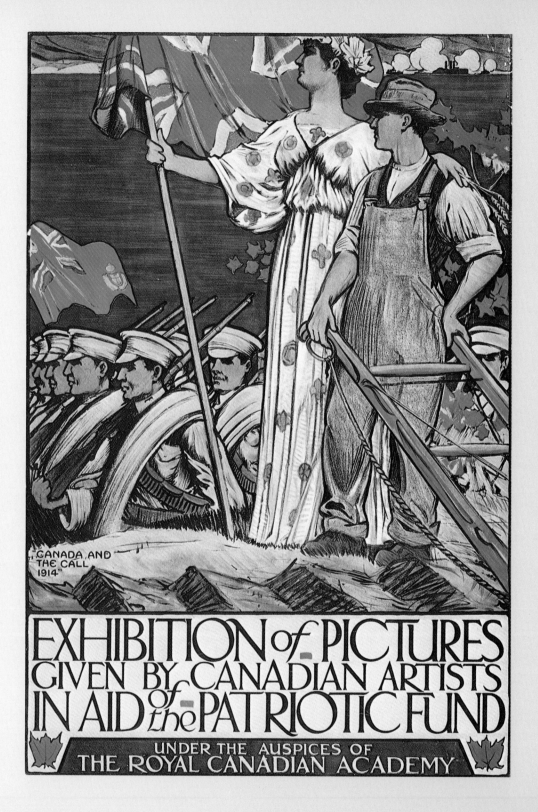

An inspirational poster advertising an art exhibition to aid the war effort, 1914, by J.E.H. MacDonald. People in all walks of life, including artists, wanted to do their part.

In peacetime a Canadian Pacific poster invites Canadians to explore the splendour of their country.

Our Tramways

In these days of rapid transportation—by land, by sea and by air—our tramways continue to be an indispensable factor in the daily lives of the vast majority of our citizens

THOUSANDS upon thousands of people in Canadian cities are entirely dependent upon the tramways for economical and convenient transportation —from home to office and office to home. Indeed, no other means has yet been devised that will permit of masses being moved so effectively or so cheaply.

And as our cities expand—as more and more people are crowded out to "Suburbia" and to country homes—so does the value of the tramway increase.

In their great service to the public, the Street Railway Companies of Canada are supplied with many, many miles of wire and cable by the Northern Electric Company.

Information...

The latest figures available show that there are 60 Electric Railway Systems in Canada, representing a capitalization of $222,852,717, and operating 2,500 miles of track. In 1927 these railways carried no less than 781,398,194 passengers at an average fare of 6½ cents. Including transfer passengers the total was 1,023,771,748.

The Northern Electric Company also makes fire alarm systems, private telephone systems, public address systems, talking moving picture equipment; and distributes well-known brands of electrical supplies and electrical household appliances of all kinds.

Northern Electric
COMPANY LIMITED
A National Electrical Service

252M

"It's Better because it's Canadian"

NO empty patriotic boast is this: "It's better because it's Canadian"!

Facts support it, detail by detail . . . cold, unalterable facts!

Canadian shops and factories and mills are the ones that cling to the proud tradition of an ultra-conscientious industrial age.

Canadian workers in metals and woods and fabrics are known for their superior individual craftsmanship.

From Canadian forests comes lumber, supremely adaptable to lathe, plane and chisel. From Canadian mines come ores of iron, copper and nickel, the like of which no other nation boasts. From Canadian farms come wool and curled hair for use in upholstery, admired the world over.

And out of these Canadian materials are built General Motors of Canada cars . . . by Canadian craftsmen, to Canadian standards, for Canadian use.

They are built to hold the place they have won in public favor under "pine and palm" . . . to maintain the favorable trade balance they have helped to establish for the Dominion . . . to fulfill the demands of varying conditions in every corner of the Empire.

And because they are designed and constructed to scorn the rigors of stern winters, the hardships of corduroy roads in pioneer districts, the ruts of rolling prairies, the rock trail and the jungle path—

—Canadian Cadillac, McLaughlin-Buick, Oakland, Oldsmobile, Pontiac, Chevrolet . . . are better made of better stuff, are better inspected and better serviced . . . are better prepared "for better or for worse" . . . because they are Canadian.

GENERAL MOTORS of CANADA LIMITED, OSHAWA, ONTARIO

CADILLAC CHEVROLET McLAUGHLIN-BUICK
OLDSMOBILE OAKLAND PONTIAC

GENERAL MOTORS of CANADA Limited

G.M. 11-27C

An advertisement in *Mayfair Magazine,* October 1929, emphasizes the importance of public transportation.

An advertisement in *Canadian Automotive Trade,* October 1926, points out the advantages of buying Canadian.

Brisk Business all Winter

Start your customers with "Maple Leaf" Anti-Freeze and "Alco-Meter" Service, and they will keep coming back all Winter.

To keep the slump out of your Winter business you must plan to keep your customers interested in your Winter service. Tell them about "Maple Leaf" Anti-Freeze and "Alco-Meter" Service, and invite them to leave their car with you for a few hours to put it in condition for Winter driving.

Make your customer a flat rate for this work, including the "Maple Leaf" Anti-Freeze, and tell him to come back as often as he wishes, but not less than once a week,

for an "Alco-Meter" test. **This will make a busy place of your garage or service station all winter, and your customers will appreciate the interest you take in their cars.**

Don't stock Anti-Freeze mixtures of unknown ingredients. Beware of Anti-Freeze compounds that are "Chemically Treated," they usually contain Calcium Chloride or other chemicals **that are injurious.** You are not looking after your customer's interest if you ask him to take chances with his car.

MAPLE LEAF ANTI-FREEZE ALCOHOL

FOR SALE BY ALL LEADING WHOLESALERS

If your wholesaler doesn't list MAPLE LEAF, write us direct

Canadian Industrial Alcohol Co., Limited, Montreal

Distributing Warehouses—Montreal, Toronto, Winnipeg, Vancouver

Another advertisement in the same issue of *Canadian Automotive Trade* offers service station operators useful tips on how to keep their business active in winter.

CANADIAN AVIATION *for March, 1929*

A Link With the Future

THE Great Cities of the Future! Lofty towers piercing the clouds . . . the heavens filled with commerce . . . the earth a lowly pedestal from which vast masses of masonry reach up to dim heights . . . stupendous monuments to man's conquest of the air!

And today, as if in anticipation, man is becoming air-minded.

Have you ever thought of all that the aeroplane has done! Have you ever thought that man's dominion of the air is an accomplished fact? Do you realize that the pioneer phase of aviation has passed . . . that the great doors of the Future are flung open to YOU?

The Reid Rambler is a link with the future. Already its Cirrus engine has won world-wide

A certificate of Airworthiness by the Director of Civil Aviation, Ottawa, is supplied with every Rambler.

acclamation by flights from London to Capetown– and back; from England to Australia; by winning the King's Air Cup in 1926 and 1927.

Its great strength is assured by wings and fuselage constructed of metal throughout. Its ease of control, its simplicity of construction, its economy of operation and maintenance . . . these qualities combine to make it the ideal plane for use by Flying Schools, Forest Patrols, Training Schools and . . . by the Private Owner.

The Reid Rambler is everywhere welcomed by men with forward-looking minds—men who bring distant markets infinitely nearer—who accelerate all their business activities by using this perfect expression of sane, swift, safe transportation.

With its simplified dual control, you may quickly learn to fly the Rambler or, if you prefer, employ a pilot. Be in the vanguard of progress. Link up with the Future.

Write today for descriptive literature and prices.

RAMBLER
The Only All-metal Light Aeroplane

Curtiss-Reid Aircraft Company, Limited, Montreal
Airpark - - St. Laurent, Que.

An advertisement for a Canadian-built aircraft in *Canadian Aviation*, March 1929, offers the artist's impression of the world of the future.

Sing a Song of Sixpence

Sing a song of sixpence,
  A pocketful of dough;
What? The timbers weren't safe?
  The inspector didn't know.

Sing a song of sixpence,
  Of dividends to sign,
Families need food you see,
  And that's why miners mine.

Sing a song of sixpence,
  Machines displacing men;
Songs of wealth and poverty,
  "They cut our pay again."

Sing a song of sixpence,
  A paycheck lean and thin,
"Judge, the children needed shoes —
  I took them." "Lock him in!"

Sing a song of labour,
  You men who dig the coal;
Only men who are organized
  Dare say each owns his soul.

Mildred Gaimes in The Nova Scotia Miner,
Glace Bay, Nova Scotia, 10 May 1930.

"Miners' Houses, Glace Bay," 1921,
  by Lawren S. Harris.

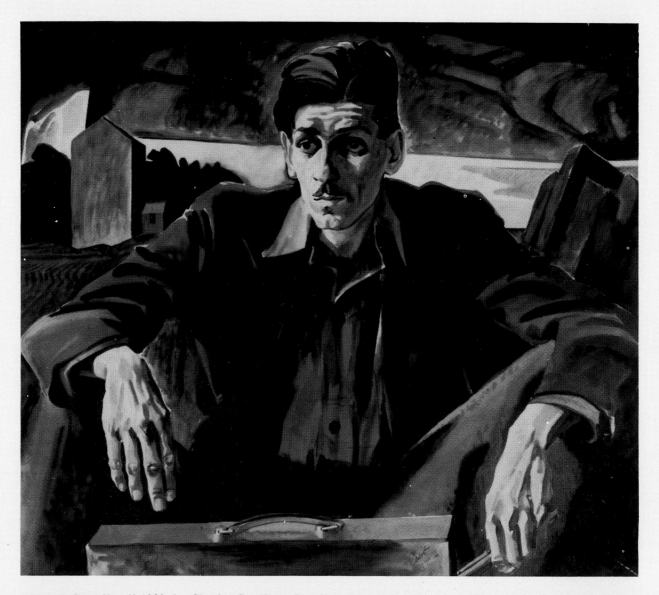

"Young Canadian," 1932, by Charles Comfort. Comfort, born in Scotland in 1900, emigrated to Canada in 1912. After seeing the first exhibit by the Group of Seven in 1919, he decided to be a painter. At the time he was already working for a commercial art firm. Comfort was appointed Director of the National Gallery of Canada (1960), the only artist to hold the position thus far.

"*S.S. Imogene* Leaving for the Icefields," 1973, by David Blackwood. Every year, around mid-March, huge ships would leave for the icefields to hunt seals. Thousands of Newfoundlanders died during the years of sealing, an industry all but finished by the 1930s. The *S.S. Imogene* was one of the last ships to make the trip to the ice. Blackwood's grandfather was the captain.

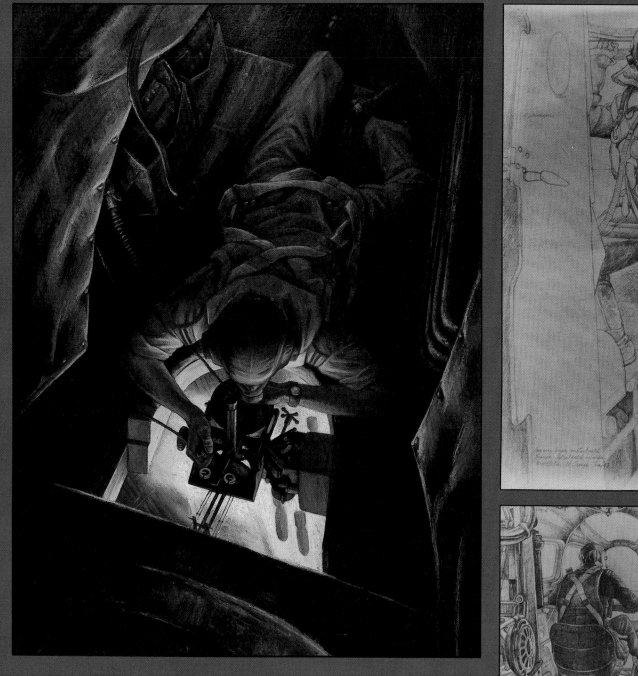

Above: "Bombs Away," 1943, by Paul Goranson showing action on a Halifax bomber. Goranson was an official war artist. At the right are some sketches by Goranson. He made notes on each sketch to remind himself of the colours in case he decided to turn it into a finished painting. *Top:* "Flight engineer;" *Lower Left:* "Plotting the course;" *Lower right:* "Dorsal gunner."

"Tank Advance," 1943, by Lawren P. Harris (son of Lawren S. Harris who painted "Miners' Houses" on pages 16 and 17). Harris was an official war artist sent to cover the Italian campaign. High on a hill above the camouflaged tanks are the ruins of the abbey of Monte Cassino. The monastery had been heavily bombed by the Allies in their attempt to take the hill.

Hockey Hassles

William dreaded arguments, and there always seemed to be arguments in hockey games. A common cause was the lack of a net. For goal posts, two oak poles had been driven into the ground before flooding, but without a net it was often difficult to tell which side of the post the puck had gone. William was a poor skater and preferred not to play on skates, so he was made goalie. This put him right in the center of the arguments. All the boys joined in. Sometimes, one side pretended to be generous and give in on a goal. But usually the side that shouted the loudest and longest won the point.

William made his own shin pads by cutting off old trouser legs and sewing them up and down at regular, spaced intervals. Into these narrow pockets he slipped thin slats from apple boxes and then attached the pads to his legs with rubber sealing rings from his mother's preserve jars.

The goalie's stick was easier to make than those of the offensive players. William had only to nail two layers of support slats on the side of a board. But other boys spent days examining branches and small trees on their way home from school in the hope of finding one suitable for a hockey stick. Some simply nailed two thin boards together neatly at the right angle, and hoped they would not come apart at a crucial moment during the game. A lucky few got real hockey sticks for Christmas. Jesse, the star player, was among the lucky and it was often he who argued with William over which side of the post the puck went.

William Kurelek looking back from 1973 to his prairie childhood during the Depression and World War II.

Left: "New Brunswick Potato Diggers Admiring Autumn Colour," from *Kurelek's Canada* by William Kurelek published in 1978 by Pagurian Press.

Right: "Hockey Hassles," from *A Prairie Boy's Winter* by William Kurelek published in 1973 by Tundra Books.

"Reflections," 1947, by Robert Hurley. A familiar western landscape under a dramatic prairie sky.

"Winter Sun," 1961, by A.J. Casson. In 1982 Casson, one of the artists who joined the Group of Seven, was still living and painting at the age of 84 in Kleinburg, Ontario.

A Haida Legend

One day soon after the great flood the Raven walked upon the beach. The mischievous Raven was bored. In frustration he complained to the empty sky. To his delight, he heard an answering muffled squeak.

Right at his feet was a huge clamshell. He looked more closely and saw that it was full of little creatures.

Well, here was something to break the monotony of his day. But it wasn't much fun as long as the silly things stayed in their shell. So he leaned his great head close, and used his bell-like crooning voice to coax them to come out and play in the wonderful new shining world. First one, then another of the shell dwellers clambered out as curiosity overcame caution. Very strange creatures they were: two legged like the Raven, but there the resemblance ended. No glossy feathers, no thrusting beak; instead of strong wings, thin sticklike arms — these were the original Haidas, the first humans.

For a long time the Raven amused himself with his new playthings. He watched as they explored their new world. Sometimes they helped each other in new discoveries. As often they squabbled over some novelty they found on the beach. He taught them clever tricks at which they were very adept.

The descendents of these children of the coast grew to challenge the stormy North Pacific and wrest from it a rich livelihood. They built the strong, beautiful homes of the Haidas. They decorated them with powerful carvings that told the stories of the great families and the gallant beasts and monsters that shaped their world. For many generations they grew and flourished, built and created, fought and destroyed, and lived according to the changing seasons and the unchanging rituals.

It's nearly over now. Most of the villages are in ruins. The people who remain are changed. The sea has lost much of its richness. Great areas of the land itself lie in waste. Perhaps it's time the Raven found a way to start again.

as retold by Bill Reid

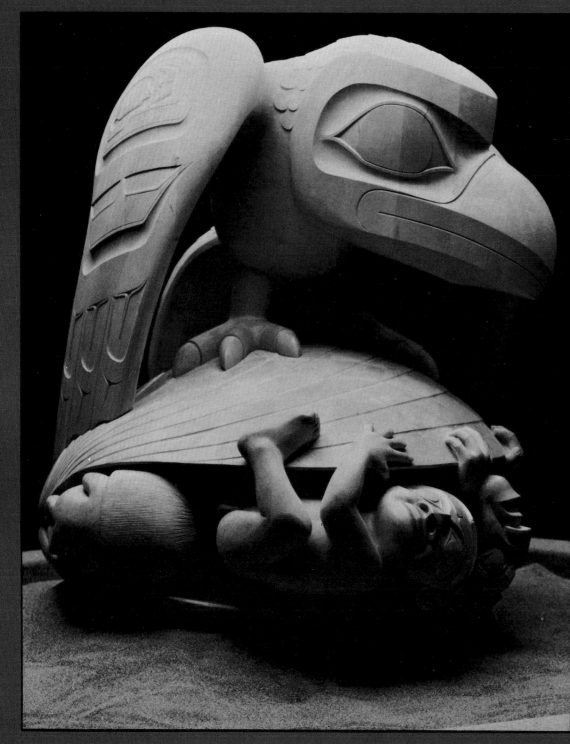

"The Raven and the First Humans" by Bill Reid.

"Mother Earth and her Children." Cree artist Carl Ray has illustrated a legend common to many native peoples in North America as far west as the prairies.

An Iroquois Legend

Once long ago a Sky Woman fell through a hole in the sky to the wide waste of waters below. Two swans saw her falling and caught her on their backs.

"What shall we do with this Sky Woman?" asked one of the swans. "We cannot hold her up forever."

"We must call a meeting," said the other.

The water animals came together to decide what to do. Big Turtle said, "If someone will dive down and bring up some earth from below, I will hold the earth on my back. Then we shall have land for the Sky Woman to live on."

So the water animals took turns in diving. First the muskrat tried. When he came up, Big Turtle looked into his mouth but could find no earth. Then the beaver made a deep dive and came up. He too, had no earth in his mouth. Others tried, but none brought up any earth.

Finally, Little Toad tried. He stayed under the water a long time. When at last he came up his mouth was full of earth. The animals spread the earth over Big Turtle's back.

Then a strange thing happened. The amount of earth began to grow until Big Turtle was holding a whole island on his back. The Sky Woman stepped off the swans' backs and started to make it her home.

The island continued to grow until it was as large as all of North America. Sometimes, they say, Big Turtle grows weary and moves his back to shift the load. Then the earth shakes. People cry: "Big Turtle is moving!"

as retold by Marius Barbeau

Left: "Trans-Canada, No. 1," by Arthur Horsfall. This dreamlike vision is inspired by the idea of the highway crossing all obstacles in its path.

Above: "Light House and Schooners," by Joseph Norris. In this vivid yet "primitive" approach to art, the frame is part of the picture.

Still from *The Man Who Planted Trees*, an animated film by Frédéric Back, produced by Société Radio-Canada. Illustration and narrative combine to tell an absorbing story about a man who changed an arid landscape into a thriving and beautiful scene by planting trees. *The Man Who Planted Trees* has won numerous international awards, including an Oscar for Best Animated Short Film in 1987.

"The Migration," 1964, by Joe Talirunili,
an Inuit artist from Povungnituk in northern
Quebec. The sculpture is in stone and ivory.

A nation's postage stamps reflect the ideas, places, and stories important to its people. Canada's first stamp, the ''threepenny beaver'' was designed by Sandford Fleming. Since that time the post office has worked with Canadian artists to produce some of the world's most interesting stamps.

Developing Skills in History

Your study of history involves not just the learning of certain information. Like most of your courses, it should also involve preparing you for your life as a citizen. As a citizen, you will be required to have certain skills.

Whether you are a member of your union, run your own business, are a nurse or a police officer or move into one of the professions, to be a successful citizen you will have to have certain skills:

a) Ability to **process** information —
You must be able to read newspapers, magazines, books, and training manuals, or to understand movies, videos, or other forms of graphic visual presentation. You must then be able to select the key ideas from the material, and record it in a meaningful way.

b) Ability to **think and organize** —
You will have to be able to think about information, to analyze it, to make comparisons, and to assess its value or importance.

c) Ability to **communicate** in writing and orally —
You will be expected to express your ideas in writing in paragraph form so that others can understand you. You will also be expected to develop more complex ideas into longer reports. Sometimes you will be expected to explain your ideas to others in a group orally or in a more formal report.

d) Ability to **work cooperatively** with others —
Living in a democracy requires that we work cooperatively with others — informally in small groups or in larger organizations.

The skills which you will be learning in your course this year then, are not just the academic skills of a history student; they are life skills which most of you will need and use for the rest of your lives.

Recording Information

Authors express their ideas in sentence and paragraph form. However, for you to remember and understand these ideas you must:
a) *SELECT* the key facts or ideas
b) *RECORD* these ideas in simple point form

Recording Your Ideas in Note Form

YOUR TASK

1. On your note paper put an appropriate HEADING at the top.
2. Draw a RULE, approximately 6 cm from the left side of the page. Record all of your notes in point form to the RIGHT side of this rule.
3. Summarize each idea in a few words and record them to the right of the rule in POINT FORM.
4. Leave at least a one-line SPACE after each note.
5. Your point form summary does not have to record *all* of the information. Select the MOST IMPORTANT INFORMATION.
6. The space to the LEFT of the rule can be used:
   — to add additional information
   — to number and summarize each point in a KEY WORD.

Sample Note (See page 39)

FREE LAND IN THE 1890s
1. Free land in U.S. already filled
2. Clifford Sifton — 1896 — Minister of Immigration
3. Encouraged immigration to the Canadian West
4. Wanted settlers from the U.S.
5. Encouraged immigrants from all over Europe
6. Flood of new immigrants opened the West, and changed Canada

Chapter One

A New Century
ADVANCE ORGANIZER

1

At the turn of the century Canada was mainly a rural society. Most people lived by farming, logging, or working in construction. The local community was the centre of most activities. Baseball and hockey games, songfests and church get-togethers were major social events.

Although the horse and buggy was still the most common method of transportation, the automobile was slowly becoming known as a new, freakish alternative. No one suspected the effects that this strange invention was to have on the new century.

2

In 1896 the minister of immigration put out a call for settlers to break new land in the Canadian West. This attracted, for the first time, many immigrants from the southern and eastern countries of Europe. Many of these pioneer families became wheat farmers. Farming methods were changing: horse-drawn and steam-powered machinery was slowly replacing the rake and sickle.

3

Industry was finding new uses for Canada's natural resources. New methods of processing them were also being developed. Timber supplied building materials and pulp and paper. Minerals such as copper, iron and nickel were used in construction and in machine equipment. Minerals and timber both found wide use in the railway building boom. Railway expansion continued until the coming of World War I in 1914.

Word List

alliance   immigrant   province
compromise   industry   reciprocity
economy   merger   resource
empire   pioneer   union

4

Factories and stores were thriving. Cities grew. People found jobs in construction and manufacturing. These jobs were usually poorly paid. Most cities became places of startling contrast. Factory and store owners lived in large comfortable houses. Their employees were usually forced to live in slum districts. To protect themselves from poor wages and working conditions, the workers banded together to form and strengthen their unions.

5

Most French Canadians were opposed to involvement in the Boer War, and were against helping to strengthen Britain's navy. English Canadians sided with Britain. The country was divided. Prime Minister Laurier sought compromises to both issues.

6

Many Canadians wanted freer trade with the United States. Competition would lower prices. Big business was against this. The Liberals wanted freer trade; opposition leader Robert Borden sided with business. The Conservatives defeated Laurier in the 1911 election.

7

Women were pressing for the right to vote. The most active groups were on the Prairies, where they were supported by farmers' organizations. Nellie McClung was a key figure in the struggle in both Manitoba and Alberta. In 1916 Manitoba granted the vote to women. Other provinces soon followed. Only Quebec refused women the vote until 1940.

Canadians at the Turn of the Century

A visit to Toronto Island might include a game at the stadium and stroll past the hotels to picnic on the beach.

What was life like in 1900? Try to place yourself back in time. Your life would have been quite different.

Many young people left school early. In the country, they were needed on the farm. In the city, their wages helped to pay for the family's food and rent. The work was heavy and the working hours long.

A Rural Society

Most people in Canada lived on farms. Halifax, Montreal, and Toronto were major cities, but much smaller than today. The railway made Winnipeg the gateway to the west. Vancouver was the boomtown of the West Coast. Regina, Calgary, and Edmonton were still pioneer cities.

Most still earned their living by the sweat of their brows. Farming was the main industry. Others worked in logging camps to provide lumber for the growing cities, the railways, and the treeless prairies. Still others worked in construction—on the rapidly expanding railways or on the roads, sewers, and buildings of the new cities. Women worked in factories, as servants for the rich, as teachers and store clerks, and on their own farms and homes.

Living close to home

The automobile was a strange sight on the roads of 1900. Most people depended on the horse and buggy for travel. Long journeys were made by train. People spent their lives close to home and their interest was centred on the local community. Life revolved round the town band, or the local baseball or hockey team.

The age of paid professional singers, comedians, or sports stars was still to come. There was no radio or television to tell of the outside world. Even newspapers were not common in many homes. The church played a great part in people's lives. They looked forward to Sunday, the day of rest. In rural areas, going to church gave an opportunity to meet neighbours and catch up on local news and gossip. Most people provided their own entertainment. A singsong round the family piano or dancing to a treasured violin brought from the old country—this was the high point of a family gathering. A night out meant watching local talent in a play or a concert at the church hall.

Boy Scout parade, Calgary, 1910. Boy Scouts were organized throughout the British Empire in 1908. Girl Guides started two years later.

List at least 10 ways in which living in Canada in 1900 was different from today.
Select 3 ways in which life was better in 1900 and 3 ways in which it is better today. Explain your reasons.

Pick-up hockey, Saskatchewan.

A New Century

The 1800s had been a peaceful period — a period of gradual change. In 1900 most Canadians expected that the twentieth century would continue in that way. But the years ahead would be stormy and fast-changing.

Prime Minister Wilfrid Laurier said: "The nineteenth century was the century of the United States. The twentieth century belongs to Canada." Perhaps this century has not developed quite as he expected. Canada has taken part in two world wars. At other times Canadian statesmen have helped to keep world peace. There have been periods of prosperity but also times of hardship. The English and French cultures Laurier knew have grown and changed. Sometimes they have worked together. Sometimes they have seemed to be at each other's throats. Native Indians and Inuit have spoken up for their rights in their own land. Immigrants from all over the world have brought new cultures and traditions. Most Canadians lived in the country in 1900. Now most live in cities. Canada at the end of the twentieth century is a very different place from the Canada Laurier knew.

Tom Longboat (Cogwagee, Cyclone Jack)

1887 — born on the Six Nations Reserve, Brantford, Ontario.
1900 — ran away from school. Started to work. Raced at local town field days.
1905 — came second in Victoria Day 8-km race at Caledonia. Decided to train seriously for distance running.
1906 — ran and won 4 spectacular races. Toronto *Globe* headline: "Longboat Always Wins."
1907 — won 40-km Boston Marathon in record time. Became Canadian hero, especially in southern Ontario.
1908 — ran in Olympics in London but collapsed after 32 km. Turned professional. Within 2 months ran and won 3 pro marathons. Was famous world-wide, and an inspiration for other Indian kids.
1909 — his contract sold twice "like a racehorse to make money." Lost some races. Papers blamed "Indian laziness" and said he was drinking too much. Was actually training at his own pace and had the odd friendly drink but was upset by contract problems.
1911 — bought contract and organized races himself.
1912 — broke his own record for 25.8 km twice.
1916 — served in army in France as dispatch runner.
1917 — competed and won in regimental games in France.
1919 — won 5-km race in "Grand Army of Canada Sports Show" at Toronto Island Stadium. Public had lost interest in pro running. Got farm work in Alberta. Wanted to raise family near home. Worked in factories in Toronto, Hamilton, and Buffalo.
1926 — got job with Toronto streets department.
1927 — at age 40, won 6.5-km race at Hamilton.
1945 — retired from streets dept. to Six Nations Reserve.
1949 — died and buried there according to longhouse tradition.

Settling the West

Until 1896 most immigrants to Canada had come from France or the British Isles. In Quebec, most of the people were descendants of French settlers who had come to Canada 300 years before. In the other provinces, most were English, Scottish, or Irish. There were a few German settlements such as Lunenburg, Nova Scotia, and Berlin, Ontario (now Kitchener). The original native peoples were scattered across the country. Some were in reserves or in the distant lands of the North. Others had moved into the cities.

During the 1800s many people had emigrated from Europe. Most of them had gone to "the great melting pot," the United States. The United States was an independent country. It had no ties to Britain. People from other parts of Europe could feel welcome.

Not having a yoke of oxen to break the heavy soil, Doukhobor women pull the plough in this pioneer community near Yorkton, Saskatchewan.

"Without animals, nothing can be done. We are starting a new village over there. We must let the people for the new village have horses to haul logs to build homes and barns before winter. That means no rest for the animals — poor things. So to give them some rest, we humans hitch ourselves to the ploughs."

Adapted from Salt of the Earth *by Heather Robinson*

Where did most immigrants come from before the 1890s?
What was Sifton's new immigration policy? How did it change the Canadian population and culture?
Compare immigration policy today with the policy in 1900.

1900 1910 1920 1930 1940 1950 1960 1970 1980 1990 2000

Immigration could be a lonely and frightening experience. This family waits outside the CPR station in Winnipeg.

Free Land

But now the free land in the United States had been filled. In Canada, the government wanted settlers to open up the Prairies. Clifford Sifton became the minister in charge of immigration in 1896. He advertised Canadian free land throughout the United States. He also encouraged settlers to come from all over Europe. He knew that only strong, healthy people could survive in the West. There they would have to break new soil, put up farm buildings, and make it through the tough Canadian winter.

Sifton's policies started a flood of immigration to the Canadian West. The outbreak of World War I brought this to an abrupt halt. Yet Canada had been changed forever. Alongside the Bourassas, Cartiers, and Lafleurs; the O'Keefes, Carrs, and Macdonalds; people with names like Richler, Diefenbaker, Mazankowski, Schreyer, and Ghiz would take their places as citizens and leaders of Canada.

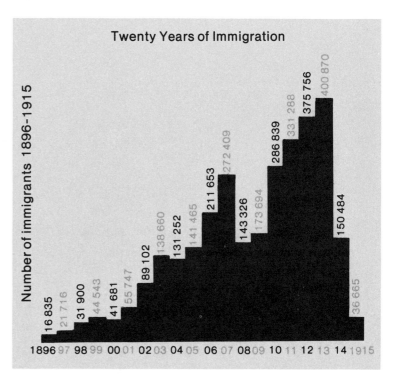

Twenty Years of Immigration

Number of immigrants 1896–1915

16 835 — 1896
21 716 — 97
31 900 — 98
44 543 — 99
41 681 — 00
55 747 — 01
89 102 — 02
138 660 — 03
131 252 — 04
141 465 — 05
211 653 — 06
272 409 — 07
143 326 — 08
173 694 — 09
286 839 — 10
331 288 — 11
375 756 — 12
400 870 — 13
150 484 — 14
36 665 — 1915

Settlers and their goods leave Edmonton for Lloydminster.

The New Immigrants

I think a sturdy peasant in a sheepskin coat, born on the soil, whose forefathers have been farmers for ten generations, with a stout wife and a half-dozen children is good quality.

Clifford Sifton

An English Immigrant

When I left school I went to Oxford University, but I had no training for a job. So I decided to emigrate to Canada. My uncle gave me $200 to help get me started.

I worked on a farm near Regina, and then another near Saskatoon. After 18 months, I had saved $1500. I was a wealthy young man.

I bought a horse and buggy and spent a month driving around looking for land. I found a good farm of 128 ha. The land company wanted $12.50 a hectare. I put $500 down. I hired a man to help me with the ploughing. As he turned that land over, those furrows rolled out like the waves of the sea.

I had about 60 ha broken and ready for spring. That winter I worked for a lumber yard in Regina. In spring I moved onto my farm with a seeder and four good horses. I brought some lumber, a keg of nails, and tarpaper, to build a shack. By this time I was pretty deep in debt but I knew what I was doing. I got that new Marquis wheat that everyone was talking about. That was the finest wheat I've ever seen. Hard and wonderful for milling and it made the finest bread in the world.

When I harvested that crop in October, I had enough money to pay off the land company, enough to buy my farm implements, enough to build a decent house and a barn, and enough to think that I was king of the world. And I was.

Adapted from The Pioneer Years *by Barry Broadfoot*

Students at Plum Ridge School, Manitoba, were mainly the children of Ukrainian settlers. Schools tried to teach good citizenship and loyalty to the British Empire. For many immigrant children, learning the customs and language of their new homeland was difficult and confusing.

Russian Jewish immigrants at Quebec City, 1911. Many groups of immigrants came to Canada to practise their religion freely.

By 1905 there were enough settlers in the West that two new provinces — Saskatchewan and Alberta — were created.

While immigrants from Europe were breaking new soil on the Prairies, Chinese, Japanese, and Indians were coming across the Pacific to work in the fisheries, mines, and lumber camps of British Columbia. The Asians were often resented by white Canadians. The government developed immigration rules that would make it difficult for Asians to enter Canada.

FOCUS

Imagine you are an immigrant to Canada in 1900 and write a letter to your parents describing life in your new homeland. Compare the problems faced by immigrants in 1900 to the problems faced by immigrants today.

Polish Immigrants

About 1905 the first Polish immigrants came to Manitoba. Up until then we'd had people from Ontario, and from the States, England, Germany, and Scandinavia.

At the immigration hall in Winnipeg they'd send them out to look at the land that was left. This was usually swampy or covered with poplar, but they usually took it. 64 ha of free land looked pretty good when all you needed was $10.00 for the registration fee. A peasant had about 2 ha in Poland or Russia if he had anything at all. But they worked hard and they learned. If you could get one for a hired hand, you were lucky.

At first they lived with their animals. This used to shock some of the oldtimers. The houses were small. They cut poles out of the bush and laid them one on top of the other for the walls. They laid smaller poles side by side for the roof. They plastered the walls with a guck of straw and mud and lime. The roof had straw on it and then a thick layer of dirt. You'd be surprised how cozy they were.

They liked music. They made their own violins. You could buy a violin at Eaton's for $2-5 but they'd spend a whole winter working on one. When they started coming to our dances, they could sure make the night lively.

When they started coming to our July 1 picnics, their children were the best behaved kids on the lot. One word from mother, and that was it.

Many of the Polish kids never went to school. A whole generation of those kids must have grown up never knowing how to read or write or do their sums. That's about all education was in those days anyway — the three Rs with some history and geography thrown in. If you could find Africa on the map you passed geography.

However, they finally realized the importance of education. One of us could still leave school at grade 8 and go into the city and make good. But if you had a "ski" or a "chuck" on the end of your name and you went to the city, you were on the end of a pick and shovel for the rest of your days. So they wanted the best school, the best teacher, the best of everything for their children.

Adapted from The Pioneer Years *by Barry Broadfoot*

Dr. Barnardo's orphans, Saint John, N.B. Between 1870 and 1935 over 80 000 children came to Canada from orphanages in England. They were sent to work in people's homes and on farms. In return for their labour they were to receive room and board and religious and moral instruction. Inspectors were supposed to check the conditions the children lived in. But it was often a long time between inspections, and some children were overworked and badly treated. On the other hand, others remember their Canadian "families" with affection and gratitude.

Within the past ten years, a nation has been born. We used to describe ourselves as English, Irish, Scotch, and French. Today our children boast they are Canadians, and the latest arrivals from Austria and Russia help to swell the chorus, "The Maple Leaf Forever."

Adapted from Strangers Within our Gates *,1909*

The Land

Most people in Canada lived on farms. Farming families tried to raise as much of their own food as possible. This meant they had a cow or two, some chickens, and perhaps a pig. They grew their own vegetables. But most of the farm was used to make money.

On the Prairies, the "cash crop" was wheat. In Ontario and Quebec, dairy farming was most common. Prince Edward Island farmers found their clay soil grew good potatoes. Fruit orchards did well in sheltered areas—the Annapolis Valley in Nova Scotia, the Niagara region of Ontario, and the Okanagan Valley in British Columbia. When the cash crop was sold, farmers could buy things they could not grow.

A new grain elevator at Estevan, Saskatchewan.

Manpower, horsepower, and steampower bring in the harvest, Alberta, 1907.

Mechanized Farming

By 1900 modern inventions were making farm work easier. Horse-drawn mowers and binders were replacing sickles and rakes. There were even steam-powered tractors to break up the soil and plough the land. Many farmers could not afford to own these machines. They rented them instead. Sometimes they hired a crew of workers with the machines. Sometimes groups of neighbours got together. They used the machines on each farmer's fields in turn.

There was still plenty of physical work to be done. Animals had to be cared for, eggs gathered, water hauled, firewood chopped and split.

Farming, especially wheat farming, was a booming business for Canada. The country advertised the Prairies as "the bread basket of the world" and "the granary of the empire."

How were modern inventions changing farming in the 1900s? Compare the life of a farm boy in 1900 to the life of most young Canadians today.

Why was the Women's Institute useful and important?

 **Art Gallery page 5**

Adelaide Hunter Hoodless

1857 — born on farm in Brant County, Ontario.

1881 — married John Hoodless. They had 5 children.

1889 — youngest child died from drinking impure milk. As a result, she decided to help women learn proper sanitation, child care, and home management.

1890s — persuaded school boards to start courses in "domestic science" for girls and "manual training" for boys. Helped found a national YWCA, the National Council of Women, the Victorian Order of Nurses.

1897 — Made a speech to Farmers' Institute at Stoney Creek, Ont. Suggested rural women needed an organization to encourage good home management. The first Women's Institute was formed. The idea soon spread to other rural communities across the country.

1903 — Persuaded William Macdonald, a tobacco millionaire, to found the Macdonald Institute (now part of University of Guelph) to teach domestic science.

1905 — Macdonald founded Macdonald College (now part of McGill University, Montreal).

1910 — Hoodless died while lecturing in Toronto.

1915 — Margaret Watt who had worked in Women's Institutes in B.C. started one at her new home in England.

1933 — Watt elected first president of Federated Countrywomen of the World in Stockholm, Sweden. Today there are Women's Institutes in 108 countries. In Canada there are 3350 branches with 72 000 members.

We sure knew how to work. We were doing things around the yard before we were 5 or 6. I hunted up brooding hens and got them back to the henhouse. I went for the cows. I handed dad things when he was fixing a piece of machinery, oiling it, or replacing a part he'd fixed. In the summer I'd load up my wagon with a jar of water and one of lemonade, and sandwiches and cookies. I'd take afternoon lunch to the field where the men were working.

When I was 7, I milked my one cow, and then it got to be two cows. By the time I was 9, I was doing a man's job with the cows.

When I was 11, I handled the team of four horses for ploughing. Other times, I helped load the hay on the wagon.

If you were a boy, by the time you were twelve, you'd pretty well given up the business of school. There didn't seem to be much sense to going any more. Each year you stayed away, the harder it got to go. What fifteen-year-old fellow wanted to sit with a bunch of eleven-year-olds? I don't think that there were any laws about when a fellow had to go to school or when he didn't. A lot of fellows never went beyond the third or fourth grade. I got to the sixth and I could read and write and do arithmetic. Usually a fellow married a girl who had gone through school. If it came to doing figures, she could do it. A lot of those farm wives did all the figuring, and books in those days.

Adapted from The Pioneer Years *by Barry Broadfoot*

BUY THIS EATON DISC DRILL 63⁰⁰

Forests and Mines

As wagons with wheels could not move freely in the forests, logs were usually brought out on sleds during the winter. Four horses were needed for a load like this.

When Europeans first came to Canada, Quebec, Ontario, and the Maritimes were covered with white pine forests. Lumbering was big business. Timber was needed in Europe. By 1900 people in the United States wanted to buy Canadian timber as their own forests were largely used up. Canadian cities and towns also needed more and more timber. Farmers on the Prairies needed timber to build their homes and barns. The railway building boom created a demand for wooden trestles and ties. The spread of electricity and the telephone required utility poles. Being a lumberjack was a good way to make a living.

As time went on, it became harder to find the big trees that produced the best timber. They had already been cut. Lumberjacks began to move west to the cedar and Douglas fir forests of British Columbia. The timber they cut was sold to the Prairie provinces, the United States, and Asia.

In the East, the end of the big trees was not the end of the forest industry. The trees that were left were ideal for making pulp and paper. Newspapers all over the world were requiring more and more paper. Canadian forest companies moved in to supply this need.

Unfortunately, little was done to conserve the forests. When trees were cut, new ones were not planted. Waste branches and cuttings were left in the bush where they created a fire hazard.

Forest products are Canada's largest industry. Only later did Canadians realize that forests have to be looked after if this valuable resource is to survive.

Mining

When people thought of the "new world" 400 years ago, they thought of new sources of gold and riches. The lure of gold led to two gold rushes in Canada. In

A paper mill, Ottawa, 1908.

FOCUS Why was *a)* pulp and paper in eastern Canada, *b)* gold on the Cariboo and Klondike, *c)* oil at Turner Valley important to the growth and development of Canada?
How important are pulp and paper, gold, and oil to Canada today?

1900 1910 1920 1930 1940 1950 1960 1970 1980 1990 2000

Frontier College provided evening classes to help mining, railway, and lumber workers get an education. This class in "civics" was for immigrant miners from Scandinavia working in a newly opened nickel mine near Sudbury.

Alberta's first oil well, Turner Valley, 1914. The first oil discoveries in Canada were made at Petrolia and Oil Springs, Ontario, in the 1850s.

the 1860s the Cariboo gold rush took place in British Columbia. In 1898 would-be miners swarmed into the Klondike in the Yukon.

Coal, copper, iron, and nickel were less glamorous than gold, but they were far more useful. By 1900 industries all over the world needed minerals. New ways of processing minerals were being developed, and new uses found for them.

The rocky Canadian Shield north of the settled areas of the country proved to hold new wealth. In earlier days *coureurs de bois* had ranged the forests of the shield for furs. Lumberjacks felled its mighty trees. Now prospectors looked under the forest floor for minerals. New mining towns sprang up overnight, especially in northern Ontario. In other parts of the country too — Nova Scotia, and southern British Columbia — the development of our mineral wealth increased.

City Life

Today Canada is an urban society. Over three quarters of Canadians live in cities. In 1900 things were very different. More than half the people lived on farms. One quarter lived in small villages and towns. Less than a quarter lived in cities.

Immigrants were pouring into Canada. Most wanted to go to the rich farmlands of the West. Many never got there. They were too poor to buy the equipment and supplies they would need to set up a farm. They found jobs in the lumber camps and the mines. They helped build the new railways. They also came to the cities looking for work in the factories.

Population Statistics

	1901	1911		1901	1911
Halifax	40 000	47 000	Hamilton	53 000	82 000
Saint John	41 000	43 000	Winnipeg	42 000	140 000
Quebec	70 000	80 000	Regina	2 200	30 000
Montreal	330 000	490 000	Saskatoon	113	12 000
Ottawa	60 000	87 000	Edmonton	4 200	30 000
Toronto	210 000	380 000	Calgary	4 400	44 000
			Vancouver	30 000	120 000

Children follow the ice wagon on a hot summer day hoping for a chip of ice to suck — a turn-of-the-century popsicle!

The Cities Grow

Canadian manufacturers were doing well. They made tractors and threshing machines for the new farms. They built buggies, bicycles, and automobiles. Steel mills turned out nails, wire, pots and pans, railway tracks, locomotives. Flour, canned meats and vegetables, brooms, stoves—all the things people needed for everyday life—came out of the factories.

There were plenty of jobs. As well as immigrants, people who had grown up on farms and in small towns moved to the cities to make some money.

Cities across the country grew by leaps and bounds. Still more jobs were created: digging sewers, paving streets, building streetcar lines. Even people with few skills and little knowledge of English or French could usually find some sort of work.

The grocery store.

How did Canadian cities change in the early 1900s?
Why did some cities grow faster than others?
List at least 5 differences between the lives of middle class people and working class people in the early 1900s?

Art Gallery page 7

Two kinds of homes.

Contrasts

Factory and store owners lived in large beautiful houses on tree-lined streets. The houses and grounds were kept clean and tidy by armies of servants. Most city dwellers weren't so fortunate.

The supply of housing did not keep up with the numbers of people coming into the cities. Most people were very poorly paid. They could not afford decent homes even if they were available. Many downtown areas became "instant slums." Immigrant families of ten lived in one run-down room. Water was not always safe to drink. There was nowhere for children to play except the street.

City councils and concerned citizens knew these conditions were bad, but they didn't know what to do about it. The idea of planning the growth of cities to avoid problems was still very new. They did their best. They provided electric lights and a clean water supply. Then established public health clinics. They improved public transportation. They set up parks and playgrounds so people could relax and play in pleasant surroundings.

The Toronto Playground System — early 1900s

29 soccer fields	8 bowling greens
9 rugby fields	2 croquet grounds
98 tennis courts	2 quoit grounds
3 lacrosse fields	33 hockey cushions
10 cricket creases	39 skating rinks and toboggan slides

Immigrant children found that where you came from didn't matter on the playground.

Recording Information in Paragraph Form

One of the characteristics of a successful citizen is the ability to express one's ideas clearly in sentence and paragraph form. Following are some suggestions to help you to develop the *skill* of paragraph writing. After you have learned this skill, you can adapt the pattern to more creative paragraph writing. (Remember: even Wayne Gretzky had to learn his father's skating drills before he became capable of the skills of a professional hockey player.)

Writing a Paragraph

Writing a paragraph is one of the first building blocks in developing the skills of a writer.

A paragraph is a group of sentences about one topic. But there is a pattern to writing a paragraph.

Each paragraph should include:

a) *Introduction* or main idea in opening or topic sentence

b) *Body of Paragraph* — several statements which explain or support the opening sentence

c) *Conclusion* — a statement suggesting the importance of the paragraph

Sample Paragraph

New Inventions of the 1920's
New inventions improved the lives of most people in the 1920s. — INTRODUCTION

New electrical appliances cut down on some of the hard work of running the house. The radio permitted people to listen to their favourite entertainers or "Hockey Night in Canada." Probably the most important invention was the automobile. The assembly line, developed by Henry Ford, made it possible for many people to afford to buy a new Model-T car. — BODY OF THE PARAGRAPH: SUPPORTING STATEMENTS

These new inventions made life easier and more enjoyable than it was in the difficult times before World War II. — CONCLUSION

When you write a paragraph, it should follow this pattern.

YOUR TASK

1. Following is an introductory sentence for your paragraph:

    In the election of 1911, the Conservatives were opposed to free trade.

    Write a paragraph which will include:
    a) the introductory sentence;
    b) three or four supporting statements;
    c) a concluding sentence stating what you think was the importance of the issue.

2. Write at least *one other* paragraph, using one of the following sentences as your introductory sentence:

    — Lumbering was a very important industry in the early 1900s. (page 44)
    — Living in the city in the early 1900s had many disadvantages. (page 47)
    — Electricity changed the way of life in the cities in the early 1900s. (page 50)

3. Write a paragraph on one of the following topics. By now, you should be able to provide your own introductory sentence.

    — The auto industry in Canada (page 53)
    — Nellie McClung (page 53)

- Liberal (or Conservative) policy in the 1911 election (page 59)
- Causes of the Winnipeg General Strike (page 96)
- Agnes McPhail (page 98)
- Changes in the role of women in the 1920s (page 100)

Creative Writing

Many successful history writers use their imaginations to attempt to re-create past events. Their work is based on extensive research. However, after collecting as much information as possible, they use their imagination to re-create the past events in as realistic and interesting a manner as possible.

Some examples of creative writing are *diaries, letters,* and *journals.* These record facts but also provide writers with an opportunity to use their imagination. Remember, you must research the information as accurately as possible before writing in a creative manner.

YOUR TASK

After using your text and other sources, write one of the following:

a) a letter in 1900, explaining why you think that the twentieth century may "belong to Canada";

b) a letter from an immigrant to Canada in the 1900s to a relative back in Europe, describing life in Canada;

c) a letter from a city dweller (rich or poor) in the 1900s describing life in the city;

d) or another letter on your choice of topic.

Making a Biographical Card

One aspect of the study of history is the study of the *people* who helped to shape history. The study of *biographies* in history is one of the most interesting aspects of the study of history. Throughout your book, you will find many brief summaries, or "bio-cards", of the lives of some important people in our history (e.g., Tom Longboat, page 37; Adelaide Hunter Hoodless, page 43; Henri Bourassa, page 55; Nellie McClung, page 59).

YOUR TASK

1. Do further research on *one* of the following in the *Canadian Encyclopedia,* the *Dictionary of Canadian Biography*, etc.:
   - Wilfrid Laurier
   - Timothy Eaton
   - Emily Murphy
   - Sam McLaughlin
   - Foster Hewitt
   - or another Canadian
2. While doing your research, record your information in point form.
3. After you have completed your research, record the information using some of the following organizers (you may suggest others):
   - DATE AND LOCATION OF BIRTH
   - EARLY CHILDHOOD, FAMILY LIFE, EDUCATION
   - ACHIEVEMENTS
   - IDEAS
   - IMPORTANCE
4. Record the information in point form in no more than one page.

Industry and Unions

In the first 10 years of the twentieth century the output of Canadian industry more than doubled. In some areas, such as iron and steel, Canadians were producing 5 times as much in 1910 as they had in 1900.

Value of Production (in thousands of dollars)	1900	1910
Tobacco	8 000	13 000
Boots and shoes	7 500	16 000
Clothes	20 000	44 000
Furniture	4 300	8 000
Farm machinery	5 000	11 000
Iron and steel	3 100	15 000
Automobiles	—	2 500
Electric light and power	2 000	13 000

Electricity

One of the things that made this growth possible was electricity. From 1880 Canadian rivers and waterfalls were dammed to produce electric power. Electric motors replaced the horses that used to draw city streetcars. Electric lights made streets and homes brighter. Electric appliances—vacuum cleaners, irons—soon appeared, making life easier for the homemaker. The greatest changes were in factories. Electricity brought in new and faster ways to make pulp and paper, sew clothes, and grind wheat into flour.

Mergers and Take-overs

The bigger the factory, the more efficiently it could produce. Gradually large companies started to dominate the scene. Sometimes several small companies came together and "merged" into one. At other times one company would "buy out" its competitors.

Small local producers found they were losing business. Rural brewers found people preferred to buy from Molson in Montreal, O'Keefe in Toronto or Labatt in London. Instead of selling flour ground in the local mill the storekeeper stocked Ogilvie's, Five

This factory in Winnipeg in 1904 had electric light, but the sewing machines were probably still operated by foot treadles.

What will electricity do for you? To encourage the installation of electricity, Ontario Hydro loaded this truck with electric equipment. Among the items on display are a circular saw and a washing machine. This helped both manufacturers and the electric company sell their products.

FOCUS

How did electricity change life for many Canadians? Why would most farmers and loggers not be able to share these benefits? If you worked in a factory in the early 1900s, why might you have wanted to join a trade union?

Roses, or Robin Hood flour. Companies like Burns of Calgary, Swift, and Canada Packers took over the meat-packing business. Small town stores could not carry the variety of goods that people could buy from Eaton's catalogue.

A broom factory in 1896. Employers found they could pay children far less than adults for doing many tedious and unpleasant jobs. Unions fought to have laws passed to stop children working. They wanted to protect the children. They also wanted to make sure children did not take jobs away from adults. The first child labour law was passed in Ontario in 1908. Other provinces followed. By 1914 scenes like this were rare in Canada.

World Federation of Miners' strike, South Porcupine, Ontario, about 1912.

The Growth of Unions

Industry was changing fast. Profits were growing. The last thing on the minds of many mill owners and factory bosses was the life of the workers. Machinery was designed for efficiency, not safety. Work places were dark, uncomfortable, and poorly ventilated. Hours were long and wages low.

Workers had started to organize unions to demand better wages and working conditions in the 1830s. By 1900 many advances had been made. Some laws protecting workers and unions had been passed. But employers did not like dealing with unions. Many battles were still to be fought between management and labour.

Big business did not take over completely. Many small companies survived, and others started up. Some people wanted a more independent way of life than working for others gave them. They scraped and saved until they had enough to open their own restaurants, barber shops, laundries, clothing stores, bakeries, or fruit stalls. Immigrants followed trades they had learned in the old country and worked as tailors, jewellers, music teachers, or shoemakers. Often they worked as hard or even harder than they would have in a factory. Their reward was that the profit, however small, was theirs and theirs alone.

Railways and Automobiles

The Canadian Pacific Railway was a great success. It carried settlers to the West. It brought the wheat crops to the ports of Vancouver, Montreal, and Quebec. New towns were growing along its tracks.

However, the CPR did not have enough railway cars to ship grain at harvest time. Settlers were moving into new areas of the West and North where the railway did not reach. Many western farmers thought the CPR should have some competition. This might bring down the freight rates they had to pay to ship their grain.

New Railways

In the early 1900s railway-building fever again swept Canada. Investors saw an opportunity to make a fortune by putting money into new railways.

The Grand Trunk Railway in eastern Canada decided to build a western extension. It would be called the Grand Trunk Pacific. The Manitoba government supported the Canadian Northern Railway as a western alternative to the CPR. Common sense said the two groups should co-operate. Greed got in the way.

Both groups had friends in Ottawa. They asked the government for financial help. Instead of deciding which plan was better, the government gave money to both. Prime Minister Laurier believed more railways were necessary.

The railway-building boom continued until 1914. World War I changed things. The government could no longer afford to provide money.

Then, economic reality burst the investors' dreams. There was not enough grain or other freight to support three transcontinental railway systems. Some of the new railways went bankrupt. The federal government was forced to take them over. In 1922

Railway building, 1902-1914
Grand Trunk Pacific
Canadian Northern
Great Northern (B.C.)
National Transcontinental
Timiskaming and
   Northern (Ont.)
Hudson Bay
   (Sask. and Man.)
Canadian Pacific
   (branch lines)

Number of Telephones

Year	Number
1900	52 000
1902	71 000
1904	95 000
1909	239 000
1911	354 000
1914	542 000

Figures are not available for the years 1905 to 1908.

Telegraph and telephone wires were installed alongside the railway. Alexander Graham Bell's invention was changing Canadian life, especially in the country. People on isolated farms found the telephone was vital to keeping in touch. Many city people did not feel the need for a telephone in their homes until much later in the century.

they were combined with other railways that were losing money to form Canadian National Railways. The CNR has been owned and operated by the federal government ever since.

Why was there a second railway-building boom in the 1900s? Why were the new railways combined to form the CNR in 1922? Describe the role of Sam McLaughlin in the early Canadian automobile industry.

Four means of transport: Grand Trunk Pacific train, Model T Ford, ox cart, and electric streetcar. Edmonton, 1912.

The Automobile

The railway was the fastest and most comfortable way of travelling. Rich and poor all used the train. But some Canadians were thinking about a new form of transport—the automobile.

Driving the new invention was not always easy. A Russell car on Yonge Street, Toronto, 1913.

Sam McLaughlin worked for his father at the McLaughlin Carriage Company at Oshawa, Ontario. Sam had seen Russell cars built by the Canada Cycle and Motor Company in Toronto. He decided it was time for the McLaughlins to start making cars.

Sam thought it would be too expensive to design his own engine. He arranged a deal with the Buick Company in Michigan. Buick supplied the engines and McLaughlin built the bodies. The tie with the Americans proved to be good business. In 1907 the

McLaughlin tries an alternate energy source, early 1900s.

McLaughlin Carriage Company produced 193 cars. In 1915 the carriage-making business was sold in order to make room to build Chevrolets. In 1918 General Motors bought the entire company. Sam McLaughlin became president of the new Canadian branch plant.

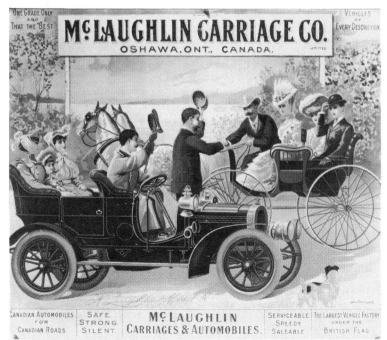

Canada and the British Empire

English Canadians and French Canadians have often differed. In 1900 most English Canadians were descendants of people from the British Isles. The idea of loyalty to the crown and to the British Empire remained strong. French Canadians did not share this feeling. Why should they be loyal to the British Empire? New France had been taken over by the English. To French Canadians, Britain was a foreign, conquering power. Why should they take part in British wars?

The Boer War, 1899-1902

These questions came up during the Boer War. Gold had been discovered in South Africa and the British wanted control of it. The area had been settled by the Boers. The Boers were Dutch pioneers and did not want to be ruled by Britain. Many English Canadians wanted to send soldiers to help the British.

Many French Canadians felt they should be on the side of the Boers. The British were conquering the Boers just as they had conquered New France. Most believed the Boer War had nothing to do with Canada. They were completely opposed to sending soldiers.

Prime Minister Laurier thought of a compromise. Canadians could volunteer to fight with the British in South Africa. Nobody would be forced to go. The volunteers would be paid by the British government. Yet neither side was satisfied. English Canadians felt Canada had not done enough. French Canadians felt that even the token force was too much.

The Naval Question

In Europe, Britain and Germany were competing for power. For hundreds of years Britain had had the most powerful navy. "Britannia ruled the waves." The British wanted to keep it that way. By 1900 Germany was

---

We French Canadians belong to one country, Canada. Canada is for us the whole world. The English Canadians have two countries, one here and one across the seas.

Wilfrid Laurier, quoted in Montreal La Presse

Those who cut your fathers to pieces on the Plains of Abraham are asking you today to go and get killed for them.

Quebec politician, 1911

There is Ontario patriotism, Quebec patriotism, and western patriotism. Each hopes it may swallow up the others. But there is no Canadian patriotism. We can have no Canadian nation when we have no Canadian patriotism.

Henri Bourassa, 1907

British Canadians will find a way, through the ballot box or otherwise, to rid themselves of the influence of this inferior and disloyal race.

Toronto News

One Fleet,
One Flag,
One Throne.

Slogan of the Conservative party in Election 1911 designed to appeal to feelings of loyalty to Britain.

I am branded in Quebec as a traitor to the French, and in Ontario as a traitor to the English. In Quebec I am attacked as an imperialist, in Ontario as a separatist. I am neither. I am a Canadian.

Wilfrid Laurier, 1911

Why did French and English Canadians have different views about the British Empire in the early 1900s?
Explain the different viewpoints of French and English Canadians to a) the Boer War, b) a Canadian navy.

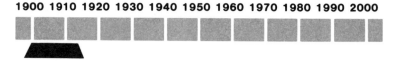

catching up. The British asked Canada, Australia, and the other countries of the Empire for help to keep the British navy strong. English Canadians thought this was the right thing to do. Canada should give money to Britain to buy a dreadnought (a new super-battleship).

Most French Canadians could not support this. Henri Bourassa was the editor of a Montreal newspaper, *Le Devoir*. He had left the Liberal party because he disagreed with Laurier over the Boer War. He said Canada should not give money to Britain in this way. It would only involve Canada in future British wars. French Canadians wanted to stay out of wars in Europe. Canada would gain nothing from them.

Once again, Laurier tried to compromise. He suggested that Canada should have a navy of its own. Some small ships would be built to protect Canadian shores. In case of war, this "Canadian navy" would fight alongside the British navy.

The leader of the Conservative party, Robert Borden, wanted to give money directly to the British navy. A small Canadian navy would be just silly—a

"tin-pot" navy. Most English Canadians sided with Borden and the Conservatives. French Canadians felt that once again the English Canadian majority had given in to Britain.

The new Canadian prime minister, Robert Borden, and the young British first lord of the admiralty, Winston Churchill, in London, 1912.

The naval question was a major issue in the election of 1911. Laurier and the Liberals lost this election. Laurier was never prime minister again. His policy of compromise seemed to have failed.

Henri Bourassa

1868 — born in Montreal, grandson of Louis-Joseph Papineau, leader of 1837 rebellion.
1890 — at age 22, elected mayor of Montebello. Also owned *L'Interprète*, a local newspaper supporting the Liberal party.
1892 — won interest of Laurier, leader of the opposition.
1896-1907 — elected as Liberal, but split with Laurier over Boer War. Continued to support all other Liberal policies. Fought for more balanced immigration so French Canada would not be swamped by English-speaking immigrants, and for equal status for French and English languages.
1908-12 — sat in Quebec legislature.
1910 — founded *Le Devoir,* to become one of Canada's most outspoken newspapers. Its first battle was over reciprocity which Bourassa claimed would lead to U.S. interference.
1911 — attacked Laurier's naval policy. Did not want Canada involved in foreign wars, though supported ties with Britain.
1917 — campaigned against conscription. Labelled a traitor by most English Canadians. Invited to speak in Ottawa, a riot broke out and he had to leave without speaking.
1918 — feeling his vision of Canada was impossible, went into semi-retirement. *Le Devoir* became less controversial.
1925-35 — returned to Commons as Independent. Devoted himself to local issues. Defeated in 1935 election.
1935 — advocated support of the CCF. Was a friend and admirer of J.S. Woodsworth
1952 — died in Montreal.

Reciprocity

In the 1800s Canada was still a colony of pioneer farmers. The United States was already an industrial country. This meant that American manufacturers had a headstart. They had bigger factories. They had a larger market for the goods they made, because there were more people in the United States. Therefore, they could sell things more cheaply.

The National Policy

John A. Macdonald and the Conservatives wanted to encourage Canadian industry. If people bought Canadian goods, money would stay in the country. Canadian manufacturers would make profits. There would be jobs for Canadians. The Conservatives developed a plan they called the National Policy. Goods coming into the country would have to pay a tariff or duty. This meant people would buy Canadian products because they would be cheaper than imported ones. The National Policy helped the Conservatives get elected in 1878.

How the tariff protected Canadian industries:

Cost of imported stove	$40	Cost of Canadian stove	$46
Import duty or tariff	$12		—
Total price in Canada	$52	Total price	$46

High or Low Tariffs?

The tariff policy was popular in industrial areas— Quebec, Ontario, and Nova Scotia. But the settlers in western Canada saw things differently. They wanted to buy cheaper manufactured goods from the United States. Because of the tariff, they had to buy more expensive goods made in eastern Canada. Many farmers in eastern Canada also objected to the tariff.

By the 1890s the country was split on the tariff. The factory owners and workers of eastern Canada supported the tariff—its protected profits and jobs.

The *Toronto Star* supported the idea of reciprocity.

Farmers and people in the West opposed the tariff. They wanted a free trade policy which would let them buy goods at the cheapest world price.

The Conservatives supported the tariff policy. The Liberals wanted freer trade. However, when they were first elected, Laurier and the Liberals kept the tariff. In the early 1900s many farmers and consumers urged them to change the policy. Then in 1910 the Americans offered a deal. They would let more Canadian wheat and other products enter the States. Canada would lower the tariff on many American goods. This is called *reciprocity*. In a reciprocity agreement each side gives something to the other.

The Election of 1911

In 1911 Laurier called an election on the reciprocity issue. The Liberals campaigned for lower tariffs with the United States. They hoped to win support from the

FOCUS

What is a) a "protective tariff, b) "free trade"? Why did Canadians from different regions disagree on tariff policy? Compare the attitudes towards free trade in 1911, with viewpoints in your province today.

Art Gallery page 4

farmers and workers in the East as well as the settlers on the prairies.

The Conservatives under Robert Borden were strongly opposed to reciprocity. They argued that it would lead to cheaper American goods flooding the Canadian market. This would be the end of many Canadian industries. It would lead to unemployment in the cities. More than that, Canada would fall more and more under American control. In the end, Canada might have to join the United States.

Big business interests in Canada did not want reciprocity. They threw their support behind the Conservatives. They bought advertisements in newspapers across the country. They appealed to people's feelings of loyalty to the king and empire. They claimed Canada would soon become totally American if there were freer trade.

These tactics made a great impression in Ontario, Manitoba, and British Columbia—areas which had been settled largely by British immigrants. In Quebec the battle had little to do with reciprocity. The naval question was the big issue there. Henri Bourassa joined the fight against the Liberals because he thought Laurier's "pro-British" policy betrayed Quebec's interests.

Robert Borden at the meeting that planned the Conservative campaign to win the election of 1911.

Laurier was an impressive speaker in both English and French, but even his active campaign style could not win the election of 1911 for the Liberals.

The result of the election of 1911 was Conservatives 133, Liberals 86. Where the elected members came from was more significant. Some regions had voted heavily Conservative, others heavily Liberal. The split caused anger and resentment. Similar splits would cause problems in the future.

Results of the election of 1911		
	Con.	Lib.
B.C.	7	0
Alta.	1	6
Sask.	1	9
Man.	7	2
Ont.	73	13
Que.	27	37
N.B.	5	8
P.E.I.	2	2
N.S.	9	9
Yukon	1	0
TOTAL	133	86

Votes for Women

At the turn of the century more than half of Canadian adults had no vote. Women were not recognized as responsible human beings. Their fathers or husbands looked after them and controlled their property.

Some people, both men and women, were beginning to realize that this was unfair. It was also dangerous, because a woman had no legal protection. If her husband abused her, her property, or her children, the law could do nothing. Thus the matter of votes for women was tied in with other social issues.

Temperance and Women's Rights

One social problem that worried many people in the 1800s was the abuse of alcohol. Societies were set up to promote temperance, or moderation in the use of liquor.

Their concern was justified. Pay envelopes were often handed out in the local tavern. Workers would stay for a friendly drink. A man with a drinking problem would have more than one — he might have drunk most of his wages before starting home. If his wife also worked, he could legally demand her wages to spend as well. Because of the "demon drink," some families went without food, heat, and clothing.

Many people felt that the only answer was prohibition, or banning the sale of alcohol completely. The Women's Christian Temperance Union became the leader in the battle for prohibition. In 1878 a federal act allowed local areas to vote on the issue.

Temperance workers were usually concerned with promoting good family life. So it is not surprising that many of the same people were involved in the struggle for laws to give women a fairer say in marriage. By the turn of the century nearly all provinces had passed Married Women's Property Acts to allow women at least some control over their own property.

Many politicians thought this was enough. But the reformers wanted more: they wanted the abuse of alcohol to be stopped by total prohibition, and they wanted votes for women.

The Vote

It was on the Prairies that the movement for votes for women really got underway. There, farmers knew the importance of women's work and felt it should be properly recognized.

Manitoba was the scene of the most active struggle. In the early 1900s, the campaign for votes for women was led by an author, mother, and temperance worker named Nellie McClung. In 1912 McClung joined a group of Manitoba women in the Political Equality League. Her keen mind and quick tongue soon made her the league's chief spokesperson.

McClung: The hand that rocks the cradle does not rule the world. If it did, the world would be a sweeter, cleaner, safer place than it is now.

Male heckler at a meeting: Don't you wish you were a man right now, Nellie?
McClung: Don't you wish *you* were?

McClung: Woman's duty lies not only in rearing children but also in the world those children must one day enter.

Premier Roblin: I don't want a hyena in petticoats talking politics at me. I want a nice gentle creature to bring me my slippers.

McClung: You'll hear from me again and you may not like it!
Premier Roblin: Is this a threat?
McClung: No, it's a prophecy!

Man voting for the first time in 15 years: You bet I came out today to vote against giving these fool women a vote. What's the good of it? They wouldn't use it!

McClung: The time will come when women will be independent enough to refuse to have their food paid for by men. When women will receive equal pay for equal work. When all avenues of activity will be open to them.

FOCUS

Why were many men and women concerned about "temperance"?
How did Nellie McClung help bring about better conditions for women?
Today women still struggle for equality. Name some issues.

1900 1910 1920 1930 1940 1950 1960 1970 1980 1990 2000

Women campaigned across the country for the right to vote.

Premier Rodmond Roblin was determined that women should not get the vote. On 27 January 1914 he told the legislature the idea was "illogical and absurd. Making women equal to men would cause strife. It would break up the home. Women are too emotional."

The next night the Political Equality League held a "mock parliament" in a local theatre. All the members were women. They debated giving the vote to men. "Premier" Nellie McClung was against it: "If men start to vote, they will vote too much. Politics unsettles men. If men get into the habit of voting, who knows what might happen?".

Everyone thought it was a great joke. But it would take two more years and a change of government before Manitoba gave women the vote. Nellie's "bonny fight, knock-down fight, drag-out fight, uniting the women of Manitoba in a great cause," was finally over. Unfortunately, the McClungs had moved to Alberta, so she was not there to enjoy her triumph. Three months later, women got the vote in Alberta too.

McClung became a member of the Alberta legislature. She worked for the social issues which had convinced her that women were needed in politics.

Nellie McClung

1873 — born on a farm in Chatsworth, Ont.
1880 — family moved west to Manitoba.
1889 — taught grades 1-8 in one-room school.
1894 — became active in WCTU.
1896 — married Wes McClung. They had 5 children.
1908 — wrote 1st novel, about temperance
1911 — McClungs moved to Winnipeg. Nellie joined Canadian Women's Press Club, campaigned for laws to improve conditions for women factory workers.
1912 — helped found the Political Equality League. Worked for votes for women in Manitoba until Wes McClung was transferred to Alberta in 1914.
1916 — women granted the vote in some provinces.
1921 — elected as Liberal member of Alberta Legislature. Supported such measures as old age pensions, mothers' allowances, better conditions in factories, a minimum wage, prohibition, birth control, easier divorce, public health nurses, no matter which party introduced them.
1924 — referendum ends prohibition in Alberta.
1926 — defeated in election by 60 votes, probably because of prohibition stand.
1927 — joined Emily Murphy and 3 other Alberta women in court case to establish that women were "persons" and could be appointed to the Senate.
1936 — appointed to first board of governors of CBC.
1939 — on Canadian delegation to League of Nations.
1951 — dies at Victoria, B.C.

Women get the vote:
1916 Manitoba
     Saskatchewan
     Alberta
1917 British Columbia
     Ontario
     Canada (some women only)
1918 Nova Scotia
     Canada (all women)
1919 New Brunswick
1922 Prince Edward Island
1925 Dominion of Newfoundland
1940 Quebec

Support for votes for women came from farmers' organizations, labour unions, the Methodist church, and many newspapers across the country, as well as from women's organizations such as the WCTU, Women's Institutes, and the Canadian Women's Press Club.

Questions and Activities

Test Yourself

Match the people in column A with the descriptions in column B.

A	B
1. Tom Longboat	a) founded the first Women's Institute.
2. Wilfrid Laurier	b) changed the family carriage factory into an automobile-making business.
3. Clifford Sifton	
4. Adelaide Hunter Hoodless	c) fought for women's right to vote.
5. Robert Borden	d) was a world champion marathon runner.
6. Nellie McClung	e) was the minister in charge of immigration in the early 1900s.
7. Sam McLaughlin	f) wanted a separate Canadian navy.
	g) opposed the policy of reciprocity.

Let's Discuss It

1. What sorts of problems did immigrants to Canada face in the early 1900s? Which of these problems do immigrants still face today? What different sorts of problems do they face today?
   Discuss what the government should do to help immigrants. What can immigrants themselves do to help them adjust to life in their new country?
2. What problems did women face in the early 1900s? Which of these problems have been solved or reduced? Which still exist today?
   Select one problem that women still face in today's society. How would you solve or reduce that problem?
3. Why did workers join trade unions in the early 1900s? Why do they join trade unions today?
   Hold a debate on the topic: Resolved that trade unions are as necessary today as they were in the early 1900s.

Let's Find Out

1. In the early 1900s many immigrants settled in the same area as others of their national group or religious background. In this way they often formed their own communities. Do some research on one of the following groups.
   a) Chinese   e) Mennonite
   b) Doukhobor   f) Mormon
   c) German   g) Polish
   d) Jewish   h) Ukrainian
   Divide your report into two sections: Origins in the Old Country, and Development in Canada.

2. Find out more about one of the following people. Write a brief biography, explaining his or her achievements and importance.
   a) Clifford Sifton   d) Nellie McClung
   b) Henri Bourassa   e) Tom Longboat
   c) Sam McLaughlin
3. Interview a local businessperson or farmer. Find out what his or her views are on free trade today.
4. Interview a local trade union member. Find out why he or she thinks unions are still necessary.
5. Do some research on the history of a railway in or near your community. Your report might use the following organizers:
   a) Plan for a Railway
   b) Building the Railway Changed the Community
   c) How the Railway Changed the Community
   d) State of the Railway Today
   If there is no railway near your community, find out about the alternate means of transportation the community has used in the past and is using today.

Be Creative

1. With a small group of other students, prepare a folder about settlement on the Prairies. Your folder should include:
   a) a *map* of Canada showing the ports where settlers arrived in Canada, the routes of the railways that took them to their new homes, and the location of settlements.
   b) a *poster* advertising free land in Canada
   c) a *description* of Canadian immigration policy under Clifford Sifton and its results
   d) a *drawing* of a settler's home
2. At the turn of the century, electricity greatly changed the way of life for many Canadians. Write a newspaper article describing how your life today would be changed without electricity. Your opening might be "Our community has been without electricity for almost a week, and life is so different."
3. Find out more about life in the cities in the early 1900s. Present your findings in the form of a diary entry that might have been written by a teenager in a poor working class family or by a wealthy factory owner. Do you think that anything should have been done about the differences between the rich and the poor? If so, what and by whom?
4. Do further research about the Boer War. Should Canada have been involved? Assume you were living at the time and write a letter to your member of parliament explaining your views.

You Are There

It is 1911. A vigorous election campaign is being fought on the issue of reciprocity, or lower tariffs with the United States. You attend meetings held by both the Liberal party and the Conservative party in your riding. The candidates make the speeches below.

How will you vote? Why? Try to persuade other voters to agree with you. Write a letter to relatives living in another part of Canada explaining the attitude of people in your region.

Borden in Ontario.

The Conservative Candidate

My fellow Canadians:

In 1879, John A. Macdonald introduced a protective tariff. This was a customs duty which was added to the cost of manufactured goods imported from the United States. We all know that because American manufacturers are producing goods for a larger market, these goods are often cheaper than Canadian goods. Without the tariff, American goods would flood into Canada. The entire farm implement industry, stove, shoes and clothing manufacturers, would go out of business. The cities of Hamilton, Winnipeg, Halifax, Montreal and Toronto would lose their main industries. Workers all across eastern Canada would lose their jobs. Without these industries, we would be a nation of farmers, fishermen, and lumberjacks — a land of "hewers of wood and drawers of water" providing raw materials for others to process.

No, my friends, low tariffs, or "Reciprocity" would not only cause mass unemployment; it would be the first step towards Canada losing its existence. If you follow the Liberal policy, we will all soon not only buy our manufactured goods from the U.S., we will soon be part of the United States. We would lose our ties to Britain and the Empire.

If you want a prosperous, independent country, vote for the Conservative party. Vote to maintain the protective tariff.

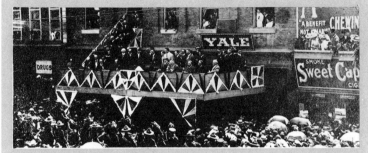

Laurier in Alberta.

The Liberal Candidate

People of Canada:

For many years we have had a protective tariff. This policy has helped the factory owners in the big cities like Toronto and Montreal. They have become wealthy selling their goods in a protected market. But at whose expense?

I say it is the farmers of the Prairie provinces who have paid the price. I say it is the farmers and people of the small valleys of eastern Canada who are losing out. It is the fishermen of British Columbia and the Maritimes. It is the lumber workers of Ontario, Quebec, New Brunswick, and Nova Scotia. These people have had to pay higher prices for Canadian goods. They could have bought less expensive goods from the United States. And the farmers of the West would not have had to pay those high freight costs to bring goods from Ontario and Quebec.

But this is only the beginning. Our tariffs have caused the Americans to place tariffs of their own against our grain, fish, and lumber.

I say reduce the tariffs. If elected, the Liberal party will arrange a treaty with the Americans. If we agree to reduce tariffs on manufactured goods from the U.S., they will reciprocate by reducing tariffs to let in our raw materials.

Fellow Canadians, we have a great future if we increase our trade. Join with the Liberal Party. Let us reduce the tariffs. Let us have a policy that benefits all Canadians, not just the wealthy factory owners in eastern Canada.

Developing Inquiry Skills

We live in a very complex world that is often difficult to understand. We are often dependent on the newspaper and T.V. journalists for our information and our opinions.

As independent citizens, we should be able to inquire into problems to help to form our *own* opinions. This involves our ability to:

— *examine* information
— *focus* attention or raise questions
— *organize* information into an interpretation or theory
— *research* for additional information
— *analyze* our data to modify our ideas
— *communicate* our ideas to others in writing or orally

When you can manage these skills, you are on the road to becoming an independent thinker.

YOUR TASK

To construct a *chart,* using inquiry skills on the topic:
Immigration to Canada Between 1896 and 1914

This is a very large topic. Therefore, you should be narrowing your study on one aspect of the topic, such as:
"Problems faced by immigrants in the period 1896-1914".

METHOD

1. *Focus your research*
   Ask yourself which kind of problems immigrants might have faced in this period? You will be able to think of some possible problems which immigrants faced:

   — Which problems did they have in *getting to* Canada?
   — Which problems did they have finding a *job*? or a *home*?
   — Was there *discrimination* against immigrants?
   — Did they have *financial* problems?
   — Were *loneliness* and *isolation* problems?
   — Was *language* a problem?
   — Which *other* problems might they have had?

These questions should help you to focus your research.

2. *Organize*
   As you do your research, use the questions as *organizers* to collect your research.

Type of Problem	Problem
Transportation	
Financial	
Employment	
Discrimination	
Money	
Etc.	

Collect your data under these headings as you read and do your research.

Developing Communication Skills

3. *Locate more information*

You will usually find that your textbook does not have enough information to answer these questions. Using the school or public library, consult additional books to find further information.

4. *Recording your information*

As you do your research, record the information under the headings which you have provided; e.g., employment problems

5. *Communicating your information*

There is little value in learning information unless you can *communicate* it to others. This could be in several forms:

— written — in sentences and paragraphs, or in chart form
— oral   — *telling* other people
— graphic— creating *pictures* to illustrate a situation to others

For this activity, record your information in chart form.

Problems Faced by Immigrants to Canada, 1896-1914

Problem	Description
Financial	
Language	
Etc.	

Writing a report for several paragraphs

A common method of communicating your ideas is in a brief report of several paragraphs. These reports should always be written using proper sentence and paragraph form. Each paragraph should be about *one* aspect or part of the overall topic.

Your report should always include:

a) *an introductory paragraph* — this should explain the main idea of your topic.
b) *several supporting paragraphs* — each paragraph should explain, in detail, one part of the overall topic (the number of paragraphs will vary according to the length of your report).
c) *a concluding paragraph* — this will give your opinion as to the importance of the topic.

YOUR TASK

Write a six-paragraph report comparing the problems faced by immigrants in the 1890s, with problems faced by immigrants today. (You can use the information from your chart as a guideline for your report.)

Write your answer in six paragraphs. Following are some suggestions for paragraph topics:

Paragraph 1 — Problems faced by immigrants in general
Paragraph 2 — Problems faced by immigrants in the 1890s
Paragraph 3 — Problems faced by immigrants today
Paragraph 4 — Similarities of problems
Paragraph 5 — Differences of problems
Paragraph 6 — Your comments or conclusion on this comparison

Chapter Two

Canada Goes to War
ADVANCE ORGANIZER

1 By the 1900s, Europe was divided into two armed camps. One consisted of Germany, Austria and Italy — the Triple Alliance. The other was made up of the British Empire, France and Russia — the Triple Entente. Only a spark was needed to set off an explosion of war. It came on 28 June 1914, when the crown prince of Austria was assassinated. Within one month the two alliances were at war.

2 Canadians volunteered to fight for the British Empire in 1914. Few knew what war would be like. Soldiers had little or no protection except for the trenches that they dug on the battlefield. They lived in these night and day. For months on end they fended off the enemy while trying to gain a little territory. This went on for four years. Often a long and bloody battle meant winning or losing only a few metres of ground. In battles like those at Ypres and Vimy Ridge, Canadians gained a new pride in their country.

3 At the beginning of the war, planes were used mainly to observe the movements of enemy troops. Then pilots began carrying rifles and firing upon enemy aircraft. Soon machine guns were mounted on the planes, bringing the war in the air to full force. Many Canadians were among the best fighter pilots of the war. The airplane changed the face of modern warfare forever.

Word List

armaments	fortify	regulation
armistice	income tax	suffrage
artillery	mobilize	tradition
conscription	regiment	trench

4

Disasters at sea were not limited to the war front. One thousand passengers drowned when the British liner *Lusitania* was sunk by a German submarine. In the Halifax harbour, two supply ships collided. One was laden with high explosives. The resulting explosion killed and maimed thousands.

5

With war came the need to produce wartime machinery and equipment. New factories were opened. 500 000 soldiers were overseas, and workers were in short supply. Women served as munitions workers in the new war factories. They also replaced men in other important jobs in Canadian society. To pay for the war, the government issued Victory Bonds and introduced new taxes.

6

The Canadian army was made up of volunteers. By 1917 so many soldiers were being killed and wounded, volunteers could not replace them. The Conservative government introduced conscription, forcing young men to join the army. This policy caused one of Canada's major crises. Most English Canadians felt loyal to the British Empire, and were in favour of conscription. But almost all French Canadians were opposed to forcing people to fight in a foreign country. Conscription caused bitter hostility between French and English Canadians, and seriously threatened the unity of Canada.

7

On 11 November 1918 the armistice was declared, ending the war. The Allies had won. Canadian troops could finally return to their country. But the cost to all sides was enormous: 50 000 Canadian soldiers lay buried in the cemeteries of France and Belgium. All told, more than 13 million soldiers lost their lives in the war.

The Road to War

In August 1914, most of the major countries of Europe became involved in the First World War. The previous 100 years in Europe had been relatively peaceful. True, Germany and Italy had expanded their territories, sometimes by war on neighbouring states. However, from the end of the Napoleonic wars in 1815 to the outbreak of this war there had been no major war. Yet all this was to end in 1914; the remainder of the 20th century would be troubled by wars, revolutions, and international conflict.

A number of factors contributed to the outbreak of war:

1 — The emergence of Germany as a major power
By 1871, Bismarck had united the German-speaking peoples into a powerful nation. They wished to be recognized as one of the major powers of Europe. The traditional German respect for the army and military traditions were personified in their leader, Kaiser Wilhelm II. By the early 1900s, German leaders were trying to increase Germany's power by increasing the size of the army and navy.

2 — Conflict over colonies
In the early 1900s, Britain, France, Spain, and Portugal had acquired large colonies in Asia and Africa. By the 1890s, German political and industrial leaders were demanding that Germany also acquire colonies. These would be sources of raw materials for expanding German industries. Because most possible colonies had already been conquered, this demand brought Germany into conflict with other European powers, particularly Britain and France.

3 — The Naval and Arms Race
In the early 1900s the British navy was the largest navy in the world. Its main duty was to protect Britain's far-flung colonies. But, if Germany was to have a colonial empire, it too would require a large navy. As

Wilfrid Laurier,
prime minister 1896-1911

Robert Borden,
prime minister 1911-1919

Germany began to build a navy, the two powers raced to see who could build the biggest navy.

Similarly, an arms race developed between Germany, on the one side, and France and Russia on the other. They worked to see who could have the largest and best-equipped army. The resulting naval and arms races increased tension and hostility in Europe.

4 — The Alliance System
Rivalries in Europe led each country to seek allies for their protection. By the early 1900s, two rival alliances were established:

The Triple Alliance — Germany, Austria-Hungary, and Italy

The Triple Entente — France, Russia, and Britain

By 1914, Europe was divided into two armed and hostile camps. All that was needed to cause an explosion was a political incident, a spark.

The Spark
On June 28, 1914, an assassination in Serbia provided that spark. The explosion threw Europe into a bloody war that lasted for four years. On June 28, 1914, Archduke Ferdinand, the heir to the Austrian throne, was killed by a Serbian terrorist in Sarajevo. The Austrians sent Serbia an ultimatum which the Serbs could not accept. The Austrians invaded and Russia came to the aid of its Serbian allies.

Within one month all of the members of the rival alliances were drawn into the conflict. Germany and Austria-Hungary (Triple Alliance) were fighting

How did the arms race and the alliance system
a) prevent the war, b) contribute to the outbreak of the war.
Compare the alliance system and arms race to conditions in the
world today.

against France, Russia, and Britain (Triple Entente).
Because Canada was a member of the British Empire,
Canada was automatically involved.

The shot fired in Sarajevo started a war that lasted
four years and killed millions, including over 60 000
Canadians.

HMS Dreadnought, built in 1906,
gave her name to a new class of
fighting ships.

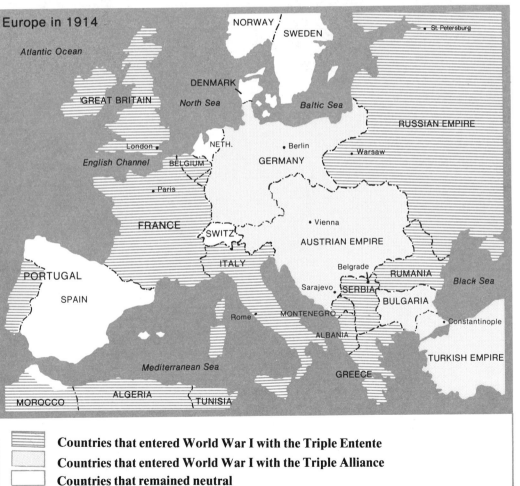

Europe in 1914

Countries that entered World War I with the Triple Entente

Countries that entered World War I with the Triple Alliance

Countries that remained neutral

The Steps to War, Summer 1914

28 June	Archduke Ferdinand is assassinated at Sarajevo.
23 July	Austria sends ultimatum to Serbia.
25 July	Serbia replies, rejecting one term.
28 July	Austria invades Serbia.
29 July	Russia mobilizes army along borders with Austria and Germany. Germany declares war on Russia.
3 August	Germany declares war on France.
4 August	Germany invades Belgium. Britain declares war on Germany.
5 August	Canada and the rest of the British Empire are at war.

Italy left the Triple Alliance with
Germany and Austria and came into the
war on the side of France and Britain.
Japan also fought against Germany in
World War I, taking over German bases
in China.

The War Begins

In the late 1800s Germany had tried to keep on friendly terms with Russia. If war came, Germany expected it to be with France. This would mean battles to the west — a western front. If Russia joined in on the side of France, it would mean battles to the east — an eastern front.

When Germany allied with Austria, Russia's friendship was lost. Russia became France's ally. How could Germany avoid a war on two fronts at once?

The Schlieffen Plan

General von Schlieffen developed a plan. He figured that the Russians would take a long time to mobilize their army. Therefore he planned to move rapidly against the French. He would mislead the French as to where the main attack would come from. The French army would concentrate along the German border.

In a two-front war, the whole of Germany must throw itself upon one enemy: the strongest, the most powerful, the most dangerous enemy. That can only be France.

General von Schlieffen

Wearing kilts and pith helmets quite unsuitable for modern war, the 48th Highlanders leave Toronto for overseas on a rainy September day in 1914.

A famous recruiting poster.

Meanwhile, the German army would invade France from the north. They would sweep across the flat lands of Belgium and northern France to the English Channel. Then they would turn toward Paris like a curved claw. They would fall on the capital from the west. All this would take about six weeks.

The French would be knocked out of the war. The Germans could then turn all their armies against the Russians.

How the Schlieffen Plan Worked

The Schlieffen plan was based on a gamble. Over 70 years before, France, Germany, and Britain had agreed that Belgium should be neutral. The gamble was that Britain would not object to the invasion of Belgium. But when the war started, the British did object. They used the invasion as a reason to enter the war.

You will be home before the leaves have fallen from the trees.

The German Kaiser speaking to his troops, August 1914

What was the main aim of the Schlieffen Plan?
Why did it fail?
How did its failure affect the war on the western front?

General von Schlieffen had died in 1913. The new German generals decided to use his plan. But they made a few changes. Instead of approaching Paris from the west, they turned south too soon. This meant the French army from the French-German border could reach them. And they were also attacked by French and British troops moving out from Paris.

The German advance was halted on the Marne River. The Schlieffen plan had failed. Instead of knocking France out of the war, the Germans found themselves bogged down. On the western front they faced the combined armies of France, Britain, and their empires, including Canada.

Instead of a short, swift campaign, it became a long, dreary, and horrible war. Four years of trench warfare had begun.

The lamps are going out all over Europe. We shall not see them lit again in our lifetime.

Edward Grey, British foreign secretary, August 1914

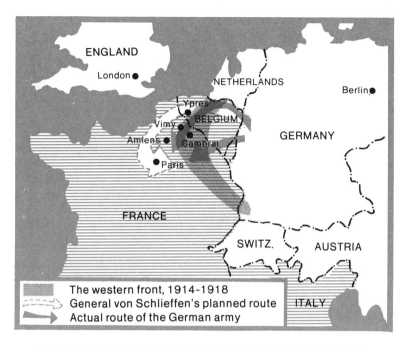

The western front, 1914-1918
General von Schlieffen's planned route
Actual route of the German army

Canada, a daughter of Old England, intends to stand by her in this great conflict. When the call to duty comes, our answer goes at once: "Ready, aye, ready."

Wilfrid Laurier, leader of the opposition, August 1914

Sam Hughes

1853 — born in Darlington, Ontario. After attending teachers' college and the University of Toronto, taught until 1885. Was member of volunteer militia.
1885-97 — owner and editor of newspaper in Lindsay, Ontario.
1892 — elected as Conservative MP.
1899 — served as volunteer in Boer War.
1911 — appointed Minister of Militia and Defence in new Conservative government.
1914-16 — organized Canadian Corps. Refused to allow Canadian troops to be divided among British regiments. As an Irish Protestant, hated Roman Catholics and seemed to antagonize French Canadians. His vanity, and violent temper also created problems for officers working under him.
1916 — was asked to resign as minister because of his unpopularity. Though he was a forceful administrator, he lacked judgement.
1921 — died at Lindsay, Ontario.

War in the Trenches

Mud. Barbed wire. Lice. Hardtack and bully beef. Rain, sleet, and snow. Mud. Rats. Shell holes full of stagnant water. Bodies. Machine-gun bullets. Sandbags. More mud.

Digging In

The Schlieffen plan had failed. The Germans could not advance. The French and the British could not drive them back. Both sides set about fortifying their positions.

They dug trenches to protect their troops. Each trench was a ditch about 2 m deep topped with sandbags. Soldiers could stand in the trench without being seen by the enemy. Between the front-line trenches was a narrow strip called no man's land. Rifle and machine-gun fire spattered across no man's land whenever a soldier detected a movement in enemy territory. Shells flew from the artillery behind the front lines, spraying shrapnel everywhere.

Over the Top

Sometimes the officers would order an advance. This meant "going over the top" of the trench and across no man's land fully exposed to the enemy's fire. Sometimes the troops managed to capture the enemy's front line. The enemy retired to their reserve trenches. Barbed wire was stretched across the new patch of no man's land. A few metres of land had been lost or won. Hundreds of soldiers might have been killed in the process. Then the whole dreary business started all over again.

Soldiers fought, ate, and slept in the trenches. Eventually they would be relieved for a few days by fresh troops. In winter they froze in the snow and sleet. Spring rains sometimes filled the trenches waist-deep with icy water. In summer the rich farmlands of Belgium and northern France turned to mud. For 4 years the war went on.

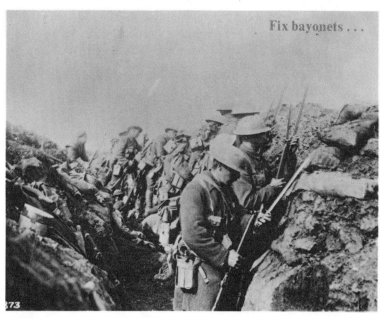

Fix bayonets . . .

. . . and over the top.

Why is there such a difference between the two letters from the front? Imagine you are a soldier in the trenches and write a letter about fighting conditions. Your letter could begin, "We have had a horrible week in the trenches..."

1900 1910 1920 1930 1940 1950 1960 1970 1980 1990 2000

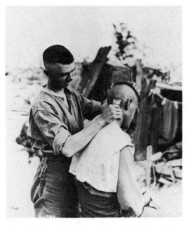

A soldier with a close haircut was less likely to suffer from head lice.

Machine guns, shellfire, and newer, more efficient bombs caused injuries never seen before.

On 1 July the Royal Newfoundland Regiment went over the top at Beaumont Hamel on the Somme River. The regiment was mown down by enemy machine-gun fire. Of the 840 officers and men who took part in the action, 293 were killed and 468 injured. Only 79 were present at a roll call following the battle.

Taking a wounded soldier out on a stretcher, the battle of the Somme, 1916.

Two Letters Home

Before heavy action: 24 March 1915

We have been put in the trenches for a week with British troops. Then we'll be taken back for further training. Then we will be in the trenches for 5 weeks, and then we get a rest.

Our German friends opposite have a sense of humour. One day they stuck a toy horse up above their trench. Our chaps shot it down. They put it up again with a bandage round its neck.

They call out things like "We no shoot, you no shoot."

"If you come halfway, we'll give you cigarettes."

"Hello, B.C., how'd you like to be walking down Hastings Street?"

Our men are so light-hearted—full of life and ginger. Somebody is going to be badly hurt when these boys let loose.

After heavy action: 15 May 1915

We were called out from Ypres about 5 o'clock. The sky was a hell of bursting shrapnel. We lay in reserve until nearly midnight. Then they told us to take the wood. We charged across 500 m of open country. We lost many men during that charge.

I saw poor Charlie go down and stopped to help him, but he urged us on. Then Andy fell, shot right through the head. When we got to the edge of the wood we found a trench just dug by the Germans. This is when the hell began. They had 2 machine guns, and the fire was like hailstones on a tin roof. Somehow they missed a few of us, but other fellows were cut in half by the stream of lead.

I have often wanted to see a fight. Never again. I remember the next morning, all the dead and dying lying about in twisted shapes. War is hell.

We are going back to the base to be reorganized. We had 26 officers before, and 2 after, so you can see it was pretty bad. I shall try to transfer, as most of my nerve has gone.

Canadian and German wounded help each other through the mud to the field hospital.

A Tale of Two Battles

In October 1914 the first Canadian troops arrived in England. The British officers sneered. These "colonials" were sloppy. They didn't even salute properly! The only way to lick them into shape would be to divide them up among British units. They would be no use in their own regiment.

The Canadian minister of militia, Sam Hughes, was furious. He refused to let the Canadians be divided up. As a result, Canada had her own army. The Canadian Corps soon proved its worth.

Ypres

After training, the Canadians arrived in Europe in March 1915. They were sent to Ypres, a city near the Belgian coast. The object was to stop the Germans breaking through to the English Channel. Since the failure of the Schlieffen plan the year before, there had been little fighting here.

The Germans wanted a way to break the stalemate. They decided to use a new weapon — poisonous chlorine gas. On 22 April a gentle breeze blew toward the allied lines — perfect for a gas attack.

The Canadians had been assigned a section of the front-line trenches. To the left were troops from the French colony of Algeria. The Algerians saw a green cloud drifting across no man's land. As it reached the trenches, they found themselves choking and gasping for breath. Those who were not suffocated fled.

Gas masks were issued to everybody, including the horses, after the battle of Ypres.

People had talked about gas warfare. However, the Allied commanders did not think it would be used. So the Canadian soldiers had no gas masks. All they could do was to soak cotton pads in urine and hold them over their faces. The acid in the urine neutralized the chlorine. Then they moved into the gap to prevent a German breakthrough. They held on for two whole days. Finally British relief troops took over.

The Canadians had proved themselves. Nobody sneered at them after the battle of "Wipers."

John McCrae was our brigade surgeon. "In Flanders Fields" was born of fire and blood during the battle of Ypres. Our headquarters were in a trench on the top of the bank of the Ypres Canal. John had his dressing station in a hole dug in the foot of the bank. Wounded men were actually rolled down the bank into his dressing station. Many times during the 16 days of battle, he and I watched the regiment burying their dead whenever there was a lull. "The crosses row on row" grew into a good-sized cemetery. We often heard "the larks still bravely singing" high in the air between the crash of shells and the reports of the the guns in the battery just beside us. He wrote "In Flanders Fields" between the arrival of batches of wounded.

General Morrison, Colonel McCrae's Brigade Commander

In Flanders Fields
John McCrae

In Flanders fields the poppies blow
Between the crosses, row on row,
That mark our place; and in the sky
The larks, still bravely singing, fly
Scarce heard amid the guns below.

We are the Dead. Short days ago
We lived, felt dawn, saw sunset glow,
Loved, and were loved, and now we lie
   In Flanders fields.

Take up our quarrel with the foe:
To you from failing hands we throw
The torch; be yours to hold it high.
If ye break faith with us who die
We shall not sleep, though poppies grow
   In Flanders fields.

FOCUS

Canadian soldiers played a brave and important part in the fighting in World War I. Describe the battle of a) Ypres, b) Vimy Ridge. For each battle explain why the part played by the Canadian army was especially important.

Art Gallery page 9

Vimy Ridge

"Zero hour will be 5:30 a.m."

The word spread through the Canadian army on Easter Sunday, 1917. Every soldier was aware that Vimy Ridge was the key to the German lines. If the Allies were to break the stalemate of the war, Vimy Ridge would have to be taken. In two years of tough fighting, Canadians had done well. The doubtful honour of storming Vimy Ridge would fall to them.

The soldiers looked across no man's land. About 100 m across the mud was the front line of German trenches. It would be sheer hell to get across. That night they got a final hot meal, and a shot of rum to heat their stomachs. It might also give them courage.

For the past two weeks the artillery had been firing shells into the enemy lines. Easter Monday dawned cold, with sleet and snow falling. At exactly 5:30 the command was given to go over the top. Covered by more shellfire, 15 000 soldiers moved in the first wave

Germans captured at Vimy.

of attack. They valiantly struggled across the mud and through what was left of the barbed wire. The return fire from German machine guns and artillery was murderous. But the Canadian shellfire had wiped out the German frontline! In the snow, the soldiers had passed it without knowing it. They surprised the second line of defence. Some fled, but others surrendered to the Canadians then and there. Despite massive losses, by midmorning the Canadians had seized the heights. Vimy Ridge was in Allied hands.

Vimy Ridge was the first great Allied victory since the beginning of the war. Canadian pride got a great boost that cold morning in northern France.

But this pride was dampened by the cost. In just a few hours, 3 598 brave Canadian soldiers had died.

The artillery bombardment before the battle of Vimy Ridge.

Triumphant Canadians return from Vimy Ridge.

The War in the Air

The Wright brothers built the first successful airplane. They flew it at Kitty Hawk, North Carolina, in 1903. Six years later John McCurdy flew the *Silver Dart* at Baddeck, Nova Scotia. The *Silver Dart* had been designed by McCurdy and Alexander Graham Bell.

However, airplanes were regarded as "too expensive a luxury for Canada to indulge in." At the outbreak of World War I Canada had no airplanes and no pilots.

This attitude did not appeal to young Canadian flying buffs. Many went to Britain to join the Royal Flying Corps. They were among the best fighter pilots of the war.

Aircraft Design

By 1914 aircraft design had not advanced greatly. Most planes flew at about 150 km/h. They had open, single

A Canadian aircraft factory. The planes were sent to Europe with the wings detached to save space aboard ship.

Billy Bishop in the cockpit of his single-seater fighter, the French-designed Nieuport 17. The machine-gun controls are on the upper wing just above the pilot's head. The gun fired above the propeller. It could be raised or lowered but not swung from side to side. Bishop scored 36 of his confirmed victories in this plane.

seater cockpits. At first planes were used mainly to observe enemy troop movements. The thrill of flying united all pilots — British, German, French. As their planes passed above the lines of battle, they would wave to each other. But then some pilots started to bring rifles into the cockpit. They shot at enemy planes in order to stop information reaching the enemy generals. The friendly game was over. The war in the air had begun.

The next step was to mount a machine gun on the plane. The problem was to avoid hitting the propeller. One British design mounted the gun behind the pilot. The French placed it above the propeller, on the top wing of the biplane. The Germans had a gun timed to fire through the propeller without hitting the blades. When the British tried this system, it did not always work perfectly. These guns had fixed mounts. The only way to aim the gun was to point the entire plane directly at the target.

Draw a picture of an airplane at the beginning of the war. Imagine you are Billy Bishop and write a letter describing a dogfight. Your opening could be: "Our 3 planes took off on a sunlit morning. Suddenly we sighted 3 enemy planes . . ."

Some Canadian World War I Air Aces	Enemy aircraft destroyed
Billy Bishop V.C. (Owen Sound, Ont.)	72
Raymond Collishaw (Nanaimo, B.C.)	60
Donald MacLaren (Vancouver, B.C.)	54
Billy Barker V.C. (Dauphin, Man.)	50
Fred McCall (Vernon, B.C.)	34
William Claxton (Gladstone, Man.)	31
Albert Carter (Pointe de Bute, N.B.)	31

V.C. stands for the Victoria Cross, the highest military honour in the British Empire. King George V awarded the Victoria Cross to 10 airmen—including 3 Canadians. Altogether, 68 Canadians won the Victoria Cross during the war.

Dogfights

Meetings of enemy aircraft became deadly "dogfights." Pilots tried to get on the tail of an enemy plane where the enemy could not return the gunfire. Being shot down usually meant instant death. Pilots did not carry parachutes. If they did, they might bail out. Their officers wanted them to try to save the planes instead. The expected life span of a pilot was three weeks before being shot down.

One of the leading "aces" of the Royal Flying Corps was a Canadian, Billy Bishop. He shot down 72 enemy planes. The greatest flying ace was Manfred von Richthofen, the famous Red Baron. He shot down 80 planes.

The Red Baron's Last Flight

One day in April 1918 Richthofen took his pilots on their usual daily patrol. They were met by a British squadron led by Roy Brown of Carleton Place, Ontario. Soon the two groups were in a fierce dogfight.

Wop May was on his first combat flight. The young Canadian realized his guns were jammed and drifted out of the battle. The Red Baron moved onto his tail. Preparing for the kill, he did not notice that Roy

Wilfred (Wop) May

1896 — born in Carberry, Manitoba.
1902 — family moved to Edmonton where father opened a farm equipment shop.
1916 — joined Canadian army. As soon as possible, transferred to Royal Flying Corps.
1917 — after training, assigned to observation flights. Wanted more excitement so requested transfer.
1918 — in first combat flight was saved from Red Baron by Roy Brown. Did not have the record of "kills" some Canadian aces had, but was convinced he wanted to fly.
1919 — returned to Edmonton. Wop was expected to join family firm, now a car dealership — had changed with times — as a mechanic. But Wop wanted to fly. Rented a JN4 Canuck. Delivered city newspapers to small towns by dropping them over the side of the plane; did stunt flying at town fairs; gave flying lessons.
1924 — Married. Quit flying to take steady job. It didn't last: Wop was soon flying again.
1929 — Flew vaccine north to Fort Vermilion to combat a midwinter diphtheria epidemic. Trip took 3 days in an open plane. Returned to find himself an instant hero; the country had followed the trip through radio reports. In December flew 1st official airmail to Aklavik.
1932 — Helped RCMP find Albert Johnson, "The Mad Trapper of the North" by tracking from the air. In the shootout when mounties on the ground caught up with him, Johnson was killed, a mountie badly injured. May flew the man back to Aklavik for emergency treatment.
1935 — Gave up active flying due to loss of right eye.
1940-45 — taught in Commonwealth Air Training Plan.
1942 — set up northern Parachute Rescue Squad to rescue U.S. pilots lost while ferrying planes to bases in Alaska.
1946 — planned commercial air route to Japan
1951 — manager of a company making jet planes.
1952 — died while hiking in Utah with 17-year-old son.

Brown had moved behind *him*. Brown got the German ace in his gun sights and knocked him out of the sky.

A Canadian had downed the legendary Red Baron.

The War at Sea

Workers at Alexander Graham Bell's laboratory at Baddeck, N.S., turned to building lifeboats.

When the war began, Canada had only the beginnings of a navy. Wilfrid Laurier had decided Canada should have her own navy, not contribute to Britain's. Canada had two mid-sized cruisers. The *Niobe* was based in Halifax and the *Rainbow* in Vancouver. Canada's navy did little fighting at sea. But by the end of the war, the Royal Canadian Navy had grown to about 100 ships, mostly small coastal vessels.

Atlantic Trade

Canada's main part in the war at sea was in shipping Canadian troops and Canadian products to Europe. Through most of the war, the United States was neutral. Americans sold goods to Britain, France, and Germany. But they sold more to Britain and France. Most Americans were sympathetic to the Allies.

Britain tried to block goods being sent to Germany. The British navy mined the North Sea so neutral ships could not get to German ports. Meanwhile the German navy wanted to stop goods reaching Britain. They declared a war zone in the waters around the British Isles.

The Germans used submarines to attack ships bound for Britain. In 1915 a German submarine sank the *Lusitania,* a British passenger liner. Over 1000 people died, including 114 Americans. The tragedy contributed to anti-German feeling in the United States.

The British started to collect ships into large groups called convoys. Convoys would sail together from Quebec, Halifax, or St. John's. They could be protected from submarines by warships. The convoy system greatly reduced the number of ships sunk.

Halifax after the explosion.

1900 1910 1920 1930 1940 1950 1960 1970 1980 1990 2000

The Halifax Explosion

Thursday 6 December 1917 dawned clear and mild in Halifax. At 7:30 the *Mont Blanc*, a French freighter loaded with benzene, picric acid, and TNT, started to move through the Narrows to Bedford Basin, the city's inner harbour. She had come from New York to join the next convoy across the Atlantic. At about 8:00 the *Imo*, a Norwegian tramp steamer carrying relief supplies for Belgium, headed out through the Narrows.

In the city, factory workers were already at their jobs. Children were assembling in school playgrounds. Offices and stores were getting ready for the day's business. Ships must take care as they pass in the Narrows. As the *Mont Blanc* and the *Imo* drew close to each other, they signalled their intentions. But suddenly the *Mont Blanc* was across the *Imo's* bow. At

Two young victims of the explosion.

8:43 the *Imo* rammed her. The two ships drifted apart. People in the city out enjoying the winter sunshine watched as a wisp of smoke rose from the harbour. At 9:06 the *Mont Blanc's* cargo of high explosives blew up.

Schools, factories, stores, and houses in a 5 km² area were completely destroyed. Part of the two-tonne anchor of the *Mont Blanc* was found 4 km away. Over 2000 people died and another 9000 were injured. That night, with 10 000 people homeless, the temperature plunged to -8°C and a blizzard was on the way.

Within days relief supplies began to pour in from Canada and as far away as Jamaica and New Zealand. The state of Massachusetts sent a special relief committee.

The Halifax explosion was the biggest man-made explosion the world had known to that time.

The War at Home

Wars have always been fought by soldiers in the front line. World War I was the first war to involve all sections of society. In Canada, far from the battle lines, people were making their contribution.

Farming

The war disrupted farming in Europe. Canada had been exporting wheat to Europe for many years. But now Europe needed far more. Canadian farmers had to fill a large part of this need.

By the end of the war "sodbusters" in the West had doubled the land used for wheat farming. Cheese exports tripled. Pork and beef exports shot sky high.

> Do you know that last year's grain crop in Europe was half its normal size? That 90 million food animals have already been slaughtered? That over 60% of the 50 million soldiers fighting the war came off the farms? In addition, thousands of ships are being sunk by enemy submarines. Most of these ships are carrying food. Our duty is simple: Produce more and waste nothing.
>
> *Speaker from the Department of Agriculture to a housewives' group, Victoria, B.C.*

Industry

Canadian business also found new markets. Before the war factories produced goods for the Canadian market. Few tried to compete outside the country. Most of our exports were raw materials—to be processed elsewhere.

Now businesses saw new opportunities. Canadian companies started to make armaments for the Allied forces. Steel companies turned to making shell cases. Others made fuses and explosives. By 1917 one-third of the shells used by the British were made in Canada.

A Ukrainian family brings in the harvest.

Red Cross supplies for the battlefields of Europe.

Canadians made guns, airplane parts, and ships. Aluminum, nickel, railway track, and timber were all sent to Europe. Uniforms, equipment, and medical supplies were made for the Canadian army.

What new Canadian industries were created by World War I?
What is "profiteering"? Give 2 examples during the war. What do
you think should happen to wartime profiteers?
List 3 ways the government raised money to pay for the war.

Art Gallery page 10

Profiteering

Most Canadians worked hard to help the war effort. City workers gave up their free time to help farmers bring in the crops. Women turned to new kinds of jobs. Businessmen and government officials worked long hours without extra pay. All this activity created great opportunities for profit.

Most businessmen were content to take a fair mark-up. But some tried to "corner the market" on a product. They would not sell until they could get the best price. Others used cheap materials and did sloppy work. The boots the first Canadian troops were given wore out in less than two months! Canned meat for soldiers sometimes came from diseased animals. Some industrialists used bribery to get government contracts.

Ordinary people did the same sort of things. On one hand, some made up parcels for soldiers and planted "war gardens" with vegetables. On the other, some hoarded supplies, wasted food, and tried to get around government regulations.

Victory Bonds

War is expensive. Canadians paid no income or profit taxes. The government could not raise enough money by other means. How was the war to be paid for?

To raise money, Canada issued Victory Bonds. Canadians were urged to buy bonds to help the war effort. After the war they could cash in their bonds and get their money back with interest. Most bonds were bought by banks and large companies. But ordinary citizens did their part as well.

Two new "temporary" taxes were introduced. The first was a business profits tax. The second was an income tax. These taxes are still with us.

An armament factory.

Women at War

Even before World War I women were breaking out of their traditional role. Many wanted to be more than housewives and mothers. Women stayed in school longer. Some went to university. A few even became doctors and lawyers. But these were special cases. It was almost impossible for women to get hired for many jobs. And women could not vote.

The Needs of Industry

The wartime industrial boom created a problem. The young men who would normally work in industry were in the army. Women moved into the war factories. By the end of the war, over 20 000 women were employed making guns, shells, and aircraft. And they held skilled jobs. Before the war, women had only done routine work. Skilled jobs had been for men.

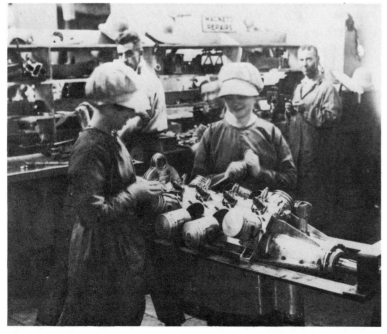

Overhauling a Curtiss OX-5 aircraft in the repair section at Camp Mohawk. Desoronto, Ont.

Women also replaced men in many civilian jobs. They became streetcar drivers, secretaries, and office managers. They moved onto the farms to help bring in the crops.

Women without paying jobs were also doing their part. They knitted socks for soldiers, sent them letters and care packages, visited the families of men who had been killed. Women supported the Canadian Red Cross and other volunteer organizations.

Letters with news of home from a mother or sweetheart helped make life more bearable for soldiers at the front.

The Army Medical Corps

The wounded soldiers on the western front needed medical care. Over 3 000 women became army nurses and ambulance drivers. Most of them served overseas. They willingly shared the dangers of warfare with Canadian men.

The Right to Vote

The efforts and achievements of women could not be ignored forever. Women wanted the right to vote. World War I meant they got that right. But the federal government granted it in a rather grudging way.

OCUS

What new roles did women play during the war *a)* in industry, *b)* in the army medical corps?
How did the part played by women help them to obtain the vote in federal elections by 1918?

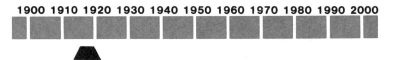

1900 1910 1920 1930 1940 1950 1960 1970 1980 1990 2000

An ambulance driver was responsible for keeping her engine in good running order.

In 1917 Prime Minister Borden decided the government needed conscription, the right to force men to join the army. Some people would not like this. It was time for an election. Borden wanted to use the election to prove conscription was "the will of the Canadian people." Before the election, the government passed the Wartime Election Act.

This act took the vote away from citizens who had emigrated from "enemy" countries. (They might vote against conscription.) It gave the vote to women—but not all women. Only army nurses and close relatives of soldiers would be allowed to vote. (They would probably support conscription: if other men had to go to war, their men might have a better chance.)

Obviously this act was unfair to other women. In 1918 all women were given the vote. But they still could not be elected to Parliament. That right did not come till 1920. In 1921 Agnes Macphail was elected to the House of Commons.

The first steps had been taken. The long struggle for real equality had just begun.

About halfway through the war a new form of warfare was begun, warfare that could hit behind the battle lines. Pilots started to drop bombs on military and civilian targets. This funeral was for Canadian nurses killed in an air raid on a hospital in May 1918.

WOMEN AND WORLD WAR I   81

Conscription

For most of the war, the Canadian army relied on volunteers. At first, many young men were excited at the idea of fighting for their country. They rushed to volunteer. They could hardly wait to get overseas.

The horrors of the trenches soon changed this. From 1915 to 1917 Canadian soldiers gained a high reputation for courage. As a result they were often chosen for the toughest battles.

In April 1917 Canadians fought at Vimy Ridge. That month over 10 000 Canadian soldiers died. Less than 5 000 volunteered to join the army. The volunteer system was not recruiting enough soldiers to replace the losses.

Prime Minister Borden had promised that his government would not introduce conscription. They would not force men to join the army. Now he felt he had to break that promise. An election was coming. The campaign was one of the fiercest and angriest in Canadian history.

Why aren't YOU?

When the war broke out, the country went mad! People were singing in the streets. Everybody wanted to go to war. We hadn't had a war since the Boer War in 1899. Everybody was going to be a hero, and I wanted to be a hero too!

But I wasn't big enough. I was only 150 cm tall and weighed 40 kg. I was 19 but looked 15. Finally a drill sergeant said, "We need buglers!" So I joined the army as a bugler.

Bert Remington of Montreal, who had emigrated from England in 1910

Me? I was probably as patriotic as most, but mainly I was restless. I joined up because it was a chance to see the world.

Robert Swan, Yarmouth, N.S.

An anti-conscription parade in Montreal, 24 May 1917.

People against Conscription

The biggest group of people against conscription were the French Canadians. When the war started, many had volunteered to enter the army. The Royal 22nd Regiment, the "Vandoos" (from *vingt-deux*) was a French-speaking unit. It had a great fighting record right through the war.

The minister of militia had been Sam Hughes, an Irish Protestant. Hughes did not try to understand the French Canadians. He hated Roman Catholics. He sent Protestant clergymen as recruiting officers to Quebec. He insisted that French soldiers be trained in English. Borden fired Hughes in 1916, but it was too late to save the situation in Quebec.

FOCUS

What was conscription? Why did Borden think it was necessary? Why did some Canadians object to conscription? How did the conscription crisis and the election of 1917 appear to split the country?

1900 1910 1920 1930 1940 1950 1960 1970 1980 1990 2000

Conscription means national division and strife. It will hurt the cause of the Allies more than a few thousand extra soldiers will bring them help and comfort. *Henri Bourassa*

French Canadians had felt no duty to support Britain during the Boer War. Some felt the same way now. This was a European war. They were being asked to save Britain, not Canada. Wilfrid Laurier, the leader of the opposition, did not feel this way. He urged French Canadians to join the army. But he did not think they should be forced to do so.

In the West, many settlers objected to conscription. They had come to Canada to get away from European wars. In many countries governments could force men into the army. They thought they had escaped that way of life. Now it seemed to be coming to Canada.

Farmers everywhere objected. Their part of the war effort was to provide much-needed food. Who would work with them it their sons were taken away?

vote against the vernment means: ou are here for life

A vote for the Government means: Another man is coming to take your place

Soldiers at the front were encouraged to vote for the government and conscription with posters like this.

What the Government Did

Prime Minister Borden was convinced that conscription was necessary. Those in favour of conscription had to win.

First he asked Laurier to join him in the government. Laurier could not do this. Although he supported the war effort, he was against conscription.

Borden then approached other Liberals. Some of them were for conscription. Several Liberals joined the Conservatives in a new party. They called it the Unionist Party.

The government took the vote away from immigrants who might be against conscription. It gave the vote to soldiers overseas and to women who would be for it. Borden promised farmers that their sons would not be forced to go. (This promise was broken after the election.)

Voting up the line, December 1917.

The Election of 1917

The results of the election were Unionists 153, Liberals 82. Only 20 of those 82 were from outside Quebec. But the results did not show the true feelings of the people. Many English-speaking Canadians did not want conscription. In fact, if the soldiers' votes were taken out, nearly half the people voted against it.

The conscription issue aroused many bitter feelings. Canadians were divided as they had not been since the execution of Louis Riel.

The War Ends

The stalemate on the Western Front in France and Belgium continued into 1918. Neither side seemed capable of winning the decisive battle that would bring victory. Soldiers on all sides wondered why they were involved in this hell on earth. The fighting on this front offered little hope and, for many, certain death.

In 1917, the Russian people, under communist leadership, revolted against their leaders. They demanded "Land, Bread, and Peace". Soldiers and sailors mutinied and refused to fight. By the end of 1917, the Russians had signed a separate peace treaty, the Treaty of Brest-Litovsk. Germany then turned all of its armies against the allies on the Western Front.

The United States Enters the War

In 1917, the United States entered the war on the side of Britain and France. Germany knew that within a year a great new supply of American troops would arrive in France. The German General Ludendorff

The first Remembrance Day. Each year at 11 a.m. on 11 November Canadians and citizens in many other countries of the world pause to remember those who served in time of war.

decided on a final offensive before the American forces arrived.

In April 1918, the final German offensive began. Over 3 000 000 soldiers attacked, supported by a massive artillery barrage. The German forces advanced over 60 km; it appeared that the breakthrough had been achieved.

Advancing down a road during the battle of Amiens, August 1918.

Canadian troops enter Cambrai, October 1918.

How did each of the following affect the stalemate on the western front: a) use of tanks, b) revolution in Russia, c) entry of the United States into the war?
What is the origin of Remembrance Day?

1900 1910 1920 1930 1940 1950 1960 1970 1980 1990 2000

However, British, French, and Canadian forces pulled back to new defence lines; the German offensive slowed down. Reinforcements were collected for the allied counter-attack. For the first time these forces included thousands of American troops. The counter-attack began in July 1918. This allied advance forced the German army to retreat. By August, the German army was in total retreat.

In Germany there were riots because of food shortages and protests against continuing the war. Some members of the German Navy mutinied and refused to go to sea. By October, it was obvious that Germany and its allies had lost the war and the negotiations for peace began.

On November 11, the armistice was signed. At 11 a.m. on the 11th day of the 11th month, the bloody war came to an end. The problem then was how to arrange the peace.

Over 8 million soldiers had died. More than 20 million more would live out their lives with wounds, shell shock, gassed lungs, lost limbs, sight, or hearing. An equal number of civilians were also victims of war.

The cemetery at Étaples, France, "where many brave Canadians rest." More than 60 000 Canadians died overseas during the four years of World War I. Many returned, with permanent injuries, to a greatly changed Canada. Ironically, the swine flu epidemic during the autumn of 1918 killed almost as many Canadians as had died overseas during the full course of the war.

The Treaty of Versailles

The November 11 Armistice ended the fighting. Germany agreed to withdraw its troops within its own borders, to surrender its fleet to Great Britain, and to disarm its army.

The victorious powers met at Versailles outside of Paris to draw up the peace treaty. Strong differences of opinion existed among the allied leaders. Georges Clemenceau, the French Premier, was determined that Germany must be punished for the invasion of France in 1870 and 1914. He demanded a harsh peace treaty.

On the other hand, President Woodrow Wilson of the United States wanted a more generous peace settlement. Wilson had previously drawn up the "14 Points" as a basis for a settlement. These included such ideas as "national determination for all peoples", freedom of the seas, open peace treaties rather than secret agreements. One major proposal was for a League of Nations to guarantee world peace.

Germany expected a treaty based on the idealism of the 14 points. Instead the Treaty of Versailles was a compromise agreement, including many of the harsher terms of Clemenceau and Prime Minister Lloyd George of Great Britain.

Treaty of Versailles

— Germany lost control of all colonies
— Alsace-Lorraine was transferred from Germany to France
— the rich Saar coal region was to be run by France for 15 years
— part of eastern Germany was given to Poland
— the Austrian and Turkish empires were broken up into separate countries

Military Controls
— German Army was restricted to 100 000 men and was to have no tanks or heavy guns
— Germany was not to have an air force
— the German Navy was to include only small ships

Reparations
— Germany was to pay money and goods to France and Belgium to repair damages of the war

War Guilt clause
— Germany was forced to sign a statement that it had been the primary cause of the war

Canadian troops arriving in Montreal, Quebec, for demobilization, 1919.

What were the expectations of the following about the 1919 peace settlement: a) France, b) United States, c) Germany? Which parts of the Treaty of Versailles caused resentment in Germany? How did the Treaty contribute to World War II?

1900 1910 1920 1930 1940 1950 1960 1970 1980 1990 2000

Reaction to the Peace Treaty

The French and British considered the treaty to be, on the whole, fair and just. Both sides had lost hundreds of thousands of their youth in the horrible battles of the Western Front. Both were determined that the treaty should do everything possible to prevent the outbreak of another world war.

On the other hand, most Germans were shocked by what they considered the harsh and unfair terms. The payment of reparations threatened to crush their struggling industries. The loss of key lands to France, Poland, and Czechoslovakia offended their sense of nationality. The limitations on their armed forces offended their sense of national dignity. Finally the war guilt clause offended their sense of justice.

In the years after 1919, the sense of injustice festered like an open wound. A myth developed that Germany had been ''stabbed in the back'' by non-military citizens within the country and not defeated on the field of battle. Many waited for the arrival of a new leader to help them to avenge their defeat.

Fifteen years later, in 1933, Adolph Hitler appeared to be that leader (*fuhrer*) who would lead Germany to avenge the Treaty of Versailles.

During the 1920s, while Hitler was in prison, he wrote his book *Mein Kampf* (My Struggle). He stated this about the Treaty of Versailles: '' . . . these points have been burned into the brain and emotion of this people until finally in 60 000 000 heads, in men and women, a common sense of shame and a common hatred would become a single fiery sea of flame, from whose heat a will as hard as steel would have risen and a cry burst forth: 'Give us arms again!' ''

EUROPE AFTER 1919

In 1923 Hitler was jailed for plotting to overthrow the government. While in jail, he wrote *Mein Kampf,* a book which explained his political aims. On his release Nazis welcomed him as a hero.

Questions and Activities

Test Yourself

Match the people in column A with the descriptions in column B.

A	B
d 1. Archduke Ferdinand	a) opposed conscription for Canada during World War I.
f 2. General von Schlieffen	b) was the leading German air ace.
c 3. Wilfrid Laurier	c) insisted Canadian soldiers fight together in their own unit.
e 4. John McCrae	d) was assassinated at Sarajevo in an incident that led to the outbreak of World War I.
5. Sam Hughes	
g 6. Billy Bishop	e) wrote a poem about soldiers on the western front.
7. Manfred von Richthofen	f) planned the German invasion of France.
	g) was the leading Canadian air ace.

Do Some Research

1. Find out more about the development of one of the following weapons during World War I. Draw a picture and use it to explain the importance of the weapon during the war.
   a) the fighter plane   c) the submarine
   b) the machine gun   d) the tank
2. Do further research on the changing role of women during World War I.
   a) as nurses and workers   b) as workers on the homefront
      at the battlefront   c) in getting the right to vote
3. Interview members of the Royal Canadian Legion about Remembrance Day.
4. Find out more about the causes and effects of the Halifax explosion.

Ideas for Discussion

1. Think about the role played by the following groups during the war.
   a) farming families   d) soldiers
   b) city families   e) nurses
   c) armament workers   f) politicians
   Rank these groups in order of importance. Compare your ranking with that of other members of the class.
2. "War brings out the best in people and the worst in people." In small groups, compose two lists: The Best in People and The Worst in People. Compare your lists with those of other groups of students.

3. Here are two different opinions on the Treaty of Versailles. Read them and decide which you agree with most. Discuss the treaty with your classmates, giving reasons for your views.

> I think the Treaty of Versailles was fair. Germany had caused the war. She had invaded Belgium, a neutral country, without excuse. Germany had been trying to expand for 75 years. She had to be punished and she had to be weakened. When the new soviet government in Russia wanted to withdraw from the war, Germany imposed much harsher terms in the Treaty of Brest-Litovsk than the western allies did in the Treaty of Versailles.
> This kind of treaty was the only way to guarantee that a strong Germany would not cause another war. If the treaty was enforced, it would keep peace in Europe.

> I think the Treaty of Versailles was too harsh. The war had not been caused by Germany alone; Austria and Russia were just as guilty. Making Germany pay all that money for the war meant her economy could not recover. Germany should not have had her colonies and so much territory taken from her.
> After the war the Allies and the Germans would have to live together. But the treaty was so unfair, the Germans were bound to be resentful. They would look for a chance to get back what they had lost. This might lead to another war.

Hold a class debate on the topic: The Treaty of Versailles was a main cause of World War II.

Be Creative

1. Prepare a newspaper on the Canadian contribution to World War I. Your newspaper could include maps, interviews, letters, statistics, pictures, editorials. Try to cover as many aspects of the war as possible, including recruitment and training, providing supplies and equipment, volunteer work, as well as the actual fighting on land, sea, and air.
2. What does your school do for Remembrance Day each year? Design a Remembrance Day program for your class or school.
3. With another student, choose a person who played a prominent role at the time of World War I. Conduct an interview, with one of you playing the interviewer and the other the historical person. You will need to do further research in order to prepare questions and answers that will highlight the role the person played in World War I.

You Are There

It is 1917. The country is about to vote in an election. The main issue is whether the government should introduce conscription. If you were one of the people described here, what would be your opinion? Why would you feel that way? Write a letter to a newspaper explaining how you feel conscription would affect the war effort, national unity, English Canadians, French Canadians, and recent immigrants.

Albert Jackson was born in London, England. He emigrated to Toronto in 1913. He was brought up to believe strongly in the British Empire and to be completely loyal to King and country. He is convinced Germany caused the war and that she has to be stopped. Canada, as part of the British Empire, is directly  involved in the war. Most of his friends in England are already in the army. He believes that all people have a duty to support the war and do whatever the government orders.

Mary Porter was an army nurse in France. She  was wounded during an air raid and has been sent home to Vancouver. She has two brothers with the Canadian army. Jack is hoping for a transfer to the Royal Flying Corps. Ed has just been awarded a DSO (Distinguished Service Order) for saving the life of a companion wounded while going over the top during the battle of the Somme. Jack is engaged to Mary's best friend, Susan. Before she left France, Mary was aware that Canadian regiments were not operating at full strength because there were not enough volunteers to replace those killed or wounded.

André Savard's family have farmed on the shores of the St. Lawrence for nearly 300 years. He is one of nine children and has recently married. He and his wife are expecting a baby. When the war broke out, he did not even hear about it for a month or so. He does not see how a war being fought over 5000 km away can possibly affect him. He knows that his cousin Pierre from Quebec City has volunteered and is now a sergeant with the Royal 22nd Regiment. He himself does not want to fight or kill people in a distant land. He is happy to let others fight if they believe in the cause. André sees his life in terms of his village, his farm, and his family.

Stefan Klemens brought his family to Saskatchewan in 1901. They came from Austria to escape the almost constant warfare. Now Stefan farms the 64 ha of land given him by the government when he arrived. He is married with six children. It has been a struggle to provide for his large family, but now they are doing well. Last year they harvested a large grain crop, and got a good price for it. He does not know how he would manage without the help of his sons Kurt (22) and Hans (19). Last week, Greta (7) came home from school in tears because the kids called her a Hunky. It bothers Stefan that Canada is fighting a war against the land where his parents and sisters still live.

Bill McAdam was born and raised in Nova Scotia. His family came here from Scotland over a hundred years ago, and he thinks of himself a loyal son of Nova Scotia. When the war broke out, many of his friends volunteered to join the army. He is still under the age limit of 18 and has not decided whether he will volunteer or not. He sometimes wonders what Canadians are doing fighting in France. His neighbours, Charlie Armstrong and George Macdonald, have already been killed, and nobody knows if Robert Cormier will ever recover from that gas attack. Yet he considers himself a good Canadian and Canada is at war. He has a strong sense of duty. He wonders what would happen if people didn't join up.

Shirley Evans lives in Hamilton and is the mother of three children — Karen (19), Timothy (16), and Daniel (9). Shirley does volunteer work for the Salvation Army. Her group serves refreshments to soldiers on the troop trains that pass through the city. Lately they have helped tend the trainloads of wounded soldiers returning home.  Karen's fiancé, Jim Lee from down the street, was killed in action at Vimy Ridge. The Evans family shares the grief of the Lees, who have lost their only son. Timothy had planned to join his father's automobile sales company, but he expects to be in uniform soon. Shirley hopes the war will end before he is old enough to join up.

Drawing and Interpretation of Maps

YOUR TASK

1. a) Compare the map of Europe in 1914 (P. 67) with the map of Europe after 1919. (P. 85)
   b) Locate at least six new countries created following the Treaty of Versailles.
2. Draw (or trace) your own map of Europe in 1919, after the Treaty of Versailles. The following suggestions will help you to make your map clear and understandable.

Guidelines for Drawing Maps

a) Trace the boundaries and coastlines in pencil.
b) When completed, go over boundaries in ink or coloured pencil.
c) Show all coastlines in an identifiable colour (e.g., blue)
d) Use colour for *meaning,* as well as for making the map attractive. Shade countries in different colours to show their location.
e) Label all important places and features by *printing* legibly, and horizontally (where possible).
f) Print a *title* in a prominent location (at the top or bottom).
g) Where appropriate, put a *legend* to explain the use of colour on your map.

Refer to the map on page 87.

Constructing a Time Line

As a student of history, you gradually will develop a sense of time or chronology. It is important to know *when* things happened. This is not just to memorize unimportant dates; you should know the *sequence* of events, because frequently one event *causes* a later event.

Your text provides a time line at the top of many pages, to show when a particular event occurred. You should develop the skill of placing events in a sequence, and seeing how and if one event affected or caused a following event.

YOUR TASK

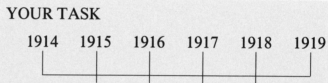

1914 1915 1916 1917 1918 1919

1. Construct a time line from 1914-1919. Locate the following events in their order on the time line:
   — Declaration of war by Britain and France
   — Signing of the Treaty of Versailles
   — Battle of Ypres
   — Armistice
   — Application of Schlieffen Plan
   — Battle of Vimy Ridge
   — Beginning of Stalemate (trench warfare) on Western Front
2. When you have completed your time line, write an explanation to show how each event affected a later event.

Oral Reports

When we listen to the radio or watch television, we depend on the ability of people to communicate. Communication by talking clearly is essential for all citizens and employees today.

In your history program, you will have opportunities to:

— discuss events in small groups;
— make oral reports to the rest of your class;
— make reports based on your research;
— participate in interviews and panel discussions.

Canadian soldiers rest in their "billets", having recently advanced on Passchendale.

YOUR TASK

1. With a group of three or four other students, consider three or four interviews you have recently heard on the radio or television. After considering these interviews, write down five characteristics of good oral communication. Compare these with others made by your classmates.

2. *An Oral Report*
   a) Select a person from your text or other sources. (The following people from World War I are suggestions only):

      — General Schlieffen
      — a Canadian soldier after the Battle of Ypres
      — a Canadian soldier following the Battle of Vimy Ridge
      — a Canadian nurse in World War I
      — a woman working in a war factory
      — a citizen opposed to conscription
      — a citizen in favour of conscription

   b) Research the ideas and actions of your subject.
   c) Present your report to the class as if you were that person.

3. *An Interview*
   Work with another student to research your topic. Prepare your report with one student acting as the interviewer, and the other as the subject. Present your interview to the class.

Chapter Three

Boom and Bust
ADVANCE ORGANIZER

1 After the war, returning soldiers expected to find security and well-paying jobs. Instead, factories were closing or cutting back production. Prices had nearly doubled. With the war over, there was no longer a demand for wartime supplies. Workers had to be laid off until new markets were found.

Canadian unions were much stronger than they had been before the war. They were ready to demand higher wages and shorter working hours. The unions joined forces in a general strike in Winnipeg in 1919. Over 30 000 workers left their jobs and the city ground to a halt. The strike lasted over a month. A clash between mounted police and the strikers led to two deaths and many injuries. The strike itself failed, but Canadian unions had demonstrated their strength to industry and government.

2 Women continued their struggle for equal rights. Emily Murphy and Nellie McClung teamed up in a court case to prove women could be appointed to government positions, including the Senate. Women took greater part in business and industry, but still met with prejudice.

3 Business gradually recovered in the 1920s. Jobs became plentiful again, and wages increased. For many it was a decade of plenty. People could afford to enjoy new luxuries of the period, such as movies and phonographs, radios, and automobiles. It seemed that the new prosperity would last forever.

Word List

assembly line	dominion	prohibition
communism	drought	revolution
conspiracy	flapper	socialism
Depression	prejudice	stock market

4

To increase their growth, big businesses sold shares of their companies on the stock exchange. Prices were based on supply and demand. But in the excitement of buying and selling, shares were bought and sold at ever-increasing, unrealistic prices. In 1929 the bottom dropped out of the stock market. The Great Depression had arrived.

With the stock market crash, entire nations could neither buy nor sell. Workers were laid off. Men roamed the country looking for jobs that did not exist. Often they ended up in hobo camps outside the towns. The price of wheat fell to one quarter of what it had been in 1929. To make matters worse, the Prairies suffered a five-year drought. Life was bleak on the farm and in the city during the thirties.

5

During the twenties and thirties Canada relied less on Britain to handle world affairs. The Statute of Westminster was passed by the British parliament in 1931. This confirmed Canada's independence. With the founding of the Canadian Broadcasting Corporation and the National Film Board, Canada was developing her own voice as a nation. By 1939 the country was a respected member of the world community. In that year World War II began. Airplane and armament factories opened up, creating jobs. The Great Depression was over. Amid all this activity, one lingering question remained: Is war the only way to end a depression?

After the War

The war was over! Canada's soldiers were coming home to take up their lives again. What would they find? How would a grateful nation welcome her heroes?

The troop ships tied up at the government docks in Halifax. From there the troop trains steamed westward. Cheers greeted them at every station. On the hometown platform family and friends hugged their brave boys with pride in their eyes. The next day the ex-soldiers headed down Main Street. The first thing they noticed was the prices. Why did everything cost so much?

Rising prices, Ottawa, 1919.

Welcome home!

Wartime Economics

During the war, industry had grown greatly. Canada had supplied shells to the western front. Ships were built and maintained for the Atlantic convoys. The steel industry boomed. Soldiers needed boots, clothes, blankets. Many factory owners became very wealthy. Farmers grew more wheat. Because of the great demand, prices had risen. The soldiers found goods cost nearly twice as much as they had in 1913.

Canadians who had stayed at home were also feeling the pinch. Wages had risen during the war, but only about 18%. They had not kept up with prices. In "real income," what their money would actually buy, workers were much poorer.

To add to people's troubles, many industries were now going through a slump. War supplies were no longer needed. Factories were closing or cutting back. The jobs that remained were already filled. Nobody needed to hire ex-soldiers. They had expected a better deal after their sacrifices in the fields of France.

Who was to blame? Some soldiers blamed the immigrants who had come to Canada before the war. They felt these newcomers, whom they regarded as aliens, had the jobs that were rightfully theirs. Others blamed the economic system and the "profiteers." They wanted a better deal for everybody.

Worker's Unrest

The surviving war veterans returned to Canada in 1919, after having fought "the war to end all wars". They hoped to settle down with their families, find secure jobs, and live better lives.

Why were many ex-soldiers dissatisfied when they returned to Canada after World War I?
What was the One Big Union? How did the O.B.U. plan to use general strikes?

 **Art Gallery page 12**

Returning soldiers march to protest the lack of jobs, Thanksgiving Day, 1920.

Robert Boyd Russell

1888—born in Glasgow, Scotland.
1900—became an apprentice machinist, learning how to build machines and engines from engineers' drawings.
1911—immigrated to Winnipeg. Got job in CPR machine shop. Soon started to organize union.
1914-18—refused to support war. Felt ordinary people were being asked to work harder and go and fight for nothing while bosses sat back and made fat profits. Union leaders in East supported the government and the war. Only leaders from West seemed to agree that the real war was with the bosses.
1919—helped start the One Big Union and organize the Winnipeg General Strike. Was arrested, tried, and sentenced to 2 years in prison.
1920s—travelled and gave speeches to gain support for O.B.U., but the idea was losing ground. Some members returned to regular trade unions, others joined the Communist party.
1930s—backed idea of one industrial union for all workers in one industry. Supported new CCF party.
1956— secretary of Winnipeg branch of CLC.
1964 — died in Winnipeg.
1967 — R.B. Russell Vocational School in Winnipeg named in his honour.

Unfortunately, the postwar economic conditions did not match their dreams. On their return, they were faced with high prices and low wages; many could not even find a job. The government appointed a royal commission to examine the causes of unrest among the workers.

It was conditions such as this which created great unrest among workers. If the existing political parties would not meet the workers' needs, they would organize trade unions to get what they wanted.

In March 1919, a group of workers met in Calgary to organize the One Big Union (OBU). They aimed at uniting all workers in one union. Following the conference, the labour leaders returned to their homes to organize more workers. Their aim, if necessary, was a general strike of all workers.

Would this be the way to get their demands?

The first opportunity came in Winnipeg in May 1919.

The worker coming home sees his children under-clothed. He dresses them up the best he can, and across the road he sees the people in the heights of luxury, driving around in limousines. I had this remark passed about my children;...their children came across the road to play with mine, and a woman came to the door and called them back, "Come away from those children, they are liable to be diseased." That remark was made to my children.

For the best part of my life I have been fighting for my country. I am drawing a life pension now. During the War I fought against labour organizations. There were placards: "Fight this War, and then come back and fight your own war." We are here to-day to fight our own war...

from *Canadian Worker in the Twentieth Century* by Irving Abella and David Miller, Oxford University Press, 1978, p. 125.

The Winnipeg General Strike

The RNWMP charge the strikers on "Bloody Saturday."

On 1 May 1919, 2000 building and metal workers went on strike in Winnipeg. They wanted higher wages (85¢ an hour) and shorter hours (44 hours a week instead of 60). The Metal Trades Council also wanted to be recognized as a union with the right to bargain for the workers. The employers refused to negotiate.

The workers appealed to the Winnipeg Trades and Labour Council. The council asked all the city's union members if they would strike in sympathy. If all workers went on strike, the city would be paralysed. The employers would have to give in. The members voted 11 000 for a general strike, 600 against. The strike began on 15 May.

By 11 a.m., the city ground to a halt. Firemen, streetcar drivers, telephone operators, storekeepers, garbage collectors, street cleaners, butchers, bakers, dairy workers—all left their jobs. Non-union workers came out too. Within three days over 30 000 people were off the job. The police wanted to strike. The Strike Committee asked them to keep working in case they were needed to keep order. The committee also asked bakers, milkmen, and other essential workers to go back to work.

A Divided City

For six weeks Winnipeg was a city of two rival camps. The strikers were led by the Strike Committee. Businessmen and employers organized the "Citizens' Committee of One Thousand."

The Citizens' Committee said they wanted to maintain essential services, but their main purpose was to break the strike. They feared the workers wanted more than just higher wages. They claimed the strike was a communist plot. This might be the beginning of a revolution in Canada. The union leaders seemed to speak in the same terms as the Russian Bolsheviks. The Citizens' Committee urged the federal government to step in.

After a month the strike was petering out. Many workers could not afford to stay out any longer. They started to drift back to work. All might have ended peacefully. But then the government decided to act. They brought in extra members of the Royal North West Mounted Police. They organized and armed a volunteer police force. The mayor banned all public marches.

The volunteer police march up Main Street.

Why did the Trades and Labour Council call a general strike?
What events led to the violence of Bloody Saturday?
Do you think the strike was a communist plot? Why or why not?
Explain 4 ideas of J.S. Woodsworth. Why were they important?

The ONE BIG UNION is Bolshevism Pure and Simple

NOTE THE STRIKING PARALLEL

Bolshevism	One Big Union
Extract from the constitution of "The Federation of Unions of Russian Workers in the US and Canada," the almost pure Bolshevik organization plant controlled by paid agents of Lenine and Trotzky.	Extract from the official stenographic record of the proceedings at the Western Canada Labor Conference at Calgary last March, where the One Big Union movement was launched by labor delegates from all western cities, including 29 from Winnipeg.
Fundamental Principle of the Federation	**Resolution Creating the One Big Union**
The struggle between the classes still continues at the present time and will terminate only when the laboring masses are organized in ONE UNION and USE FORCE to take possession of all wealth through the violence of Social Revolution.	"Resolved that this conference place itself on record as favoring the immediate re-organization of the workers along industrial lines, so THAT BY VIRTUE OF THEIR STRENGTH, the workers may be better prepared to ENFORCE ANY DEMAND they consider essential to their maintenance and well-being."

Business interests said the people behind the strike were communists.

The Arrests

On 17 June the strike leaders were dragged from their beds at gunpoint. They were taken to Stony Mountain penitentiary. Protests erupted all over the country. Why had these people been arrested? What law had they broken? In Winnipeg a group of ex-soldiers decided to hold a protest march. That Saturday they led the strikers down Main Street. They were met by Mounties swinging clubs and firing pistols.

In the riot which followed, two people died. The volunteer police were called in. They patrolled the streets with machine guns. "Bloody Saturday" would long be remembered by Canadian workers.

A week later the Strike Committee called off the strike.

A Communist Plot?

There is no proof the strikers were planning a revolution. It is most likely they were simply trying to get higher wages and better conditions. But the leaders did not talk that way. Their angry speeches led many to believe there was a plot to overthrow the government. Seven of those arrested were convicted of conspiracy. They received sentences of up to two years in prison. Five were never brought to trial. J.S. Woodsworth, a church minister, social worker, and writer, and two others were acquitted.

The general strike had failed. Workers found other ways to try and solve their problems. However, people had become more aware of these problems. The trade union movement gained support. Some of the strike leaders, such as J.S. Woodsworth, turned to politics. They brought the workers' viewpoint into parliament.

When wilt thou save the people, Lord? O God of mercy, when?
The people, Lord, the people. Not crowns and thrones, but men.
Labour Hymn, 1919

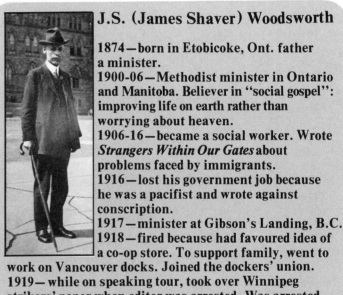

J.S. (James Shaver) Woodsworth

1874—born in Etobicoke, Ont. father a minister.
1900-06—Methodist minister in Ontario and Manitoba. Believer in "social gospel": improving life on earth rather than worrying about heaven.
1906-16—became a social worker. Wrote *Strangers Within Our Gates* about problems faced by immigrants.
1916—lost his government job because he was a pacifist and wrote against conscription.
1917—minister at Gibson's Landing, B.C.
1918—fired because had favoured idea of a co-op store. To support family, went to work on Vancouver docks. Joined the dockers' union.
1919—while on speaking tour, took over Winnipeg strikers' paper when editor was arrested. Was arrested himself for an editorial he wrote. Charge dropped when prosecutor discovered one passage was quote from Bible.
1921—elected in Winnipeg as Independent Labour MP. Communists opposed him because he said socialism should come democratically, not by revolution. In Ottawa spoke on behalf of workers. Uncovered RCMP spies in labour unions. Fought for old age pensions, unemployment insurance, fair treatment for immigrants.
1933—chosen as leader of new CCF party.
1939—stood alone in parliament to oppose Canada's entry into World War II. Even his own party could not support his pacifist beliefs, but all respected his views.
1942—died at Vancouver, B.C.

Women Are Persons

Women first were given the right to vote in the West. In 1918 the federal government gave women the vote on the same basis as men. By 1922 women could vote in provincial elections in all provinces except Quebec.

Women also began to run for office. In the Alberta election of 1917 two women, Louise McKinney and Roberta MacAdams, were elected. In 1921 two more, Nellie McClung and Irene Parlby, entered the Legislature. In British Columbia Mary Ellen Smith became the first woman cabinet minister in the British Commonwealth. At the federal level, Agnes Macphail was the first woman to enter the House of Commons.

Women in provincial legislatures worked for social changes. They pressed for laws on better housing, health, and education. They wanted laws to make marriage fairer to women. They asked for minimum wage laws and safe working conditions. Naturally, these measures were not achieved by women alone. Men supported them too. But it was a sign of changing attitudes that laws like these were being passed.

It seemed that women were finally able to take an equal place with men in public life. Yet very few women were actually running for office. Even fewer were being elected. And there was one branch of government where they were not accepted at all. This was the Canadian Senate.

Agnes Macphail

1890—born near Owen Sound, Ont.
1900s—attended high school and teachers' college at Stratford, Ont. Taught school in Ontario and Alberta.
1921—elected as United Farmers' of Ontario MP for her knowledge of farmers' problems and her work in farm co-op movement.
1921-40—As first woman MP, found she had to speak on women's issues even though she'd never been active in the women's rights movement. Said what women needed was absolute equality, not special favours. Her real interest was in helping the powerless—farmers, workers, the old, the handicapped. Worked for old age and disability pensions, better health care, prison reform. With J.S. Woodsworth supported Nova Scotia miners in a bitter dispute with their employer and the government. As a socialist and pacifist, often supported Woodsworth and later the CCF party's policies.
1940—defeated in federal election because of pacifist views. Worked as newspaper columnist.
1943—elected to Ontario legislature.
1945—lost election because of heart attack.
1948—re-elected to Ontario legislature as CCF member.
1951—retired from politics.
1954—died in Toronto of a heart attack.

The lord chancellor of Britain on his way to deliver the Privy Council's judgement in the "persons case." The procession is part of a ceremony hundreds of years old. The British Privy Council was the final court of appeal for Canadians until 1949. In that year Canada asked Britain to amend the British North America Act to make the Supreme Court of Canada the final court.

FOCUS

How did Agnes Macphail work to help "the powerless"?
Who was Emily Murphy? How did she and the "Alberta Five" gain
for women the right to be appointed to the Senate?

1900 1910 1920 1930 1940 1950 1960 1970 1980 1990 2000

Emily Murphy

In 1916 Alberta had appointed Emily Murphy to be a judge. She was the first woman judge in Canada. In her first day in court a lawyer challenged her. He said that only a "qualified person" could be a judge. According to British law, only men were "persons."

That word "persons" kept cropping up. The British North America Act, Canada's constitution, said senators should be "qualified persons." Did that mean women could not be senators? In 1921 the Montreal Women's Club asked Prime Minister Borden to appoint Murphy to the Senate. He said this was impossible.

Women's groups thought this was unfair. For many years Murphy had worked for poor people, blacks, Chinese immigrants, Indians, children, women. She would make an excellent senator.

In 1927 Murphy teamed up with McClung, Parlby, McKinney, and a long-time women's rights worker, Henrietta Muir Edwards. They fought the "persons case" in the courts. The Supreme Court said women were not persons. It based its decision on conditions at the time of Confederation. No one then had expected women in public office. When the BNA Act mentioned persons, it did not mean women.

The "Alberta Five" took their case to the final court of appeal. This was the British Privy Council. The council ruled that women were persons. "The exclusion of women from all public offices is a relic of days more barbarous than ours."

After her long battle, people expected Emily Murphy would be made the first woman senator. She was not. In 1930 Liberal Prime Minister Mackenzie King appointed Cairine Wilson of Montreal to the Senate. Wilson was a Liberal. Murphy was a Conservative. Some thought King just wanted to ignore her because she had caused so much trouble.

McClung and Murphy

Nellie McClung fought against the abuse of alcohol. She urged governments to introduce prohibition which forbade the sale of alcohol. Emily Murphy wanted to change the drug laws. She thought drug addicts should be treated as sick people, not as criminals. She felt sentences for drug dealers should be more severe.

Both women were writers. McClung wrote novels, short stories, and essays. Most of her writing was about women's issues or prohibition. Murphy, under the name Janey Canuck, wrote about western life. Her book *The Black Candle* was different. It was about the drug trade. It was regarded as a textbook on the subject all over the world.

In 1938 the Canadian Federation of Business and Professional Women's Clubs presented this tablet in honour of the "Alberta Five." The tablet was unveiled by Prime Minister King. Nellie McClung, the only one of the five to attend the ceremony, is at the right.

New Fields for Women

During and after World War I women were granted the right to vote. At about the same time reformers achieved another goal. Prohibition, or a ban on the sale of alcohol, was introduced.

Officially the ban was part of the war effort. The grain used to make alcohol could be used for food instead. But people expected there would be social benefits from the ban. They thought family life would improve. There would be fewer broken homes and abused wives and children. For a few years after the war, prohibition was in force in every province of Canada.

Unfortunately, prohibition did not work as people hoped. Those who really wanted to drink found the alcohol somewhere. Criminals turned to bootlegging—making and selling liquor illegally. By 1924 most provinces decided liquor control was better than a liquor ban. If people could buy alcohol legally, the criminals would be forced out of the business. The government could make money from liquor taxes. The licensed beverage room replaced the illegal speakeasy.

However, the temperance workers had made their point. Society had become aware of the problem. Alcohol abuse is not as widespread as it was in the late 19th century. Drinking still causes many social problems, but help is now available for alcoholics and their families.

Because prohibition was such a sensitive issue, the government asked the people to vote on it in referendums.

The United States kept prohibition after it had been given up in Canada. There were big profits to be made rum-running from the Maritimes to New England, across the Great Lakes, down the Pacific coast, and all along the border. As an American official said, "It's impossible to keep liquor from dripping through a dotted line." The United States gave up prohibition in 1933.

Working

During the war women had turned to jobs they had never done before. When the men came back from the front they took over most of these jobs again. Still, women now had a better foothold in the world of work outside the home.

Yet society had its prejudices. It was not considered respectable for a married woman to work. Many employers automatically fired women when they married. Also, many of the gains of the war and the twenties were lost during the Depression of the thirties. Then people thought it was unfair for a woman to hold a job—especially a well-paying job—instead of a man. They thought the man needed the job more.

FOCUS

What social problems did people hope prohibition would solve? Why did governments change from prohibition to liquor control? What gains did women make in the 1920s in employment and recreation? How were some of these gains lost in the 1930s?

CHIC SILK FROCKS FOR MISSES WITH THE GAY AIR OF YOUTH

8⁹⁵ 12⁷⁵ 14⁵⁰ 10⁹⁵ 11⁵⁰ 13⁷⁵

T. EATON Cᵒ

Sports

Women found new freedom in sports. They played basketball, hockey, and baseball, often for company-sponsored teams. Women's basketball was broadcast on radio. Sunnyside Stadium in Toronto drew 6000 spectators for women's baseball. Crowds for men's games were often not as large.

In 1928 Canadian women went to the summer Olympic Games for the first time. The track and field team won medals in nearly every event.

Women's sports had only a brief period of glory. As professional sport grew, companies stopped sponsoring women's teams. Women's teams began to have trouble getting time in public sports arenas. The "real" athletes (men and boys) were seen as more important. By the thirties women were discouraged from active sports. Some doctors claimed it might harm their ability to have babies. This attitude lasted well into the fifties. Girls in school continued to play some games but often with "girls' rules." Instead of taking part in hockey and football, girls became cheer-leaders. Team sports for adult women became rare.

Beauty contests like this Miss Toronto contest would have been considered immoral before the twenties.

Clothing

The new woman needed new styles of clothing. She wanted the freedom to move easily. The young "flapper" was not going to climb into the corsets and long skirts her mother wore before the war.

By 1928 skirts barely covered the knee. Clothes were loose and comfortable. Women gave up long hair and hairpins for "bobbed" and "shingled" haircuts. Other freedoms followed. It was not uncommon to see flappers smoking—and even drinking—in public. Needless to say, their parents did not always approve.

Elsie MacGill

1905 — born in Vancouver, B.C., daughter of Helen G. MacGill, a journalist and women's rights worker.

1917 — mother appointed a juvenile court judge, one year after Emily Murphy became 1st female judge.

1927 — Elsie was 1st woman to graduate in electrical engineering from University of Toronto.

1929 — 1st woman to graduate in aeronautical engineering from University of Michigan. Caught polio. Became lame.

1933 — did further work in aeronautics at Massachusetts Institute of Technology (MIT).

1934-37 — worked at Fairchild Aircraft, Longueuil, Que. Helped test-fly first Canadian designed and built all-metal aircraft.

1939-43 — in charge of engineering on Canadian-built Hawker Hurricanes and U.S. Navy Helldivers (planes launched by catapult from aircraft carriers) at Canadian Car and Foundry, Fort William, Ont.

1943 — married Eric Soulsby, an executive at Canadian Car. Opened her own consulting business.

1946 — at ICAO (International Civil Aviation Organization), helped set up airworthiness regulations.

1947 — chaired Stress Analysis Committee for ICAO.

1955 — published *My Mother the Judge*.

1967 — served on Royal Commission on the Status of Women. (Mark, son of Nellie McClung, worked for Commission.) Continued consulting business into the 1970s.

1980 — died on visit to sister in Cambridge, Mass.

The Boom Years

Industry took time to change gears from wartime production. An economic slump started in 1919 that lasted into the early 1920s. Then businesses started to make

High rigging, B.C.

The railways met the Pacific at Vancouver where wheat, lumber, and minerals were transferred to ships for the world market. →

British Columbia

Timber exports to the world.
A new smelter at Trail.
Vancouver — Canada's third largest city.
Port of Vancouver — Gateway to Pacific.

During the 1920s and 30s the airplane became a vital link in Canada's developing transportation system.

The Prairies

New motor-driven tractors and other farm machinery.
New types of grain needing a shorter growing season lead to opening of northern Prairies to farming.
New mines at Flin Flon, Man.
Construction of railway and new port at Churchill, Man., so wheat exports could be shipped through Hudson Bay.

Hanna, Alberta, a typical prairie town on the CNR.

FOCUS

Describe the economic development in the 1920s in your region of Canada.
Which region or regions did best during this period? Which did worst?

Ontario

New hydro-electric plants.
Massey-Harris expands farm machinery factories.
American firms like Esso, Ford, GM, GE set up Canadian branch plants.
Hamilton steel mills expanded.
More lead, nickel, zinc, silver, and gold mines open in northern Ontario.

Quebec

Expansion of pulp and paper industry.
New hydro-electric plants.
Electricity used at Arvida to power new aluminum smelter.
Cities like Sorel, Trois Rivières, Chicoutimi attract new industry.
Canada's largest port and greatest city, Montreal, continues growth.

The Maritimes

Fishing, farming, and part-time lumbering still main way of life.
Some growth in coal and steel industry in Cape Breton.
Ports and shipbuilding decline.
Few new industries — Maritimes considered too far from main population centres.

Hydro-electric plants were set up wherever water power was easily available. This new turbine being assembled at Chippewa on the Niagara River was typical.

New facilities at the bustling port of Montreal attracted business from the smaller, less modern ports of Saint John and Halifax in the Maritimes.

A new office building, Toronto.

The assembly line.

Fishing schooners, N.S.

Tourists, P.E.I.

Easy Street

Modern inventions became part of everyday life in the 1920s. People could buy electric stoves, washing machines, irons, vacuum cleaners, toasters. They didn't look like the models we use today. They had few automatic features. But the homemaker of the twenties could rely on many of the same electrical appliances to take the drudgery out of housework.

Home Entertainment

Evenings in many homes were spent round the kitchen table building and adjusting the home-made crystal radio set. The problem with crystal sets was that there was no amplification. The listener had to wear earphones. For family listening big electric radios in fancy wooden cabinets dominated the living room. Of course, there wasn't much on the air during the day. There were few Canadian stations except in the big cities. At night, though, the radio could pull in stations from halfway across the continent—Montreal, Calgary, Boston, Toronto, Salt Lake City, Winnipeg. Saturday night was "Hockey Night in Canada." Families from Glace Bay, Nova Scotia to Medicine Hat, Alberta, gathered at the radio to listen for Foster Hewitt's excited cry, "He shoots. He scores!"

Near the radio was the phonograph. Which was better, an electric or a hand-wound model? The new electric ones were far less work and kept the record turning at a constant speed. Hand-wound models could be taken on picnics for outdoor listening.

A range cost more than twice as much if you wanted to cook with the technological wonder, electricity, than if you were prepared to put up with the fuss of wood or coal.

List 5 inventions that used electricity. Explain how each made life easier or pleasanter in the 1920s.
What are the advantages of producing goods on an assembly line?
In what ways has the automobile changed our way of life?

The "EMPIRE" Electric Vacuum Cleaner 37.50

Eatonia "GOOD VALUE AND RELIABILITY"

EATONIA Toaster Stove 4.35

Curling Tongs 1.95

EATONIA Electric Iron 3.50

Electric Coffee Percolator 9.95

Automobiles

Parked in front of the house was the family automobile, probably a Model T Ford. Henry Ford had just about cornered the market on economy cars. He invented the assembly line. By having each worker do a single job on many cars, he was able to produce cars more cheaply. In 1917 the "Tin Lizzy" cost $495. By 1925 so many cars were rolling off Ford's Canadian assembly line at Windsor that the price had dropped to $424.

Of course, the car was not much use in winter. Even if it started, the roads were too bad to travel. Most motorists put the car up on blocks until spring.

Driving at other seasons could be a risky business too. Many farmers make a little extra money by lending their horses to pull motorists out of the mud. Most country roads were earth. Gravel was used on main highways. In the cities, some streets were paved.

An early tent trailer.

Buying on Time

With all these wonderful items in the stores, it seemed a shame to do without. Almost anything could be bought on the "easy monthly payment plan." Next year, or even next week, the investment on the stock market might pay off. Then the family could sell Tin Lizzie and buy a McLaughlin-Buick or a Hudson Super Six.

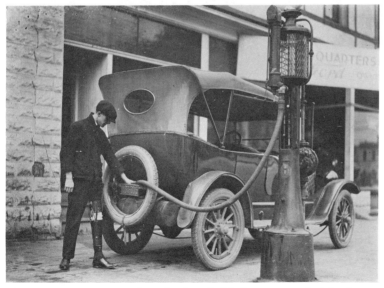

This gas station attendant had probably been wounded during the war.

Not all homes had ice boxes or refrigerators, so the daily milk delivery was an important convenience right into the 1960s.

On the Town

Now that people worked only 9 or even 8 hours a day, they had time for pleasure. The entertainment industry boomed during the 1920s. Those looking for an evening out had plenty of choice.

Vaudeville and Burlesque

In the early years of the century theatres were built in many Canadian cities and towns. Many were part of a chain controlled by Ambrose Small, a Toronto businessman. Travelling theatre companies used these theatres to perform the latest plays from London or New York. Vaudeville, a type of variety show, was very popular. More daring people went to burlesque shows. At burlesque, between the stand-up comics and the skits you could see the ladies of the chorus line, the exotic dancers, and the strip-tease artists.

The Palace in Montreal sold tickets to "bargain matinees" for 25¢. On Saturday afternoons children's tickets were even cheaper.

The Movies

The biggest entertainment of all was the motion picture show. There were movie houses in every city and town across the country. Many people felt the week was not complete without an evening laughing and crying with Charlie Chaplin, falling in love with Rudolph Valentino, or holding their breath while the dashing hero bravely rescued Mary Pickford from the bad guys. By the end of the decade, people flocked to see—and hear—the new miracle, the talking picture. *The Jazz Singer,* starring Al Jolson, spelled the end of the silent movie era.

"America's sweetheart," Mary Pickford, was born in Toronto.

FOCUS

What were vaudeville and burlesque shows?
How did talking movies affect live theatre?
Describe an evening out you might have enjoyed. Your opening
might be: "How shall we choose where to go tonight?"

Music and Dance

In the evenings young people flocked to the night
clubs to listen to the latest music fad — jazz.
Many adults, of course, thought jazz was horrible.
However, they told each other it was a passing fancy —
it couldn't last long.

For more active amusement people went dancing.
In the dance halls live orchestras played the latest
popular tunes. The tango, the Charleston, and the
black bottom were all the rage.

Many theatres did not
switch entirely to movies
until the 1930s. The New
Orpheum in Vancouver
advertised "Vaudeville
and Photoplays."
Showing the feature film
Shanghai Bound provided
a break for the singers,
comedians, and dancers
who were the live
entertainment. The
Orpheum is now the home
of the Vancouver
Symphony Orchestra.

The Dumbells

The Dumbells were the idea of Captain Mervyn Plunkett. Before
the war, Plunkett had been in the hardware business in Orillia,
Ontario. He had also worked for the YMCA. The YMCA sent him
to France to entertain Canadian troops at the front. Soldiers
needed to laugh, and Plunkett wasn't getting the results he
wanted. So he became a talent scout. He brought together a group
of soldiers who could sing, act, and play the fool. They called
themselves the Dumbells.

The Dumbells were asked to perform before King George V and
Queen Mary in London. In 1921 they took their zany show "Biff,
Bing, Bang" to the Ambassador Theatre in New York. A critic
said, "It took a bunch of Canadian soldiers to show Broadway
what speed is." They turned down an offer to make a movie so
they could take the show back to Canada. Each year, until the
talkies killed vaudeville, the company toured the country. They
played all the large city theatres. They performed in small town
schoolhouses and church halls. Once they had to climb a fence
and cross a field to get to the barn which was their dressing room.

The Dumbells used no women in their shows because there had
been no women in the original wartime group. The men acted and
sang all women's parts. "Marjorie" played by Corporal Ross
Hamilton was always a great hit. Many could not believe
Marjorie was really a man.

Marie Dressler was born in Cobourg, Ont., in 1869. At 17, she
ran away from home with a touring opera troupe. A comedy star,
she appeared in plays in New York and London. Her Hollywood
breakthrough came with the talkies, though she first appeared
in a movie in 1914. Here she appears with Frankie Darrow and
Wallace Beery in one of her most popular films, Tugboat Annie.

The Golden Age of Sports

In the 1920s Canadians from all walks of life took part in sports. Town and village teams all competed for space on hockey rinks, baseball diamonds, and soccer fields.

Canadians were also making a name for their country in international and professional sports. The 1928 Olympic Games were a high point. The Canadian track and field team, particularly the women, who were competing for the first time, won medal after medal.

Female Athlete of the Half Century

The daughter of Russian immigrants, Bobbie Rosenfeld shone in almost every sport she tried. She was a star in Toronto in softball, tennis, basketball, and hockey. But her greatest success was in track. In the 1928 Olympics in Amsterdam she won a silver medal in a dead-heat in the 100 m race. She went on to lead the Canadian women's team to a gold medal in the 400 m relay. In the 1930s Rosenfeld was a sports columnist for a Toronto newspaper.

Male Athlete of the Half Century

Like Rosenfeld, Lionel Conacher was representative of the time before athletes specialized. He grew up in the slums of downtown Toronto. He was a champion in every sport he played. He played hockey for the Montreal Maroons and football for the Toronto Argonauts. He was an all-star in baseball and lacrosse and a champion boxer and wrestler. Later he became a member of Parliament. He died while playing softball at the age of 57.

Percy Williams of Vancouver trained for two years for the 1928 Olympics in Amsterdam. He came first in both the 100 m and 200 m races. He was described as "the greatest sprinter the world has ever seen." No other Canadian has ever won two Olympic gold medals.

The most successful team in Canadian history was the Edmonton Grads. Members of the team were all graduates of McDougall Commercial High School in Edmonton. Started in 1915 by school coach Percy Page, they dominated basketball for the next 25 years. During this period they won 502 games and lost 20. Once they won 147 games in a row. They represented Canada at 4 Olympics and won each time. In 1940 their practice facilities were taken over by the army, and the team folded.

FOCUS Who were the Canadian athletes of the half-century? Why do you think they were chosen for this honour?
Why are the 1920s remembered as the golden age of sports in Canada?

The *Bluenose* was built as a fishing schooner in Lunenburg, Nova Scotia, in 1921. Skippered by Captain Angus Walters, she competed in races against the best schooners in Canada and the United States. She won almost every race. In 1938 the *Bluenose* was sold as a cargo boat. She sank in a storm off the coast of Haiti in 1946. Today the *Bluenose* is remembered on the back of the Canadian dime.

In 1963 an exact replica, *Bluenose II* was built in the same shipyard. She is owned by the Nova Scotia government.

Howie Morenz, "the Stratford streak," became the star of the Montreal Canadiens. He was the fastest skater in the NHL. Sports writer Jim Coleman described him this way:

"When Howie Morenz picked up the puck, circled behind his own net, and started for the opposing goal, he lifted you right out of your seat. He appeared to fly above the surface of the ice. He could skate faster than Davey Keon. He could shoot as hard as Bobby Hull. He was as strong as Gordie Howe."

The women's Olympic relay team, 1928. The uniforms of the Canadian athletes were considered quite daring in 1928. By 1932 women from all over the world were wearing "brief" uniforms like these to compete in the Olympics in Los Angeles.

Ethel Catherwood, "the Saskatoon lily," contributed to Canada's success at the 1928 Olympics by winning the gold medal in the high jump.

Did the Twenties Really Roar?

During the twenties more people were able to afford the comforts of life than ever before. For example, by 1928 one out of two Canadian families owned a car. Rich factory owners made big profits. Even middle class Canadians could invest in the stock market.

What was happening to the others, the half who could not afford cars? Life was particularly hard on immigrants in the cities. They arrived not knowing the language and with few skills. Employers took advantage of them, paying them as little as possible. Women, too, were paid much less than men doing the same type of work. Wages of factory workers stayed low. The company might be making huge profits, but workers did not share in them. Businessmen priced goods as high as possible. Often the workers could not afford to buy the things they had helped produce. As a result, unsold goods piled up in warehouses and stores.

Most people thought the boom would go on forever, but some economists saw danger signals. They did not like the unequal distribution of wealth. The rich got richer while workers and farmers did not have enough money to buy their share of goods.

Children look for pieces of coal among the cinders dumped outside the coal-gas plant, 1923.

The International Picture

Countries like the United States, Canada, Britain, France, Italy, and Germany were dependent on international trade. If something happened to upset the trade pattern, all countries would suffer. For example, Canada's economy was based on the export of lumber, pulp and paper, wheat, and minerals. What would happen if other countries could no longer afford to buy our exports?

The Stock Market

By the 20th century, many businesses were too big to be owned by one person or one family. Big companies financed themselves by selling shares on the stock market. The price of shares was determined by supply and demand. If a lot of people wanted to buy, the price was high. If more wanted to sell than to buy, the price dropped.

Careful investors made sure they got their money's worth. They checked that the company had good prospects. But as the excitement of buying and selling took over, some people forgot what the whole business was about. Shares were traded at higher and higher prices. Often the price bore no relation to the real value of the earnings and profits of the company.

Daring investors took risks. They bought "on margin." They paid the stock broker 10% or 15% of the price of the shares. Later, when the price had risen, they sold. They could then pay the broker what they owed and still make a profit. Of course, the deal was that the broker could make a "margin call" if the stock fell. Then the investor would have to pay all the money owed. No one worried about margin calls. Stocks might dip a little, but in the long run they always rose. Why should things ever change?

FOCUS
Why did many *a)* immigrants; *b)* women; *c)* factory workers not share in the prosperity of the 1920s?
Explain what happened to cause the stock market crash of October 1929.

Canada **Art Gallery pages 16-17**

The Crash

Nobody knew on 3 September 1929 that the stock market had reached its peak. After that, prices began to slip, but this had happened before. Most investors thought there would be a turnaround soon.

This time there was no turnaround. Brokers started to make margin calls. Investors couldn't pay up. The brokers were forced to "sell them out."

On Thursday 24 October thousands of shares bought on margin were dumped onto the stock market. There were no buyers. Prices took a nose dive.

When the news hit the newspapers, other investors panicked. On 29 October, "Black Tuesday," things were even worse. This time the sellers were small investors rushing to sell out before they lost everything. The bubble had burst.

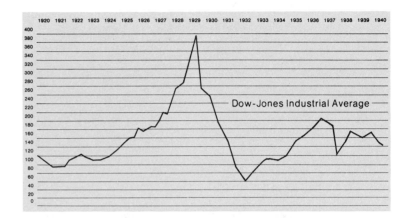

Dow-Jones Industrial Average

The New York Stock Exchange three days before the crash. By 1929 economic conditions in Canada were closely tied to those in the U.S.

It is likely that more than half of the Canadian people were never anything but poor between the wars, although they were worse off in the thirties than before. For these people the twenties had not roared. The decade has come to seem almost a golden age of prosperity. This is probably because *nostalgia* has a bad memory. Also, for many Canadians, the Depression seemed so terrible that whatever came before it was bound to seem more attractive by comparison.
from The Dirty Thirties *by Michiel Horn*

Here am I, working all day long for $25 a month, while the poorest man in the mines has $4 a day and only works 8 hours. It sure is the limit!
Helmi, an immigrant woman from Finland working as a domestic servant, speaks her mind in Painted Fires, *a novel by Nellie McClung.*

. . . A pupil went to school till he was 14. If you passed high school entrance at 13, you could quit and go to work. The boys were apprenticed to some trade. I think the rate was $4 a week, 10 hours a day, and 5 hours on Saturday.

Q. What would be a typical house of that class?
A. The average home is a shack of three or four rooms.
Q. Do they have running water?
A. Yes, but no baths. At least 80% have no hot water.
Q. What about child mortality?
A. The parts of town where juvenile delinquency is highest are the parts where the greatest number of children die. The two go together.

Two quotes from The Canadian Worker in the Twentieth Century *by Irving Abella.*

The Great Depression

The panic that caused the stock market crash had started in the United States. It quickly spread to all countries involved in trade. The crash triggered the Great Depression.

The Downward Spiral

After the crash small investors thought they would still get by. For many of them investing in the stock market had only been a sort of hobby. True, their savings were gone, they had nothing to fall back on. But most people had never invested in the stock market anyway. They hadn't had enough money in their pay envelope to do more than feed, clothe, and house the family. Like those who couldn't afford to invest, small investors still had their jobs. They thought nothing more could happen to them.

They were wrong. Many Canadian products were made for export. When the crash came, foreign countries bought much less. Prices fell. Canadian farmers still had unsold wheat in storage. Many Canadian companies had been overproducing. They already had goods piled up in warehouses. There was no point in producing more. They closed down or cut back until the backlog was sold. Their workers were laid off. Those lucky enough to keep their jobs had to accept pay cuts. Unemployed people did not have the money to buy luxuries like radios and vacuum cleaners. Workers who make these products were laid off too. Next came the workers who supplied the raw materials. Soon people could not afford to buy shoes, coats, dresses. A sad spiral had set in.

By 1933 one in five Canadian workers had no job. There was no system of unemployment insurance. Two million people were "on relief."

A Depression Dictionary

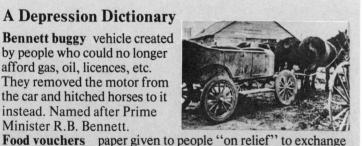

Bennett buggy vehicle created by people who could no longer afford gas, oil, licences, etc. They removed the motor from the car and hitched horses to it instead. Named after Prime Minister R.B. Bennett.

Food vouchers paper given to people "on relief" to exchange for basic food supplies. Vouchers were used instead of money because it was assumed people would spend money foolishly.

Funny money term used to ridicule Social Credit party's plan to give all citizens a credit to spend of $25 a month.

On relief or **on the dole** receiving public welfare.

Pogey public relief, welfare. **Pogey house** hostel for people with no place to live. Also **pogey pants**, etc.

Riding the rods hitchhiking on a freight train by climbing onto the undercarriage. Actually this was too dangerous to be practical. Most hobos sneaked inside the cars or rode on the roof.

Soup kitchen place giving free meals to poor people, usually run by municipal relief office, a church group, or private charity.

A soup kitchen. Unemployed men seated for a free meal. It satisfied their stomachs, but was often a blow to their pride.

OCUS

Compare the upward economic spiral of the 1920s with the downward spiral of the 1930s.
How did people survive during the Dirty Thirties when there were few jobs and no unemployment insurance?

1900 1910 1920 1930 1940 1950 1960 1970 1980 1990 2000

Evicted because they cannot pay the rent, Montreal.

CONTRASTS

The Prosperous Twenties	The Depressed Thirties
Industrial expansion	Industry slowing down
New businesses opening	Bankruptcies and business failures
Stock market values high	Stock market values low
Prices high	Prices low
Wages high	Wages low
Plenty of jobs	Few jobs
Mood of optimism	Mood of pessimism

Freight hopping.

Learning to Survive

Perhaps the worst part of living through the Depression was the shame of being out of work. People had been taught that if they were poor, it must be their fault. Only lazy people failed. Every time they lined up at a soup kitchen or accepted food vouchers, the despair went deeper.

A woman seeking a well paying job was frowned on because "Men needed the jobs more." On the other hand, many women accepted low wages. Therefore they sometimes found jobs when there were none for men. They left their husbands to keep house and went out to work long hours for $3 or $4 a week. Society said that men should be the breadwinners. Every day husbands, brothers, sons, lost a little more self-respect.

People did not give up. They made do. They patched old clothes. When the clothes fell apart, they wore flour sacks. They put wads of newspaper in worn-out shoes. They used tea leaves and soup bones three and four times. When there was nothing left at home, they set out across the country looking for work.

Riding the Rods

They stole into empty freight cars. They hitch-hiked along the highways. Perhaps there would be work on the next farm or in the next town. A knock on the farmhouse door got them a meal but no work. When they lined up at the factory gates, the sign was always out: No Help Wanted.

In summer they slept beside open fires in "hobo jungles" on the edge of town. In winter they might be allowed to sleep on a jailhouse floor.

For many, this way of life went on for ten years. These were the Dirty Thirties.

EFFECTS OF THE DEPRESSION   113

The Prairie Dustbowl

No work in Edmonton. This family from Saskatoon is on the move again.

The worst place to be during the Depression was on the Prairies. In 1929 wheat had fetched $1.60 a bushel. In 1932 farmers could hardly get rid of it for 38¢. In 1933 world conditions started to improve a little. Some factories in eastern Canada took on a few more workers. Mines were being reopened. On the Prairies, though, the troubles had only just begun.

Drought

The summer of 1931 had been very dry. In 1932 the rains came again. In 1933 the drought returned. There was no real rain for five long years.

Crops depend on the soil on the surface of the land. The subsoil beneath contains no nourishment. Without rain, the fertile prairie topsoil turned to dust. Strong winds whipped it up into a black blizzard. Farmers stood in sorrow as the land that fed them blew away. They watched the few wheat plants that survived the wind storms shrivel and die in the parched subsoil.

With the drought came the grasshoppers. They hatched by the millions in the prairie desert. Farmers looked up to see dark clouds of hoppers blotting out the sun. When they had passed by, nothing would be left alive. One farmer reported they had even stripped the bristles from his broom. Only the metal band that had held the bristles and a chewed handle remained.

In the bumper crop of 1928 Saskatchewan had produced 8 750 000 tonnes of wheat, or 1.6 tonnes per hectare. In the worst year of all, 1937, production fell to 920 000 tonnes, or 0.2 tonnes per hectare.

What did farming families do, hit by the double blows of Depression and dustbowl? They went barefoot. They dressed in flourbags. They burned

Feb 11, 1935

Dear Sir –

Please don't think I'm crazy for writing you this letter, but I've got three little children, and they are all in need of shoes as well as underwear but shoe's are the most needed as two of them go to school and its cold, my husband has not had a crop for 8 years only enough for seed and some food, and I don't know what to do. I hate to ask for help. I never have before and we are staying off relief if possible. What I wanted was $3.00 if I could possible get it or even some old cloths to make over but if you don't want to do this please don't mention it over radios as every one knows me around here and I'm well liked, so I beg of you not to mention my name. I've never asked anyone around here for help or cloths as I know them to well.

Yours Sincerly
Mrs. P. E. Bottle

Prime Minister Bennett, who was a millionaire, received many letters like this one from Alberta. He sent Mrs. Bottle $5.00.

Give 3 reasons why the Prairies were the worst place to be during the Depression.

Write a report on conditions on the Prairies for a newspaper in your community during the 1930s.

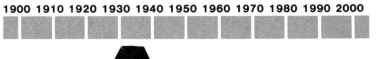

1900 1910 1920 1930 1940 1950 1960 1970 1980 1990 2000

wheat instead of wood—it was cheaper. They ate gopher stew. They gave up the telephone, the newspaper, the car. They fell behind on their mortgage payments. When the bank foreclosed, they were forced off the land. Others just gave up. They headed for the cities of Ontario or moved farther west to British Columbia. Over one quarter of the wheat farms on the Prairies were abandoned during the thirties.

Most families just hung on. Perhaps next year the rains would come. They might have a good crop. The price they got for it might cover the cost of growing it.

In 1938 the rains came again, but so did hail and grasshoppers. It was not until 1939 that things returned to normal. And it took World War II to bring the price of wheat back to a profitable level.

Dust storm on the Prairies.

The farmers in Saskatchewan are in desperate circumstances. Only about half of them have sown seed this year, and much of that seed has blown out. The soil has drifted completely over fences to a depth of 60 cm on one road.
Quoted in The Dirty Thirties *by Michiel Horn*

The church at Brussels, Ontario, sent us a railway car of mixed fruit and vegetables, apples, potatoes, beets, carrots, onions, cabbage — 26 000 kg in all. We also received clothing, mostly second hand, but all good.

The United Church — particularly from Ontario — surely responded nobly. Over 130 carloads of fruit and vegetables were donated to Saskatchewan, and the railways transported it all free.
Quoted in The Dirty Thirties *by Michiel Horn*

Here's how it was. Let me tell you. The wind blew all the time, from the four corners of the world. From the east one day, the west the next. If you were working outside, you didn't notice it too much, but the women did. Ask my wife — but she's dead now — she said the wind used to make the house vibrate. It was just a small wind, but there, always steady and always hot. A hot sucking wind. It sucked up the moisture. So this wind just blew and blew, and we had dust storms and times when we kept the lanterns lit all day.
Quoted in Ten Lost Years *by Barry Broadfoot*

The On-to-Ottawa Trek

The Depression was probably hardest for young single men. When employers had to cut staff, they let the young and single go first. They assumed older, married employees needed the jobs more. While young women were often unemployed as well, it was considered natural for them to be supported by their families.

The young men set off to look for work in other cities across the country. Usually there were no jobs anywhere. City relief officers worried about these drifters. They did not want to have to support them. They had enough trouble giving food and clothing to their own people. So they tried to make the newcomers move on.

But what if these desperate people turned violent? What if communist agitators organized them? There could be a revolution! The cities demanded action from Ottawa.

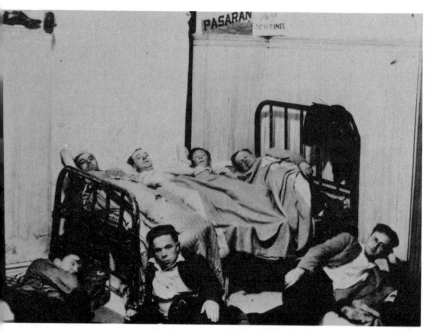

A flophouse during the Depression.

Relief Camps

The federal government decided to stop any revolution before it started. Relief camps were set up to get the drifters off the roads, out of the cities, and out of trouble. Men in the camps worked 8 hours a day. They built roads, dug ditches, planted trees. In return each received work clothes, a bed, food, and 20¢ a day. The camps were run by the Department of National Defence.

Men found the camps to be a cross between an army camp and a prison labour camp. After the work was over there was nothing to do. Conditions were terrible. One bunkhouse was 24 m by 7.3 m. It had no windows. The 88 men slept 2 to a bunk.

Men in the camps felt cut off from the world. There was no future for them. They were not even allowed to vote.

Reaction

In June 1935 over 1000 camp workers from the Vancouver area jumped some empty freight cars. They were headed for Ottawa to complain directly to the prime minister. On the way, other discontented workers joined them. People in the cities they passed through welcomed them, fed them, and wished them well. Even the train crews co-operated.

The government was terrified. They had set up the camps to avoid trouble. They had even forbidden the camp workers to form committees. Now a mass movement had begun. The On-to-Ottawa trek had to be stopped.

The trekkers were met in Regina by the RCMP. Eight delegates were allowed to go to Ottawa to meet with Prime Minister Bennett. It was a stormy meeting. Soon each side was calling names. Bennett called the

FOCUS

Why did the government set up relief camps?
Why did camp workers start the On-to-Ottawa trek? What happened? Think of a recent mass meeting or march to try to influence government policies. What happened at it?

leader a criminal. The leader called Bennett a liar. Bennett refused to listen to their demands. The delegates returned to Regina determined to continue the trek.

The On-to-Ottawa Trek reaches Regina.

The Regina Riots

On 1 July, Dominion Day, the trekkers held a meeting to raise money in the Market Square. The police were afraid the crowd might get out of hand. Soon after the meeting started, a large furniture van pulled up at each of the four corners of the square. At the blast of a whistle the vans opened and out poured Mounties and city police waving batons. In the words of one trekker, "We took it for a few minutes, and then we let go against them."

The riot lasted until late evening. The On-to-Ottawa trek was over. The government realized that the relief camps were a failure. Within a year they had been closed down. Closing the camps, of course, did not solve the problems of the unemployed.

Depression Across Canada

If one worker in five was out of a job, four were still working. The hardship was great, but the country survived. How did people in each region cope? Everybody suffered to some degree, but those who produced goods for export had the biggest problems.

The factories of southern Ontario and Quebec produced goods which were mainly sold in Canada. They were protected by high tariffs. This kept foreign goods out. Some factories were able to keep going, even though they were producing much less. The tariff wall meant they could keep prices high. However, this made things even harder for those who needed the goods.

Farmers in Central Canada and the Maritimes had mixed farms—a little wheat, some corn, a vegetable garden, some cattle and poultry. If they could not sell their produce, they could at least trade, or barter it. The local storekeeper knew his customers had no cash. He would gladly accept a few dozen eggs and a barrel of apples in exchange for a pair of shoes. The Maritimes had missed out on the boom of the twenties anyway. Conditions in the Depression were worse, but Maritimers were used to hardship.

British Columbia was almost entirely dependent on export. Lumbering, mining, and salmon fishing were the major industries. There were no markets and no jobs.

The Prairies were hardest hit: First they could not sell their wheat. Then the dustbowl meant they could not even grow it.

Bennett and King

"Prosperity is just around the corner." In 1930 the Liberals under Prime Minister Mackenzie King were prepared to sit and wait for prosperity to arrive. When the provinces (which mostly had Conservative governments) asked Ottawa to help look after the unemployed, King refused to give them "a five-cent piece."

R.B. Bennett

The voters were angry. They elected the Conservatives under R.B. Bennett to form a new government. The Conservative approach to the Depression was not very different from the Liberals'. Both believed it was best for business to "find its own level."

Laissez faire is French for "Let it be," or "Leave it alone." This is the name given to the economic theory that business and industry will make the most profits if the government does not try to control them. If they make good profits, there will be more money, and everybody will be better off. In the 1920s it seemed that *laissez faire* worked well. Some economists knew the crash was coming, but governments in North America and western Europe thought it was wrong to interfere with the economy. Even after the crash they did not feel they could (or should) do anything to get things moving again.

Bennett did try to protect jobs in Canadian factories with high tariffs on imports. He suggested lower tariffs on goods from countries which would offer the same deal to Canada. He managed to get Commonwealth countries to agree to this idea at a conference in Ottawa in 1932. However, ordinary people did not feel any effects from this policy. They were still out of work. The lines outside the soup kitchens got longer.

In 1933 U.S. President Roosevelt promised Americans a "New Deal." Instead of leaving business to run itself, the New Deal brought the government into the economy. Slowly things started to improve in the United States.

In hard economic times people lose confidence in their political leaders. Mackenzie King won this election in 1926, but lost to the Conservatives under R.B. Bennett in 1930. In 1935 the voters chose King and the Liberals again.

Letters to Prime Minister Bennett

Chichester, Que.
March 13 1935

Dear Mr. Bennett.

I am a little boy 11 years old I live in a very back wood place and I am very poor there is a big bunch of us I am going to school My little Sister and I we have three miles to go and break our own path but we dont mind that if we were only able to buy our books, the Quebec books are very expensive so I just thought I would write you maybe you would give us enough to buy our books if you dont I Guess We will have to stop and try and earn a little money to help out our father please excuse paper and pencil as I have no better Hoping to hear from you real soon I am

Yours Loving Friend
Albert Drummond

Please answer soon soon soon

Murray Harbour P.E.I.
March 24 1935

Dear Sir:

I am writing you to see if their is any help I could get.

As I have a baby thirteen days old that only weighs One Pound and I have to keep it in Cotton Wool & Olive Oil, and I havent the money to buy it, the people bought it so far and fed me when I was in Bed. if their is any help I could get I would like to get it as soon as possibile.

their is five of a family, Counting the baby.

their will be two votes for you next Election

Hoping too hear from you soon

Yours Truly.
Mrs Jack O'Hannon

FOCUS

What is *laissez faire*? Do you think this policy is effective during a depression? What was Bennett's New Deal? Why did the voters elect King in 1935?

Bennett was a rich man, but he could not solve the problems caused by the Depression from his private fortune. However, when he received letters from desperate citizens he often responded with gifts of money or clothing.

Calgary June 18th 1935

Dear Mr. Bennett,
   Do please raise the Old Age Pension to at least thirty dollar per month. So many of your very old friends, myself included, have really not enough to exist on.
   Very best wishes for your good health,

Sincerely,
Alma Ward

May 20/31

Mr Bennette
   Since you have been elected, work has been imposible to get. We have decided that in a month from this date, if thing's are the same, We'll skin you alive, the first chance we get

Sudbury Starving Unemployed

Regina Sask.
May 24/35

Dear Sir:
   You will. no doubt be surprized to recived this requaist.
   I thought that you would have second hand clothing that would not be suitable for you to wear. as I am straped for clothes fit to wear to Church I disided to write to you
   My best suit is over 8 years old and pretty well frayed
   Judging you by your picture I beleve you are about the same size as myself
   I might say my people and I have allways been stunch Conservatives I wouldn't ask a Liberal party if I had to go naked.
   I was 69 years of age May 22/35
   I voted as a farmer's son when I was 18 years old for Sir John A McDonald's Goverment and Im still on the list

I am yours respectfuly
J.A.Graydon

1900 1910 1920 1930 1940 1950 1960 1970 1980 1990 2000

In 1935, just before an election, Bennett introduced a "Canadian New Deal." It included many of Roosevelt's ideas. It proposed an 8-hour workday, a minimum wage, unemployment insurance, and price control.

"King or Chaos"

The Liberals under Mackenzie King poured scorn on Bennett's plans. They used the slogan "King or Chaos." The voters also were not impressed. Why had Bennett waited for five years while Canadians rotted without jobs? They felt the New Deal was just a way to try to get votes.

The Liberals swept to victory in the election of 1935. They had few real policies. However, by this time everyone realized that governments had to act to help people out of the Depression. The situation was confused by federal and provincial jealousies. The federal government had most power to raise money through taxes. Social policies like unemployment relief, which cost money, were provincial responsibilities. It seemed an impossible situation.

In 1937 King set up a Royal Commission on Dominion-Provincial Relations. The "Rowell-Sirois Commission" recommended sweeping changes in the tax system to remove the stumbling blocks to co-operation. It suggested equalization payments to poorer provinces. It said the federal government should be responsible for unemployment insurance.

However, this report did not come out until 1940. By that time the Depression was over. World War II had started. The unemployed had found jobs — in the army and the arms factories.

The Depression was not ended by R.B. Bennett or Mackenzie King. It was ended by Adolf Hitler.

The New Politics

From the depths of the Depression sprang new political ideas. The Liberals and the Conservatives both believed the problems would solve themselves, that it was not the duty of government to affect the economy. But some people were not prepared to wait. They formed new political parties.

Co-operative Commonwealth Federation — CCF

Liberals and Conservatives dominated parliament, but there were members from other political groups as well. In 1920 United Farmers groups in Ontario and the Prairie provinces came together as the Progressives. The first woman to be a member of parliament, Agnes Macphail, was a Progressive. Workers supported Labour candidates. J.S. Woodsworth, one of the leaders of the Winnipeg General Strike, was elected as a Labour member of parliament. Other members of parliament were Independents. They didn't belong to any party.

In 1933 some Progressives, some Labour representatives, and other interested people met in Regina. They formed the Co-operative Commonwealth Federation. The CCF believed in *socialism*. They wanted the government to control much of the business and industry in the country. The

The Regina Manifesto — Program of the CCF

1. **The people (the government) should own all banks and financial institutions.**
2. **The people should own key industries such as railways, mines, lumbering, telephone systems, hydro-electric companies.**
3. **There should be a large-scale program of public works (housing, roads, and public buildings) to provide jobs for the unemployed.**
4. **Laws should guarantee minimum living standards for all through programs like unemployment insurance, family allowances, old age pensions.**
5. **Farmers' land should be protected from mortgage foreclosures.**
6. **There should be a guaranteed minimum wage.**

Newly elected CCF MPs with their leader, J.S. Woodsworth, 1935. The young Tommy Douglas is seated at the left.

economy should be run on a co-operative basis for the benefit of the people. Under the private enterprise system owners ran things to make profits for themselves. The system lacked controls. Because it was uncontrolled, it had led to the Depression.

The CCF elected J.S. Woodsworth as their leader. They published the Regina Manifesto which described their program.

Many people confused the socialist CCF with the Communist party. There were some big differences. The Communists believed that change would only come through violent revolution. The CCF strongly believed that changes in the system should be made democratically. People must vote freely. The Communists said the rights of the individual were not important. The welfare of the state was all that mattered. The CCF upheld the individual's civil rights. Woodsworth was respected by all political parties when he stood up for immigrants, old people, or trade union members.

Summarize the 6 main ideas of the Regina Manifesto. Why did the CCF support each of these ideas?
What did Aberhart believe was the main cause of the Depression? How did his Social Credit party propose to end it?

William Aberhart advocating the idea of Social Credit

Poverty in the Midst of Plenty

The stores of Alberta were stocked with clothes, radios, and tractors, but people had no money to buy them. Farmers had wheat and could not sell it. If they managed to sell, the price they received was often less than the cost of sowing and harvesting it.

Far away in Ottawa, Liberals and Conservatives debated and discussed—and did very little.

William Aberhart was a school principal in Calgary. Albertans knew him as Bible Bill, the radio preacher of the Calgary Prophetic Bible Institute. In 1932 he began to talk about a new political idea, Social Credit.

The root of the Depression, he said, was that people did not have enough money to buy the things that were being produced. If people had more money, they could buy more goods. More people would have jobs. They would have more money. The Depression would be over. He proposed to credit each citizen with a monthly "social dividend" of $25.

This idea made great sense to the farmers and workers of Alberta. They trusted Bible Bill Aberhart.

You can strip down the appeal of Social Credit to the $25 a month. All of us farmers were in desperate straits. Here was William Aberhart promising $25 a month, and he was a Minister of the gospel. I asked him about that $25 after one of his meetings, and he told me I must have faith.
A farmer in Central Alberta

In the 1935 provincial election Social Credit won 56 of the 63 seats and Aberhart became premier.

The federal government ruled that issuing money was a federal power. Aberhart's provincial government had no right to give out money. Many Albertans became convinced that Canada was being run by and for eastern interests. The old parties preferred talking about laws and the constitution to helping people in need.

New parties and new politics sprang up in other parts of Canada during the Depression. In British Columbia, Liberal premier Thomas Pattullo tried to bring the provincial government into the economy with a program of "work and wages." In Quebec Maurice Duplessis came to power in 1936 with the party he founded, the Union Nationale. He is shown here with the fiery Liberal premier of Ontario, Mitch Hepburn, on Hepburn's onion farm.

Enjoying Life

Life in the thirties was not dull and drab all the time. People found their fun in many ways. If they could not afford to travel, they could still get together with friends and neighbours for a picnic. They could go swimming at the community beach. Saturdays there were often concerts in the bandstand in the local park.

Radio

Amos and Andy, Eddie Cantor, Bing Crosby, Fanny Brice, Jack Benny—these were the entertainers of the decade. If you had a radio, your pleasure was free. Soap operas ran daily. People could hardly wait to learn more of the loves, fears, disasters, and joys of Helen Trent, Our Gal Sunday, or Ma Perkins. Monday evenings Lux Radio Theatre presented radio versions of the latest movies. Other nights people pushed aside the furniture and danced to the music of the big bands.

The Canadian Radio Broadcasting Corporation (later the CBC) was established in 1932. Canadians from coast to coast could now listen to their own programs. They tuned in to the music of The Happy Gang from Toronto. They laughed at Stag Party from Vancouver. Sunday mornings boys and girls listened to the stories of Just Mary from the Maritimes. At Christmas the whole family gathered round the radio for the King's Message. French Canadian farmers were the first to receive farm news. The programs were so popular that English farm broadcasts were soon started too. J. Frank Willis gave the first on-the-spot news coverage at the rescue operations after the Moose River Mine disaster in Nova Scotia. People learned about the confrontation between Ontario Premier Mitch Hepburn and the strikers at the General Motors plant in Oshawa. Each week on Hockey Night in Canada Foster Hewitt greeted them: "Hello, Canada and hockey fans in the United States and Newfoundland."

Jeannette MacDonald in Rose Marie and Shirley Temple in Susannah of the Mounties. Mountains and Mounties were Hollywood's impression of Canada. Add some snow, birchbark canoes, handsome lumberjacks, and wicked French Canadians, and the picture was complete.

Flash Gordon movies were Saturday afternoon favourites.

Movies

In this era before television, every town had its own movie house. When there was 15¢ to spare, kids went to the Saturday afternoon show almost every week. The cartoons, the latest episode in the adventures of The Shadow or Tom Mix, a full-length movie, sometimes even a free comic book—all could be had for 10¢. The extra nickel bought a chocolate bar or

FOCUS

Which 1930s radio programs might you have enjoyed?
Describe an afternoon at the movies during the 1930s.
How did sports fans find out about the achievements of their
favourite stars and teams?

some jelly beans. A generation grew up on cowboy and Indian movies. These movies painted a distorted picture of the Indians' struggle for survival when European settlers moved in. Native people are still fighting the warped attitudes these movies created.

Few movies dealt with real life as it was in the Depression. People wanted to escape all that. They flocked to laugh at the Marx brothers, Laurel and Hardy, Charlie Chaplin, W.C. Fields. They shivered in their seats as they watched *Frankenstein* or *Dracula*. They thrilled to the adventures of Errol Flynn and Virginia Mayo in pictures like *Captain Blood*.

Canadian movies? Impossible! Everyone knew movies were made in one place only — Hollywood. Of course there were plenty of movies *about* Canada. The fact that these movies painted a pretty strange picture of the country didn't seem to bother anyone.

Sport

Is sport something people watch or something they do? Before television helped create superstars and super salaries there was a lot more "doing."

Winter in the thirties found Canadians of all ages on the ice—skating, curling, playing hockey. Spring and summer brought baseball, swimming, soccer, football. Every town had its own teams. Kids worshipped the local allstar rather than some national figure.

Professional sports were popular too. The Montreal Royals and the Toronto Maple Leafs were the only professional baseball teams. Football was beginning to attract attention. Each year the best western team travelled east to meet the eastern champions. Each year the West was defeated. Then in 1935 Fritz Hanson led the Winnipeg Blue Bombers to victory. National rivalry for the Grey Cup had begun.

The excited public followed the birth and upbringing of the Dionne quintuplets through magazine articles and radio reports. The quints became a great tourist attraction in Callander, near North Bay, Ont. They lived in a hospital built especially for them, and were used in movies and advertisements for baby food.

Then, as now, hockey was the Canadian sport. The excitement was carried across the country by the magic of radio. Kids who had never seen the Montreal Canadiens or the Toronto Maple Leafs play knew all the details of the latest game. If they missed the game on the radio, they picked up the story on the sports page of the newspaper the next day.

Young people today either don't care about the Great Depression or have an exaggerated view of it. It was tough, but it wasn't all hunger and sadness. There were picnics, corn roasts, and cheap dances. Young people fell in love and got married. People learned to cope with being poor and out of work. Many rose to heights of bravery and unselfishness they never would have reached in normal times. Babies were born, whether their fathers were employed or not, and their young mothers made do with handmade or hand-me-down layettes. . .

Do you want to know something? I don't think I'd have wanted to miss the Great Depression for the world.
Hugh Garner

Changes Between the Wars

In 1914 Canada did not declare war. Britain's declaration meant the whole British Empire was automatically involved. By 1939 things had changed. Canada issued her own declaration of war.

What is a Dominion?

When Canada became a dominion in 1867, nobody thought that this meant she was an independent country. She handled her own internal affairs, but foreign affairs were still handled by Britain. Canadians soon discovered that Britain was not always interested in what was best for Canada.

During World War I people in Canada were proud of their country and their part in the war effort. They began to feel "Canadian." At the peace treaty discussions in Versailles, Canada and the other dominions of the British Empire sat as separate nations. Canada was an independent member of the new League of Nations.

In 1923 Canadians and Americans worked out a treaty to protect halibut on the Northwest Coast. The British ambassador to Washington expected to sign the treaty on Canada's behalf. Canada announced that her own minister of fisheries would sign the treaty. No British signature was required.

The British Commonwealth of Nations

It was obvious that the new relationship of countries in the British Empire had to be spelled out. Other groups—the Boers of South Africa and the Irish—were also unhappy. They were threatening to leave the empire. The Imperial Conference of 1926 issued the Balfour Report. It stated that the dominions were free and equal. They were united by the Crown and associated as members of the British Commonwealth of Nations.

In 1931 the British parliament passed the Statute of Westminster. This act declared that the British parliament had no power over the laws of the dominions.

Canada's constitution, the British North America Act, was an act of the British parliament. When the Statute of Westminster was passed, Canadians had not worked out how they could make changes to their constitution. So Canada asked Britain to keep the power to amend the BNA Act for the time being.

A Changing Identity

As British traditions faded, the American influence on Canadian life became stronger. If Canada was to be a nation, it was important that Canadians should have a sense of their own country. This was why the Bennett government established the Canadian Radio Broadcasting Corporation. The CBC would give Canadian actors and singers a chance to display their talent. It would provide a news service to tell Canadians about things from their own point of view. In 1939 the King government set up the National Film Board. It was to make films not only for Canadians but also to tell others about Canada.

Transport by Air

Radio could take the human voice to out-of-the-way places. The airplane brought food, supplies, mail, and medical assistance. After their exploits during World War I, Canadian aces had not given up flying. Flyers like Punch Dickens and Wop May became bush pilots. Bush pilots flew under incredible conditions. They performed deeds of great bravery. But airline companies in the twenties and early thirties were small, often with only one or two planes. None could afford to serve the whole country.

FOCUS

How did the Statute of Westminster of 1931 describe Canada's position within the British Commonwealth?
Name 3 organizations in Canada established by the government.
List some Canadian achievements in art, medicine, and writing.

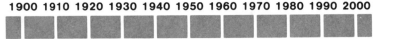

1900 1910 1920 1930 1940 1950 1960 1970 1980 1990 2000

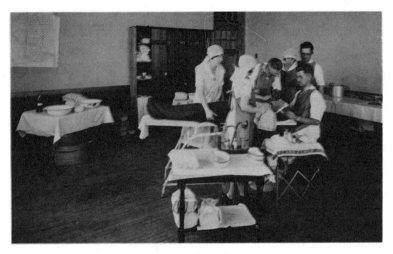

A travelling medical clinic in Alberta. Medical services to the public improved dramatically between the wars.

On TCA's first aircraft, oxygen was required over the Rockies.

The government stepped in. In 1937 Trans Canada Airlines (later Air Canada) was formed. Within two years the company had 15 ten-passenger aircraft. Former bush pilots made up the crew. To ensure the safety of passengers, all the flight attendants had to be registered nurses.

The Government in Business

Laissez faire economics said governments should leave business alone. In Canada provincial governments ran hydro-electric and telephone companies. The federal government ran a railway, and airline, a radio network, and even a film studio! In the United States private companies handled these things. Why was it different in Canada?

Here investors said the distances were too vast, the risks too great. Yet Canadians needed services and transportation. They needed to know about themselves and each other. If private industry could not provide these things, the government had to.

Achievements

Canada was no longer a colony. She was an independent nation, proud of the achievements of her citizens. Diabetics all over the world were being kept alive with insulin, the discovery of Frederick Banting and Charles Best. A Montreal hospital had become a world leader in brain surgery under the guidance of Wilder Penfield. The Group of Seven and Emily Carr had changed Canadian painting forever. Stephen Leacock was regarded as the funniest writer in the English language. Canada was a respected member of the world community.

Frederick Banting

1891 — born on a farm near Alliston, Ont.
1903 — schoolfriend died of sugar diabetes.
1916 — graduated from medical school and joined army as doctor in France.
1921 — with Charles Best began research on diabetes. Knew disease was result of a malfunctioning pancreas. Experimenting with diabetic dogs, they found that an extract of the pancreas (later called insulin) controlled sugar build-up in the blood. Found way to extract insulin from slaughter cattle for human use.
1922 — only known treatment for diabetics was practically to starve them to slow sugar build-up. Insulin tested on a 14-year-old, Leonard Thompson, who had lost so much weight he was near death. In a few weeks he regained normal health. Banting sold patent for insulin to University of Toronto for $1, profits to go to medical research.
1923 — Awarded Nobel Prize for Medicine. Upset that Best was not honoured, shared prize money with him.
1923-39 — directed Banting and Best Dept. of Medical Research, supervised work on cancer, lead poisoning, silicosis. A good amateur painter, became friend of A.Y. Jackson of Group of Seven.
1939 — investigated effects of high altitudes on pilots for RCAF.
1941 — died in plane crash in Newfoundland on way to England on "a mission of high national importance."

Questions and Activities

Test Yourself

Match the items in column A with the descriptions in column B.

A	B
1. One Big Union	a) stated the original program of the CCF.
2. Social Credit Party	
3. Regina Manifesto	b) granted Canada full independence within the Commonwealth.
4. Alberta Five	
5. Statute of Westminster	c) fought for the right of women to be made senators.
	d) wanted to give each citizen $25 a month.
	e) sought bargaining power by uniting all workers.

Ideas for Discussion

1. If a general strike like the one in Winnipeg were organized in your community, what industries and services would be closed down? How would you personally be affected?
   Do you think workers should have the right to organize general strikes? Why or why not?

2. Was prohibition a good idea? Discuss this in relation to the ways we deal with alcohol abuse today. Are today's methods more or less successful than prohibition was?
   Compare prohibition of alcohol to today's ways of handling drugs. Do you think the use of marijuana should be legalized?

3. Summarize some of the main advances in rights and freedoms for women made in the period 1914 to 1930. Compare these to advances for women made in the period since the 1960s.

4. Discuss the impact of the automobile on:
   a) shopping patterns   d) travel and holidays
   b) city and community planning   e) jobs and industry
   c) convenience   f) morality

5. In the 1930s the government set up work camps for unemployed young men. Some people suggest that a similar system, but with more freedom, should be set up for the unemployed today. There would be a choice of:
   working in local parks, public buildings, etc.
   helping the aged or handicapped
   clearing land in unsettled areas like the North
   joining the armed forces
   Hold a debate on the topic: Resolved that unemployed young people should work for the government rather than being given unemployment insurance.

6. How involved should the government be in running industries and providing services? Here is a list of organizations run by the federal government. What does each one do?
   Why did the government become involved in this area?
   a) CNR   d) TCA (Air Canada)
   b) CBC   e) Petro-Canada
   c) NFB
   List other industries and services run by the federal and provincial governments. Do you think the government should continue to be involved in these areas? Are there other industries or services that you think the government should run? Why?

Do Some Research

1. Do any members of your family belong to a trade union? Compile a list of unions that people in your community belong to. Name some other unions in Canada today. What are their objectives? How have union aims changed since the time of the Winnipeg General Strike? How have they remained the same?

2. Find out more about one of the following:
   a) J.S. Woodsworth, "a saint in Canadian politics"
   b) Agnes Macphail, Canada's first woman MP
   c) Mary Pickford, "America's Sweetheart"
   d) The mystery of Ambrose Small, theatre owner
   e) Bible Bill Aberhart
   f) Banting and Best
   g) The Alberta Five
   h) The Group of Seven

3. Write a report about an outstanding woman in Canada today in one of the following areas:
   a) industry and commerce   c) sports
   b) politics and law   d) entertainment
   Describe her background and accomplishments.

4. Do some research on automobiles of the 1920s. Describe the basic features and options that were available.
   How have automobiles changed since the 1920s? What features have disappeared? What new features have been introduced? What "options" of the 1920s are now standard equipment?

5. Find out more about one of the following:
   a) Movies of the 1920s   c) The early days of radio
   b) Movies of the 1930s   d) Records and record players
   Write a paragraph describing their main features and importance.

6. Find out more about the success of Canadians at the 1928 Olympics. Compare their record to that of Canadian athletes in more recent Olympics. Can you draw any conclusions from this comparison?

7. The Edmonton Grads were one of the most successful sports teams ever. Do further research on the Grads or another Canadian sports team of the 1920s and 30s. Your report might include information under the following headings:
   a) Beginnings   c) Star players
   b) Coaches   d) Win-and-loss records
8. Memories of the Depression. Interview a member of your family or a neighbour who lived through the Depression. Prepare a list of questions you want to ask before you start, but be ready to follow up any interesting points that come up during the interview. Your list of questions might include some of the following:
   a) Where did you live during the 1930s?
   b) What jobs did people in your family do?
   c) What wages did they make?
   d) What kind of home did you live in? Did you move during the Depression? Why?
   e) What kind of food and clothing did you have?
   f) What did you do for entertainment?
   g) What was, for you, the saddest part of the Depression?
   h) What are your happiest memories of the 1930s?
   If you record your interview on a tape, you will be able to refer to it as you write a one-page summary for the class. Some of the best sections might be edited into a class tape of Memories of the Depression.

Be Creative

1. Write a letter from a soldier who has just returned home at the end of World War I. Your opening might be: "I am so pleased to see my family and friends again, but this town sure has changed!"
2. With a group of other students prepare a folder on the changing role of women from 1914 to 1930. Your folder should include:
   a) a *poster* advertising a women's rights rally;
   b) a *speech* by a supporter of women's rights;
   c) a *picture* of women's fashions and hairstyles in the 1920s with an explanation of how these gave women new freedom;
   d) an *editorial* favouring or opposing the right of women to be senators;
   e) a *letter to the editor* disagreeing with the editorial.
3. Design an advertisement for a product or appliance that became available during the 1920s. Let your ad explain how buying the item will make life easier, more convenient, or more entertaining. Compile a class brochure called Advertisements of the Roaring Twenties.
4. Make a mural or picture-map of Canada showing industries across the country in the 1920s.

5. Write a letter to Prime Minister Bennett asking for help for you and your family. Write Bennett's reply.
6. Prepare an edition of a newspaper in your community for a specific date in the 1920s or 30s. Your newspaper might include:
   a) reports on local, provincial, national, and international events
   b) entertainment and sports news
   c) information on new inventions and scientific discoveries
   d) human interest stories
   e) editorials
   f) letters to the editor
   g) political cartoons
   h) business news on local industries and job opportunities
   i) advertisements for new products
   j) fashion news
   k) want ads
   For some of these items you will need to do additional research.

You Are There

Starting a business — a store, a factory, an industry, a mine — takes a lot of money. Most companies get this money by asking people to *invest* in the business by buying *shares* or portions of the company's *stock*. If the company does well and makes a profit, the shares will pay the investor *dividends*. More importantly, the value of the shares themselves will go up. If the company does not make a profit, there will be no dividends and the value of the shares will go down. Shares are bought and sold on the stock market.

You're a big investor!
Your Uncle Fred has died and left you $5000 on condition you invest it on the stock market.
1. Start by consulting the business section of the daily newspaper over several days in order to establish the trends in the value of stock shares.
   a) Find a stock that has gone up in value.
   b) Find a stock that has gone down.
2. Invest Uncle Fred's $5000 in stocks of your choice.
3. Record the value of your stocks each day. Remember that if you think your stock has "peaked," or if you don't like its performance, you can sell it at the going price and re-invest in another stock.
4. At the end of a month, calculate the current value of your shares.
Did you make a profit? Compare results with other members of the class.

Group Activities

In many school activities, students "learn" *from* the teacher or from a textbook. As citizens at work, in sports, or at home, we often learn by working *with* other people. In fact, most citizens learn from their friends and associates rather than from a "teacher".

YOUR TASK

— To work in a group with three or four other students, to prepare a *folder of materials* on a given topic.

Specific Topic

The changing role of women from 1914 to 1930 (or another topic of your choice)
Prepare a folder of materials including the following materials:

a) a *poster* advertising a women's rights rally;
b) a report of *speech* by a supporter of women's rights;
c) *drawings* of women's fashions and hairstyles of the 1920s, with an explanation of why women supported these new styles;
d) an *editorial* favouring (or opposing) the right of women to be involved in Parliament;
e) *a letter to the editor* disagreeing with the editorial

Procedure

1. Select your topic (or arrange with your teacher for another appropriate topic).
2. Divide the work among your group, so that each person is responsible for completing part of the group task.
3. Conduct your research on your activity. Consult other members of your group for advice and assistance.
4. Arrange to share your reports informally with each other. You should *edit* each other's work before preparing a "final draft".
5. When the work has the approval of the other group members, prepare a final draft in the most effective form.
6. When your group has completed its task, prepare a cover for your folder.
7. As a group, plan what could be the most appropriate or effective means of communicating the information to others:

   — brief oral reports
   — overhead transparencies
   — panel presentation
   — rehearsed interviews
   — skit or dramatic presentation

Evaluation of Group Activity

Your group activity may be evaluated in several ways:

1. *Teacher Assigned Mark for Group*

	OUT OF	TEACHER MARK FOR GROUP	GROUP'S SELF-EVALUATION
ORGANIZATION OF MATERIAL	3		
APPROPRIATENESS OF CONTENTS	3		
ACCURACY AND COMPLETENESS OF INFORMATION	3		
QUALITY OF WRITTEN AND GRAPHIC MATERIAL	3		
EFFECTIVENESS OF PRESENTATION TO REST OF CLASS	3		
TOTAL	15		

2. *Peer Evaluation*

Students in the group assign themselves a mark as a group.

3. *Group Assigns Mark to Each Individual*

WITHIN THE GROUP	OUT OF	STUDENT MARK
CONTRIBUTION TO PLANNING	3	
CONTRIBUTION TO RESEARCH	3	
CONTRIBUTION TO PREPARATION OF MATERIAL	3	
CONTRIBUTION TO PRESENTATION	3	
OVERALL CO-OPERATION WITHIN THE GROUP	3	
TOTAL	15	

Total Mark of Group Activity

TEACHER MARK	— OUT OF 15	_____
GROUP MARK	— OUT OF 15	_____
INDIVIDUAL MARK	— OUT OF 15	_____
	TOTAL 45	_____

Writing a Newspaper Account

The newspaper is one of our main sources of information for understanding world events today. A useful form of writing is to describe a historical incident as if you were a reporter at the time of the event.

When you write a newspaper report, you should:

- research and collect the necessary information;
- describe the events as accurately as possible, without bias or prejudice;
- answer the five "W" questions;
  — who? — where? — when? — what? — why?

YOUR TASK

1. Read several newspaper reports to see how reporters (journalists) write their accounts.

2. *Newspaper Account*
   After you have read several news reports, become a reporter and write an account of one of the following (or choose a topic of your own);

   — The Winnipeg General Strike
   — The Supreme Court Decision on the "Persons Case"
   — Stock Market Crash, October 29, 1929
   — The Dustbowl in the Prairies
   — The On-to-Ottawa Trek
   — The Election of the Social Credit Party in Alberta
   — The Birth of the Dionne Quintuplets
   — The Edmonton Grads

Chapter Four

The World at War
ADVANCE ORGANIZER

1

After World War I life was not easy in Europe. The war had left many countries heavily in debt. Some people resented the new borders that had been drawn at the end of the war. They distrusted the new democratic forms of government that had been set up. The Depression made these problems even worse. In all this uncertainty, dictators easily gained control. They offered simple solutions and promised glory for their country. They silenced all who spoke against them. In Italy and Spain, Mussolini and Franco came to power. In the Soviet Union, Stalin ruled.

2

Most dangerous of all was Adolf Hitler, who gained power in Germany in 1933. He told Germans they were the "master race." He blamed all Germany's problems on scapegoats — "non-German traitors" within the country — and the unfair terms of the treaty that ended World War I. Hitler's sweeping racism became government policy. Fear of his secret police gripped the country while Hitler urged Germans to dream of ruling the world.

3

Other nations knew Germany had real causes for complaint. They hoped that if they let Hitler take a little, Germany would be satisfied. In 1938 Hitler's armies swept into Austria and Czechoslovakia. When Poland fell to German tanks and dive bombers in 1939, world leaders knew they had to fight back. Their resistance came too late: soon most of Europe was under Nazi rule.

Word List

appeasement   fascism   ration
blitzkrieg   liberation   recruit
demilitarized   partisan   scapegoat
dictator   purge   unity

4

Canadians figured prominently in World War II. The Royal Canadian Navy organized huge supply convoys to Britain. Canadian pilots helped stop Hitler in the Battle of Britain and other air battles. Canadian soldiers fought bravely on the battlefields of Europe and Asia. They suffered a tragic defeat at Dieppe, France. They played a valiant part in the slow advance through Italy and the final invasion of western Europe after D-Day.

5

Canadians at home produced airplanes, ships, and armaments. They bought Victory bonds to help pay for the war. Food and gasoline were rationed so more supplies could go to Europe. Women entered the factories and joined the armed forces. Young people ploughed up their schoolyards to plant "victory gardens."

6

Japanese army officers also dreamed of a vast empire. They attacked China, American bases in the Pacific, and British and French colonies in Asia. Many Canadians feared and hated the Japanese who had moved to Canada. Japanese Canadians were taken from their homes on the Pacific coast and held in camps until the end of the war.

7

The war ended with the dropping of atomic bombs on two Japanese cities. This was the final horror in a war marked by crimes against humanity. Millions of Jews and other minorities had been murdered under Hitler's rule. Too many powers had been willing to prove their might through warfare. The United Nations was founded in the hope of maintaining peace for all in the future.

Dictators in a Changing World

For people in Europe the 1920s were a time of change, insecurity, and frustration. The treaty of Versailles was expected to straighten out the chaos caused by World War I. However, it created as many problems as it solved. The losers of the war felt they had been unfairly treated. The winners could not see that they had gained anything. Both felt cheated.

A New Map of Europe

The diplomats at the conference in Versailles believed every national group should have its own country. So they gave lands that had been part of Germany to Poland and to France. They broke up the Turkish and the Austrian empires into independent countries. But it was impossible to draw neat lines and put all

High-ranking officers of the Nazi and Fascist parties of Europe. Front row (from left to right): Herman Goering, Benito Mussolini, Adolf Hitler.

Germans or Slavs on one side, all Poles or Italians on the other. Within the new borders there were still minority groups. The minorities resented being part of these new countries. The majority groups feared the smaller nationalities might cause trouble.

Rise of Fascist Dictators

Before the war there had been elected assemblies in most countries of Europe. These assemblies had rarely had much power. It was the princes, kings or emperors and their advisors who made the final decisions. Now Europeans had lost faith in their old leaders. The old system had led them into a useless war. The diplomats at Versailles, under the leadership of U.S. President Woodrow Wilson, wanted to set up democratic forms of government. But these new democracies had not grown naturally. As a result, few people knew how to run a country in a democratic way. Voters had no experience to help them judge the new politicians.

Then came the thirties. The Depression caused huge social, economic, and political problems in stable democracies like Canada, the United States, and Britain. In unhappy Europe the effects were disastrous. People felt they had to find a way out of the hopelessness, frustration, and insecurity that surrounded their lives.

They were ready to follow a leader—one who promised better things. They wanted to be told their country was great—and would become greater. They were prepared to believe their problems were somebody else's fault—the foreigners, the communists, the democrats, the Jews.

It was conditions like these that led to the rise of fascism. Mussolini, Hitler, and Franco rode to power on the backs of broken hopes, fears, poverty and hatred.

Why did the new national boundaries created by the Treaty of Versailles fail to bring peace to Europe?
Why did the people fall under the influence of dictators?
Do you think a dictator could come to power in Canada today?

1900 1910 1920 1930 1940 1950 1960 1970 1980 1990 2000

The Fascist symbol, a bundle of rods and an axe, was taken from the ancient Roman Empire. The rods represented the power of corporal punishment and the axe represented the power of capital punishment.

Fascism in Italy

In Italy Benito Mussolini formed the Fascist party to fight communism and socialism. Fascists in black shirts gathered to listen to their great leader. The black shirts were a sort of uniform. They made the wearers feel like a private army. The "blackshirts" broke up trade union meetings and communist rallies with clubs and fist fights. They conducted a campaign of terror against those who protested their actions.

In 1922 Italian unions called for a general strike. Mussolini said that if the government didn't stop the strike, the Fascists would. Fascists from all parts of Italy marched on Rome. In panic, the king asked Mussolini to form a new government.

Mussolini promised great things for Italy. He introduced an economic program that was to make Italy self-sufficient. Meanwhile the blackshirts continued their bullying tactics to silence all criticism. Soon Mussolini was dictator of Italy. There was no opposition. Only Fascists were allowed to run for election.

The hammer and sickle of the Communist party symbolize the power of the workers.

Stalin's Russia

Ten years after the communist revolution, Joseph Stalin came to power in the Soviet Union. He proved to be an able but ruthless dictator. Stalin set up a "five year plan." Under the plan Soviet citizens worked and sacrificed together to expand industry. The plan was exciting because it looked to a better future. It worked, but the cost was high. Stalin conducted "purges" of those the police said were against him. They were sent to prison camps in the Arctic or Siberia. Thousands were executed in secret.

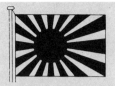

Japan was "the land of the rising sun." On the military ensign, rays spread from the sun to show how the armed forces could spread out to conquer the world.

The Army in Japan

Meanwhile, on the other side of the world, army officers prepared their nation for conquest and empire.

The Japanese emperor was considered divine by his loyal subjects. The Japanese armed forces were responsible to him, not to the elected government. In the late twenties a group of young officers took control of the army. They dreamt of a vast Pacific empire. They were supported by businessmen who wanted raw materials and a guaranteed market for Japanese industry. Government ministers who opposed them were often assassinated.

Franco's symbol was a crossbow and arrows. Adapted from the Spanish coat of arms, it represented military might.

The Spanish Civil War

In 1936 General Francisco Franco led a revolt against the government of Spain. The government was made up of several political groups, including the Communist party. Franco wanted to stamp out communism. He was supported by the army, landowners, factory owners, members of the Roman Catholic church, and the Falange (the Spanish fascists). Mussolini and Hitler sent help from Italy and Germany. Stalin supported the government side.

The world looked the other way as a democratically elected government was crushed by fascist rebels. Some were not content to stand aside. They formed the International Brigades to fight alongside the government forces. Among them were 1200 Canadian volunteers who formed the Mackenzie-Papineau battalion. Other Canadians, especially Roman Catholics, were more worried about communism than about fascism. To avoid offending anyone, the Canadian government did its best not to get involved.

The war lasted 3 years. By 1939 Franco was dictator of Spain. He ruled Spain until his death in 1975.

Adolf Hitler

In Germany the leader of the National Socialist (Nazi for short) party watched Mussolini's rise to power with admiration.

Adolf Hitler was born in Austria in 1889. After an unhappy childhood be became a homeless drifter. The outbreak of World War I found Hitler in Germany. He eagerly joined the German army. He proved an able and courageous soldier.

Germany surrendered in 1918. Soldiers everywhere cheered because the war was over. Hitler cried because Germany had been beaten. He swore revenge on the "socialists and Jewish traitors who," he said, "had stabbed Germany in the back." He joined the Nazi party. Its aim was to rebuild Germany and defeat her enemies. Hitler's passionate speeches soon made him the party leader.

An outdoor rally in Berlin, 1937.

Nazi troops prepare to march in a parade.

Being a Nazi was made exciting. Hitler organized the party on military lines. The Nazis marched through the streets of German towns. They had their own salute, their own uniforms, their own songs, their own symbol—the swastika. They listened to stirring speeches from their leader. The brown-shirted "storm troopers" broke up Communist party meetings, attacked the homes and businesses of Jews, and struck terror in the hearts of other "traitors."

Many Germans were not won over. Germany had a new democratic system of government—with 27 political parties. By 1933 the Nazis were the largest party in the German parliament, but they never won a majority in a free election. As leader of the largest party, Hitler was asked to be chancellor. He accepted on condition that he be given dictatorial powers. That evening, the Nazis held torchlight parades. Swept along by excitement, the crowds roared "Sieg Heil! SIEG HEIL!" (Hail victory!).

OCUS

List 5 reasons why many Germans supported Adolf Hitler when he came to power.
What actions did Hitler take when he came to power?
Why might young people be attracted to the Nazi party?

Why Germans Supported Hitler

Even people who had not voted for Hitler were glad to see a strong man in charge. They thought he would solve the country's problems. Few understood his real intentions.

Hitler blamed Germany's troubles on the treaty of Versailles. In many ways he was right. The treaty demanded that Germany pay for the war with money and goods. This had made life difficult for Germans in the 1920s. Hitler, his face red with rage, tore the treaty to shreds before cheering crowds.

The Depression hit Germany hard. Perhaps the Nazis could put Germany back to work.

Few Germans liked or trusted the new democratic system of government. It had never really worked. It was easy to blame democracy for Germany's problems. Hitler promised a return to strong government. His private army of storm troopers paraded through the streets. They broke up the meetings of other political parties. Many people supported the Nazis out of fear.

Hitler gave the Germans targets to blame for all their problems. His favorite scapegoats were the communists and the Jews. The Nazis preached "racial purity." They claimed Germans were the "master race." Jews, Slavs, and other minorities were to be regarded as "impure aliens."

Many saw Hitler as an inspiring leader. He had become a brilliant, hypnotizing speaker. Nazi rallies were full of colourful parades and rousing marching songs. People who attended felt they were part of a great movement.

And Hitler delivered on his promises. Germany was put back to work. New roads and bridges were built all over the country. Guns, tanks, warships, planes—all forbidden by the treaty of Versailles—started to pour from German factories. Young men flocked into the army. In 1936 they rode the new tanks down the new highways, across the bridges and into the Rhineland. The Versailles treaty had declared this part of Germany to be demilitarized forever, but Germany was on the way back to glory!

Meanwhile, all traces of democracy in Germany were being destroyed. Socialists, democrats, communists, religious leaders, teachers, scientists—all who spoke out against the Nazis—found themselves in concentration camps. Jews found they couldn't get jobs. Instead of the truth, newspapers printed Nazi propaganda; radios blared it forth. The unions, the schools, the army, even the churches were under Nazi control. The Gestapo, Hitler's secret police, were everywhere.

The Hitler Youth was formed to inspire young people with Nazi "ideals."

The Gathering Storm

In 1919 the nations of the world had come together in the League of Nations. The League was to settle international arguments through debate. The nations wanted to prevent another war.

During the 1920s the League managed to settle a number of disputes between nations. By the 1930s things weren't working as well. Some countries had learned they could defy the League and get away with it.

Manchuria

In 1931 a group of Japanese army officers created an excuse to invade the Chinese province of Manchuria. Within weeks Manchuria was torn from China. The League of Nations was not prepared to act. Asia seemed so far away. All the League did was to refuse to recognize the new government of the province. The only result of that was that Japan withdrew from the League.

By 1937 World War II had already begun in Asia. Japan set out to conquer the rest of China and to build an empire in the Pacific.

Ethiopia and the Rhineland

In Italy Mussolini's economic program was not working. Mussolini decided a war would take people's minds off the problems of the Depression. He would rebuild the Roman Empire. He saw himself as *il Duce,* a leader greater than Julius Caesar.

His victim was Ethiopia. All through the summer of 1935 Italian troops gathered in Italy's colonies on the borders of the ancient African kingdom. In October they poured into Ethiopia. The Ethiopians fought bravely, but spears were no match for machine guns, planes, tanks, and poison gas.

Emperor Haile Selassie of Ethiopia appealed to the

Norman Bethune

1890 — born in Gravenhurst, Ont. Strong minded from early childhood, often not popular with others.
1907 — After high school worked as a logger, teacher in one-room school and with Frontier College. Started university, got bored and dropped out for a while, but by 1914 was halfway through medicine.
1914 — dropped out to join Canadian Army Medical Corps.
1915 — wounded. Returned to university.
1916 — graduated in same class as Frederick Banting.
1917-19 — served as surgeon with Canadian navy.
1920s — worked as doctor. Enjoyed easy, 20s lifestyle.
1927 — developed TB. Insisted doctors try an experimental treatment, collapsing the lung. Cured. Decided to dedicate life to helping others.
1928-33 — working in Montreal, invented many surgical instruments for chest operations.
1935 — visited U.S.S.R. Impressed by government-run system of medical care for all. On return, advocated it for Canada.
1936 — shocked at Canadian opposition to socialized medicine, joined Communist party. Volunteered to help government forces against Franco in Spanish Civil War. Set up mobile blood transfusion clinic to take blood right to the wounded in front lines of battle.
1937 — returned to Canada for speaking tour on Spain.
1938 — went to China to help Chinese forces under Mao Tse-tung in war against Japanese. Worked under incredible conditions with almost no medical supplies to help Chinese wounded. Wrote own textbooks to train medical workers.
1939 — a cut on his finger infected during an operation (was not wearing rubber gloves). Died of blood poisoning. A hero in China, not recognized in Canada until 1970s.

League of Nations. The League members agreed that Italy was in the wrong. They said they would cut off Italy's oil supplies. "Oil means war!" replied Mussolini. In fear, the League backed down. In any case, it was

FOCUS

Why did the League of Nations fail to act against Japan, Italy, and Germany?
What countries did Hitler take over before invading Poland?
How would you have dealt with Hitler at Munich in 1938?

1900 1910 1920 1930 1940 1950 1960 1970 1980 1990 2000

While Mussolini invaded Ethiopia, Hitler's armies were welcomed by cheering crowds as they entered the Rhineland.

more worried about the consequences of Hitler's march into the Rhineland. Would France declare war? France, at the urging of Britain, decided not to press the issue.

Hitler and Mussolini soon realized they had served each other well. They had kept the League from acting against either of them. With the military rulers in Japan, they formed the Rome-Berlin-Tokyo Axis. This was an agreement to support each other against communist Russia. Now Hitler had allies. He was ready to gamble that the leaders of Europe would agree to anything to avoid war.

The Appeasement of Germany

Hitler declared that his vision of the "master race" required that Germans everywhere belong to one united Germany. In 1938 he announced that Austria was to be part of Germany. The German army marched in. The Austrians had had no way of defending themselves. France and Britain said nothing. Seven million Austrians were now German. And Hitler had his next target almost surrounded.

The rich industrialized Sudetenland area of Czechoslovakia was home to 3 million Germans. Hitler claimed they were being oppressed. He threatened to occupy the area. France, Britain, and Russia promised to stand by the Czechs. At the last moment the leaders of western Europe met at Munich. They gave in to Hitler's demands rather than have another war. British Prime Minister Chamberlain went home to cheering crowds. He claimed he had achieved "Peace with honour, peace in our time." Many people in Canada and elsewhere heaved a sigh of relief. Others warned of greater threats to come.

Within months the German army swallowed up the rest of Czechoslovakia. Hitler now demanded German-speaking areas of Poland. Finally the leaders of France and Britain realized they had to take a stand. They declared they would guarantee Poland's borders.

The government of the Soviet Union decided it could not rely on the western democracies for help against Hitler. Look at what had happened to Austria and Czechoslovakia! So the Soviet Union and Germany signed a treaty not to fight each other. A secret agreement was also made to divide Poland between them. With the Soviet Union out of his way, Hitler was now ready.

On 1 September 1939 German tanks thundered across the Polish border. Bombers flattened the great city of Warsaw. On 3 September France and Britain declared war against Germany. One week later, a hastily assembled Canadian parliament voted to stand by Britain.

Blitzkrieg

The Nazi armies crushed Poland in less than a month. By October 1939 the Polish armed forces had collapsed under the pounding of German tanks and Stuka dive bombers. Hitler had taught the world a new word—blitzkrieg or "lightning war."

After the defeat of Poland came a lull in the fighting. People called this the "phony war" or "sitzkrieg." But most knew it was a time of careful preparation for the bloody struggle to come.

In the spring of 1940 Germany struck in a new wave of blitzkrieg. Denmark fell in one day, Norway in two. The Netherlands were smashed in five days. Belgium took eighteen. Even mighty France was shattered in six weeks. Hitler was master of Europe.

Dunkirk

British and French troops were pinned against the English Channel near the French port of Dunkirk. If British ships could reach Dunkirk in time, they could be rescued. The navy had few ships to spare. The word got round. English fishermen, weekend pleasure sailors, ferry captains, all took their boats across the channel. Canal boats and river tugs towed rowboats and empty coal barges out to sea. The volunteer fleet brought back 350 000 men — ten times the number the government had hoped to save.

Britain stood alone in Europe. The new prime minister, Winston Churchill, promised nothing but "blood, toil, tears, and sweat." It seemed that the war would soon be over. German forces were preparing for the invasion of Britain.

In the distant port of Halifax, Nova Scotia, ships were assembling to steam in convoy across the Atlantic. As well as fighting soldiers they carried the food and weapons needed for one of the most important battles in history — the Battle of Britain.

A convoy of ships sets out on the dangerous voyage across the Atlantic.

The Battle of Britain

On 10 July 1940 the German air force, or Luftwaffe, set out to clear the Royal Air Force (RAF) from the skies. Wave after wave of German Messerschmidts and Heinkels streamed across the channel. They spread out over Britain to their bombing targets—airfields, ports, factories. Slowly but surely the RAF was being wiped out. At one point every British fighter was in the air. Had the Germans launched another attack, no planes were available to respond.

Then suddenly the German tactics changed. The RAF had made a surprise bombing raid on Berlin. The Germans decided to "blitz" the cities in revenge. They would terrorize the civilian population into surrender. The plan backfired. The bombs rained on London

FOCUS

Was Dunkirk a victory for the Germans or the British?
Why did the Germans fail to win the Battle of Britain?
Why do you think Lord Beaverbrook was nicknamed Tornado?
What was his contribution to the war effort?

 **Art Gallery page 20**

night and day. Londoners moved into air raid shelters and subway stations. Each day they set about repairing homes, reopening stores, carrying on. British resistance grew stronger, not weaker.

However, with this breathing space the few remaining RAF Spitfires and Hurricanes could regroup. Newly trained pilots could join those who had been flying almost constantly since the battle began. New planes were coming off the assembly lines at the rate of 500 a month.

On 15 September German planes almost blackened the skies. The RAF was ready for them. When the day was over the Luftwaffe was decidedly beaten. Two days later, Hitler called off the attack. If he could not wipe out Britain, he would turn against the Soviet Union.

The Battle of Britain was won by a few hundred pilots. They included 80 Canadians as well as Britons, Poles, Americans. The Luftwaffe lost 1733 planes, the RAF 915. Canadian pilots accounted for 60 definite and 50 probable "kills."

Royal Air Force Spitfire airplanes at Duxford, England.

Max Aitken, Lord Beaverbrook (Tornado)

1879 — born in Maple, Ont., son of a minister.
1880 — family moved to Newcastle, N.B.
1895 — left school. Worked first in a drugstore, then as R.B. Bennett's law clerk.
1898 — discovered talent as business promotor. Sold insurance, bonds, re-organized Maritime coal, steel, and lumber industries.
1906 — married. On honeymoon in Caribbean bought a hydro-electric company and a streetcar company.
1907 — at age 28, a millionaire. Moved to Montreal, the financial capital of Canada. Bought Montreal Trust Co.
1910 — organized founding of Canada Cement Co. and Stelco. Moved to England. Elected as British MP.
1914-18 — as Canadian military representative in Britain, arranged that Canadian army would serve as a unit. For Canadians at home, wrote reports, hired war artists, and made 1st films of soldiers in action. Made British minister of information (wartime propaganda).
1916 — Made Lord Beaverbrook.
1918-39 — established huge newspaper empire. Warned Britain of threat of Hitler.
1940 — as minister of aircraft production, broke all rules to boost monthly production from 183 to 471. "Cannibalized" old and damaged aircraft to fix others.
1941 — as minister of supply, set up "lend-lease" program with U.S. Organized supplies for U.S.S.R. after Nazi invasion.
1946-64 — set up scholarships, art galleries, community centres, especially in N.B. Wrote 6 history books.
1963 — remarried at age 83.
1964 — died in England.

Never in the field of human conflict was so much owed by so many to so few.

Winston Churchill

THE COURSE OF WAR, 1939-1940   139

The Dieppe Raid

As France fell to Hitler's armies, Mussolini decided Italy was ready to join in. By 1941 nearly all Europe was under German or Italian control. British and Australian troops were fighting Germans and Italians in North Africa. In December the Japanese attacked American and British positions in the Pacific. The British colony of Hong Kong fell to Japan on Christmas Day. The main thrust of German might was turned against the Soviet Union.

Why the Dieppe Raid?

The Soviet Union was bearing the full weight of German attack. Stalin pressed his western allies to open a second front. If they would attack in France, the Soviet Union might get a little relief.

The British knew they were not ready to start a second front. But the whole Commonwealth was enraged at the fall of Hong Kong. The Americans, their new allies, wanted to get moving. Also Canadian soldiers in Britain had been waiting for action since the start of the war three years ago. A raid might satisfy the Soviets, the Americans, and the Canadians. It might be useful, too. It could test German coastal defences. It could help plan a full-scale invasion.

The Raid

On the morning of 19 August 1942, 5000 Canadian soldiers crouched in landing craft off the heavily fortified French port of Dieppe. They were to seize the town, destroy the port facilities and airport, and take prisoners. The key to victory was surprise.

When the first Canadians hit the beach, the Germans were ready and waiting. The ships had been spotted during the night. Also some ships had gone off course and arrived late. As a result the raid did not start till broad daylight.

German soldiers tend their wounded Canadian prisoners.

The Canadians were facing 15 km of cliffs fortified with cannon, barbed wire, tank traps, and mines. Many landing craft were blown right out of the water. In one boat of 80 men that made it to shore, 40 were killed and 20 wounded within minutes. One regiment had 96% casualties. Only a few soldiers ever reached the town.

Give 3 reasons for the decision to conduct a raid on Dieppe.
Why were Canadian troops chosen for the raid?
Do you think the lessons learned from the Dieppe raid were worth
the heavy losses? Explain.

1900 1910 1920 1930 1940 1950 1960 1970 1980 1990 2000

▲

When the smoke cleared, 900 men lay dead. Nearly 2000 had been taken prisoner. The boys from Winnipeg, Hamilton, Montreal, Calgary, Windsor, Regina, and Toronto had been savagely defeated.

A British military committee examined the causes of the failure. They noted: the foolishness of attacking a fortified beach in broad daylight; and the failure to pulverize defence positions by aerial and naval bombardment before the landing.

The report concluded: Although from a purely military point of view the results [of the Dieppe raid] achieved were disappointing, and the heavy casualties sustained regrettable, it is considered that the operation was worthwhile provided its lessons are carefully applied when the time comes to re-enter France on a larger scale.

The principal lessons appear to be, firstly, that much stronger military forces are required to

Rev. John Foote V.C.

Chaplains are priests or ministers. Their job is to give spiritual and personal guidance to soldiers. They are not fighters. They do not carry weapons. They are not sent on daring raids. When Captain John Foote, chaplain of the Hamilton Light Infantry, heard his men were going to France, he insisted on going with them.

When the Canadians hit the Dieppe beaches, Foote was in the thick of the battle. His mission was to aid wounded and dying soldiers. When it was clear the battle was lost, he worked frantically to save lives. "Every man carry a man!" he urged the retreating troops. He himself moved 30 soldiers into the boats.

As the Germans moved closer, Foote's soldiers grabbed him and dragged him into a boat. He fought them off, and waded back to the beach yelling, "The men ashore need me far more than you."

Captain Foote was taken prisoner. He was forced to march for two days without boots. He was sent to a prison camp. After the war, he was awarded the Victoria Cross for his courage.

break through the German coastal defences in any important area; secondly, that a much higher proportion of the military forces should be held in reserve until the progress made in the initial assault is known…. Unless this is done there is no guarantee that any of the beaches will be secured…. Arising out of this is the need for far more effect methods of supporting the troops….

The next time that the Allied forces landed in Europe, they benefitted from these costly mistakes. D-Day occurred on June 6, 1944, the day that Allied forces invaded Europe. Many of the disastrous errors of the Dieppe raid were avoided. The sacrifices made by Canadian soliders on the beaches of Dieppe helped reduce the casualties of Canadian, British, and American forces on D-Day.

Crippled landing craft and abandoned tanks litter the beach near the bodies of the dead and dying.

Canada at War

There is more to war than sending soldiers to the battlefield. How could Canada, Canadians, and Canada's resources best be used to fight World War II?

The War Plan

The Canadian government drew up a war plan. The plan covered the areas that were most important to Canadians. It also dealt with the areas where Canada could make the biggest contribution to the Allied war effort. The plan was carefully co-ordinated with the war plans of other countries.

1. The defence and security of Canada.
2. The production of food supplies for Britain.
3. The production of weapons and ammunition for Allied forces.
4. Training for Allied pilots.
5. Development of the Royal Canadian Air Force (RCAF) for home defence and overseas duty.
6. Development of the Royal Canadian Navy (RCN) for home defence and convoy duty.
7. Development of the Canadian Army for home defence and overseas duty.

Victory Bond drive, Prince Rupert, B.C., 1941.

Weapons of War

One thousand ships, 15 000 aircraft, 700 000 trucks. Countless guns, bombs, and bullets. Under C.D. Howe, the no-nonsense minister of munitions and supply, war products poured from Canadian factories.

Howe wanted to avoid the profiteering that had soured the war effort in World War I. A wartime prices and trade board limited prices to "cost plus 10%." Even with these controls the government was paying up to $65 million a week for war supplies.

Where did the money come from? Income taxes rose to new heights. Canadians lent their money to the war effort by buying Victory Bonds. Victory Bonds paid for two thirds of the cost of the war.

Rationing

If people had money left after paying taxes and buying bonds, there was little to spend it on. In 1942 every Canadian received a ration book. When you bought sugar, butter, meat, tea, or coffee you had to hand over some coupons from your book. When your coupons were gone you couldn't buy—except on the "black market." If you were caught, you had to pay a stiff fine.

Gas was rationed. You could fill up once a month. You couldn't buy a new car. The last car was produced in 1942.

Canadians had good jobs. They could afford good food, new cars, clothes, and appliances. Why did they go without?

Anything that Canadians could spare went to the war effort. The butter and cheese Canadians didn't eat went to the tables of Britain where rationing was much more severe. The steel that once had made washing machines went into bombers. Even the common nickel changed—it was made of zinc instead.

Describe 5 ways in which ordinary Canadians contributed to the war effort?
In times of war people often co-operate and sacrifice more than they do at other times. Why?

The Children's War Effort

Kids collected paper, metal, rags, rubber, bones. Contests were held to see who could make the biggest ball of aluminum foil. All these things could be recycled into war materials.

Lunch hour was time for the knitting circle. Socks and scarves were made for soldiers. Letter writing campaigns cheered up lonely prisoners of war. The school baseball diamond was ploughed up to plant a "victory garden" to produce food for the war.

Boys drilled as cadets. Young people were let off school to help bring in the harvest. This kind of war work meant you didn't have to write exams!

Many Canadians think recycling is an idea of the 1970s and 80s, but in the 1940s patriotic Canadians saved anything that could be re-used in the war effort.

Volunteers

Canadians volunteered to be air raid wardens. They patrolled the coasts to guard against an invasion that never came. They studied aircraft to serve as "spotters" in a bombing raid. They got together to build public air raid shelters. Wealthy Canadians gave their work to the government for a dollar a year. The war drew Canadians together in a spirit of co-operation.

> Thanks to the skill and devotion of our men and women, Canada is a granary, an arsenal, an airdrome, and a shipyard of freedom.
> *William Lyon Mackenzie King*

The Japanese Canadians

The Pacific War

War had been raging in Asia since 1937. China was weak and divided. Japan took advantage of this to expand her empire. When France fell to the Germans, Japan moved into the French colony of Indo-China. Once Hitler attacked the Soviet Union, the Japanese knew they had nothing to fear from the north. They turned their attention south to Hong Kong, Indonesia, and Malaya, and east to the Pacific.

At the American naval base in Pearl Harbour, Hawaii, sailors were turning over in their bunks. Most were looking forward to a lazy day off on that pleasant Sunday morning of 7 December 1941.

Out of the west came the Japanese bombers. In two hours the American Pacific fleet lay at the bottom of the harbour. The United States had been brought into the war.

The next day the Japanese laid siege to the British colony of Hong Kong. Among the defenders were 2000 Canadians. These troops from Manitoba and Quebec had been hurriedly sent to Hong Kong when the British realized attack was certain. They had almost no training. Some had never fired their rifles. They didn't even know you had to pull the pin before you threw a grenade.

The green Canadians fought bravely alongside the British and Australians at Hong Kong. They wouldn't give in. The battle lasted for 17 days.

On Christmas Day 1941 Hong Kong surrendered to the Japanese. The men who had defended it spent the rest of the war in Japanese prison camps. In the battle for Hong Kong 290 Canadians had died. Another 264 would die in the camps.

Today the graves of those who died defending Hong Kong lie on a hillside above the city.

Japan's entry into the war caused near panic for many people in Canada. To Canada's east, Hitler ruled in Europe. Now Japan was sweeping through Asia to the west. The fall of Hong Kong seemed like the end of the world. Canadians wanted revenge and struck out at the handiest target — the Japanese Canadians.

Canadians or Japanese?

Canadians had never been really welcoming to Asian immigrants. After 1913 few Asians were even allowed to enter the country. As a result, by 1942 more than half the 23 000 "Japanese" living in Canada had been born here. They were Canadian citizens. Few had any sympathy for Japan's ambition to take over the Pacific.

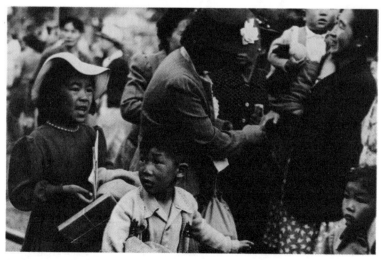

A family waits to be "relocated" to a camp in the B.C. interior, 1942.

FOCUS

What led the government to take action against the Japanese Canadians? What did the government do?
Explain why you agree or disagree with the 1988 policy to compensate the surviving Japanese Canadians for their losses.

1900 1910 1920 1930 1940 1950 1960 1970 1980 1990 2000

Most Canadians paid no attention to these facts. They decided the Japanese Canadians were dangerous. They might be spies. They might help the Japanese attack North America. In 1942 the government ordered that they be moved away from the coastal regions of British Columbia.

Many Japanese Canadians were forced to move to camps in the B.C. interior. Often families were separated. The men were sent to one camp, women and children to another. Others were sent as labourers to farms on the prairies and in Ontario.

The government held auctions to sell these people's personal possessions, their homes, and their businesses. For the buyers there were great bargains. The Japanese Canadians never got a fair price for the things they had lost.

David Suzuki

1936 — born in Vancouver. Parents born in Canada but of Japanese descent. Spoke only English at home. Father encouraged his interest in nature — birds, trees, animals, fish, insects.
1942-45 — with mother and sisters sent to camp near Slocan, B.C. Other kids jeered at him because he spoke no Japanese. White kids jeered because he was an "enemy." Only kids he had fun with were from Doukhobor community near Slocan. Later family moved to Ontario. Father told him: "You have to be ten times better than a white, because if you're just as good as a white, you'll lose out every time."
1954 — an outstanding high school student, he won scholarships to pay for his university education. Studied and taught at universities in the U.S. and Canada. Specialized in *genetics* (how characteristics are inherited through genes). Remembering own experiences with discrimination, worked with civil rights groups to fight racial prejudice.
1968 — became professor of zoology at UBC.
1970s, 1980s, and on — produced and starred in popular science shows for radio and television.

Partial Compensation for Japanese Canadians

In September 1988, Prime Minister Mulroney announced that the government would partially repay the Japanese-Canadian survivors for their losses. The terms were:
— a public apology for past injustices against the Japanese Canadians, their families, their heritage;
— $21 000 for each surviving Japanese-Canadian born before 1949;
— $24 million to establish a Canadian Race Relations Foundation;
— $12 million to the Japanese-Canadian Association for low-cost housing for elderly Japanese Canadians.

Husbands and fathers say goodbye to their wives and children.

Behind the Scenes

In a total war not all the action is on the front lines. Many important battles are fought behind the scenes. Some are out in the open. Others are highly secret.

The British Commonwealth Air Training Plan

Military leaders knew that air power would be vital in World War II. Air crew must be trained before they can go into action. Canada provided the bases for the British Commonwealth Air Training Plan.

Trainees came from all over the Commonwealth — Australia, South Africa, Britain, West Indies, and New Zealand. Volunteers who had escaped when Poland, France, and Norway fell to the Germans also trained in Canada.

Courses were short and often inadequate. The rush to get pilots and service crews ready to fight caused many accidents. In one horrible month, 500 aircraft were put out of service by inexperienced fliers. All told, there were 850 deaths during training. On the other hand, 130 000 graduates, over half of them Canadian, went on to fight the battle of the skies.

Bombers on the tarmac, Manitoba, 1943.

The Secret War

On the shores of Lake Ontario somewhere near Oshawa was Camp X. Few knew of its existence. Those who did know said nothing. Camp X was a top secret training post for spies, secret agents and sabotage experts. It was under the direction of Canadian master spy, William Stephenson.

Agents from Camp X were dropped behind enemy lines to spy and report by radio. They connected with underground movements in occupied countries to disrupt enemy activities. One agent who trained at Camp X was Ian Fleming. After the war he wrote the James Bond spy stories.

Station M was a vital part of Camp X. It was staffed by forgers, safecrackers, chemists, movie set designers, and costume experts. Station M provided agents with false passports and money, battered suitcases, and European style toothpaste, eyeglasses, shabby suits, and underwear. Everything an agent carried had to look right to enemy eyes.

The Sheepdog Navy

Far from land, on the chilly north Atlantic, Canadians and Newfoundlanders also showed courage and endurance. Some were sailors in the "merchant navy," the cargo ships that bore food, fuel, and weapons to Britain. Others were part of the Royal Canadian Navy (RCN), which shepherded the convoys. The RCN's job was to find and sink the German U boats before these submarines found and sank the ships of the convoy.

By 1943 the U boats were on the run. They were being destroyed by weapons, sonar equipment, and shore-based aircraft. By the end of the war, the RCN had 400 fighting ships, the third largest navy in the world. It had shepherded 25 000 ships across the ocean. The Atlantic lifeline had been kept open.

How did Canada contribute to the air war?
What part did the Canadian navy play in the war at sea? Why was it important?
Who was Intrepid and what did he do?

1900 1910 1920 1930 1940 1950 1960 1970 1980 1990 2000

Rough weather in the North Atlantic, March 1942.

Two Canadian Agents

"Set Europe ablaze!" Churchill told the special agents parachuted into enemy-held territory. Among the 28 Canadian agents who went into Europe, 8 died. Even today, little is known of what they did.

Guy Bieler was born in Montreal. His spine was badly injured when he parachuted into France. Even so, he organized a sabotage group. They derailed and blew up trains carrying troops and arms. They sabotaged locomotives. In the end Bieler was captured and shot.

Frank Pickersgill of Winnipeg was captured when he landed in France. Nazi double agents had given him away. He refused to break under questioning. When his captors switched from threats to bribery, he broke a bottle on his interrogator's desk, slashed the throat of an SS guard, and jumped out a 2nd floor window before being stopped by 4 bullets. In prison camp he organized resistance, helping prisoners regain some lost pride. The Nazis finally executed Pickersgill and 15 other agents by hanging them from meat hooks.

William Stephenson (Intrepid)
1896 — born in Winnipeg. As teenager invented his own secret "Morse code."
1914-18 — joined army. Survived 2 gas attacks and declared unfit for service. Falsified medical records and joined Royal Flying Corps. After 5 hours' training, flew as pilot. Shot down 26 planes, including that of Lothar von Richthofen, the Red Baron's brother. Downed himself, captured, and escaped to British lines. Wrote report on German prison camps.
1920s — interested in broadcasting, with Beaverbrook helped set up the BBC. Pushed "wild" ideas like television, splitting the atom, and laser beams. Set up film studio.
1930s — became involved with British intelligence.
1939-45 — as "Intrepid," ran British Security Co-ordination, a secret army of code-breakers, spies, robbers, assassins, and sabotage experts. Many trained at Camp X.
1979 — made Companion of the Order of Canada.
1980s — living in Bermuda, still taking active interest in world affairs.
1989 — died in Bermuda at the age of 93.

Women go to War

In 1939 Canadian women were eager to defend their country. Unfortunately, Canadian leaders saw little room for women in the war effort. As more and more men left for the battlefront, the role women could play became more obvious.

Industrial strength was the key to success in the war. Canada had vast resources. Canada's women put their brains and muscles to turning raw materials into tanks, planes, and ships. By 1943 over one million women were working in Canadian industry.

Managers had to change some of their ideas about workers and how to run a factory. Women often proved to be more careful and patient than male workers. Day care centres were set up in many plants. Production rose as workers donated free time to produce another tank or bomber. Men were often outnumbered. They sometimes had to endure female wolf whistles. They learned that in the right circumstances women could swear as well as men could.

Women volunteered to visit wounded soldiers. They sent packages to prisoners of war. They made dressings for the wounded. The family garbage shrank.

Railway workers.

Machine shop mechanics.

Housewives saved paper, scrap, fat, and bones for recycling. They made sure food was eaten, not thrown away.

Women in Uniform

Society had wanted to keep women out of the factory. It was determined to keep them out of the armed forces. When women were refused by the forces they set up their own volunteer units.

By 1941 the armed forces were in desperate need of recruits. Women were finally allowed to join up. One young woman walked 30 km to get to a recruiting station. By the end of the war Canada had 45 000 servicewomen. Many of them had been posted overseas.

These women often found themselves in the heat of battle. They were bombed, shelled, and torpedoed. Some were made prisoners of war. 244 won medals for gallantry.

List 5 ways in which women contributed to the war effort. Were women treated with full equality? Explain your answer. Imagine you are one of the Canadian heroines listed on this page. Write about your wartime experiences.

FOCUS

1900 1910 1920 1930 1940 1950 1960 1970 1980 1990 2000

The Canadian Women's Army Corps conducts a fire-fighting demonstration in London, England, 28 February 1943.

Taking a break, London, February 1943.

Women Prove Themselves

During the war women succeeded in a society dominated by men. Many men had doubted their worth. Now women gained freedom and self-respect. They knew the satisfaction of earning their own money. They also knew the injustice of getting less pay than a man for doing the same work.

After the war many women were happy to return to a more "traditional" role. Many young couples had postponed marriage and babies for the course of the war. Peace meant it was time to start a family. Women became housewives and mothers. It was not until the sixties and seventies that women began to build again on the gains they had made in wartime.

Canada's Servicewomen	Total	Posted Overseas
Canadian Women's Army Corps (CWAC)	21 624	2 900
RCAF Women's Division (WDs)	17 018	1 400
Women's Royal Canadian Naval Service (WRENs)	6 781	1 000
Nursing Sisters		4 172

Canadian Women at War

Molly Lamb Bobak—first female official war artist.

Gudrun Bjening—war propaganda film-maker for the National Film Board.

Fern Blodgett — first female wireless operator on a wartime ship. She crossed the Atlantic 78 times during the war.

Margaret Brooke — nurse. While crossing from Nova Scotia to Newfoundland, the ferry she was aboard was torpedoed by a U boat deep in Canadian waters. Held a fellow nurse, Agnes Wilkie, up in the icy water all night. At dawn a giant breaker forced them apart. Wilkie drowned, but Brooke, now unconscious, was rescued.

Kathleen Christie and **Maye Waters** — nurses stationed at Hong Kong. Aided the troops during the battle for Hong Kong and continued to help them during two years of imprisonment by the Japanese.

Elsie MacGill — chief aeronautical engineer for Canada Car (later Hawker Siddeley). This company produced 1650 Hurricanes for the air war.

Charmion Sansom — radio announcer for a London-based station. Much loved by the troops. Like other radio personnel, her real identity was kept secret until after the war.

Helen-Marie Stevens — army nurse. Heroine of a bombing raid during the London "blitz." Worked for hours aiding customers in a bombed out restaurant. She used champagne as an anaesthetic. "I did what any Canadian nurse would do."

Conscription — Again

Should a person be forced to go and fight? This question had almost split the country during World War I. Prime Minister Mackenzie King was determined to avoid another crisis in World War II. He promised his government would not introduce conscription for overseas service.

In October 1939 Premier Maurice Duplessis of Quebec called for a provincial election. Duplessis was a bitter critic of the war policy. He said the federal government was out to take power away from Quebec. If Canada was to remain united through the war, it was vital that Duplessis's Union Nationale party be defeated.

The federal Liberals threw their support to the provincial Liberal party. Three Quebec federal cabinet ministers campaigned vigorously against Duplessis. They told the Quebec people that conscription for overseas service would never be introduced by their government. They would resign first. They also threatened to resign if Duplessis was re-elected. This would leave Quebec without any influence in the federal cabinet. The provincial Liberals were swept into office.

Meanwhile Premier Mitch Hepburn of Ontario wanted to see more Canadians go to war. He accused his fellow-Liberal, Prime Minister King, of being too weak. In early 1940 King called a federal election. The Liberals won an overwhelming victory in all regions of Canada. Hepburn's political career was over. The country was united behind King.

You won't get to Berlin in an Armchair!

If Canada and the United Nations had depended upon "Armchair Soldiers" to fight this war, the Nazis and Japs would have grabbed this country long ago.

There is no "Royal Road" to Berlin. It's fighting all the way and Canada's Army needs every man it can get. That's why, today, you should volunteer for overseas

service. You'll need months of intensive training to make you fighting-fit.

Don't be a stay-at-home and let the other fellow do it. Get into a man's uniform with the G.S. badge of honour on your sleeve. If we're going to win this war, we'll have to do more than just read about it in the papers.

OVERSEAS BADGE OF HONOUR
GS
WEAR IT ON YOUR ARM

So, come on you fellows, the good old army has got to finish the job.

VOLUNTEER TO-DAY
JOIN THE CANADIAN ARMY
FOR OVERSEAS SERVICE

Home Defence

Volunteers filled Canada's fighting forces overseas. Many people felt this might not be enough. In the dark days of 1940 Parliament set up conscription for home defence only. Men drafted into this army were often jeered at because they hadn't volunteered to go overseas. Later they were called "zombies" by those who thought every young man should want to fight.

Conscription if Necessary

King had promised not to introduce conscription. In 1942 he asked the country to release him from his pledge. At that time it still did not look as if the government would need to force men into the armed

What is conscription? Why is it a sensitive issue in Canada?
Do you think Prime Minister King handled the conscription issue
well? Explain.
Would you have been for or against conscription? Why?

1900 1910 1920 1930 1940 1950 1960 1970 1980 1990 2000
▲

The War Heats Up

While the Canadian Army stayed in Britain there was
no need for conscription. For two years the issue was
avoided. After the Italian campaign and the invasion
of France, things changed. The battle for Europe had
begun and losses were high. The government tried its
best to recruit men voluntarily. Only a few joined up.
Reluctantly, in November, King ordered some of the
soldiers conscripted for Home Defence to go
overseas. These 16 000 soldiers (called "zombies" by
the regular soldiers) were sent overseas.

There was an uproar. One Quebec cabinet minister
resigned. But other French Canadians stood by King.
Louis St. Laurent, King's "Quebec lieutenant", told
Quebeckers that the decision was necessary.

Fortunately, the war ended soon after. Only 2500
"zombies" actually fought and were good soliders.

Unlike the crisis of 1917, all Canadians had been
consulted before conscription was introduced. The
unity of Canadians was strained but not broken.

Campaigning in favour of conscription.

services. The Canadian army was sitting in Britain
waiting to go into action. But King knew the situation
might change. If it did, he wanted to be ready for it.

The government organized a vote on the question.
Across the country, 64% voted to let the government
decide. Ontario, Manitoba, and British Columbia were
80% in favour. In Quebec 72% were against. Many
French Canadians felt they had been betrayed. The
unity of 1940 was crumbling. Mackenzie King tried to
cool the issue. He used the slogan "Conscription if
necessary but not necessarily conscription."

Prime Minister King casts his ballot in the 1942 referendum.

The Italian Campaign

The Tide Turns

In 1942 the tide of war turned. In North Africa British and American troops drove back Italian and German forces under Field Marshal Rommel, "the desert fox."

In the freezing Russian winter, German troops faced disaster. In the territory they had conquered the people rose up and attacked them from behind the battle lines. The decisive battle was fought at Stalingrad. In February 1943 the once proud German army surrendered. The Russians took 90 000 prisoners. Soviet forces began to roll towards Berlin. They had suffered starvation, torture, and atrocities at the hands of Hitler's troops. They were prepared to take revenge on the German people.

In the Pacific the Americans had recovered quickly after Pearl Harbour. By the end of 1942 the ships sunk there were raised, refitted, and back in action! In June the Americans decisively defeated the Japanese navy at Midway. Island by island, they crept closer to Japan. In China communist and nationalist armies were rallying against their Japanese conquerors. British and Commonwealth forces began to drive the Japanese from Southeast Asia.

Each Allied victory was paid for in blood. Winning the war had become a matter of time and of lives.

Advancing under sniper fire, Campochiaro, Italy, October 1943.

In May 1943 General Montgomery's British army and General Eisenhower's American army surrounded the German and Italian troops in North Africa. It was time to cross the Mediterranean Sea to Europe.

The Invasion of Sicily

Since the disastrous raid on Dieppe, Canadian soldiers had seen no action. Now the 1st Canadian Division was to take part in the invasion of Sicily under General Montgomery.

The battle for Sicily was fought under the blazing July sun. Within 38 days the victorious Allied troops were preparing to invade the Italian mainland. Mussolini's dreams of a new Roman Empire were shattered. His own people rebelled and threw him out of power. Hitler swiftly moved German troops into Italy. The fact that the Italians had surrendered was not going to stop him.

The Liberation of Italy

The Italian campaign was long and difficult. 92 000 Canadians fought in Italy. 30 000 were wounded or killed. A few snipers in the rugged mountains could slow an army to a crawl. And the German forces fought brilliantly. Even with the help of Italian partisans, the Allies paid heavily for each kilometre they won.

FOCUS

Why do you think the Italian people rebelled against Mussolini?
Why was the battle for Italy long and difficult?
What reputation did Canadian troops get from the way they fought
and won the battle for Ortona?

Art Gallery page 21

The battle for Ortona was a terrible lesson for Canadian troops. The Germans turned it into a series of house-to-house fights. It took a month to capture the town. The Canadians became known as experts at street fighting.

On 4 June 1944 the Allied armies entered Rome. Canadian soldiers marched with their British, American, New Zealand, Indian, South African, French and Polish comrades to the cheers of the Italian people.

While one Canadian force crept up the boot of Italy, another prepared for the greatest land-sea invasion in history. Two days later came D-Day—the long awaited Allied invasion of France.

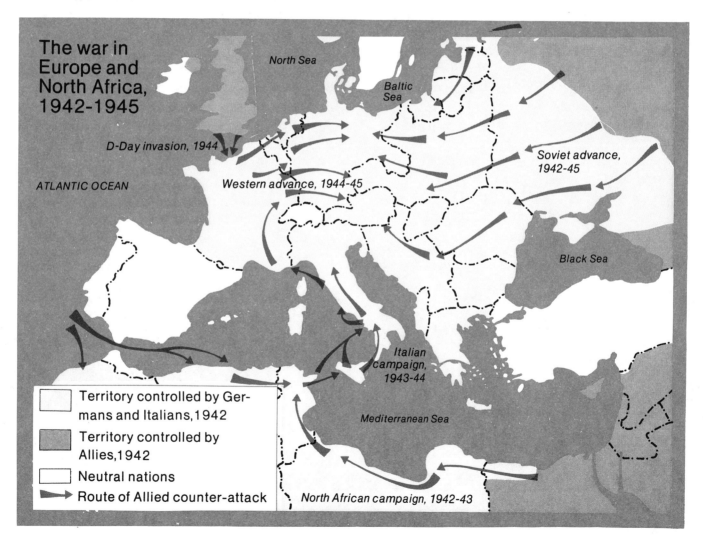

The war in Europe and North Africa, 1942-1945

North Sea

Baltic Sea

D-Day invasion, 1944

ATLANTIC OCEAN

Western advance, 1944-45

Soviet advance, 1942-45

Black Sea

Italian campaign, 1943-44

Mediterranean Sea

North African campaign, 1942-43

☐ Territory controlled by Germans and Italians, 1942

▨ Territory controlled by Allies, 1942

☐ Neutral nations

➤ Route of Allied counter-attack

D-Day to V-E Day

Everything had been carefully planned. The tide was right. The moon was right. Would the weather be right for D-Day, the big invasion planned for 5 June 1944? Or would it have to be put off for a month?

The south of England was one big army camp. Everybody knew the invasion of France was about to begin. Only a very few knew when and where the landing would be made.

On 4 June the troops were ordered to the ships. Some ships set out. Suddenly, the weather reports got worse. The landing was postponed. The ships were recalled. By the morning of 5 June, violent winds were battering the coast of northern France. The troops stayed crammed aboard the ships, awaiting further orders.

Then the weather forecasters said there would be a lull in the storm. General Eisenhower made the decision. D-Day would be June 6, a day later than planned.

The Normandy Beaches

Across the English Channel the Germans were waiting at Calais. Pilots returning from bombing raids had told them the main build-up of troops and equipment was at Dover. What they had seen were empty tents, dummy ships, plywood gliders, and inflated rubber tanks.

The invaders struck 200 km to the southwest—on the beaches of Normandy. The Dieppe raid had taught them the Germans would destroy any harbours they tried to capture. So they wouldn't use the ports. Two complete harbours were built in Britain, towed across and assembled on the spot. Fuel for trucks and tanks would flow through "Pluto," an underwater pipeline.

All through the night bombers struck at the German defences. Just before dawn, paratroopers dropped behind enemy lines. The main force hit the beaches. The liberation of Europe had begun.

Canadian troops land in Normandy.

Why was the weather an important factor in planning D-Day?
What preparations did the Allies make to be sure the invasion would be a success?
What part did Canadians play in the fighting after D-Day?

The Push to Berlin

It was 11 months before western troops met their Soviet allies near the Elbe River in central Germany. They were 11 months of hard struggle. Hitler was determined to fight to the bitter end. He was prepared to destroy Germany and the German people rather than surrender.

In the long push towards Berlin, Canadians were given the task of clearing the French, Belgian, and Dutch ports. This was slow, dangerous work. Enemy forces fought from behind strong fortifications. Every port taken meant more Allied ships could unload more tanks, weapons, and troops.

The ports fell, one by one. On 8 September 1944 Canadian forces entered Dieppe. This time they came by land and as conquerors. The stain of defeat was erased as they marched into the port.

A chaplain gives the last rites to a soldier dying at the roadside.

In 1945 Canadian forces liberated the Netherlands. The Germans opened the dykes that held back the water from the low-lying fields. Canadian troops found boats and kept moving. As the Germans retreated, grateful Dutch families poured out of their homes to welcome their liberators. Even today, Canadians are warmly received in the Netherlands.

The End of the Dictators

On 27 April 1945 Mussolini was captured and shot by his own people. His body was displayed hanging upside down on a meat hook in Milan. Three days later in his underground bunker, Hitler listened to Soviet guns bombarding Berlin. He placed a revolver in his mouth and pulled the trigger. His body was burned so it could not be displayed by his enemies. On 8 May 1945, Germany surrendered unconditionally. This was V-E Day — Victory in Europe Day.

German children surrender to Canadian troops, April 1945.

The Holocaust

When Hitler came to power in 1933 he began his war on the Jews. He ordered Germans to boycott Jewish stores. He forbade Jewish lawyers and doctors to practise freely. Jews lost the right to vote. In many places, Jews were not allowed to use public parks, swimming pools, or sports fields.

Other nations made feeble protests. They did nothing.

The First Boat People

Early in 1939 the *St. Louis* sailed from Hamburg, Germany and aboard her were 907 Jews. They were looking for a safe home far from the persecution of Nazi Germany.

They tried to land in Cuba but they were turned away. They headed for the United States but they were forbidden to enter the country. They came north to Canada but Canadians, too, turned them away.

Most countries tried to keep all immigrants out during the Depression years. Many people were particularly prejudiced against the Jews. In Canada, over 100 000 people signed a petition to stop Jewish immigration. As a result of attitudes like these, few Jews were able to escape from Europe during the 1930s. When Hitler overran the continent, they were caught in a trap.

The *St. Louis* returned to Europe where the Dutch agreed to give its passengers a home. A year later the Germans occupied the Netherlands. The Dutch were powerless to save these and other Jews. Most of the passengers of the *St. Louis* later perished in Nazi death camps.

The Holocaust

By 1941, the German policy was becoming clear — the outright extermination of all Jews in areas under German control. It was referred to as "the final solution". As a result of the German conquests in Russia, large numbers of Jews entered the slave labour camps. The Nazis decided that they would need a more systematic way of killing the Jews. As a result death camps, such as Dachau, Auschwitz, and Treblinka, were set up to quickly and scientifically kill Jews. Men, women, and children were herded into "showers" and murdered by clouds of poison gas. Later the bodies were burned in huge ovens. Hitler's plan was to eliminate every trace of the Jews from the face of the earth.

By 1945, over 6 000 000 Jews had died in Nazi death camps. Several million other enemies of the German government also lost their lives — French, Dutch, Russians, Poles, gypsies, communists, homosexuals, and Germans who opposed the Nazi régime. This mass slaughter is known as the "holocaust".

Persecution of Jews in Nazi Germany was an established fact before the outbreak of World War II. When Jewish residents were rounded up in Chemnitz and forced to clean the town, this man refused and was then paraded through the town in a garbage wagon.

What actions did the Nazis take against the Jews after 1933? Who do *you* think was responsible for the Holocaust? Explain your answer. Discuss with other class members.

1900 1910 1920 1930 1940 1950 1960 1970 1980 1990 2000

Who Bears the Guilt?

Many war criminals were hunted down and punished after the war. Hitler, who ordered the policy, died in a suicide in Berlin in 1945. Adolph Eichmann, who was in charge of the ''final solution'' was captured after the war by Israeli agents, tried as a war criminal, found guilty, and executed. The infamous Dr. Josef Mengele who carried out medical experiments on live Jews, was never captured. Some Nazis who had participated in carrying out the Holocaust, were given forged identity papers by allied authorities after the war. This was in return for giving information and services to the victorious allied powers. Some continued to live with new names in countries like Canada and the United States.

But who bears the guilt? Was it just Hitler and his fellow Nazis who gave the orders? What about the guards who ran the camps? the chemical workers who made the poison gas? the railway workers who carried thousands to the camps? the ordinary citizens who watched their neighbours disappear, and said or did nothing? And what about those who claimed that they were innocent because they simply did what they were told?

Jews on the way to the gas chamber at Auschwitz.

And what about the nations who looked the other way before the war? What about Canadians who refused to admit Jewish refugees in the 1930s?

Who bears the guilt?

The State of Israel

After the war, many Jews who survived the Holocaust wanted to escape from the persecution and destruction of Europe. Many wanted to return to what they believed was the ancestral homeland of the Jews in Palestine. In 1948, the State of Israel was created as a national home for the Jews. Although many of the survivors did arrive in Israel, it was not to be the land of peace which they expected. The creation of the State of Israel greatly offended the Palestinians and other Arabs. The resentment and conflict from this dispute has continued to the present.

The Mushroom-Shaped Cloud

On 6 August 1945 a lone American bomber flew high over the Japanese city of Hiroshima. The plane dropped a single bomb, nicknamed "Little Boy." For the first time in history an atomic bomb was unleashed on the world. By the end of the day 173 000 people were dead or dying.

The bomb drifted over the city hanging from a small parachute. It exploded with a burning white flash "brighter than a thousand suns." Shock waves mowed down buildings. Fireballs burned through the streets. Pieces of the city tore through the air. Finally a huge mushroom-shaped cloud billowed over the city.

People who looked up at the sound of the explosion had their eyes melt from the heat of the blast. Skin turned black and dripped from bones. Those who died at once were lucky. Many more suffered slow painful deaths from radiation poisoning. Decades later, deformed babies were born to the survivors of Hiroshima.

The Americans asked the Japanese to surrender. There was no reply. Three days later the same horror was repeated at Nagasaki. 80 000 more people were cremated in a nuclear inferno. Japan surrendered unconditionally on 14 August 1945 — V-J Day.

Hiroshima, ten years later. The city decided to preserve this ruined building as a reminder of the bombing.

FOCUS

Why do you think the Americans decided to use the atomic bomb?
Do you think atomic bombs will ever be used again?
What was the chief aim of the United Nations?
What 2 superpowers emerged at the end of World War II?

1900 1910 1920 1930 1940 1950 1960 1970 1980 1990 2000

The United Nations

Even before V-E Day the leaders of the world were looking for a way to maintain peace in the future. The old League of Nations had failed. They would learn from its mistakes and build a better, stronger, United Nations.

It was not going to be easy. The war had created new borders, and new hatreds. The "old" world powers—Britain, Germany, France, Japan—lay shattered and exhausted. Two new rival superpowers—the United States and the Soviet Union—had gained strength and influence.

World War II left a bitter, confused and divided world. The shadow of the atomic bomb and a new arms race lay across it. Could the United Nations keep the peace?

In the Hiroshima museum, visitors read a technical description of the bomb and the explosion.

A model shows what remained of the city after the bomb.

Halfway around the world, Ottawa celebrated V-J Day.

Questions and Activities

Test Yourself

Match the items in column A with the descriptions in column B.

A	B
1. Blitzkrieg	a) spy training centre near Oshawa
2. Little Boy	b) allied retreat from France
3. The Axis	c) city in Italy
4. The *St. Louis*	d) conscripted soldiers
5. Pearl Harbor	e) an atomic bomb
6. Camp X	f) Jewish refugee ship
7. Ortona	g) alliance led by Germany
8. Dunkirk	h) allied invasion of France
9. Zombies	i) lightning war
10. D-Day	j) American naval base in Hawaii

Who Am I?

Identify the following people from the clues.

1. I served as British prime minister during World War II. I promised the British nothing but "blood, toil, tears, and sweat." Who am I?
2. I am a scientist of Asian ancestry. My people suffered greatly in Canada during World War II. Who am I?
3. I ran a brilliant spy organization during World War II. In 1979 I was honoured by the government of Canada. Who am I?
4. I led Canada during World War II. I engineered a solution to the conscription crisis. Who am I?
5. I grew up in New Brunswick but moved to Britain. I was in charge of British aircraft production during the Battle of Britain. Who am I?

Ideas for Discussion

1. The conscription issue divided Canadians in two world wars. Arrange the classroom to look like the House of Commons. Have each student be the member of parliament for a different constituency in Canada. Be prepared to give a speech in favour of or against conscription in World War II. After the debate, hold a vote on the issue. If your class had been the House of Commons, would conscription have been introduced?
2. The decision to drop the atomic bomb on Japanese cities has often been criticized. Imagine you are an adviser to U.S. President Truman. Write a memo either supporting or attacking the plan to drop the A-bomb on Hiroshima and Nagasaki. Then hold a meeting of the president's "advisers" at which you should be prepared to defend your views.

3. Many Nazi supporters were tried for war crimes at Nuremberg after the war. However, Hitler had committed suicide and could not be brought to trial.
   Imagine that Hitler had been captured alive. Organize a trial with judges and defence and prosecution lawyers. Select students to play the parts of witnesses, members of the jury, court reporters, guards, etc.

Do Some Research

1. Find out about one of the following and write a brief report:
   a) a famous Canadian soldier in World War II;
   b) a famous general of World War II;
   c) some new weapons invented during World War II;
   d) a Canadian winner of the Victoria Cross in World War II.
2. People's memories often tell historians a different story from the one recorded in books, papers, and reports. Interview someone who remembers World War II. Find out about his or her experiences at home in Canada and/or at the battlefronts of Europe, Africa, or the Pacific. Assemble a class booklet or tape of Memories of World War II.
3. Make a map of the world showing:
   a) the major Allied powers
   b) the major Axis powers
   c) ten major battle sites
4. With a small group of other students, prepare a folder on life on the Canadian homefront during World War II. Your folder might include:
   a) posters   e) brief biographies
   b) pictures   f) advertisements
   c) songs   g) wartime regulations
   d) slogans   h) ration cards
5. Find out what life was like in Hitler's concentration camps. Imagine you have been sent to one of these camps and write a secret diary about your experiences.
6. Find out more about one of the following war heroes. Write a "biocard" like the ones that appear in this book.

Buzz Beurling   Anne Frank   Winston Churchill

7. Design a wall chart comparing Canada's involvement in World War I and in World War II. You may wish to compare some of the following items:
a) length of the war (dates)
b) number of soldiers fighting
c) number of people killed
d) important battles
e) types of weapons
f) activities on the homefront
Add other ideas of your own to complete the chart.

8. Governments often ask artists to paint pictures of wartime scenes. What can be shown in a painting that might not appear in a photograph? Study the pictures on pages 20 and 21 of the Art Gallery. Go to the library and find out more about war artists. Report to the class, explaining which war artists you feel best convey the atmosphere of war and why.

Be Creative

1. Reporting the news as it happens is always an exciting job. During wartime it is also very dangerous. Reporters from all nations risked their lives to bring news of the battlefront to people back home. Imagine you are a Canadian war correspondent. Give an on-the-spot news report about one of the following:
a) the fall of Hong Kong
b) the Battle of Britain
c) the battle for Ortona
d) the Normandy beaches on D-Day
e) the liberation of the Netherlands
Make your report as authentic as possible. You could present it as a newspaper article, a radio report, or a commentary to a news film that will be shown in a movie theatre before the main feature.

A wrecked and abandoned landing craft.

A German soldier offers a light to a Canadian prisoner of war.

2. In a group of four or five students, prepare a brief play showing a scene from the life of some Japanese Canadians during the war. Present your play to the class and watch the plays of other groups. Discuss your reactions to the plays.

3. Make a model or draw a diagram of a ship or plane used in World War II. Write a brief paragraph on its role in the war.

4. Design posters to point out the horror of war and to promote world peace.

You Are There

The Dieppe raid was a stunning disaster for the Canadian troops that took part. Today the debate still rages over the real military worth of the operation. Your class has been appointed to conduct an investigation into the Dieppe raid.

Some of you are *investigators,* whose job is to prepare questions, analyze documents, interview witnesses, and report your conclusions. Others among you are *witnesses.* You may be called upon to testify on the raid in your role as:
a) citizens of Dieppe who saw the raid
b) German officers and soldiers
c) Canadian officers and soldiers who were captured
d) Canadian officers and soldiers who escaped
e) Canadian and British officers who planned the raid
Still others are *reporters.* Your job is to report on the proceedings on a day-by-day basis.

The pictures below, taken by German photographers, may be introduced as evidence.

Canadian prisoners of war are marched through the streets of Dieppe as citizens watch from the sidewalk.

Cause and Effect in History

CAUSE → EVENT → RESULT → SIGNIFICANCE

Events in history rarely happen in isolation. They are usually parts of a *sequence* of events. One incident *causes* another, which in turn affects later events. This is what is referred to as *"cause and effect" in history*.

Dieppe — a tragic waste, or a lesson learned?

Time Sequence

When studying an historic event, you must always consider the time sequence. You therefore should examine events from this viewpoint:

Background Cause → Immediate Cause → EVENT → Results → Long-term Signficance

Past → Present → Future

— German people were dissatisfied with Treaty of Versailles
— Hitler in power with expressed ideas of expansion — 1933
— German violations of peace treaty — 1935-1938
— Annexation of Czechoslovakia — March 1939

Background causes

↓

Invasion of Poland — September 1939

Immediate cause

↓

World War II — 1939-1945

Events

↓

— Liberation of Nazi-occupied territories
— Surrender of Germany and Japan
— Disarmament of Germany and Japan — division of Europe between occupying powers (U.S.S.R. and Western nations)
— Destruction of Nazism
— Formation of United Nations

Results

↓

— Origins of Cold War Conflict
— Beginnings of U.S. and U.S.S.R. domination of world
— beginnings of Atomic Era

Long-range Signficance

↓

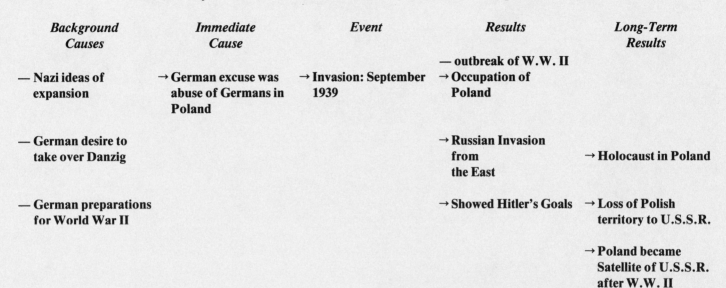

Case Study — The Invasion of Poland by Germany in September 1939

Background Causes	Immediate Cause	Event	Results	Long-Term Results
— Nazi ideas of expansion	→ German excuse was abuse of Germans in Poland	→ Invasion: September 1939	— outbreak of W.W. II → Occupation of Poland	
— German desire to take over Danzig			→ Russian Invasion from the East	→ Holocaust in Poland
— German preparations for World War II			→ Showed Hitler's Goals	→ Loss of Polish territory to U.S.S.R.
				→ Poland became Satellite of U.S.S.R. after W.W. II

YOUR TASK

Analyze the:

Background Cause Immediate Cause Event Result Long-Term Results

of *at least one* of the following:

(a) Rise of Adolph Hitler
(b) The Dieppe Raid, 1942
(c) The Internment of Japanese-Canadians in Canada
(d) The Conscription crisis of 1944
(e) The Holocaust
(f) The Dropping of the Atomic Bomb on Japan

Thousands of Japanese Canadians were sent to internment camps.

Chapter Five

Midcentury
ADVANCE ORGANIZER

In 1949, Newfoundland entered Confederation as the tenth province. Joey Smallwood spearheaded the movement for union with Canada. He became Newfoundland's first premier. The province has since progressed rapidly in many areas. Once solely dependent upon the fishing industry for its economy, Newfoundland developed the industries of mining and forestry. The province now faces the prospect of new wealth in the form of oil and deposits of natural gas.

2

A wave of prosperity swept Canada in the fifties. Western oil and natural gas reserves yielded new sources of power for Canadian industry. Pipelines for oil and gas were built. Large bodies of water were harnessed to generate electricity. Uranium deposits were found, promising future benefits from nuclear power. As new resources were discovered, new industries developed. The St. Lawrence Seaway was constructed to aid in the transport of materials.

This economic growth was largely due to foreign investment, much of it American. Such investment brought Canada a much-desired prosperity during the fifties and sixties. It unfortunately also led to future conflicts over the ownership and financial control of Canada's resources.

Word List

boom town	medicare	refugee
Centennial	nuclear	suburb
family allowance	pipeline	unemployment insurance
isolation	pollution	welfare state

3

With the end of World War II, the future looked bright for Canada. Returning soldiers and their brides were ready to raise families in these peaceful and prosperous times. Over four million babies were born in Canada during the fifties. The educational system had to accommodate the unexpected youth explosion.
For the first time, teenagers became a driving force in Canadian society. Business began looking to the new teenage market. There arose a new "pop culture," one that often rebelled against society's traditional values. It found its greatest voice in a new form of popular music: rock 'n' roll.

4

The era of the post-war boom saw Mackenzie King's resignation as prime minister. His successor, Louis St. Laurent, was defeated by John Diefenbaker's Conservatives. Diefenbaker in turn was defeated by Lester Pearson's Liberals. Labour union leaders and members of the CCF party saw the need for a strong third voice, one that would uphold workers' rights. The two groups banded together and in 1961 formed the New Democratic Party. NDP ideas have found their way into important policies such as Medicare.

5

The rebellious streak of the fifties came into full bloom in the sixties. The youth culture was now accompanied by more concrete ideas. Social and political protest was typical of the times. The new patterns of lifestyle, music, and dress reflected a desire for tolerance and peace in the world. Much of the rebellion was focused on the hopelessness of the Vietnam War.

6

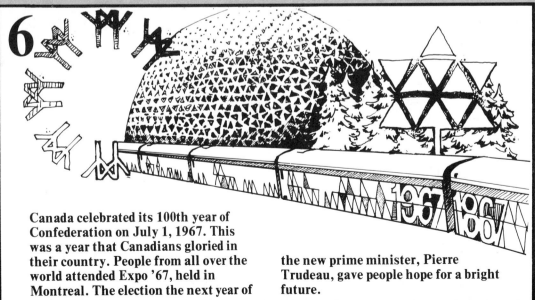

Canada celebrated its 100th year of Confederation on July 1, 1967. This was a year that Canadians gloried in their country. People from all over the world attended Expo '67, held in Montreal. The election the next year of the new prime minister, Pierre Trudeau, gave people hope for a bright future.

Adjusting to Peace

Once again Canadian soldiers, sailors, pilots, mechanics, nurses were returning home from war. Over a million men and women were coming out of uniform. Another million had worked in war-related industries. How would the Canadian economy cope with these people? Those who remembered the slump after World War I and the Depression shuddered at what might happen.

However, economic planners had learned from experience. The American government set out to help countries like the Soviet Union, Germany, and Japan that had suffered most from the war. If the factories in these countries could be reopened, if people could afford to buy clothes to wear and food to eat, international trade would increase. The whole world would benefit.

The experts were right. Economic recovery after World War II was spectacular. Canadians shared in the good fortune.

Wheat sales boomed. New resources of iron ore, oil, and uranium were developed. People went on a buying spree. Now they could get all the things that they had done without during the war. Washing machines, nylon stockings, automobiles were sold as fast as they poured out of the factories. At last there was enough meat and butter on the table to please everybody.

William Lyon Mackenzie King

Canada's prime minister, William Lyon Mackenzie King, must have been glad to see how his nation adjusted to peace.

King had been Laurier's minister of labour before World War I. He became leader of the Liberal Party after Laurier's death in 1919. He was prime minister through most of the boom period of the 1920s. When the people got tired of Bennett's Depression policies, they returned King to power in 1935. He remained in office through the war years until he retired in 1948. All told, he had been prime minister for nearly 22 years, the longest of any prime minister in the British Commonwealth.

King was a curious mixture of opposites. He never married and had few close friends. Outsiders regarded him as a practical, down-to-earth, and ruthless politician. Yet his diary reveals that this tough political

Future, past, and present prime ministers. Louis St. Laurent and Mackenzie King sit before a portrait of Laurier at the 1948 Liberal leadership convention.

FOCUS

Give 3 examples of the way Canada boomed after the war.
How did King's policies change during the period he was in power?
In what way did American influence in Canada grow after the war?
Do you think this influence was good or bad?

1900 1910 1920 1930 1940 1950 1960 1970 1980 1990 2000

realist wept for hours at the death of his pet dog. He also believed he received messages from the spirit of his dead mother.

Mackenzie King with Pat.

King's policies changed with the times. In the 1920s he had believed that government should stay out of business and out of people's lives. The Depression taught him that government could not be that simple. In 1940 he introduced a system of unemployment insurance. During the war his government brought in rationing and measures to control business profits and to strengthen trade unions. At the end of the war he established family allowances. Canada was slowly changing from a "laissez-faire state" to a "welfare state."

American Influence

Some people claim King was far too willing to allow American influence into Canada. During World War II he made military and economic agreements with the United States. By combining their operations the two nations could contribute more to the war effort. After the war this association expanded further. American companies moved in to develop Canadian resources and invest in Canadian industry. The prosperity of the 1950s was largely based on American investment. When Mackenzie King handed the reins of power to Louis St. Laurent on 15 November 1948, he saw a rich country looking confidently to the future.

Clarence Decatur (C.D.) Howe
"American by birth, Canadian by choice"
"Minister of everything"

1886 — born in Waltham, Mass., U.S.A.
1907 — on graduating from Boston Tech, went to Dalhousie in Halifax to teach in new dept. of civil engineering.
1913 — moved to Fort William (Thunder Bay), Ont. to build grain elevators. "I've never seen one of these things in my life, but I'll take the job."
1913-1929 — built elevators from Prince Rupert, B.C. to Prescott, Que.
1930s — business collapsed with Depression and dustbowl. Decided to enter politics.
1935 — elected as Liberal. Made minister of transport.
1936 — re-organized harbour system, CNR, and set up CBC.
1937 — set up TCA, Canada's first national airline.
1940 — as minister of munitions and supply, harnessed government, industry, and entire work force to support war effort, allocating materials and workers where most needed to produce tanks, planes, ships. Encouraged experts to serve country for "a dollar a year." On trip to Britain, torpedoed by German U boat. Rescued from lifeboat after 8 hours on open sea in December.
1945 — Minister of reconstruction and supply and minister of trade and commerce.
1951 — also appointed minister of defence production during Korean War.
1954 — organized all-Canadian route for Trans-Canada Pipeline for natural gas from Alberta to central Canada.
1956 — in order to get pipeline construction started that season, arranged huge loan from government. Forced the legislation through parliament by using "closure."
1957 — defeated in election mostly over closure issue. Retired from politics, but stayed active in business.
1960 — died New Year's morning at home in Montreal.

Newfoundland Joins Canada, 1949

Canada cannot be considered complete without Newfoundland. It has the key to our front door.

John A. Macdonald

The island of Newfoundland thrusts out from the coast of Canada far into the Atlantic. For centuries islanders have felt closer to Britain than to any part of North America. In 1867 they refused to join Canada. They felt they had little in common with the mainlanders. They would remain a self-governing colony of Britain.

Newfoundlanders continued to fish for cod, to jig for squid, and to hunt seal. They developed the lumbering industry in the island's interior. They mined iron ore on Belle Isle and found other deposits of copper, lead, and zinc. The merchants of St. John's sold these goods mainly in Britain and the West Indies. In return they bought the manufactured items and the farm products the islanders could not make or grow.

Depression and Newfoundland

Independence meant isolation. When the Depression hit, Newfoundlanders had nothing to fall back on. The market for lumber and minerals disappeared. Other countries could not even afford to buy fish.

By 1934 one third of the workers were unemployed. The average family income was $150 a year. There was little health care and few schools. The government was in debt. It couldn't raise enough money even to pay interest. The dominion of Newfoundland was bankrupt.

The islanders turned to Britain for help. Britain decided the island should be governed by a "commission." The commission was made up of three Newfoundlanders and three non-Newfoundlanders. All the commissioners were appointed to their jobs. None were elected by the people.

A Strategic Position

During World War II, Newfoundland's isolation came to an end. British, American, and Canadian money and technology poured into the island. Its location between North America and Europe was vital

Flatrock, an "outport" village during the Depression.

Joey Smallwood signs the documents that join Newfoundland to the rest of Canada.

What jobs did the people of Newfoundland depend on?
What happened in Newfoundland during the Depression?
Who led the campaign for Newfoundland to join Canada?
Why did Newfoundlanders decide to enter Confederation?

to both the sea war and the air war. St. John's became a headquarters for ships on convoy duty. New modern airports sprang up at Goose Bay in Labrador and Gander on the island. Aircraft from the factories of North America refuelled there on their way to the battles of Europe. Newfoundlanders became used to seeing American and Canadian uniforms everywhere.

Referendum

After the war Britain felt it was time to return Newfoundland to a more democratic form of government. A national convention was elected to discuss the future. Should the island go back to "responsible government" and run its own affairs? Should it stay with the appointed commission? Some delegates brought up a third idea— confederation with Canada. A few urged union with the United States, but this option was not officially considered.

The people voted on the three main options in a referendum. The result was unclear. No one option received more than half the votes. Another referendum was held on the two more popular options — responsible government or confederation.

The campaigning was fierce. People who worked for the government thought they would lose some of their power if Newfoundland joined Canada. The merchants were afraid Canadians would move in on their markets. Fishery workers, loggers and miners wanted more security. Joining Canada would give them benefits like unemployment insurance and old age pensions. A popular broadcaster named Joey Smallwood led the campaign for union with Canada.

This time the vote was for union with Canada. Newfoundland and Labrador entered Confederation as the tenth province on 31 March 1949. "The Last Great Step of Confederation" had been taken.

The Way the Vote Went:	1st Referendum	2nd Referendum
Commission Government	14%	dropped from ballot
Responsible Government	45%	48%
Union with Canada	41%	52%

Joseph R. Smallwood (Joey)
"The only living Father of Confederation"

1900—born in Gambo, Bonavista Bay, Nfld., the oldest of 13 children. Did not speak until age 3, "but made up for it later."
1915—organized student strikes. Quit school. Worked as apprentice printer. Continued studies while working as reporter in St. John's, Halifax, Boston, New York.
1920s—organized unions and co-ops all over Newfoundland. Once walked 1100 km to urge workers to fight a pay cut.
1930s—starred on radio as Joe the Barrelman, talking about island people, events, stories.
1939-45—made fortune raising livestock to feed troops stationed in Newfoundland.
1948—campaigned vigorously in referendums for union with Canada, saying it would lead to more jobs and security.
1949—became province's 1st premier. "I love this job. I love it to death. I love every minute of it." Stayed close to people. Always answered own phone. With financial aid from federal government, built hospitals, schools, roads. In order to provide better services, moved people from "outports" to larger centres.
1967—after Expo 67 bought several national pavilions and moved them to Newfoundland to serve as community centres and theatres.
1971 — his Liberals defeated by Frank Moores' Conservatives. Some of his schemes had been costly failures. He was said to be out of touch with younger people.
1973 — published his autobiography *I Chose Canada*. Now spends time writing and travelling in his beloved province.

The Boom in Resources

On 13 February 1947, the Alberta sky was seared by a soaring column of orange flame. After drilling 133 dry wells and spending $23 million, Imperial Oil had struck black gold! Leduc Number 1 was the first major strike in a vast new oil field.

Soon other oil companies joined the search. More fields were discovered — Redwater, Pembina, and Joffre in Alberta, Steelman and Weyburn in Saskatchewan. Along with oil, the searchers found natural gas. Canada now had her own supplies of power for industry, fuel for transportation, heat for homes, schools, and business. By the early 1960s Canada had drilled over 20 000 oil and gas wells.

Energy and Minerals

Besides oil and gas, Canada was developing other energy sources. The waters of the St. Lawrence River, Labrador, Northern Quebec, Manitoba, and British Columbia were harnessed to provide electricity.

Canada also proved to be rich in another energy source. The atom bomb that exploded over Hiroshima brought great tragedy. It also focused attention on the possibilities of nuclear power. In northern Ontario and northern Saskatchewan were deposits of uranium, the new nuclear fuel.

Factories in the United States were producing more goods than ever before. War-torn Europe and Japan were rebuilding their industries. Everyone wanted Canadian minerals. They were prepared to spend money to find them.

Soon the vast mineral wealth of Canada was being tapped. Companies sent out prospectors to pinpoint mine sites. The forest was cleared almost overnight. Mines, plants, airstrips, roads, railways, homes, stores sprang up in the wilderness. The fifties was the era of the boomtown.

The day that Leduc No. 1 blew in, 13 February 1947.

The riches from natural resources spurred industry. Steel production doubled. Factories produced heavy equipment for use in mines, on farms, and in other factories. Goods were also made for the consumer. The country went crazy for automobiles. During the fifties Canadians bought nearly three and a half million new cars.

Prospectors at work. Will this be the site of a new boomtown?

Boomtowns of the Fifties

Schefferville, Que. — iron ore.
Sept Iles, Que. — new port and railway bringing ore from Schefferville and Labrador.
Elliot Lake, Ont. — uranium.
Thompson, Man. — nickel.
Uranium City, Sask. — uranium.
Kitimat, B.C. — smelter for imported aluminum ore (bauxite) using nearby hydroelectric resources.

Name 3 sources of energy that helped create the economic boom.
What regions of Canada did best from the boom? Why?
What regions gained little from the boom? Why? What problems
grew from the resource development of the 1950s?

1900 1910 1920 1930 1940 1950 1960 1970 1980 1990 2000

Below the Surface

Few considered the longterm results of this ride to riches. There were grave problems in the making.

The boom was not shared by all Canadians. Much of the Atlantic region was barely touched by the new wealth. The Prairies still relied on wheat farming. They were rich one year and poor the next because of rapidly changing world markets. Poverty was still a reality across Canada.

Central Canada did best from the growth in activity. The main industries and cities were located here. Many of the resource developments in other provinces were owned by corporations with headquarters in Toronto and Montreal. They rarely worked in the best interests of the local area. Profit was the motive, not people.

Even the boomtowns rarely maintained their

The final weld on the Trans-Canada Pipeline, Kapuskasing, Ont., 10 October 1958.

frenzied growth. Within ten years markets dried up; towns died. Ghost towns were often all that remained of the dreams of limitless prosperity.

The landscape was often treated with little respect. Developers simply tore the wealth from the earth. They left permanent scars behind them. They poured pollution into the rivers and blew it into the air.

Canadians did not pay for the exploration and development of their resources. The money came from outside the country, mainly from the United States. This seemed fine at the time. Foreign investment meant jobs. It also meant loss of ownership and control. In 1956 American firms controlled over half the manufacturing in Canada. Of the sixty largest firms in Canada, less than half were Canadian owned. It was a trend that was increasing rapidly.

The fabulous fifties brought prosperity to Canada. They also sowed the seeds for major problems in the future.

Pipelines

How were oil and gas to reach those who wanted to use them? Trucks and railway cars could carry them, but they would have to return empty. The answer was a "one-way" transport system — a pipeline. Soon pipelines were creeping across Canada.

The first pipeline east was for oil and went partly through the United States. When the Trans-Canada natural gas pipeline was built, the Liberal government wanted an all-Canadian route. This would cost more. The minister of trade and commerce, C. D. Howe, agreed to lend the pipeline company money to cover the extra cost. The Conservatives wanted to debate the loan in Parliament. Howe cut short the debate by using a parliamentary procedure called *closure*. Parliament, led by the Liberals, approved the loan.

The Conservatives said the company would never be able to pay back the money. The voters were worried too. They thought the Liberals had been too high handed. In the next election they chose the Conservatives under John Diefenbaker. As a matter of fact, the pipeline was such good business the government loan was paid back ahead of schedule.

To the Heart of a Continent

In 1535 Jacques Cartier sailed up the great St. Lawrence River. When he came to Hochelaga (Montreal) he found he could go no further. Upstream lay a turbulent stretch of white water that is now called the Lachine Rapids.

Four hundred years later North Americans still could not travel by ship up the St. Lawrence River through the Great Lakes to Fort William, Ontario and Duluth, Michigan, on Lake Superior. In 1941 Canada and the United States signed an agreement to build a canal deep enough to allow ocean ships to reach the Great Lakes. Ten years later, the Americans were still studying the project. Canada needed the new transportation route badly. The new mining towns of Quebec and Labrador needed to get their ore to the factories of Toronto, Hamilton, Detroit, and Chicago. The West needed to move its wheat to market. The growth of industry meant Ontario needed new power sources. Hydro-electric plants could be built at the same time as the canal or "seaway."

Canada decided to build the seaway alone. This spurred the United States to action. Talks started up again. In 1954 a final agreement was reached. Each country would pay to build the part of the seaway that was in its territory.

Building the Seaway

Canadian technology got to work. Five of the seven new locks were designed and built completely by

"Moving house" to make room for the seaway.

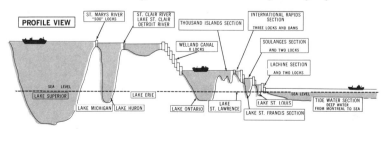

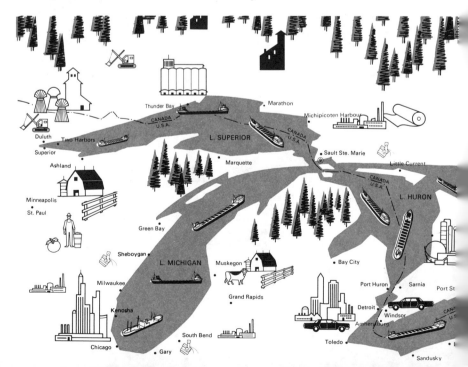

Give 3 reasons why Canada needed the St. Lawrence Seaway.
How did Canadians and Americans divide the work of building the seaway?
How did the seaway affect people in towns that were in its path?

Canadians. Giant rapids were blown to smithereens. Whole islands were demolished or created from scratch. Cross-river tunnels were carved out. Bridges were raised. When their towns and villages had to be flooded 6500 people were "relocated." Teams of historians and archeologists worked feverishly to remove relics and buildings before historic sites were submerged forever.

On 26 June 1959 Queen Elizabeth II and U.S. President Eisenhower officially opened the St. Lawrence Seaway. Merchant ships could now travel 3700 km into the industrial heart of North America. Grain ships could sail to Fort William and Port Arthur (now joined as the city of Thunder Bay) and meet the freight trains bringing wheat for world markets from the Prairies.

Work on the seaway continues to this day. The original 8.2 m depth is not enough for many modern ships. The seaway continues to adapt and modernize.

Louis St. Laurent (Uncle Louis)
"I know nothing of politics and never had anything to do with politicians."

1882—born in Compton, Que., son of a French father and Irish mother. Until he was 6, thought all children spoke French to one parent and English to the other.
1905—graduated from Laval University as lawyer. Unlike many lawyers was not interested in politics.
1914—by now married with family, saw World War I as European war, not important for Canada.
1919-39—represented both Quebec and federal governments in many cases before Supreme Court of Canada and British Privy Council.
1930—president of Canadian Bar Association.
1941—asked to join federal cabinet as leading Quebec figure to help persuade Quebeckers that conscription might be necessary. Agreed "as a patriotic duty and for the duration of the war."
1945—on Canadian delegation at San Francisco conference founding the United Nations.
1946—planned to retire but persuaded not to.
1948—chosen as new leader of Liberal party to succeed Mackenzie King as prime minister.
1949, 1953—won huge election victories. Led country in period of tremendous growth and change. Made Supreme Court final court of appeal instead of British Privy Council. Tried to bring power to change constitution to Canada but could not get provinces to agree. Started seaway and Trans-Canada Highway.
1957—narrowly defeated by Diefenbaker's Conservatives. Aged 74, retired from politics and returned to law.
1973—died in Quebec City. For many Canadians a symbol of co-operation and national unity.

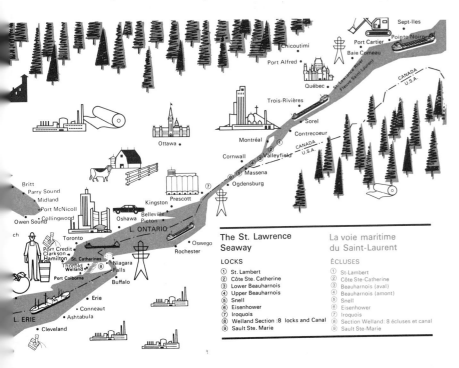

The St. Lawrence Seaway

La voie maritime du Saint-Laurent

LOCKS	ÉCLUSES
① St. Lambert	① St-Lambert
② Côte Ste. Catherine	② Côte Ste-Catherine
③ Lower Beauharnois	③ Beauharnois (aval)
④ Upper Beauharnois	④ Beauharnois (amont)
⑤ Snell	⑤ Snell
⑥ Eisenhower	⑥ Eisenhower
⑦ Iroquois	⑦ Iroquois
⑧ Welland Section :8 locks and Canal	⑧ Section Welland: 8 écluses et canal
⑨ Sault Ste. Marie	⑨ Sault Ste-Marie

locking procedures
All locks on the St. Lawrence Seaway are filled or emptied by gravity. To raise a vessel, for example, the upstream valves are opened and the water simply flows into the chamber through openings at the bottom of the walls. The following diagram illustrates the procedure:

UPPER GATE   LOWER GATE

FILLING VALVE   EMPTYING VALVE

The diagram portrays the following steps:
1: From the lower level the ship sails through the open gates into the lock and is secured to bollards near the side of the walls. The gates are closed.
2: The valves are opened and water is allowed to flow in, lifting the ship.
3: When the vessel reaches the higher level the upper gates are opened and the ship sails out.

To lower a vessel the above steps are reversed. It takes less than ten minutes to raise or lower the water level.

The Baby Boom

The population of Canada had not increased greatly during the 1930s and 1940s. Throughout the depression of the 1930s, immigration had been restricted. During World War II, there was virtually no immigration, and family life was disrupted while several hundred thousand Canadians served overseas.

Postwar Baby Boom

Following the war, the population began to increase rapidly. War veterans returned to establish new families. Approximately 48 000 war brides came to Canada after the war, with 21 000 children. The birth rate in the 1930s was 20.1 per 1000; by the 1950s, the birth rate was 28.0 per 1000. The government encouraged increased immigration from the British Isles, also welcoming displaced persons from Europe, and the disrupted peoples of Europe.

War brides arrive in Montreal, 1946. Most came from Great Britain.

Source of War Brides

	Wives	Children
Great Britain	44 886	21 358
Holland	1 886	428
Belgium	649	131
France	100	15
All others	72	28
	47 593	21 960

During the war, many Canadian soldiers married their brides while overseas. The arrival of the war brides and their children was one of the first waves of immigration after the war. Many felt a great culture shock, moving from Europe to isolated towns in various parts of Canada. As with all immigrants, they suffered the initial shock of dislocation, isolation from friends and family, and a different way of life. However, in spite of these difficulties, most stayed with their new families.

Canada became a youth-centred society. Companies making toys, child-care products, and bicycles did well. Provincial governments struggled to keep up with the mushrooming school population. They built new schools and tried frantically to find the teachers in Britain and even in Australia. They never seemed to catch up. The next year still more children were ready to meet the new teachers in the overcrowded classrooms.

Growth of the Suburbs

The face of Canada's cities changed remarkably in the postwar period. As the population increased, many new homes were needed. Many people chose to live in the more open areas outside of the cities, the suburbs.

Explain the terms "baby boom" and "war brides".
How did the postwar period affect the following — size of families; schools and education; suburbs; prosperity.

A War Bride Remembers

My husband decided to take me to visit his sister in Saskatchewan. He was hoping to make farming our future, and I was to get a first-hand look.

To me it seemed like the end of the world — great stretches of land and sky, neighbours and towns miles away.

I was scared of the livestock, the outdoor toilet didn't help matters and the quietness was something I wasn't used to. I'd come from Wolverhampton and for the first time I began to miss the things of home: the pubs, the movie shows, big stores, dances and the faster pace of life. The loneliness was unbearable at times and I became very homesick. I was also pregnant and physically ill. But I had to forget my misery and pitch in and help. Harvest was in full swing, and meals had to be prepared and taken out to the fields. Days were taken up with cooking and washing dishes, and there was no time for self-pity. I learned a lot from those days on the farm, but Saskatchewan was not for me. I don't think I'd ever have got used to the loneliness.

We went back to B.C. but were unsettled and decided to move in with the in-laws in central Alberta, the land of mixed farming. I wasn't prepared for the long, cold winter with bitter winds, drifting snowstorms and temperatures of 40 and 50 degrees below zero at times.

And living with the in-laws was not that easy. The house was cold and draughty. Water had to be hauled daily, along with wood for the stove and pot-belly heater. At night the heater had to be kept low as a precaution against overheating the pipes. In the morning we'd get up to frozen water pails and ice-cold floors. And there were the everyday problems of trying to cope until my husband found work. There were tears and depression from homesickness, especially at Christmas.

from *The War Brides* by Joyce Hibbert, Peter Martin Associates, Toronto, p. 101.

Shoppers left the downtown area, and shifted to new suburban shopping plazas. The new suburban growth contributed to an expanding economy — the construction, appliance, and manufacturing industries prospered; new roads and highways were built; almost every suburban family owned one car (soon two-car families were not unusual).

The character of the suburbs was a change from the older, more concentrated inner-city areas. The suburbs were characterized by spread-out neighbourhoods, new homes, shopping plazas, gasoline stations, hamburger stands, and superhighways.

The "happy days" of the 1950s and 1960s had arrived.

Shopping malls were designed to serve the new suburban lifestyle. Instead of going downtown to shop at a number of stores along the main street, the homemaker with several small children could use the mall for one-stop shopping convenience.

POPULATION GROWTH   175

The Fabulous Fifties

Confidence and fear. Life in the fifties revolved between these two poles. The confidence was based on the new prosperity. The fear came from the shadow of the Cold War.

Even though World War II was long past, the fifties were still years of fear. The fear of nazism had been replaced by the fear of communism. The development of the hydrogen bomb made nuclear war an ever-present possibility. International politics were tense. Yet inside Canada things seemed better than they had ever been.

The Confident Years

In economic terms things looked secure. People couldn't live as if an H-bomb was going to fall tomorrow. They enjoyed life and the new technological wonders of prosperity.

Around 1952 a new article of furniture began to appear in Canadian living rooms. The baby boom generation grew up glued to the television screen. Youngsters rushed home from school for Howdy Doody. Their older brothers and sisters watched I Love Lucy. The entire family gathered round the set to see the latest entertainers on the Ed Sullivan Show. And at last sports fans could *see* the game described by Foster Hewitt on Hockey Night in Canada.

17-inch Table Model
060-G-660. Price, delivered 189.50

21-inch Table Model
060-G-662. Price, delivered 289.50

21-inch Console Model
060-G-664. Price, delivered 309.50

THE EATON TELEVISION WARRANTY

Every VIKING Television Set carries a full year warranty on the picture tube; 90-day warranty on all other tubes and parts. While we are convinced that VIKING Television Receivers will perform as well or better than other nationally advertised makes, we suggest you recognize the distance limitations on TV reception. Only if you live well within a 100-mile radius of a powerful TV station, or if an immediate neighbour is receiving satisfactory programs, should you order a television set. If in doubt, please write for more specific details regarding your area to EATON'S Mail Order, Dept. 60

CBC camera operators prepare for the first football game on TV, fall 1952.

Advertisers used special lenses to make cars look longer than they really were, because longer, lower, and wider cars were what people were expected to want. With gas at less than 10¢ a litre, who cared about fuel economy?

FOCUS

What new item or change in the 1950s do you think has most affected Canadian life?

Describe a day in the life of a teenager in the fifties. Try to include as many aspects of "fifties lifestyle" as possible.

NEW

Shopping malls
Sunday sports
Expressways
Sputnik
Stereophonic sound
Queen Elizabeth II
Television
The Stratford Festival
Polio vaccine
Computers
Transistor radios
Jet travel

Teenagers at a rock 'n roll concert.

The Teenager

A new species of person, commonly known as a teenager, appeared in the fifties. In earlier times a child had gone straight from school to the responsibilities of adulthood. The new prosperity meant parents could afford to let their kids finish high school and even go on to college or university. This new group of students were certainly not children. They were not part of the adult world. This did not worry them. With 1 300 000 other teenagers in the country by the end of the decade, they created their own culture.

This cohesive and energetic group soon made its presence felt. Teenage fads in boys' hairstyles ranged from crew-cuts (short and bristly) to duck-tails (long and greasy). Girls wore bobby sox, sweater sets, and ruby red lipstick. Fitting in with the crowd was all important. A teenager's greatest fear was to be thought "an oddball."

Teenagers danced to a new form of music. Despite the agonized complaints of parents and church ministers, rock 'n roll was here to stay. Songs with meaningful lyrics like Shoop de doo and Da doo ron ron blared from the new transistor radios. Each week teenagers waited eagerly to hear which of their idols had tunes in the top ten — Elvis Presley, Connie Francis, or Buddy Holly? Perhaps a Canadian star like Paul Anka or Juliette, or a Canadian group like the Crewcuts made the list.

The youthful eruption of energy that is the teenager remains with us today. Being a teenager is a stage of life all Canadians pass through. However adults, then as now, did not always understand the phenomenon. The "generation gap" became a matter of concern.

Elvis Presley, Ottawa, 1957.

Side Effects

The fifties brought prosperity and excitement. But rapid change is difficult for society. Some families could not adjust. The divorce rate began to creep up. Juvenile delinquency became a problem in the large cities. The move to the suburbs increased reliance on the automobile. Traffic jams, expressways, and gasoline pollution became part of daily life.

The fifties were years of growth and change. Cities, fashions, lifestyles, and values were transformed. Canadians were sure they were living in the best society in the world. After the long years of depression and world war, the fifties were indeed fabulous.

Immigration and Refugees

Hungarian refugees in Vienna, Austria, wait to register for camps that will provide food and shelter until they are accepted as immigrants to a new country.

Immigration and Refugees

In the postwar period, more immigrants came to Canada than at any time since 1913. Many were immigrants from the British Isles; others were refugees (displaced persons) from Communist-controlled countries in eastern Europe.

Prime Minister King had stated that Canada's immigration policy would preserve "the fundamental character of the population". He meant that it would remain mainly European and white. Very few questioned that immigrants would come from Europe, excluding groups from Asia or the West Indies.

Gradually, the numbers of immigrants from Italy, Greece, the Ukraine, and other parts of southern and eastern Europe increased to change the character of

The Hungarian Revolution

In 1956 Hungarians revolted against their communist government. Within days help for the government came from the Soviet Union. Soon Soviet tanks were rolling through the streets of Budapest. Before the government regained control, thousands of people had poured across the border into Austria.

Canada offered to help. Immigration requirements were relaxed. 36 000 Hungarians were airlifted to Canada. They arrived with little more than the clothes on their backs and Canadians took them into their homes. They found them jobs. They gave them clothes and furniture. They taught them English or French. The refugees repaid their hosts well. They became hard-working and loyal citizens of their new country.

Czechoslovakia, Uganda, Vietnam

Canada has taken in large groups of refugees on three more occasions since World War II.

In 1968 the Soviet Union stepped in to prevent liberal government policies in Czechoslovakia. Many people fled the country and 10 000 of them came to Canada.

In 1973 President Idi Amin of Uganda stripped the Asians in his country of their property and told them to leave. Canada took in 5000.

In 1975 Vietnam was united under a communist government. Many people in the south, especially business people and former government workers, were persecuted. They started to leave the country in small boats. There is evidence that the government organized their departure in return for huge sums of money. By the end of 1980 Canada had taken in 60 000 "boat people."

cities like Toronto and Montreal. Canada began to lose its largely British and French nature. Trudeau was determined that Canada would be not only a bilingual country but a multicultural society as well. Immigration rules were changed to encourage immigration from new sources — from the West Indies, Asia, Africa, and Latin America, without reference to race, colour, or religion. Added to this was the so-called that has changed and enriched Canadian society over the past 40 years. The multicultural society had arrived.

FOCUS

How did postwar immigration change the nature of the Canadian society and population?
Define the term "refugee". How has the admission of refugees become an issue or problem in recent years?

1900 1910 1920 1930 1940 1950 1960 1970 1980 1990 2000

Immigration to Canada by year

Year	Number	Year	Number	Year	Number
1901	55,747	1931	27,530	1961	71,689
1902	89,102	1932	20,591	1962	74,586
1903	138,660	1933	14,382	1963	93,151
1904	131,252	1934	12,476	1964	112,606
1905	141,465	1935	11,277	1965	146,758
1906	211,653	1936	11,643	1966	194,743
1907	272,409	1937	15,101	1967	222,876
1908	143,326	1938	17,244	1968	183,974
1909	173,694	1939	16,994	1969	161,531
1910	286,839	1940	11,324	1970	147,713
1911	331,288	1941	9,329	1971	121,900
1912	375,756	1942	7,576	1972	122,006
1913	400,870	1943	8,504	1973	184,200
1914	150,484	1944	12,801	1974	218,465
1915	36,665	1945	22,722	1975	187,881
1916	55,914	1946	71,719	1976	149,429
1917	72,910	1947	64,127	1977	114,914
1918	41,845	1948	125,414	1978	86,313
1919	107,698	1949	95,217	1979	112,096
1920	138,824	1950	73,912	1980	143,117
1921	91,728	1951	194,391	1981	128,618
1922	64,224	1952	164,498	1982	121,147
1923	133,729	1953	168,868	1983	89,157
1924	124,164	1954	154,227	1984	88,239
1925	84,907	1955	109,946	1985	84,302
1926	135,982	1956	164,857	1986	99,219
1927	158,886	1957	282,164	1987	159,098
1928	166,783	1958	124,851	1988*	157,000
1929	164,993	1959	106,928		
1930	104,806	1960	104,111		

*Estimate   SOURCE: Statistics Canada

Refugees

Since 1945, a basic part of our immigration policy has been that Canada would provide a home for refugees from oppression in their homelands.

In the 1980s, several large groups of immigrants mysteriously arrived off the shores of Canada by boat, claiming to be refugees. Most people felt that their claims were abuses of the refugee policy. Yet, in spite of these abuses, Canadian policy is still to provide a home for legitimate refugees from oppression in totalitarian states. The problem remains as to how to distinguish legitimate refugees, and those seeking to abuse the system.

Sri Lankan refugees land off the shores of Newfoundland, 1986.

The Man from Prince Albert

John Diefenbaker scores a point off the Liberal government, 1948.

The Liberals had been in power so long they seemed to regard it as their right to govern the country. Many people felt they were becoming arrogant. They acted as if they knew best and didn't have to listen to anyone. When they wanted to make a loan for the Trans-Canada Pipeline, they used closure to cut off debate in parliament. In 1956 some Canadians felt the government betrayed Britain and France in the way foreign affairs minister Lester Pearson handled the crisis over control of the Suez Canal.

John Diefenbaker

In 1956 the Conservatives chose a new leader. The fiery, colourful John Diefenbaker from the prairies brought new life to the party. His skillful attacks on Liberal policies bore fruit. The voters saw him as a man who cared about the country and the "little people."

In the election campaign of 1957, Diefenbaker hit hard at "Liberal arrogance." He said they weren't achieving anything for the country. He had a "northern vision" for Canada. "Roads to resources" would open up the northland to development and settlement.

Minority Government

Diefenbaker and the Conservatives won more seats than any other party in the election of 1957. However, together the opposition parties — Liberals, CCF, Social Credit — had more seats than the Conservatives. This meant they could block any measure the Conservatives wanted passed. Diefenbaker declared he could not work this way. Early in 1958 he called another election.

Majority Government

Diefenbaker seemed to have hypnotized the nation. The result was a Tory landslide. The Conservatives won 208 seats, leaving only 57 for the other parties.

Diefenbaker worked hard to help all Canadians feel at home in their country. He invited Ellen Fairclough to be the first woman in the Federal Cabinet. He appointed James Gladstone as the first native Indian in the Senate. He chose Georges Vanier to be the first French Canadian Governor General.

Perhaps Diefenbaker's greatest joy was the passage of his Bill of Rights. This law guarantees all Canadians certain basic rights such as freedom of religion, freedom of speech, equality before the law, regardless of race, colour, religion, or sex.

Give 3 reasons why voters chose the Conservatives over the Liberals in the election of 1957.
How did Diefenbaker try to protect the rights of all Canadians?
Why was this a difficult time to be in power?

The Arrow on a test flight over Niagara Falls, 1958.

Diefenbaker was proud of his German and British background. He wanted to promote the multicultural nature of Canada without weakening her British heritage. He worried about the growing Americanization of Canadian economic and cultural life. His policies certainly helped many Canadians appreciate themselves and their country. But despite his good intentions, the politician from the prairies never fully understood Quebeckers and their view of Canada.

Disappointments

Diefenbaker is remembered for his efforts in the field of human rights. At the time, the disappointments in other areas seemed more important. He had been a brilliant opposition leader, but he and the Conservatives had little experience at governing. They made mistakes.

This was a difficult time to be in power. The great economic boom of the fifties was slowing down. At one point the government had

to devalue the Canadian dollar. "The Diefendollar" people called it, a blow to Canadian pride.

Perhaps the turning point in Diefenbaker's political career came in 1959. He decided to cancel the Arrow, a Canadian-built supersonic jet fighter. Many people never forgave him.

Minority Government Again

In the election of 1962 the Conservatives lost 92 seats. The voters' confidence in Diefenbaker's stirring speeches had been shaken. He was still prime minister, but once again he headed a minority government.

The Fall of the Arrow

Canadian aircraft manufacturers had become world experts during the war. In the 1950s the A.V. Roe Company was developing a new jet fighter, the Arrow. Engineers and air force officials said it was at least 20 years ahead of its time. Just as the first prototypes rolled out of the Malton factory and took to the air, Diefenbaker cancelled the project. He said Canada should buy American Bomarc missiles instead.

Diefenbaker was surprised at the reaction to this decision. People were furious. They said he had dealt a crippling blow to the Canadian aircraft industry. Overnight 15 000 people lost their jobs. Canadian aircraft experts became part of the "brain drain," leaving the country to find work. Worse, the American missiles needed nuclear warheads. Canadians weren't sure they wanted to be a nuclear power.

Perhaps as a result of the public outcry, Diefenbaker was never able to make up his mind to accept nuclear warheads for the Bomarcs. No Arrow. No nuclear warheads. Diefenbaker had great trouble explaining Canadian defence policy. Even his cabinet ministers lost confidence in him. This lack of decision helped lead to his defeat in parliament in 1963.

In 1967 the Conservatives chose a new leader, Robert Stanfield. Though he was bitter about the way his party had treated him, Diefenbaker continued to represent Prince Albert in his beloved House of Commons His wit and energy kept him in the public eye. Reporters knew that if they wanted a pithy comment on Liberal government policy, they could always get one from John Diefenbaker.

He lived to see his party regain power under Joe Clark in 1979. Later that year, shortly before his 85th birthday, "Dief the Chief" died as he had wanted — "a politician with his boots on."

The Quiet Diplomat

In 1957 the Liberals lost their first federal election in 22 years. Their leader, Louis St. Laurent, decided it was time he resigned.

Lester Pearson had been St. Laurent's minister of foreign affairs. He had just been awarded the Nobel Peace Prize for his role in the Suez crisis of 1956. He had suggested the United Nations send a peace-keeping force to the area. By hard work, he got all the countries involved to agree. Not surprisingly, at the leadership convention soon after, the Liberals chose Pearson.

However, the Nobel Peace Prize was not enough to win the next federal election for Pearson and the Liberals. In 1958 the Conservatives racked up the biggest parliamentary majority in Canadian history. The voters were impressed by Diefenbaker. They thought of Pearson as a diplomat, not as a politician. Pearson did not seem really comfortable in parliament. He lacked Diefenbaker's dramatic flair. He seemed more at home watching a baseball game or playing tennis than making angry speeches in the House of Commons.

In 1962 another international crisis, this time over Soviet missile bases in Cuba, gave Pearson and the Liberals the chance they needed. Diefenbaker had refused to arm Bomarc missiles in Canada and at Canadian NATO bases in Europe with nuclear warheads. Without them, the Bomarcs were almost useless. In the light of the crisis, Canada's allies and members of Diefenbaker's own cabinet pressed the prime minister to accept the warheads. When he still would not move, three cabinet ministers resigned. Pearson made a speech in parliament. He said. "We must honour our commitments." We had taken the missiles, so we had to take the warheads. This made sense to many Canadians.

Parliament had lost confidence in Diefenbaker. Early in 1963 his government was defeated in the House of Commons. He was forced to hold another election. The result was another minority government. But this time the Liberals under Pearson would try to run the country.

Walking a Tightrope

Pearson never had a clear majority in the House of Commons. This meant he had to exercise all his diplomatic skills to stay in power. In order to keep the support of the New Democratic Party (the new name for the CCF) he brought in policies they would approve. All the time the Conservatives kept sniping at Liberal policies and unearthing scandals to embarrass the government.

Lester Pearson addresses the General Assembly during the Suez Crisis. Canada played a key role in creating the first UN peacekeeping force, and continues to take an active part in international affairs.

Why was Lester Pearson awarded the 1957 Nobel Peace Prize? Construct a chart to examine the achievements of Lester Pearson. Explain in each case whether you think his achievements were positive or negative for Canada.

Diefenbaker had urged Canadians to appreciate their country's unique heritage. The Pearson government took this a step further. On 15 February 1965, Canada's official flag was raised over the Peace Tower for the first time. The Canadian army, navy and air force were unified as the Canadian Armed Forces. A system of federal-provincial conferences was set up. Pearson hoped these conferences would help the federal and provincial governments co-operate to provide the best programs and services for Canadians.

Shadows for the Future

The relationship of French and English Canadians became a matter of concern in this period. Pearson set up a Royal Commission on Bilingualism and Biculturalism. The "Bi and Bi Commission" warned Canadians that the French had good reasons to complain about their position in Canada and the way other Canadians treated them. Unfortunately, Canadians largely ignored the findings of the Commission. The government did agree that the civil service should be bilingual. Then it could serve all Canadians equally, and give all a chance at the top jobs.

Under Pearson, American control of the economy grew even greater. Finance Minister Walter Gordon tried hard to reverse this trend. However, he warned too loudly of the dangers of American domination, and became very unpopular. Canadians did not want to be told that their comfortable way of life was based on American interests.

Pearson's last full year as Prime Minister was 1967. Beneath the excitement and joy of Centennial celebrations lay problems his government had not been able to beat. The next year Pearson handed over the reins of power to a very different leader of the Liberal party. His name was Pierre Elliott Trudeau.

For 98 years Canadians discussed the idea of a national flag. Not until 1965, two years before the Centennial celebrations, did Canada acquire a flag of her own. Before then Canada had "borrowed" two British flags. The Union Jack was used at home. The Red Ensign was used to represent Canada at international conferences, to identify Canadian embassies, for Canadian athletes to carry at the Olympic Games.

Many Canadians, especially those of British origin, were quite happy with this compromise. They liked the emphasis it placed on ties with Britain and the Commonwealth. Those who had come from other parts of the world did not feel the same way. And many French Canadians resented it because it was a reminder of the British conquest of New France in 1759.

The flags Canada was using divided Canadians more than uniting them. Pearson wanted a symbol all Canadians could identify with. In 1964 he announced Parliament would choose an official flag.

In the election of 1891, John A. Macdonald's Conservatives used this poster to appeal to loyalties to Britain.

A committee studied over 2000 designs submitted from across the country. Slowly the choice was narrowed down and modified to the single red maple leaf we know today. However, the debate in parliament was long and furious. It took 33 days and 252 speeches before the flag was approved.

The bitterness of the flag debate led people to expect that the new flag would be rejected by many. On the contrary, it met almost universal acceptance. It became more than a flag. It appeared on T-shirts, knapsacks, coffee mugs, and bumper stickers. Canadians today have trouble remembering what all the fuss was about in 1964.

The New Democratic Party

Canada has two major political parties, the Liberals and the Conservatives. Third parties have found it hard to survive in this country, especially in federal politics.

After World War II the CCF had trouble attracting voters. The Liberals under Mackenzie King had "stolen" many CCF ideas such as old age pensions and unemployment insurance. Many Canadians thought of the CCF as a party of the past. It had sprung from the bleak despair of the Depression that few wanted to remember. CCF slogans warning of the evils of capitalism seemed out of place in the booming fifties. In fact, against the background of the Cold War, they seemed dangerously radical. Some business people and journalists attacked the CCF as being "commie."

The party was almost wiped out of federal politics in the great Diefenbaker landslide election of 1958. CCF supporters felt it was time for a new vehicle for their hopes.

The Labour Movement

At the same time, Canadian labour unions were becoming more involved in politics. Traditionally, since the disastrous Winnipeg General Strike, unions had kept out of political affairs. This attitude was changing.

Business was booming. Giant corporations donated money to the Liberal and Conservative parties. They expected these parties to reflect the interests of big business.

As business grew, so did labour. The two clashed in long and bitter strikes. Government leaders tended to be on the side of business. Labour unions often found themselves with few allies in government. More and more labour leaders were feeling the need for political power. In 1956 the unions formed the Canadian Labour Congress. The CLC was an "umbrella" organization that would help them work together.

Union leaders were still looking for a political party to represent their views and interests. Two years later representatives of the CCF and the CLC agreed to start a "New Party," which would revive the CCF and provide workers with a political voice.

The idea of a New Party caught fire. New Party clubs held conferences across the country. In 1960 a New Party candidate was elected to parliament — even though the party did not yet officially exist.

The Birth of the NDP

In 1961 the largest political convention in Canadian history met in Ottawa. The delegates gave the New Party its official name, the New Democratic Party. The NDP

Mayor Charlotte Whitton welcomes the delegates.

was an alliance of labour leaders, farmers, intellectuals, and former CCFers. They elected as their leader a tough

Why did the CCF lose support after World War II?
Which two groups formed a "New Democratic Party"?
What is medicare? Do you think it has been successful in
fulfilling its aims?

1900 1910 1920 1930 1940 1950 1960 1970 1980 1990 2000

▲

witty orator, Tommy Douglas, the premier of
Saskatchewan. The country now had a clear choice from
the increasingly similar Liberals and Conservatives. When
the delegates left for their homes across the country, they
were sure that Canadian politics had been changed
forever.

In a sense, they were right. The NDP found greater
acceptance than the CCF. Since 1961 the NDP has won
provincial elections in Saskatchewan, Manitoba, and
British Columbia. The party has shown increasing
strength in Ontario.

However, in federal politics the NDP has remained a
distant third. In western Canada the NDP is the major
alternative to the Progressive Conservatives at the federal
level. It has found it difficult to win seats in the Atlantic
provinces and to maintain its level of support in Ontario.
In Quebec the party is almost non-existent.

Journalists and other politicians no longer dismiss the
NDP as commies and pinkos. The Liberals have often
taken NDP policies and made them their own. This has
been especially true in the areas of social welfare and
control of the economy, particularly of natural resources.

In the 1980 federal election the party gained the
support of over 2 million voters and won 32 seats. Under
dedicated principled leaders like Tommy Douglas, David
Lewis, and Ed Broadbent, the NDP has won the respect
of voters, politicians, and the press. The "New Party" has
come a long way.

Medicare

Perhaps the greatest contribution the NDP has made to
Canadian society is universal free medical care. "Medicare"
was first introduced by the CCF-NDP to Saskatchewan in 1962.

Doctors in the province were violently opposed to the plan. It
restricted the amount doctors could charge for their services.
Medical fees would be paid by the government not the patient.
The doctors claimed this would destroy the "doctor-patient
relationship." The government, under Premier Tommy
Douglas maintained that good medical care was a right that
belonged to everyone, not just those who could afford to pay.

The doctors fought by going on strike. The government issued
an international appeal. Doctors who believed in the idea of
medicare came from other countries, especially Britain. They
gave free medical care to the people of Saskatchewan until the
issue was settled.

Eventually the striking doctors accepted the program. It soon
became clear that medicare did not destroy the doctor-patient
relationship. Nor did it greatly affect doctors' incomes.

The Liberals in Ottawa watched the Saskatchewan
experiment with interest. The government of Lester Pearson
soon offered all the provinces medicare on a "shared cost"
basis. Today all provinces have some sort of medicare program.
Medicare does not always work smoothly, but residents in
Canada have access to medical care regardless of the size of
their pay cheque.

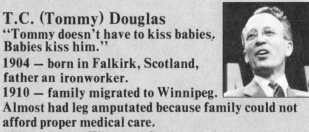

T.C. (Tommy) Douglas
"Tommy doesn't have to kiss babies.
Babies kiss him."

1904 — born in Falkirk, Scotland,
father an ironworker.
1910 — family migrated to Winnipeg.
Almost had leg amputated because family could not
afford proper medical care.
1919 — during Winnipeg Strike sided with workers.
1922 — lightweight boxing champion of Manitoba.
1930 — became Baptist minister at Weyburn, Sask.
1933 — helped start CCF.
1935 — elected to House of Commons for CCF.
1944-61 — led CCF government of Saskatchewan, first
socialist government in North America. Introduced
government hospital plan, air ambulance system, and
medicare.
1961 — chosen as 1st leader of federal NDP.
1962 — defeated in federal election by opponents of
medicare. Ran again in B.C. by-election and elected.
1970 — refused to approve War Measures Act during
Quebec October Crisis.
1971 — resigned as leader but continued as MP to 1979.
1986 — Tommy Douglas died, acclaimed as a fighter for
ordinary Canadians.

The Swinging Sixties

Changing the world was almost a way of life during the sixties. The decade was one of rebellion, excitement, and creativity. People, especially young people, seemed to question everything. They "organized." Groups were ready to do battle for the causes they believed in.

Social change was never more obvious than in the world of fashion. A fashion fever swept the world. Extremes were the order of the day. The miniskirt invaded the school, the factory, and the office. Only the most daring women, however, sported the topless bathing suit. Men replaced white shirts with bright colours and patterns. Narrow ties gave way to flamboyant wide ones. At the same time appearances lost their importance. What one looked like mattered less than what one was.

Miniskirts attract no attention in this Winnipeg lunchtime crowd.

Human relationships were altered dramatically when the birth control pill was introduced in 1960. Canadian attitudes to personal morality and sexuality changed. The idea of trial marriages became less shocking than it had been in the conservative past.

Canadian family life showed signs of cracking under the pressure of unrelenting change. Divorce became more common. The "generation gap" that had appeared in the fifties widened to reveal the divisions that existed in many families.

The sixties heralded a search for identity. People looked to religious cults, psychology and even drugs in order to discover "reality." Young people in particular turned to "grass" and "acid" in their search for understanding in a confusing and changing world. The problem of drug abuse is a terrible legacy of the "swinging sixties."

"You say you want a revolution," but "All you need is love!"

Name some changes that took place in Canadian society during the 1960s. In your opinion what was the most important event or change of the decade?
Why do you suppose the 1960s were termed "the swinging sixties"?

Peace and Love?

Peace and love were the watchwords of the decade. Yet violence was evident everywhere. For many people it came to a head in the brutal Vietnam War. This revealed that the United States could be ruthless in pursuing its goals. Young Americans were drafted into the armed forces. As the sixties became the seventies thousands of "draft dodgers" burned their draft cards and fled to Canada to avoid fighting in a war they could not believe in.

The fifties had been a time where everyone had known what was right and what was wrong. The turmoil of the sixties changed all that. The world would never be as self-satisfied and sure of itself again. Yet the decade ended on an optimistic note. As Canadians watched in amazement, an American astronaut set foot on the surface of the moon. His words matched the decade: "One small step for man; one giant step for mankind."

Movements of the Sixties

Canada's native people fought back in the face of racism and neglect. Indian and Métis leaders like Harold Cardinal, Howard Adams, and Kahn Tinehta Horn called attention to the plight of their people. They demanded justice and equality from Canadian society.

Women became aware of their inferior role in Canadian society. The women's liberation movement burst out into the open. Conservative Canadian men had been quite comfortable with the idea that women were there to make their beds, cook their meals, and look after their children. Now they reeled from shock as women questioned this concept.

Women protested and marched for changes in abortion laws, divorce laws, and employment practices. More and more women entered the work force. Some needed the pay cheque. Some were eager for a career and identity of their own.

The province of Quebec emerged from long isolation. Quebeckers protested the place their province held in Confederation. A group of extremists, the Front de Libération du Québec (FLQ), rocked Canada with repeated bombings and robberies. More peaceful Quebeckers who wanted Quebec to separate from Canada formed the Parti Québécois.

Canadian students were no longer willing to accept the ideas of their parents and teachers without question. They organized strikes and sit-ins and refused to write exams. Sometimes these activities led to riots and violence. Students campaigned for everything from an end to war and poverty, to an end to marks and fees.

Demonstrators protest the war in Vietnam and Canada's role in selling arms for U.S. troops fighting there.

Canada's 100th Birthday

1867 | 1967

There had been no plan to select a popular Centennial song. But Bobby Gimby's CA-NA-DA was so bright and sparkly it was quickly adopted.
Judy LaMarsh, secretary of State

On 1 July 1867 four provinces had come together to form the Dominion of Canada. The new nation's motto was "From sea to sea." Six other provinces joined the confederation until the motto became a reality. Territories to the north were added, and the nation was bounded by a third sea, the Arctic Ocean. In area, Canada was the second largest country in the world. In 1967 Canadians set out to celebrate their country's 100th birthday. All across the land, in every village, town, and city, they planned how they would mark Centennial year. They held parades, dances, banquets, and carnivals. They built libraries, schools, concert halls, and stadiums. That year Canadians gloried in being Canadian.

Expo 67

Canada invited the entire world to help celebrate! The city of Montreal was host to a world fair, or exposition. Man and His World was the theme of the show. It soon became known to Canadians as "Expo 67."

For one beautiful and unforgettable summer, Expo took us into the future that can be ours.
Robert Fulford

Montreal was chosen for its charm, vibrancy, and international flavour. It was the largest city in Canada and the largest French-speaking city in the world after Paris. Montrealers, led by Mayor Jean Drapeau, set out to make Expo the biggest and best party ever.

Bowsman, Manitoba, held a privy parade, with balloons.

FOCUS What sort of things did Canadians do to celebrate the first hundred years of Confederation?
Do you think that there will still be an independent Canada to celebrate its 200th birthday? Explain.

Expo was held on three islands in the St. Lawrence River. One of the islands was totally man made! Early in 1967 futuristic domes, and towers began to rise. They were carefully planned to blend with each other, the newly landscaped parkland, and the waters of the river. And these were only the shells that held sights, sounds, and ideas the world had never seen before.

A world fair is an advertising display. Each country wants to show itself at its best. The last world fair had been held in 1956 in Brussels, Belgium. Since then there had been great progress in such fields as film, architecture, and science. These developments had grown behind the walls of studios and laboratories. Many were on show at Expo 67 for the first time.

People walked through the glorious array of national pavilions. They saw technology put to work in exciting ways they had not dreamed possible. They listened to the babble of strange languages and felt that Man was truly enjoying the beauty and riches of his World. Canadians and their guests learned new ways of seeing, thinking, and living.

After we have all seen Expo, how can we ever again be content with the cities in which we live?
Ron Haggart

A Good Year

Centennial year came at a happy time for Canada. Most Canadians could not remember the hopelessness of the Depression. Many could not remember the shock of World War II, which had ended 22 years before. Even the Cold War, when people lived in fear that some American or Soviet general would "push the button" and start a nuclear war, was fading from people's minds. Canadians lived in peaceful and prosperous times. They forgot their own differences within the country. They did not worry about gloomy economic forecasts. They simply enjoyed their pride in Canada and her place in the world.

Bells pealed from coast to coast. People danced in the streets. Ships in our harbours blew their horns. Aircraft showered our towns with thousands of tiny flags, and the flares the air force dropped over Trenton, Ontario, were so brilliant you could see them 50 miles away. Soldiers marched, 100 gun salutes boomed. Alberta's birthday cake for Canada weighed 1600 pounds. People on foot, on horses, in canoes, and even in wheelchairs set out on zany journeys to prove their love of country. In Vancouver 100 girls dressed as candles to form a living birthday cake. In a Halifax park Bluenosers downed 20 000 cups of clam chowder. In Saskatchewan every July 1 baby got a silver spoon.
Harry Bruce

Questions and Activities

Who am I?

1. I led Newfoundland into Confederation with Canada. I became known as "the only living Father of Confederation." Who am I?
2. As prime minister, I gave Canadians their first Bill of Rights. My political supporters knew me as "the Chief." Who am I?
3. I was called "the king of rock 'n roll." Teenagers greeted me with screams of delight whenever I appeared. Who am I?
4. I set up the CBC and TCA (now Air Canada). I had so many jobs in government I was nicknamed "Minister of Everything." Who am I?
5. I won the Nobel Peace Prize in 1957. I was prime minister when Canadians got their own national flag. Who am I?
6. I was premier of Saskatchewan from 1944 to 1961. I became the first national leader of the NDP. Who am I?
7. We were the most popular musical group of the sixties. We came from England, but our music conquered the world. Who are we?

Ideas for Discussion

1. What would have happened in Newfoundland if Newfoundlanders had voted *not* to enter Confederation in 1949? Write your thoughts down in a brief paragraph. Be prepared to read your paragraph aloud during a class discussion.
2. List the good and bad results of the boom of the early fifties. Hold a class debate on the topic: Resolved that the economic boom of the fifties created more problems than it solved.
3. With a group of other students discuss the statement, "Parents rarely understand teenagers — and teenagers rarely understand parents."
4. Canada underwent a "baby boom" in the 1950s. Today Canadians are having fewer children or none at all.
   a) Suggest reasons for this drop in the birth rate.
   b) What does the drop mean for the future of our country? Some possible areas for discussion are schools, the labour force, immigration, and supporting the elderly.
5. What are the characteristics of a good prime minister? Working in small groups try to decide which of the following best fulfills the role of prime minister:
   a) Louis St. Laurent
   b) John Diefenbaker
   c) Lester Pearson
6. How has rock 'n roll changed the world? Have these changes been good or bad? In your opinion what song, singer, or group has had the greatest influence? Why?
7. If you had a choice, would you have preferred to live during the fifties or the sixties? Why?

Do Some Research

1. Visit the library to find out more about the province of Newfoundland since it joined Canada in 1949. You might use the following headings:
   a) Geography   d) Towns, Villages, and Outports
   b) Culture and Traditions   e) Political Leaders
   c) Transportation   f) Economic Development
2. Research the recent history of a "boomtown" in your region. Why was the town established? Has the town continued to develop? What do you think will be the future of your boom town?
3. Find out more about the cancellation of the Avro Arrow project by the Diefenbaker government. Make a list of the reasons for this decision and the arguments against it. State your personal conclusions clearly and firmly.
4. Write a brief biocard of an important Canadian of the fifties or sixties. Here are a few suggestions:
   a) Judy LaMarsh   e) Normie Kwong
   b) Marilyn Bell   f) K.C. Irving
   c) Paul Anka   g) Maurice Richard
   d) Kahn Tinehta Horn   h) W.O. Mitchell
   Make a class folder or wall display for your biocards.
5. Summarize the achievements or changes won by one of the protest movements of the 1960s.
6. Find out what projects your community undertook to celebrate Canada's 100th birthday. Were these projects a good idea?

Be Creative

1. Make a working model to demonstrate how a lock operates on the St. Lawrence Seaway.
2. Divide into teams and prepare time capsules for the fabulous fifties or the swinging sixties. Include photo records, magazines, records, souvenirs, fashions, news items. You might celebrate the end of your project with a theme party.
3. Write a newspaper article on one event in the celebration of Canada's 200th birthday. Use exciting headlines and pictures to present your story. Place your articles together in a class bicentennial newspaper. (Do you think we will still have newspapers in 2067?)
4. Prepare a department store catalogue for the 1950s. Compare this catalogue with a modern version. What differences do you find in the products available, design, prices?
5. Compare the hit songs of the fifties and sixties with each other and with the songs of today. What differences do the songs reveal about attitudes to
   a) values   b) technology   c) teenagers   d) love

You Are There

In periods like the fifties Canadians regarded almost all economic development as "progress." In the sixties people began to look at some of the side effects of development. They wondered if it was all worth it. Certainly development in some form is necessary for the economic health of a nation. When we examine the question of development today, how do we count the cost?

A Pulp and Paper Mill at River Rock

River Rock is in northern Canada. In the early years of the century copper was discovered nearby. Miners and their families soon created a small town on the banks of the Rocky River. Merchants moved in to open stores. Teachers, lawyers, restaurant owners, and doctors came to offer their services to the community.

River Rock is a pleasant place, surrounded by rich forests. Rushing streams tumble into still lakes that teem with fish. The town is friendly. People enjoy living here.

Three years ago the mine closed because the ore had run out. Now young people are leaving town in order to find work in the big cities to the south. Stores have closed because business is

poor. The town council cannot raise the money to provide the services a modern community needs. Many residents rely on unemployment insurance and provincial welfare benefits. It seems that for the last three years the town has been limping along from one government grant to the next.

Recently U.S. Conglomerate Inc. has shown interest in River Rock. The company plans to develop a giant pulp and paper

A major issue is confronting you, the people who care about the town of River Rock. You are going to a public meeting to discuss it. On a piece of paper jot down the concerns you want raised at the meeting. Be prepared to make a statement, ask questions, or add comments to make sure these concerns are discussed. Keep an open mind. Others may have points you have not thought of.

What is the future for River Rock?

mill. The forests in the valley can be harvested. The Rocky River can be dammed to provide power. All that is needed is the go-ahead from the town council. Then the company will build the mill, provide jobs for local residents, and make profits for its share-holders. River Rock could boom once again.

For weeks all of you — citizens of River Rock, representatives of U.S. Conglomerate, town councillors, and others — have been discussing the proposal. Tonight a public meeting is being held in the school auditorium. A number of groups with special concerns have asked to speak at the meeting:

a) *The town council,* led by Mayor Irene Nadeau: You know the town desperately needs jobs. The taxes paid by the company will help provide new roads, schools, recreation centres, libraries.

b) *Young people* in town: You are eager to get jobs in a highly skilled industry. You also love your valley and fear that its beauty may be destroyed.

c) *Senior citizens:* You want the valley to remain as it was when you were young. Yet you also want your children and grandchildren to be able to live and work in River Rock.

d) *Native people* on the reserve nearby: You are afraid the company will ruin your traditional hunting and fishing grounds.

e) *Jonathan Goldstein's* and *Alice Chan's* families: You have recently moved to River Rock because of its beauty and isolation. You mistrust big business, especially American corporations. You fear the company will be out for profit at any cost.

f) *U.S. Conglomerate's* managers: You feel there is a great future for an operation in River Rock. But millions of dollars will have to be spent in start-up costs. There will be no profits for several years. You are prepared to comply with "reasonable requests" on the way you set up the mill. But you do not want expensive interference from local government. If you feel the citizens are not behind the idea, you are prepared to invest elsewhere.

Chapter Six

From Trudeau to Mulroney
ADVANCE ORGANIZER

1

In the late 1960s, Pierre Trudeau offered a youthful and vigorous approach to government affairs. His fresh ideas and moral strength appealed to the young, and gave new hope to the older generation of voters. World leaders were impressed with his ideas on foreign policy. Trudeau's main objective was a unified Canada. He sometimes achieved his aims by tightening federal controls, which often angered the provinces.

2

In 1973 the oil-producing countries of the Middle East raised their prices. Canadian companies were forced to spend more money for the energy used to make their products. The prices of manufactured goods increased. The workers demanded higher wages to keep pace with the rising prices. Some businesses couldn't afford to keep all their employees. Largely because of this, unemployment rose.

3

In the 1960s, immigration policies meant to be fair to all attracted people of many nationalities to Canada. These people brought with them their own traditions and values, and their own approaches to day-to-day living. Unfortunately many were met with prejudice and hostility in their new country. Although multiculturalism is heartily encouraged by the federal government, racism is still a problem in some Canadian cities.

Word List

budget	energy crisis	multiculturalism
common market	environment	negotiate
conservation	equality	racism
consumer	inflation	standard of living

4

The original natives of Canada are the Inuit and Indian peoples of the North. But industry's desire for northern oil and gas may displace them from their homeland. They are fighting a continuing battle to maintain their way of life in the face of modern technology.

5

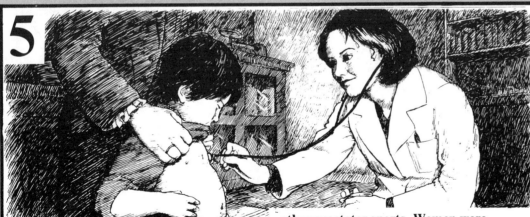

Many trends in society and culture developed in the seventies. There was greater activity in modern music, theatre, dance and film. More people participated in hockey, soccer, and other spectator sports. Women were more vocal than ever before in asserting their social and working rights. The general public and the business world began to accept the need for women's equality.

6

By the 1980s, many Canadians were beginning to be unhappy with Pierre Trudeau and the Liberal Party. They were concerned about unemployment, inflation, and the increasing national debt. In 1984, they elected a Conservative, Brian Mulroney, as Prime Minister of Canada with a landslide majority. He was determined to reduce the national debt, and to provide more jobs. He was returned again as Prime Minister in the 1988 election.

Trudeaumania

The sixties had been a time for youth, colour, and liveliness. Canadians were tired of the same old faces that had dominated the political scene for so long. In the high spiritedness that surrounded Centennial year they wanted fresh blood. Pierre Elliott Trudeau seemed the ideal man. The new minister of justice was much younger than most politicians. He enjoyed sports, dancing, parties, sexy clothes. He had done exciting things like standing up to big business and the Quebec government during the Asbestos strike and visiting communist China in a period when it was cut off from the western world. He had new ideas, a strong sense of justice and a deep love for Canada. Surely this was the man to lead Canada into the seventies. When Pearson resigned in 1968, Trudeau was chosen as leader of the Liberal Party. As soon as he was sworn in as Prime Minister he decided to hold an election. He would take advantage of the mood of the country.

The Campaign

Wherever Trudeau appeared to give a speech, it was a little like a rock concert. Teenagers cheered and screamed themselves hoarse. The crowds swarmed to get close to their hero. Women tried to kiss him (which he clearly enjoyed). People were thrilled by his clear vision of a just society where all Canadians' rights were respected; where all could enjoy the good things of life.

Candidates from other parties had little chance against the Liberals. Voters had been swept off their feet by the new Liberal leader. They were also tired of the compromises minority governments had to make. Canada had not had a majority government since 1962. Voters felt that this was what the country needed in order to get things done. When Canadians went to the ballot box in 1968, they gave Trudeau the majority he had requested.

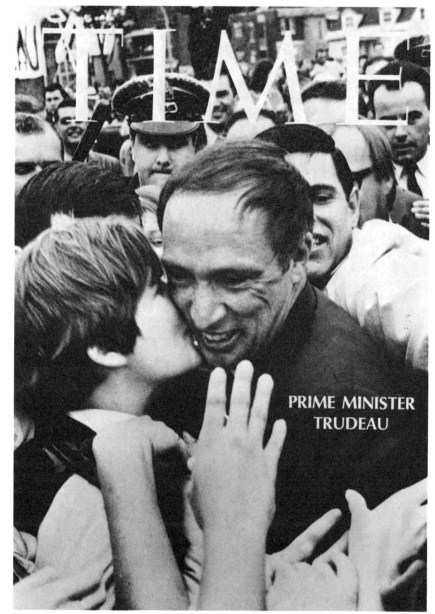

It is every politician's dream to be on the cover of *Time* magazine. Pierre Elliott Trudeau made it because of the excitement and enthusiasm that surrounded his stunning election victory in 1968.

FOCUS Why were voters attracted to Pierre Trudeau in 1968?
Name two areas in which he made changes in Canadian politics.
What were Trudeau's greatest strengths and weaknesses?

1900 1910 1920 1930 1940 1950 1960 1970 1980 1990 2000

By the late 1970s cartoonists often portrayed Trudeau as a rich, uncaring person who did not understand the everyday problems of ordinary Canadians.

The Just Society

The 1970s were difficult years. The economy slowed down and it was a time of high unemployment and inflation. Tensions grew between English and French, between "old" Canadians and recent immigrants. Native Peoples demanded fairer treatment. Women demanded true equality with men. Many of these matters were beyond the control of the government. But people had high expectations of the changes that Trudeau would make. His election slogan in 1968 was "the Just Society". When he could not solve many of these problems, many Canadians felt disappointed and angry.

Nevertheless, under Trudeau there were some symbolic changes. He appointed Bora Laskin as the first Jewish Chief Justice of the Supreme Court. Pauline McGibbon of Ontario and Ralph Steinhauer of Alberta became the first woman and first Native Indian Lieutenant-Governors of their provinces. Len Marchand became the first Native Indian to be a cabinet minister. Jeanne Sauvé became the first woman Speaker of the House of Commons and, later, the first woman Governor General of Canada. Yet these important symbolic moves were described as mere "tokenism" by militant Native Peoples and by the feminists.

French Canada

One of Trudeau's crusades was to extend the rights of French-speaking Canadians in other parts of Canada. He said that if French Canadians did not have language and legal rights outside of Quebec, they would remain isolated in Quebec — a French-speaking ghetto or "reserve". His goal was to create a country where English- and French-speaking Canadians could share equal language and legal rights.

The Official Languages Act was passed in 1969 to ensure Canadians could be served by the federal government in either French or English. This meant many civil servants had to learn a second language. Companies doing business in Canada were also required to mark their products in both languages. The act only applied to matters under federal control. Trudeau was unhappy that he could not persuade the provinces to follow the federal lead.

Canadian unity was the matter which concerned Trudeau most. In many ways he seemed to be fighting a losing battle. In the early years, the main threat seemed to come from Quebec. By 1980 provincial leaders in many regions of the country were disagreeing with the prime minister. They thought he was trying to take away some of their powers. Many citizens were confused. Which was more important, the province or the country?

Economic Problems

The postwar period from 1945 to the early 1970s was a period of almost uninterrupted economic growth in Canada. Industries were expanding, and there was great demand for our agricultural, forest, and mineral products. There was a shortage of workers, and jobs were plentiful. Wages increased each year, inflation remained low. Canadians eagerly bought the new signs of prosperity, — new homes, large cars, stereo sets, and colour television sets.

By the early 1970s, the economic expansion began to slow down. Unemployment began to increase. Wage increases fell behind the rate of inflation. Farmers had to borrow money at high rates of interest to pay for new equipment. What had happened? Why was there such a change after 30 years of continuous growth?

Energy Crisis of the 1970s

Much of the world's supply of oil comes from the Middle East. In 1973, the Organization of Petroleum Exporting Countries (OPEC) combined to control the selling price of oil. Within a year, the price of oil jumped from $8 a barrel to over $12 a barrel. By 1980, the price was over $30 a barrel and seemed to be going higher and out of control.

Oil and petroleum products are now essential to the way of life of all industrial countries. This is especially true of countries like Canada in the cold area of the northern hemisphere. It is not only essential to operate cars and home heating, but many industries use petroleum products. The result of high oil costs was a period of higher consumer costs and inflation.

The Wage-Price Spiral

When companies were forced to spend more to make their products, they had to raise their prices. When workers saw prices going up, they demanded higher wages from their employers. They felt they should be able to keep buying products the way they always had. When employers paid higher wages, they had to raise their prices again. A "wage-price spiral" set in.

This was not the only effect of the rise in oil prices. It also led to increased unemployment. Business leaders did not know how high oil prices were going to go. They were afraid to invest in new ventures in such an uncertain climate. There were few new companies looking for workers. Many older companies found that they could not sell as much at the higher prices they now had to charge. Many people who had jobs in these companies were laid off.

Saudi Arabian delegates at an OPEC conference in the 1970s.

How did each of the following contribute to Trudeau's defeat in 1979: energy crisis; FIRA; provincial opposition; the deficit?

1900 1910 1920 1930 1940 1950 1960 1970 1980 1990 2000

The 1970s

The 1970s were clearly the Trudeau era. His personality and policies dominated Canada throughout that period.

He was concerned that Canadian industries be protected from being taken over by foreign (mainly U.S.) companies. He was influenced by the ideas of economic nationalists such as Walter Gordon. Gordon pointed out the danger to Canadian independence of having too much foreign control of Canadian resources and industries. In 1974, the government formed the Foreign Investment Review Agency (FIRA) to screen takeover bids for any Canadian industry or resource. FIRA slowed the increase of foreign ownership and pleased Canadian nationalists. At the same time, the reduction in American investment added to the slowdown in the economy. Many were not so concerned with the source of investment; they were concerned more with economic growth — and jobs. This issue continued to divide Canadians throughout the 1970s and 1980s and may continue to be a problem.

Provincial Opposition

Trudeau believed in a strong federal government. He believed that only if the federal government retained strong powers could it deal with the problems facing Canada as a whole. However, many provinces felt that their interests were not being served by the federal government. This was so not only in Quebec. Premiers Brian Peckford of Newfoundland, Peter Lougheed of Alberta, and William Bennett of British Columbia demanded greater rights for their provinces. The annual federal-provincial meetings became full of controversy and heated. The particular issue was control of resource revenues, particularly from oil and gas. Many felt that the atmosphere of conflict and confrontation was due to Trudeau's uncompromising attitude. Trudeau said that someone had to stand up for the powers of the central government against the de-centralizing interests of the provinces.

Trudeau was more concerned with political and constitutional matters than with economic questions.

An Increasing Deficit

Throughout the 1970s the government faced decreasing revenues from taxes. But as unemployment increased, more money was needed for unemployment insurance and other social programs. Until the 1970s, governments had aimed at balancing their budgets. By the mid-1970s, the government chose to pay for its needs through deficit budgeting — spending more money than it raised through taxation. By the late 1970s, the annual deficit was over $12 billion per year; by the 1980s the annual deficit was $38 billion. Trudeau's opponents pointed out that the country could not go on indefinitely with such annual increases to our national debt.

Election 1979

By 1979, Canadians were ready for a change. The Progressive Conservatives campaigned under their new leader, Joe Clark, promising to bring the budget under control. The election results were:

Progressive Conservative — 136
Liberal   — 114
New Democratic Party   — 26
Créditistes   —   6

Political Change

From 1968 to 1979, Canada had only one prime minister; from 1979 to 1984 we had four prime ministers.

Joe Clark (1979-80)

Prime Minister Joe Clark was elected with only a minority government. (The total number of opposition seats was greater than the number of Conservative seats.) That should have indicated the need for cautious government. Instead, Clark decided to govern as if he had a majority and to take the consequences. Eight months later, the government was defeated in the House of Commons and had to call an election. The results of the 1980 election were:

Liberal	— 147
Progressive Conservatives	— 103
New Democratic Party	— 32

Trudeau returns 1980-1984

"Welcome to the 1980s," said Trudeau on his return as Prime Minister. In his second term, Trudeau concentrated on his primary concern, a new constitution.

In the referendum vote in 1980, Quebeckers had rejected the idea of "sovereignty-association" proposed by Premier Lévesque and the separatist Parti-Québécois. Trudeau and other Liberals had promised that if Quebeckers voted "*non*" in the referendum, he would revise the constitution to make it more in keeping with the needs of Canadians in the 1980s.

Trudeau set out on the giant task of constitutional reform. Although most people supported changes in the constitution (British North America Act, 1867), it was almost impossible for all provincial leaders to agree on reform.

Trudeau had three main goals:
1. Patriation — the right to amend the constitution (which remained with the British Parliament) must be given to Canada.
2. an Amending Formula — to develop a system to amend the constitution acceptable to the premiers. This would protect provincial rights, particularly the interests of Quebec.
3. a Charter of Rights and Freedoms — to provide a guarantee of the rights and freedoms of all Canadians within the constitution. The charter would protect the rights of Canadians from abuses in any laws passed anywhere in Canada.

The process was slow and difficult. Finally on November 5, 1981, an agreement was reached to satisfy all of the premiers — except Premier Lévesque of Quebec. The new Constitution Act was signed by the Queen and came into effect in 1982.

Trudeau's dream of a new constitution had been achieved — but at a price. Lévesque and other Quebec officials rejected the new constitution and the fact that it was imposed on Quebec despite their opposition.

The paradox remained. In trying to satisfy the needs of the people of Quebec, the government had satisfied the wishes of the other provinces. Quebec had been left out, as dissatisfied and isolated as ever.

Trudeau — Speech to National Press Club, 1969
"Living next to you (the U.S.) is in some ways like sleeping with an elephant. No matter how friendly and even-tempered is the beast, one is affected by every twitch and grunt."

Why did Trudeau want to reform the Constitution?
Explain why each of the following was a problem in the process of patriating the constitution:
a) the Charter of Rights; b) support from Quebec

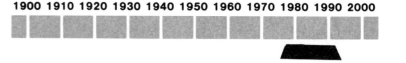

1900 1910 1920 1930 1940 1950 1960 1970 1980 1990 2000

Trudeau in International Affairs

Trudeau was more popular and respected in other countries than within Canada. His speeches and statements on international affairs were well-received in countries around the world. In 1970, he established diplomatic relations with Communist China for the first time. He attempted to develop new ties with Latin America, an area that Canada had often ignored. While Americans emphasized the East-West split between Communist and Western nations, Trudeau warned of the even greater danger of the North-South split. He emphasized the perils of ignoring the needs of the countries of the southern hemisphere. Most of these countries had immense economic, educational, and health problems.

In his last years in office, Trudeau embarked on a crusade for world peace. He sought to bring about nuclear disarmament and to reduce the threat of nuclear war. Though his efforts were praised, he was not successful in reducing hostility between the U.S. and the U.S.S.R.

In November 1981, the Prime Minister and the provincial premiers had their final discussions that led to the Constitution Act of 1982.

End of an Era

National Energy Policy

In the 1980s, most of the Canadian oil industry was owned by American oil companies. Trudeau and many of the Liberals wanted to have greater Canadian control of production and pricing. The rise in energy prices in the 1970s had been due to international factors beyond Canadian control. The hope was to have greater control in the industry to protect Canadian consumers.

In 1981, they introduced the National Energy Program (NEP):
1. to increase Canadian self-sufficiency in oil by increasing production of oil, particularly in the off-shore areas (Arctic and Atlantic);
2. to establish Petro-Canada as a Canadian-owned company in the oil industry;
3. to reduce tax concessions to the oil-producing companies, and to transfer excess revenues to the federal government.
4. to maintain a separate Canadian oil price, independent of the inflated world price.

The intention of Trudeau and the Liberal government was to use the tax revenue gained from increased oil prices to finance the increasing demand for social legislation (e.g., medical care, pensions, unemployment insurance).

The NEP did not work out as planned. Oil producers were opposed to the government policies. Many, seeing opportunities for profits being reduced, pulled out of Canada to develop new oil wells in the United States. Albertans, led by Premier Lougheed, felt that they had been betrayed. They believed that the federal government was using revenues from the oil industry to finance social legislation for other Canadians. For the first time, Albertans had an opportunity to acquire and enjoy the profits of their resources. Many Westerners believed that Trudeau and the Liberal government were depriving them of this opportunity.

Westerners believed that, once again, their interests had been sacrificed to the needs of eastern Canadians. For the first time in decades, Western separatist parties began to rally support.

Construction of the Norman Wells to Zama pipeline — the first buried crude oil pipeline in Canada's North.

FOCUS

Examine the National Energy Policy, using the following organizers: goal, achievements, weaknesses.
Who were the four Canadian Prime Ministers of the 1980s?

1900 1910 1920 1930 1940 1950 1960 1970 1980 1990 2000

Trudeau departs

Trudeau had then been Prime Minister for 15 years, longer than any other Prime Minister except Mackenzie King. Most of his political goals had been achieved. However, the country remained in an economic recession. Many Canadians, including many Liberals, were waiting for his retirement.

On February 29, 1984, Trudeau "went for a walk in the snow". When he returned, his mind was made up; he announced his retirement the next day.

Trudeau had dominated Canadian life as no other prime minister had done since Sir John A. Macdonald. He had left a legacy of achievements.

For many, his retirement came none too soon. He was very unpopular in the West and among business people across Canada. His strong will had helped to create a mood of conflict between the provinces and the federal government. In 15 years, he had helped to change the country greatly; but for Canadians who were looking for a new style of leadership, his departure was welcomed.

John Turner 1984

John Turner was elected as the new leader of the Liberal Party and became Prime Minister in July 1984. He had been a member of the Liberal cabinet up until 1975. In that year, he retired after disagreeing with Trudeau over Liberal policies, and became a corporate lawyer in Toronto.

Nine days after becoming Prime Minister, Turner called an election. The Conservatives were also led by a new leader, Brian Mulroney. In the election campaign, Mulroney captured the mood of the country, which was ready for a change. The election result was one of the greatest landslides in Canadian history.

Progressive Conservatives — 211
Liberal — 40
New Democratic Party — 30
Independent — 1

John Turner had been prime minister for only two months.

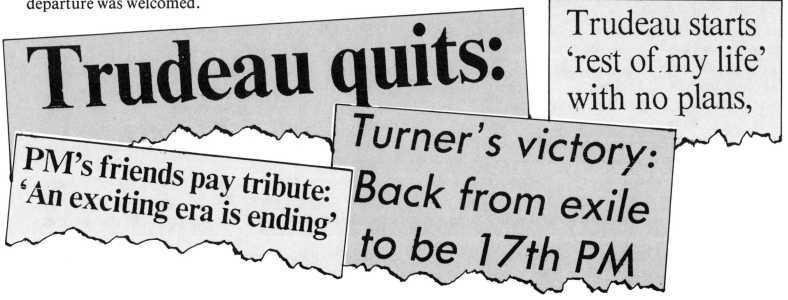

Trudeau quits:

Trudeau starts 'rest of my life' with no plans,

PM's friends pay tribute: 'An exciting era is ending'

Turner's victory: Back from exile to be 17th PM

The Mulroney Era Begins

The return of the Conservatives with a huge majority showed that Canadians were ready for new directions. Prime Minister Mulroney had promised to stimulate the economy and provide "jobs, jobs, jobs". He also pledged to reduce the annual deficit, to encourage the growth of private industry, to reduce the conflict between the provinces and the federal government, to strengthen the Canadian defence role, and to improve relations between the United States and Canada. However, early in his term of office, a series of problems developed which caused many to withdraw their support of his government. Within three years, eight cabinet ministers had to resign because of scandals or suspected conflict of interest. The government was accused of widespread patronage appointments. Mulroney was accused of being indecisive in carrying out his policies. The government appeared to have lost its direction and, by 1986, was running third behind the Liberals and the New Democratic Party in public opinion polls.

An Improved Economy

Gradually the economy began to improve. Industries expanded and jobs were created faster than at any time in previous years. Unemployment dropped from a national average of 11% to 7%, although remaining high in parts of the Maritimes and Quebec. The Canadian economy grew at a faster rate than any other Western nation in the period from 1984 to 1988.

Efforts to reduce the deficit were only partly successful. The annual deficit was reduced from $38 billion per year to $28 billion; yet the Conservatives were still a long way from their goal of eliminating the deficit.

Laws were passed to encourage business. Taxes were reduced on corporations. FIRA, which had

Industry and employment increased during the first years of Mulroney's term as Prime Minister.

restricted American investment, was replaced by Investment Canada, which actively sought more American investment. Prime Minister Mulroney announced to an American audience, "Canada is open for business." The NEP was cancelled to encourage further American investment in the oil industry.

Canadian economic nationalists opposed these changes as examples of a Canadian sell-out to the United States. But, in the atmosphere of prosperity, many others saw only the increased number of jobs and new companies and were less concerned about increasing American investment.

Explain what you think are the three greatest differences between the ideas and policies of Pierre Trudeau and Brian Mulroney. With which leader do you agree? Explain why.

Meech Lake Accord

Prime Minister Mulroney had promised to reduce the conflict between the provincial premiers and the federal government. He had also promised to find a compromise which would return Quebec within the constitution.

In April 1987, he invited all of the premiers to attend a conference at the government's private retreat at Meech Lake, Quebec. To the amazement of most, an agreement was reached which has since been known as the Meech Lake Accord:

1. Quebec was to be described as a "distinct society" with special features distinct from the other provinces;
2. provinces would have the right to appoint Senators and Supreme Court judges from among their residents;
3. future changes in the structure of the federal government (size of the Senate or of Supreme Court; creating provinces out of territories) would have to have the support of all provinces thus giving each province a veto;
4. provinces could opt out of national social programs and receive federal funds for their own programs if they were in the "national interest".

The accord was to go into effect when approved by the federal government and by each provincial government.

The accord satisfied all of the demands of the Quebec government, and was rapidly approved in Quebec. The agreement was supported by the leaders of all three federal parties, and by early 1989 had been approved by all provinces except Manitoba and New Brunswick.

The Meech Lake Accord promised to bring Quebec back into Confederation and to reduce federal-provincial conflict, but was not accepted by all provinces. A new series of Canada-wide panels and discussions began in 1991. In the summer of 1992, several meetings of the provincial leaders, including Quebec and Native leaders, produced another constitutional formula, recognizing Quebec as a "distinct society" and Native Peoples' right to self-government, and proposing a revamped Senate and House of Commons.

Prime Minister Mulroney and Premier Robert Bourassa

Foreign Policy Changes

The Armed Forces

The Conservative government had promised to improve and increase the strength of the Canadian armed forces. New tanks, armoured vehicles, and guns were purchased. The air forces were equipped with the CF-18, the newest American fighter.

The Arctic

In 1986, the United States sent the icebreaker *Polar Sea* through the Arctic northern passage without informing the Canadian government. The U.S. claimed that the passage was an international waterway. Canadians claimed that this was a Canadian passage. In reality, Canada had done little to establish its control of the Arctic area.

In 1987, the government announced that it would consider the purchase of nuclear-powered submarines to patrol our shores, including the Arctic. They would be able to monitor and control the movement of any submarines, Soviet or U.S., and establish the Canadian claim to the Arctic. Most people supported the idea, but questioned the cost of at least $8 billion. Nevertheless, all agreed that something would have to be done to assert Canadian rights to the northern coastal waters.

The United Nations

Prime Minister Mulroney surprised most people by appointing Stephen Lewis, a former leader of the NDP in Ontario, as the Canadian ambassador to the United Nations in 1984. Lewis turned out to be one of his best appointments. Not since the days of Lester Pearson had there been such a strong Canadian presence in the United Nations Assembly. Lewis spoke out strongly, particularly on issues relating to the needs of countries in the Third World. By 1989, Canada was again recognized as a leading middle power at the UN. In 1988, in recognition of Canada's more-prominent role, Canada was appointed as a member of the Security Council for a period of two years.

Canadian forces on manoeuvres in the Arctic.

"Nearly every Canadian has threads to other places through ancestry and emigration or simply by travelling and working abroad and making friends. At one time, most of the strong threads stretched only to the United States and Europe. But over the last twenty years of immigration, many of the threads now reach beyond the Pacific to Asia and southward to the Caribbean and Latin America, and pull Canada into a more central place in the world."

New Democratic Party International Affairs Committee, April 1988

Summarize the main changes in foreign policy introduced by the Progressive Conservatives after 1984, using the following organizers: Arctic defence; Role in the United Nations; Role in the Commonwealth.

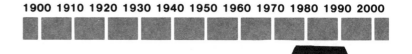

The Commonwealth

Canada is a leading member of the Commonwealth, a number of English-speaking nations from around the world. Most had been colonies within the former British Empire. After World War II, the British Empire had evolved into the Commonwealth.

During the 1980s, the Commonwealth faced serious problems. The need for aid to underdeveloped members continued. But the issue which caused the greatest problem was the question of racism in South Africa. British leadership and respect in the Commonwealth had decreased as a result of Britain's failure to strongly oppose the South African policy of *apartheid*.

Prime Minister Mulroney spoke out strongly in favour of all Commonwealth countries imposing economic sanctions (refusing to trade with South Africa). He tried to persuade Britain's Prime Minister Thatcher to support sanctions. Despite his failure in this, his strong attacks on South African policies made Mulroney one of the leaders in the Commonwealth by the late 1980s.

Apartheid

South Africa had imposed a policy of "apartheid" or apartness between blacks and whites. Blacks were not only kept apart but denied the basic rights of citizenship — the right to vote, to own property, and to travel with freedom around their country. This denial of basic human rights provoked opposition from other members of the Commonwealth. In 1961, South Africa was forced to withdraw from membership in the Commonwealth. The issue of racism, however, continued to be an explosive issue facing the people of South Africa and other Commonwealth members.

The Election of 1988

In the election at the end of their first term, Mulroney and the Conservatives campaigned on their record. Canadians showed their support by again returning the Conservatives with a reduced but clear majority.

Progressive Conservatives — 169
Liberal — 83
New Democratic Party — 43

For the first time since the days of Sir John A. Macdonald, Conservatives had won two consecutive elections. Their victory in Quebec indicated that French Canadians had shifted their support, after 100 years of favouring the Liberals.

Many Canadians were still concerned about the impact of free trade on Canada's future. Others wondered about the impact of the Meech Lake Accord. Yet the majority had put these concerns aside. They had faith in the future, and that future in the 1990s would be led by Brian Mulroney.

Free Trade with the United States

"Free trade with the United States is like sleeping with an elephant. It is terrific until the elephant twitches, and if it ever rolls over, you're a dead man..."

"The dangers (of free trade) are to the structure of the economic base of Canada, and over sovereignty as a nation. American priorities aren't necessarily Canadian priorities."

Brian Mulroney, 1983

"I have spoken today to the President of the United States to express Canada's interest in pursuing a new trade agreement between our two countries."

Prime Minister Brian Mulroney speaking to the House of Commons, 1985

What had changed Prime Minister Mulroney's mind between 1983 and 1985?

During the early 1980s, the American and Canadian economies had experienced a serious recession. By the mid-1980s, many spokespersons for the Canadian business community began to demand that Canada make a new trade agreement with the United States. They felt that this was the only way to guarantee access to a larger economic market. Further, it would prevent the United States from establishing tariffs preventing the entry of Canadian products and resources into the United States. By 1985, the Conservative Party had accepted free trade as the basis of its new economic policy.

After two years of negotiations, the trade agreement between Canada and the United States was signed. It still had to be passed by the American Congress and the Canadian Parliament. The main ideas of the agreement were:
— all remaining tariffs between the two countries would be eliminated by 1998;

— any restrictions on American investment in Canada would be greatly reduced;
— export of Canadian energy resources (oil, natural gas, and hydro-electricity) would be increased; in case of an energy shortage, resources would be shared between the two countries;
— the Auto Pact was not to be affected;
— the U.S. would respect the right of Canada to protect some of its cultural industries (radio, television, magazines, newspapers) from American investment;
— future trade disputes would be settled by an arbitration board consisting of Canadians and Americans.

The **free trade question** was the dominating issue in the election of 1988, with Canadians almost equally divided on the issue.

Supporters of free trade claimed that it would:
— reduce prices of some imported American goods for Canadians;
— establish access for Canadian goods in the larger American market;
— increase overall Canadian prosperity and economic opportunities, and therefore increase the number of jobs for Canadians;
— increase efficiency in Canadian industries by forcing Canadian companies to compete with American industries;
— improve opportunities for the export of surplus Canadian energy (oil, natural gas, hydro-electricity);
— establish Canada as a part of a large economic unit, in competition with other large trading blocks in Europe and Japan;
— guarantee to protect Canadian culture;
— protect Canadian industries and resources from future American protective legislation.

Summarize your argument either for or against free trade. Summarize the argument for the other side, from the viewpoint of a person in another region of Canada.

1900 1910 1920 1930 1940 1950 1960 1970 1980 1990 2000

Opponents of free trade argued that the free trade agreement would:
— not significantly reduce prices of imports from the United States because 80% of imports were currently not affected by tariffs;
— tie Canadians to the American market, restricting future trade agreements with Japan and Pacific Rim countries, and with the European Economic Community;
— cause many Canadian industries to close because of increasing imports of goods from the United States;
— cause Canada to lose control of its energy program;
— threaten some of our Canadian social programs, such as unemployment insurance, hospital and medical programs, federal subsidies to less-developed regions of Canada;
— tie Canada to the United States in such a way as to increase the Americanization of Canadian culture and the Canadian way of life.

The debate over free trade was the leading issue in the election of 1988. Conservatives were solidly in support of the new trade agreement; most Liberals and New Democrats were opposed. Canadians were almost equally divided on this crucial question affecting Canada's future. The only solution was to let the people decide.

In the election of November 1988, the Conservatives obtained another majority.

The Canadian people had made their decision, and the free trade agreement came into effect in January 1989.

In summer 1992, after months of discussion, a North American Free Trade Agreement was reached among negotiators for Canada, the United States, and Mexico, to be ratified by the governments of the three countries.

Duty-free imports — January 1, 1989
Free trade between Canada and the United States starts today as items, such as computers, skis, whiskey, and motorcycles, can begin moving across the border duty-free.

Today, skates, skis, furs, frozen fish, computers, and animal feed will no longer be subject to duties when shipped across the border.

Also today begins the reduction of tariffs by 20 percent on a wide range of goods, such as machinery, furniture, paint, paper products, and hardwood.

On each January 1, the tariffs will be cut another 20 percent until those goods are duty-free on January 1, 1993.

Such products as clothing and textiles, appliances, most processed foods, footwear, drugs, and cosmetics won't become duty-free until January 1, 1998.

People protest against free trade during a parade in Toronto.

New People for a New Society

Who should be allowed to come to Canada? At the turn of the century Clifford Sifton wanted "sturdy peasants in sheepskin coats." The need for farm workers decreased once the West was settled. In 1905 Frank Oliver, the new minister of immigration wanted only "the right class of British immigrant." Until World War II the government made it difficult for people like Asians, Jews, and eastern Europeans to immigrate. It did not think they would "fit in" to Canadian society. This policy was enforced when several hundred Sikhs from India aboard the *Komagata Maru* were turned away from Vancouver in 1914. In 1939, 907 Jews aboard the *St. Louis* were not allowed to enter Canada.

After World War II Canada accepted many refugees from Europe as a humanitarian gesture. However, the basic rules remained the same: white people from the British Commonwealth, the United States, and France were preferred, then other Europeans. Numbers of non-white immigrants were severely limited.

Changing Attitudes

By the 1970s many Canadians felt this immigration policy was a scandal. People should not be judged on the colour of their skin, where they came from, or the language they spoke at home. The choice of immigrants should be based on Canada's need for workers in certain fields and the ability of the immigrants to fill that need.

In 1976 the Canadian government announced a new immigration policy. Immigrants would be judged on a system which awarded points for education, job skills, and a knowledge of English or French. No weight would be given to race or country of origin.

The change was immediate. As living conditions improved, fewer people from Europe wanted to leave their homeland. On the other hand, many countries in Asia, Africa, and the Caribbean were poor. Opportunities for good jobs were few. It was hard to get an education. Many people in these countries decided they would have a better chance in Canada.

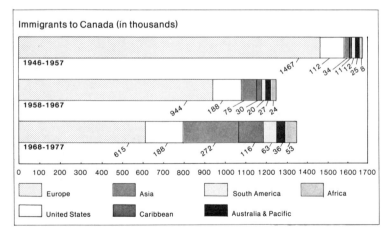

Immigrants to Canada (in thousands)

1946-1957   1467 112 34 11 12 25 8

1958-1967   944 188 75 30 20 27 24

1968-1977   615 188 272 116 63 36 53

0 100 200 300 400 500 600 700 800 900 1000 1100 1200 1300 1400 1500 1600 1700

- Europe
- Asia
- South America
- Africa
- United States
- Caribbean
- Australia & Pacific

Even before 1976 immigration policy was changing, and more immigrants from "non-white" countries were entering Canada.

Vietnamese refugees wait to talk to immigration officers on their arrival at a Canadian airport.

FOCUS

In the past, what groups of people found it difficult to enter Canada?
How did Canada's immigration policies change during the 1970s?
What does the expression "visible minority" mean?

1900 1910 1920 1930 1940 1950 1960 1970 1980 1990 2000

IMMIGRATION SELECTION CRITERIA*
A Summary of the Point System

Factors	Criteria	Max. Points
1. Education	One point for each year of primary and secondary education successfully completed.	12
2. Specific Vocational Preparation	To be measured by the amount of formal professional, vocational, apprenticeship, in-plant or on-the-job training necessary for average performance in the occupation under which the applicant is assessed in item 4.	15
3. Experience	Points awarded for experience in the occupation under which the applicant is assessed in item 4 or, in the case of an entrepreneur, for experience in the occupation that the entrepreneur is qualified for and is prepared to follow in Canada.	8
4. Occupational Demand	Points awarded on the basis of employment opportunities available in Canada in the occupation that the applicant is qualified for and is prepared to follow in Canada.	15
5. Arranged Employment or Designated Occupation	Ten points awarded if the person has arranged employment in Canada that offers reasonable prospects of continuity and meets local conditions of work and wages, *providing* that employment of that person would not interfere with the job opportunities of Canadian citizens or permanent residents, and the person will likely be able to meet all licensing and regulatory requirements; *or* the person is qualified for, and is prepared to work in, a designated occupation and meets all the conditions mentioned for arranged employment except that concerning Canadian citizens and permanent residents.	10
6. Location	Five points awarded to a person who intends to proceed to an area designated as one having a sustained and general need for people at various levels in the employment strata and the necessary services to accommodate population growth. Five points subtracted from a person who intends to proceed to an area designated as not having such a need or such services.	5
7. Age	Ten points awarded to a person 18 to 35 years old. For those over 35, one point shall be subtracted from the maximum of ten for every year over 35.	10
8. Knowledge of English and French	Ten points awarded to a person who reads, writes and speaks both English and French fluently. Five points awarded to a person who reads, writes and speaks English *or* French fluently. Fewer points awarded to persons with less language knowledge and ability in English or French.	10
9. Personal Suitability	Points awarded on the basis of an interview held to determine the suitability of the person and his/her dependants to become successfully established in Canada, based on the person's adaptability, motivation, initiative, resourcefulness and other similar qualities.	10
10. Relative	Where a person *would* be an assisted relative, *if* a relative in Canada had undertaken to assist him/her, and an immigration officer is satisfied that the relative in Canada is willing to help him/her become established but is not prepared, or is unable, to complete the necessary formal documentation to bring the person to Canada, the person shall be awarded five points.	5

*Members of the family class and retirees are not selected according to these criteria; Convention refugees are assessed against the factors listed in the first column but do not receive a point rating.

A Changing Population

As the new policy took effect, the face of Canada changed. White Canadians sat next to blacks and Asians on city buses. Children born in Canada found their new classmates were from Uganda, India, or Trinidad. The line-up in the supermarket included people from all over the world.

When immigrants arrived from Europe they looked the same as Canadians. As a result they were accepted because few even knew they were immigrants. The new immigrants were a "visible minority" — easily recognized as being different. Many Canadians found this interesting and exciting. Others found it frightening. People often fear what they do not understand. Their fear can turn to prejudice and hate.

Prejudice made life difficult for many immigrants. Some found themselves the target of racial attacks. They found they could not get good jobs, not only because of the problem of unemployment but also because employers demanded "Canadian experience." They found landlords would not rent to them even though in most cases discrimination in housing is illegal.

Fairer rules for immigration are only the beginning of the answer. A just society must ensure fair treatment for all once they have arrived in Canada.

Multiculturalism

During the 1970s one million people immigrated to Canada. They were eager to become a part of their new society. They also wanted to preserve the customs and traditions of their native country.

Assimilation or Integration?

Should immigrants forget their homeland and culture and become like other Canadians as soon as possible? Some people believe that immigrants should be *assimilated:* cut off their ties with their homeland; forget their original cultural identity; and become "Canadian" like everyone else. This is comparable to the American idea of the "melting pot" where all immigrants become part of one identical society.

Others suggest that immigrants should be gradually *integrated* into Canadian society. Immigrants should be encouraged to retain important aspects of their original culture, such as Ukrainian dancing, the Scottish kilt, or Islamic religion. It is thought that Canada would be a richer society if Canadians were free to retain their original culture,

while being integrated into a Canadian identity. This would be the Canadian "mosaic" — a multicultural society.

In 1971 Prime Minister Trudeau announced that his government supported the idea of the mosaic, or multiculturalism. They would encourage Canadians to take pride in their customs and traditions. Money was set aside for cultural programs.

Economic Impact of Immigration

Some people believed that immigrants take the jobs of Canadians. They wanted the government to cut down on immigration as long as there was any unemployment in Canada. Supporters of immigration suggested that if we followed this policy we would always have a restricted immigration policy, because we are likely to have unemployment in the near future. It was also pointed out that immigrants *create* employment. Every immigrant family purchases clothing, household appliances, furniture, utensils, and other necessities. After a short period, most

Dragon dance.   Shumka dancers.   Native peoples' dance   Sword dance.   Canoe race.

FOCUS Compare the American "melting pot" with the Canadian "mosaic." Prepare a chart to examine the case for and against an **ASSIMILATED** and an **INTEGRATED** society. Use the headings *Description, Case for,* and *Case against,* as organizers.

1900 1910 1920 1930 1940 1950 1960 1970 1980 1990 2000

immigrants require housing and a car. The need for these goods and services provides employment for thousands of Canadians.

It has also been pointed out that the birth rate in Canada, since the introduction of "the pill" in the 1960s, has declined to such a degree that the population of Canada will start *to decrease* by the year 2010. Some have suggested that Canadians should suggest increased immigration. The Canadian economy will not maintain our existing standard of living unless the population is maintained or increased.

Racism

A person's culture is more than songs, meals, and holidays. It is an everyday affair. It is what one wears, how late the kids can stay out at night, how long they stay in school, attitudes to work, ways of relaxing.

Different cultures have different attitudes to family life. In some cultures children are indulged. In some they are expected to obey their parents without question. Rules for girls may not be the same as rules for boys.

Some people ask questions if they don't understand something. Others think asking questions is pushy and rude. Some accept whatever treatment they are given. Others stand up for their rights. What seems a chance remark to one may be an unbearable insult to another.

Differences like these lead to misunderstanding, fear, and hate. Colour of skin, shape of eyes, religious practices, eating habits, and style of clothing can all be the focus of hatred. This type of prejudice is known as racism.

The problem of racism is most severe in the big cities. School boards, police forces, social workers, city governments have all tried to deal with the issue. Often in doing so they are accused of racism themselves. Like other Canadians they may not recognize how their words and actions may be seen as racist by others.

Canadians face a serious challenge. The multicultural mosaic is threatened when people cannot tolerate differences. The alternative is a forced melting pot in which everyone would lose a little.

At the market.   Clog dance.   Loyalist Days.   Caribana parade

Canada's Native Peoples

The native peoples were the first Canadians. Before European settlers came, they lived a life in tune with nature. This special relationship with the environment was highlighted in their religions. The spirit of the land was an important symbol. Conservation was the principle behind the way they hunted and fished.

European traders taught the native people to value the fur more than the animal that bore it. Then settlers moved in and took over the land. Sometimes a treaty was made between the native people and the new government. The native people were usually allowed small areas of "reserved" land and an annual pension that was little more than welfare. For this, they had given up the vast land they regarded as their heritage.

By the 1970s many native people felt the government treated them as permanent welfare cases. Their traditional way of life had vanished. Settlers had destroyed the natural forests and grazing lands where they had hunted. They had lost the customs and values they cherished. They owned only their restricted reserves. If they left the reserves to seek work, they found they did not possess the skills required in the modern cities. They were trapped in a lifestyle that robbed them of their self respect.

Canada's native people suffered from an unemployment rate of over 50%. Some were victims of alcoholism. They were twice as likely as other Canadians to commit suicide. Native people lived in the poorest parts of Canadian cities. On the reserves housing, sewage systems, schools, and recreation facilities were all far below standard.

> If I could just get the people from Treasury Board to come out and visit the reserves it would be easy to get more money. If they could just see the schools, the housing, the roads and the lack of running water.
> *Warren Allmand, minister of Indian Affairs, 1976*

A government "white paper" is a statement of proposed policy. In a formal ceremony, native Canadians present a "red paper" containing their views on native affairs in response to a government white paper.

The Search for Solutions

Native people faced a basic problem. They wanted an adequate standard of living like other Canadians. They also wanted to retain the old relationship with the land. There were vast expanses of land they claimed were theirs but the government said the land no longer belonged to them.

Instead of letting the government have its way, the native people took their case to court. Native lawyers argued that their ancestors had never meant to give away their lands. The government had merely acted as if they had. They also argued that the government had not lived up to its side of the terms of the treaties.

The first native land claim case to reach the courts was the Nishga claim to 10 000 km² near the Nass River in northern British Columbia. The Nishga fought the case all the way to the Supreme Court of Canada. The ruling went against the Nishga, but 3 out

FOCUS

Why did the native people's traditional way of life disappear?
What problems did they face *a)* in the city, *b)* on the reserve?
What arguments did they use to defend their land claims?
Name other steps they are taking to improve their status.

Art Gallery pages 26-27

of 7 judges disagreed with the verdict. Even though the native people lost the case, this was encouraging. The government had at least been forced to listen to them and reply to their arguments.

Later the same year the Supreme Court of the Northwest Territories ruled that the Northwest Territories Indian Brotherhood "might have a claim" to one million km² of land. Partly because of this ruling the Canadian government set up the Mackenzie Valley Pipeline Inquiry.

The James Bay hydro-electric project in northern Quebec was built on land native people had lived on for 5000 years. The Cree and Inuit were able to negotiate a treaty that should have given them adequate land, money, health services, and local self-government. However, they claim that already the Quebec government has not lived up to its part of the bargain. They are not being allowed the language rights specified by the treaty. In 1980 a number of Cree babies died because of inadequate health care.

By the end of the 1970s Canadians were listening to the concerns of native people. Native organizations had been stronger and more outspoken. They had established their right to negotiate for their traditional lands. They were dealing with the social problems of native people both on and off the reserves. They were regaining pride and a sense of purpose. Perhaps native people could play an active part in Canadian society without giving up their customs and values.

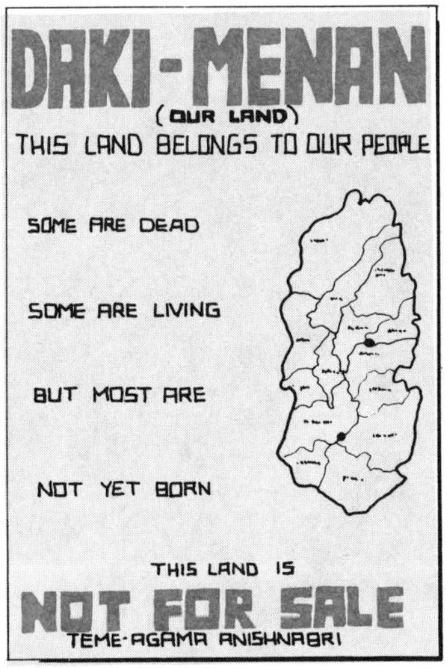
DAKI-MENAN
(OUR LAND)
THIS LAND BELONGS TO OUR PEOPLE
SOME ARE DEAD
SOME ARE LIVING
BUT MOST ARE
NOT YET BORN
THIS LAND IS
NOT FOR SALE
TEME-AGAMA ANISHNABAI

Chief Dan George

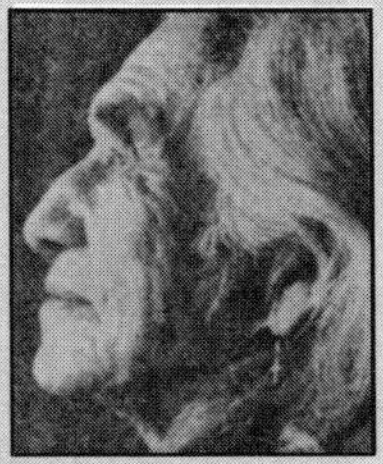

"Let no one forget this: we are a people with special rights guaranteed to us by promises and treaties. We do not beg for these rights, nor do we thank you because we paid for them. We paid with our culture, pride, and self-respect. We paid we paid and we paid until we became a beaten race, poverty-stricken and conquered."
from "Lament for Confederation"

1899 — born on a Coastal Salish reserve on Burrard Inlet, B.C. Attended a mission boarding school in North Vancouver.
1916 — started work as a logger.
1920 — became a longshoreman on Vancouver docks.
1947 — badly injured in dockyard accident. Became an entertainer. Soon known all over Burrard Inlet.
1951 — elected chief of his tribe. Lost election in 1963. Later made honorary chief of Shuswap and Squamish tribes.
1960 — cast as Antoine in CBC TV series *Cariboo Country.*
1965 — appeared in Walt Disney film *How to Break a Quarter Horse.*
1967 — as a leading spokesman for native peoples, delivered his "Lament for Confederation" at centennial celebrations in Vancouver. Explained how Indian people had been poorly treated and their interests ignored in 100 years of Confederation.
1970 — starred as Ol' Lodgeskins in *Little Big Man.* Nominated for an Oscar.
1972 — chosen as national chairman for Brotherhood Week. Continued work in film and TV while living on his reserve.
1981 — died in a Vancouver hospital

We want to carry on our own economic and community development so that Indian people can share in the things all Canadians want, and can do so within the framework of an Indian value system. That is what our struggle is all about.
George Manuel, president, National Indian Brotherhood, 1969

Northern Frontier, Northern Homeland

In Canada's North native people can still live close to the land and sea. They now hunt and fish with the aid of modern tools like guns, snowmobiles, and motorboats. Yet their attitudes to nature and conservation remain.

Beneath the Arctic Ocean lie vast resources of oil and gas. The energy crisis of the 1970s meant southern Canadians wanted access to these resources. When a large gas field was discovered in the Beaufort Sea, the easiest way to transport the gas seemed to be by pipeline. A pipeline was planned along the Mackenzie River Valley.

There were problems to overcome. The route stretched for 2000 km before it even reached the Alberta border. Most of the land it would pass through was *permafrost* — frozen all year round. This meant the pipeline would have to be built above ground.

Otherwise the heat from the pipeline would melt the permafrost and cause the line to sink.

Many Canadians in the South thought these engineering problems were all that had to be worried about. The gas was needed in southern Canada. The project would create many jobs. In the South, factories would produce steel pipe and equipment. People would move north to work on the actual construction. Native people could work on the pipeline. Northern businesses would have more customers and hire more workers. The pipeline seemed to be a good idea.

Others thought differently. They feared the pipeline would damage the northern environment. The government decided the project had to be studied before it was started. Justice Thomas Berger was appointed to conduct the Mackenzie Valley Pipeline Inquiry.

The changing northern environment. An oil rig on an artificial island in the Beaufort Sea. In the 1970s oil companies started to build entire islands like this one. The dredge ship *Beaver Mackenzie* at the right pumps a mixture of water and sand from the ocean floor and slowly a new island is formed.

Give 3 arguments in favour of a northern pipeline.
Give 3 arguments against a northern pipeline.
Do you think the pipeline should be built? Explain.
Should native people have their own government in the North?

 **Art Gallery pages 30-31**

The Inquiry

Berger listened to the pipeline experts in Yellowknife. He also took his inquiry to 35 native communities in the Mackenzie Valley and the Western Arctic. He wanted the Inuit and Dene (Den-nay) peoples of the area to be able to speak to the inquiry "in their own villages, in their own languages, in their own way."

He found nearly all the Inuit and Dene were against the pipeline. They were afraid drilling in the Arctic Ocean would disturb the fish and sea mammals and pollute the water. They said the pipeline would cut across the migration routes of the caribou. They did not want southern-style industry in the North. They wanted to hunt and fish in the old ways. The pipeline would destroy their way of life.

Berger's final report suggested that the pipeline be delayed 10 years. This would allow time to solve the native people's problems. He agreed  that the Inuit and Dene should have "special status" within Canada. They wanted a new political area in the North controlled by a government of native people. This would allow them to preserve their way of life.

The Canadian government agreed with only part of the report. They felt the pipeline was too important to wait 10 years. They did not accept the idea of "special status." They did agree that native claims had to be dealt with before the pipeline was started.

There are many more people in southern Canada than in the North. They need northern oil and gas. Native people in southern Canada have lost their old way of life. In the North, many aspects of the traditional culture still survive. Should the needs of the majority of Canadians come before the desire of the Inuit and Dene to preserve their way of life?

Pitseolak

"My name is Pitseolak, the Inuit word for the sea pigeon. When I see pitseolaks over the sea, I say, 'There go those lovely birds — that's me, flying!'"

About 1900 — born on Nottingham Island, Hudson Strait, N.W.T. Had a happy, healthy childhood near Cape Dorset, Baffin Island. Father taught her Inuit legends and beliefs in the spirit world. Learned skills expected of Inuit women: food preparation, treating animal skins, sewing clothes, repairing tents and kayaks.

Married childhood friend, Ashoona. They had 17 children, 5 are still living. Became well known for beautiful embroidery on caribou and seal skins brought to her by Ashoona.

Ashoona died on a family hunting trip. Life was hard for Pitseolak and the family.

1950s — James Houston, government administrator and himself an artist, encouraged Inuit to sell soapstone carvings and other crafts to make the money they needed in the new cash-based North American society. When a friend, Oshweetok, recognized possibility of printing Inuit drawings, Houston helped people of Cape Dorset develop their own techniques to make prints. Suggested to Pitseolak that she draw "the old ways." Her drawings and prints based on the legends learned from her father have sold well all over the world.

She has been drawing "the old ways and the monsters" ever since. "I'll keep on doing them. I'll make them as long as I am well. If I can, I'll make them even after I am dead."

Woman Power

The First Phase of Feminism

In the early 1900s, women had struggled to get rights equal to those of men. They had achieved the right to vote and to hold government positions. Increasing numbers had gone to university; a small minority of those became lawyers and doctors.

However, the battle for full equality had just begun. During World War Two, an increasing number of women entered the work force, or served as members of the women's divisions of the armed forces. After the war, the long-held attitude emerged again — a woman's place was once again in the home. When asked their occupation in the 1950s and 1960s, most women replied that they were "just" housewives. Although there were exceptions in the fields of teaching and nursing, most women who were in the workforce were usually in lower-paid positions, such as office workers or clerks, with few opportunities for promotion.

If women were accepted as equals, why did they not succeed at the same rate as men? The answer was that they were *not* accepted as equals with men in most roles. Women were not encouraged to seek equality. Society, including most women themselves, seemed to accept their inferior status.

The Demand for Women's Liberation

The period from the mid-1960s to the 1970s was a period of great social unrest and upheaval throughout North America. Starting with the civil rights movement in the United States, the movement quickly spread to other groups demanding fewer controls and greater freedom. Native Peoples, university students, and women began demanding changes in their favour.

There had always been women demanding improvements for women, but they had been regarded as voices crying in the wilderness. By the 1960s, these isolated voices had become a loud chorus. The period from the 1960s on has been described as the second wave of feminism.

If one person could be described as the person who ignited this movement, it would be Betty Friedan. In her book *The Feminine Mystique,* she captured the mood of restlessness, discontent, and frustration of women all over North America. She was joined by many Canadian women and organizations led by such women as Laura Sabia and Doris Anderson. As a result of demands by Canadian women, in 1967 the federal government created the Royal Commission on the Status of Women to examine the condition of women in Canadian society and to make recommendations for improvements. The committee published its report in 1970.

Report of the Royal Commission on the Status of Women (1970)

The report included 167 recommendations, dealing with the rights of women in the workforce, in education, legal rights, and with the rights of women to government and administrative positions. Many of the recommendations providing for greater equality of opportunity for women in the workforce were implemented. Others dealing with the rights of women to maternity leave, to publicly supported daycare, and to "equal pay for work of equal value" became the issues of the 1980s and 1990s.

The significance of the Report was that it raised women's issues to such prominence that they could no longer be ignored. In 1973, the federal government established an Advisory Council on the Status of Women to report to the Minister of Labour. In recent years, a cabinet minister has had the specific responsibility of looking after women's issues. In the 1980s, women lobbied successfully to have equal rights for women included within the Charter of Rights. Political leaders were then obliged to discuss or debate women's issues in federal election campaigns. The number of women in the federal parliament has slowly but constantly increased.

What is to be done?

From a woman's viewpoint, the struggle is still not over. In the 1980s, the women's movement sought legislation to guarantee
- equal pay for equal work;
- publicly supported daycare;
- fully paid maternity leave for a minimum period;
- a reduction in the wage gap between women and men;
- abortion on demand

REAL Women

Not all women have supported the women's movement. REAL (Realistic, Equal, Active for Life) Women emerged as a rival group who opposed many of the ideas of the women's movement. They sought to improve the position of women, while defending the traditional role of women within the household. As a result, they were opposed to abortion on demand and to publicly supported daycare, both of which they felt would disrupt traditional family life.

YOUR TASK

1. Do further research on one of the issues facing women today. Prepare an oral or written report on the issue.
2. Do further research on a women's organization and on Real Women. Compare their views on at least two issues. Which organization do you think provides the best solution to the issues facing women today? Prepare a written or oral report to compare their views.
3. Class debate. Prepare an argument for one side of the following debate: "Resolved that women have achieved equality with men in Canada today."

Is There a Canadian Culture?

What is culture? In its broadest sense it is an entire way of life. Many use the word to mean the books, magazines, and papers people read, the music they listen to, the films, TV, and live theatre they watch.

During most of the twentieth century popular "culture" in Canada came largely from outside the country. People enjoyed American movies. They read books published in the U.S., Britain, and Europe. When television started in the fifties nearly all the popular shows were American. If Canadian artists were known in Canada, it was usually because they had become famous in another country.

Many Canadians were concerned about this. They argued that the problem was largely a matter of *access*. Canadian talent could not become known if it wasn't given a chance to perform. Movie houses should show some Canadian films. Rock concerts should feature some Canadian groups. Theatres should use Canadian actors in Canadian plays. Schools should teach children with Canadian textbooks, stories, and poems. Art galleries should display Canadian paintings and sculptures. When people saw how good Canadian culture was, they would become interested in it.

Government Support of Canadian Culture

Some people felt that many aspects of Canadian culture could not survive in competition with foreign, especially American, cultural activities. American radio and movies were too well-established, too well-funded, for competition from smaller Canadian companies. As a result, in Canada, various levels of government have either created cultural organizations or have assisted Canadian talent. This is in contrast with the United States, where radio, movie, and television companies are all privately owned. With the large American audiences, they can operate at a

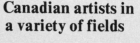
Canadian artists in a variety of fields

Alice Munro, novelist.

The rock group, The Spoons

Norval Morrisseau, painter.

The Royal Winnipeg Ballet, Canada's oldest ballet company.

Margaret Atwood, writer

FOCUS

Name 5 organizations that support and develop Canadian culture.

For discussion — Is it necessary to have government support to maintain a distinctive Canadian culture?

Art Gallery page 33

profit. In the smaller Canadian market, this could not always be possible.

1 — In the 1930s, the government created the Canadian Broadcasting Corporation (CBC) to provide a radio network for all areas across Canada. (This was expanded to include television broadcasting in the 1950s.)

2 — In 1939, the National Film Board was established to provide films about Canada, produced by Canadians. The NFB has produced excellent documentaries, features, and cartoons. Many have won Oscars and other international awards.

3 — In 1951, the Canada Council was created. This was to give money to artists, writers, actors, and other Canadian creative people to enable them to present their works to all Canadians. As the Centennial Year approached, in 1967, interest in Canadian culture

Stratford, Ont., probably Canada's best-known theatre.

blossomed, and interest in Canadian artists continued to grow in the 1970s and 1980s.

4 — In 1968, the Canadian Radio and Television Commission (CRTC) took over the job of granting licenses to radio and television stations. In 1970, the CRTC announced that in order to keep their licences, radio and television stations would have to broadcast a certain percentage of Canadian material. This would give Canadian artists an opportunity to perform and become known.

In order to supply this "Canadian content", recording companies started looking for Canadian talent. Singers like Anne Murray and Gordon Lightfoot and groups like Rush, Trooper, and Bachmann Turner Overdrive were signed up. Once Canadians heard their music on the radio, they wanted to see them in person. Booking concert tours became easier for Canadian musicians. On television, Canadian actors were hired to perform in series like "The Beachcombers" and "King of Kensington".

5 — Telefilm Canada was established to encourage Canadians to make feature-length films. With Telefilm Canada's help, such successful films as *The Apprenticeship of Duddy Kravitz* and *Why Shoot the Teacher?* were made. On the other hand, Telefilm Canada also gave money to films like *Meatballs*, which some people thought hardly seemed representative of a distinctive Canadian culture. Some people protested that many of the films were not "Canadian" at all. They had American stories and American stars. They were shot in Canada only to get Canadian financing.

During the 1970s and 1980s, Canadians continued to enjoy books, films, and movies from other parts of the world. They were also showing increased interest in the work of Canadian artists and performers.

Fitness and Sport

Sports are fun. Canadians at all times in history would agree with that statement. Yet they might not agree on what it meant. In 1900 Canadians assumed it meant sports were fun to play. By 1970 most Canadians thought it meant sports were fun to watch. During the seventies professional sports became big business. Several times a week Canadians could buy tickets or turn on their TV sets to watch "the big game."

Canadian Football League

The Canadian Football League founded over 100 years ago, is one of the oldest professional sports leagues in Canada. Since the 1930s it has featured an intense rivalry between teams from eastern and western Canada. This rivalry climaxes in the Grey Cup game every November. In 1948, the Calgary fans brought examples of western hospitality and exhuberance to the Grey Cup game in Toronto. Ever since, the Grey Cup game has been the occasion of a national festival bringing West and East together in friendly rivalry.

However, since the 1980s, the CFL has been in financial trouble in several cities. The games used to draw capacity crowds in cities like Montreal, Toronto, Edmonton, and Vancouver. Lately, the teams began to have difficulty in attracting enough supporters to maintain the teams' payroll. In 1987, the Montreal team went bankrupt. Also, there were serious financial difficulties in Ottawa, Hamilton and other cities.

Many felt that the publicity, "hype", and wide television exposure of the National Football League in the U.S. had reduced the CFL to a second-rate status. Some suggested that this was a foretaste of what would result from free trade with the United States. In effect, some Canadian activities would be replaced by the more expensive and better-promoted American models.

Hockey

Many Canadians regard hockey as their national sport. Yet for years Canada had only two professional teams — the Montreal Canadiens and the Toronto Maple Leafs — in the National Hockey League. In the seventies investors decided that more money could be made out of the interest in hockey. They began to start new teams like the Vancouver Canucks — and a new league.

In 1972 the World Hockey Association was formed. It had twelve teams, four of them in Canada. The two leagues competed for fans and players. Hockey salaries soared as star players were lured from one league to the other.

The WHA survived until 1978 on a shaky footing. Then it became clear that it was not making enough money to continue as a league. A deal led to some WHA teams joining the NHL. They included the Edmonton Oilers, the Winnipeg Jets, and the Quebec Nordiques. In 1980 the Calgary Flames also joined. The NHL, which had six teams in 1967, now had twenty-one, seven of them in Canada.

Canadians dominated international hockey from the 1920s to the 1950s. Then, teams from the Soviet Union began to defeat the best Canadian amateur teams. Canadians consoled themselves with the theory that their professional teams were still superior.

In 1972 the first great test of the best Canadian and best Soviet players took place. Team Canada was expected to win easily. In fact, only a dramatic last-minute goal by Paul Henderson in the final game in Moscow let Canada squeak through to victory.

Since the 1970s, there have been many hockey games between the best Canadian professional teams and the best European and Soviet teams. Since the first international tournament in 1972, the teams have learned a great deal from each other. Canadians have learned from the European emphasis on skating, passing, and playmaking. European and Soviet teams have learned to play a more robust, physical style of hockey. The results usually produce the most exciting hockey games played each year.

Paul Henderson's winning goal

Examine what you think are the three most important sporting events in your area or province this year. Use the following organizers to examine your selection: fitness of participants; fitness of spectators; commercial involvement; other factors.

Amateur Sport and Participaction

For years Canada had paid little attention to amateur sport. This began to change during the 1970s. In 1976 the summer Olympic Games were held in Montreal. Canadians naturally wanted to put on a good showing. Government and private industry gave grants to help amateur athletes with their training.

Two years later the Commonwealth Games were held in Edmonton. Graham Smith won six gold medals for Canada in swimming. Diane Jones Konihowski amazed spectators with her skill in the pentathlon.

As interest in amateur sports events increased, Canadians became more aware that in general they were in poor physical shape. In 1971, Participaction was established as a private company to encourage Canadians to lead healthier and more active lives. participaction has been very successful in encouraging Canadians to be more fit by walking, swimming, jogging, cycling, skiing, and other forms of sport and activity.

5,491,989 THAT'S HOW MANY CANADIANS ARE CROSS-COUNTRY SKIERS

Way to go, Canada!

PARTICIPACTION

By the 1980s many Canadians were once more thinking of sports as fun to do as well as fun to watch.

Baseball

Big-league baseball came to Canada when the Montreal Expos joined the National League in 1967. The Toronto Blue Jays entered the American League in 1976 and almost made it to the World Series in 1985.

Diane Jones Konihowski

1951 — born in Saskatoon. As child, kept busy with gymnastics, ballet, figure skating, drama.

1963 — started training with Bob Adams who had competed in decathlon in 1952 Helsinki Olympics.

1969 — entered University of Saskatchewan. In sports concentrated on pentathlon (hurdles, shot put, high jump, long jump, 800-metre run).

1970 — lost confidence in herself and performed poorly. Quit track and ballooned up to 82 kg.

1971 — moved back home to "Mom's cooking" and a correct diet. Started a ten-year training program aimed at winning an Olympic gold medal in the penthathlon.

1975 — won pentathlon at Pan-American games in Mexico.

1976 — came sixth, ahead of all other Canadians, in pentathlon at Montreal Olympics.

1977 — married John Konihowski, a fellow track star and member of the Edmonton Eskimos football team.

1978 — won pentathlon before her home fans at Commonwealth Games in Edmonton.

1979 — voted Canadian Woman of the Year. Trained for Moscow Olympics.

1980 — forced to miss her chance for an Olympic gold medal when Canada joined boycott of Moscow Olympics because of Soviet invasion of Afghanistan.

Questions and Activities

Test Yourself

Match the persons or groups in column A with the sport or field of entertainment in column B.

A	B
1. Pitseolak	a) international sport (e.g. hockey)
2. Anne Murray	b) creative writing
3. Edmonton Oilers	c) soccer
4. Dan George	d) baseball
5. Rush	e) art
6. Montreal Expos	f) WHA and NHL hockey
7. Alice Munro	g) singing
8. Team Canada	h) rock music
9. Vancouver Whitecaps	i) acting

Ideas for Discussion

1. Compare the ideas and policies of Pierre Trudeau and Brian Mulroney. Use at least five of the following headings as organizers for your comparison:
   relations with provincial leaders; energy policy; attitude to the national debt; attitude about powers of the federal and provincial governments; attitude to French-Canadian, English-Canadian relations; attitude towards the Meech Lake Accord; attitude towards the United States; belief in the role of government in the economy.

2. Prepare one side of the argument for a class debate: Resolved that the free trade agreement will strengthen Canada's economy and cultural identity.
3. "There is no Canadian identity." Brainstorm arguments for and against this idea.
4. Petro-Canada, established in 1975, is a "crown corporation," meaning it is owned by all Canadians.
   a) Do you think it is a good idea for Canadians to "own" an oil company?
   b) If you saw two service stations offering gas at the same price and one of them was a Petro-Canada station, would you take your car there or to the other station?
5. Name jobs that before the 1970s might have been considered "for men" or "for women" in the following areas:
   a) offices   d) hospitals
   b) factories   e) schools
   c) farms   f) homes
6. Are boys and girls treated equally in your school? Provide specific examples to support your idea.
   Write a letter to the school board outlining any changes you feel should be made in your school. Be sure to send a copy of the letter to your principal.

Do Some Research

1. Analyse a recent strike in your community.
   a) What was the position of the workers?
   b) What was the position of the management?
   c) What was the final settlement? Were workers and management both satisfied?
   d) How did the strike affect your community?
   e) What are your personal reactions to this strike?
2. Do some research about one of your favourite Canadian sports or entertainment personalities. Write a biocard. Pass the cards around the class and then assemble them in a class folder.
3. Do you think the "point system" of selecting immigrants is really fair? How would you change it or improve it?
4. There is prejudice in Canada not only against immigrants from other countries but also against other groups that people perceive as "different." Find out more about one such group. What can you do to help them become fully accepted as part of Canadian society?

Be Creative

1. Write a letter to a local newspaper outlining your ideas on an aspect of one of the following:
   a) sexual equality   c) Canadian culture
   b) native rights   d) immigration policy
2. Organize a radio or television program to re-enact a famous sporting event of the 1960s or 1970s. Present your program to the rest of the class.
3. Present a visual or sound collage on one of Canada's most famous musicians, singers, artists, actors, dancers, or writers.
4. Organize a multicultural "caravan" or pageant in your class or school.
5. Design a Participaction exercise program your family might enjoy.

You Are There

You and the other members of your class work for Alpha Corporation. Your jobs involve assembling high technology radio and radar equipment. The work force is about 75% female and 25% male. Four weeks ago, you and the other members of your union voted to go on strike. You have been walking the picket lines ever since. The union's strike fund has given you some money, but not nearly enough to cover your living expenses.

Now your union negotiators and the company have agreed on issues affecting wages, fringe benefits, and safety. However, issues of special importance to the women working in the plant have been rejected by the company.

Union leaders have called a meeting today to decide whether to accept the company's offer or to continue the strike. As you enter the hall in a nearby community centre, you are handed a sheet summarizing the state of negotiations. You read the list of accepted and rejected demands, and make up your mind on how you will vote. When the meeting is called to order, you should be prepared to speak up for your point of view.

Would your position be any different if you were male or female? Why or why not?

Electronic Workers' Union Local 198

Report of the Strike Committee

Fellow workers, as you know, our negotiating team has been meeting with Alpha Corporation representatives. Last night we began to feel we were getting somewhere. The company has finally agreed to some of our demands, but not all. However, we felt we should put the offer to a vote, even though it is not entirely satisfactory.

UNION DEMANDS	COMPANY POSITION
1. Wage increases as requested over a two-year contract period.	Accepted.
2. Better fringe benefits including a dental plan.	Accepted.
3. Improved pensions.	Accepted.
4. New, tougher safety regulations.	Accepted.
5. Six months' paid maternity leave.	Rejected.
6. Day-care facilities in the plant.	Rejected.
7. Improvement of washroom facilities. (As we all know, the plant was built for an all-male work force.)	Rejected.
8. Equal pay for work of equal value.	The company says it has the right to decide the pay levels of jobs.
9. More equal opportunities for promotion.	The company claims opportunities are already equal and that it does not discriminate against women.

Comparison — Then and Now

"The further backward you can look, the further forward you can see."

— Winston Churchill

"Those who ignore their history, are doomed to repeat it."

— George Santayana

Does history repeat itself?
If you know what happened previously, does that mean that you know what will happen in the future?

Most historians believe that history does *not* repeat itself. The complex of events and people are so varied and different that they can never be exactly duplicated.

Then, you are probably asking, "Why *do* we study history?"

The events of your life usually do not repeat themselves exactly. However, we would all agree that our memory of previous experiences helps us to understand present conditions and make more intelligent decisions affecting our future lives.

Similarly, an awareness of previous historical events may help us to understand related events; it will help us to understand and to make more informed and intelligent decisions about current issues.

Conditions and events in history at different times are often similar but are *never* identical. Therefore, in studying history, it is sometimes useful to compare past events with contemporary or recent events. You will usually find both *similarities* and *differences*.

Having knowledge about the Stock Market Crash of 1929 would help in understanding the

Almost eighty years later, people are still discussing the pros and cons of free trade.

Stock Market Crash of 1987. There were similarities, but also significant differences. Knowledge of the earlier crash helped some economists to predict that there would likely be another crash, but did not help in determining when, to what degree, and with which consequences.

YOUR TASK

Compare two events, one historical and the other more recent. You should select your own *focus* questions to help to organize your comparison. Point out both *similarities* and *differences*.

We are a trading nation. Since the beginning of our history, since the time of the voyageurs we have been trading people. Our survival depends on our ability to trade . . . .

I am convinced that this agreement strongly benefits both nations and will provide tangible benefits for all regions of Canada . . . It provides increased opportunity for trade, for investment and for growth. It provides better prices for consumers . . . We have negotiated this agreement on terms that uphold the national interest and strengthen the unique fabric of Canadian society.

Prime Minister Brian Mulroney, 1988

The F.T.A. (free trade agreement) is far superior to any other alternative that is available in terms of Canada's trading relations with the United States. Furthermore, it could provide an encouraging example and precedent for the world and thus help break the logjam that has been holding up a GATT breakthrough and thereby threatening a worldwide trade war. Finally, the FTA provides Canada with a hedge against such a disaster, since it assures Canada of much-improved access to its most important market.

John Crispo, economist and professor

Select *one* of the following topics:

HISTORIC EVENT	MORE RECENT PERIOD
Problems faced by immigrants, 1890-1914	Problems faced by immigrants today
Reciprocity issue of 1911	Free Trade issue of 1980s
Conscription crisis, in World War I	Conscription crisis, in World War II
Unemployment conditions in 1930s	Unemployment conditions today
Social conditions in the 1950s (or 1960s)	Social conditions today
Problems facing women in 1900s (or period of your choice)	Problems facing women today
A topic of your choice	Conditions of today

Method

1. Select *focus* questions to research your topic.
2. *Organize* a chart to show similarities and differences.
3. *Research* further information to clarify similarities and differences.
4. *Record* your information in chart form.
5. *Assess* your comparison to see if there are more differences than similarities or vice versa.
   Draw your own conclusion and present supporting information.
6. *Communicate*
   Prepare your chart in a final copy form. You should be prepared to present your comparison to other members of the class in an oral report.

Chapter Seven

Canada and the World
ADVANCE ORGANIZER

1

Out of the ashes of World War II rose the United Nations. The UN was created to prevent future wars and to promote world co-operation. Most countries, including Canada, are members of the United Nations. Canada has solidly supported the UN with money, people and materials. Canadian soldiers have served in several UN peace-keeping operations.

2

Since the introduction of atomic warfare in World War II, an all-out war can now mean the destruction of our entire world. For this reason there has come about a new form of war, called the Cold War. The Cold War is a war of nerves. The major powers threaten each other with displays of military strength rather than outright warfare. Canada lies between the two main rivals — the United States and the Soviet Union.

To help keep peace and to protect Canadian interests, Canada has joined two major alliances. These are NATO and NORAD. Canada supports NATO to protect Europe against aggression by the Soviet Union or its allies. Canada and the U.S. form NORAD, whose goal is to protect North America from enemy attack. Membership in these alliances could at some time involve Canada in a major war.

3

Not all of Canada's foreign ties are of a military nature. Canada is a member of two non-military organizations — the Commonwealth and la Francophonie. The Commonwealth is a free association of peoples once ruled by the British Empire. La Francophonie is a free association of French-speaking nations of the world. Both of these bodies provide Canada with friendships all over the globe.

4

Canada is concerned about a number of trouble spots in the world. Of increasing importance are the Third World countries. These are the poor, often starving nations of Africa, Asia, and South America. Their people account for well over half of the world's population. Canada has given money and supplies, and has sent people as advisers to help improve conditions within these countries.

At the opposite end of the economic scale are the Arab countries of the Middle East. These countries have vast quantities of oil and therefore hold power over other countries. Canada needs oil from the Middle East, and values the Middle East as a trading partner. To help ease tensions, Canadian soldiers have served as peace-keepers for the United Nations in the Middle East as well as other parts of the world.

Word List

acid rain	cultural nationalist	Mixed Economy	Third World
boycott	Francophonie	multinational	United Nations
Cold War	ideology	NATO	veto
Commonwealth	Market-Economy	satellite	Warsaw Pact

5

Although Canada and the United States share the same continent, it is surprising how little the people of each country know each other. Stereotypes have been created by the movies, television, and other media. Although many of the stereotypes are old ones, for the most part they are still with us. A clear, unbiased image of each other would make for easier social and economic relations. With the increasing tensions in the world today, such mutual understanding would greatly benefit both countries.

6

At the turn of the century Canada considered its ties to the British Empire the most important. Between the wars Canada began to stand independently in foreign affairs but seldom looked beyond its borders. Since World War II Canada has taken full part in both continental and world affairs. Now the most important aspect of Canadian foreign policy is our relationship with the Americans. The United States is our most important trading partner and military ally. Canada and the U.S. share many political, cultural, and economic interests. However, they sometimes disagree over the handling of different problems. In the end, each country tries to protect its own interests. Americans have invested in Canada and promoted Canadian economic growth. At the same time Canadians are anxious to maintain control of their own companies. Still, each country is likely to become more dependent on the other in years to come. It is important that Canada and the U.S. keep their alliance an open and friendly one.

The United Nations

As World War II entered its final days in Europe, representatives of 50 nations met in San Francisco. Their dream was to build an organization to maintain peace and promote friendly relations among all countries of the world. They called this organization the United Nations.

After World War I a similar organization, the League of Nations, had been formed. The League of Nations had not been able to control the actions of nations like Japan, Italy and Germany because other member nations had refused to act against them. The delegates at San Francisco were determined to learn from the mistakes of the League of Nations.

The United Nations was to be much stronger than the old League. It would help solve all important problems facing the world — political, economic, social and cultural. In short, the United Nations was to be a centre of international co-operation.

Six Languages

The United Nations is a fascinating but gigantic and confusing organization. An army of interpreters is required to translate debates. Delegates may speak in any of six official languages — Arabic, Chinese, English, French, Russian and Spanish. About 150 countries are members of the UN. The headquarters are on the banks of the Hudson River in New York City, but the UN has offices in many countries all over the world.

When the United Nations building was opened, Canada's gift was the nickel-bronze doors that lead to the General Assembly. The panels of the doors represent four themes — peace, justice, truth and brotherhood. Surely these themes are central to the work of the United Nations.

It took the Nations of the world many meetings to decide how the United Nations should be organized. Its structure is the result of compromise.

The General Assembly is the central body of the UN. All other agencies report to it. Each member nation is represented here. Each has one vote. The General Assembly meets once a year to debate important issues.

The Security Council is responsible for maintaining peace and security. Britain, China, France, the Soviet Union, and the United States — the world's big powers — are permanent members. The General Assembly elects 10 non-permanent members for two-year terms. The 5 permanent members each have a *veto,* or the right to forbid action by the council. Many people think this veto power is a serious weakness in times of crisis.

The Secretariat is the permanent staff of the United Nations. It is headed by the Secretary General. The Secretary General is responsible for the day-to-day running of the UN. Another duty is to bring matters that threaten international peace to the attention of the UN. The job requires great diplomatic skill.

Agencies of the UN include many international councils and organizations to deal with specific international concerns. Here is a list of some of these agencies:
ILO (International Labour Organization)
IMF (International Monetary Fund) and World Bank
FAO (Food and Agriculture Organization)
UNESCO (United Nations Educational, Scientific, and Cultural Organization)
UNICEF (United Nations Children's Fund)
WHO (World Health Organization)

FOCUS

What is the main purpose of the UN?
Note 5 ways in which the UN has made the world a better place.
Collect newspaper articles to examine *one issue* in which the
United Nations is involved today.

Girls in Mersa,
Ethiopia, collect
water for their
families from a
UNICEF sponsored
water system.

1981-1990

The UN's Work

The United Nations Organization has tried to live up
to its basic principle and goals. Though it has not
always succeeded, it has had a number of successes.

1 — *Collective Security*

In June 1950, the North Korean army (encouraged by
the U.S.S.R.) invaded South Korea (backed by the
U.S.). The United Nations declared this invasion an
act of aggression and sought support from other UN
members to repel the invasion. The largest military
contribution came from the U.S. However, forces
from over 30 countries, including Canada, fought the
war to stop the North Korean invasion. (Over 20 000
Canadian soldiers fought in Korea, and 312 were
killed in action.) This was the first and only "police
action" fought by UN forces to resist an act of
aggression.

2 — *Peace-keeping*

Lester Pearson was the first Canadian to receive the
Nobel Peace prize. In 1956, he suggested that a United
Nations peace force be created to keep the peace after
the Arab-Israeli War. Canadian forces were a part of
the first UN army, the "blue berets", in the Gaza and
Sinai area. Since then, Canadian forces have been
leading members of UN peace-keeping forces. They
have served in Cyprus, Kashmir, the Congo, and
more recently in the Iran-Iraq area.

3 — *International Aid*

The UN provides funds for developing nations for
agricultural and industrial development, for technical
assistance, and for medical and educational
assistance. However, it cannot solve all of the world's
problems. It is limited by the amount of money that it
has available, money donated by the member nations.
Many nations facing their own economic problems
have reduced their contributions to the UN.

4 — *A Forum for Meetings and Discussions*

The UN provides a neutral meeting ground for
countries around the world to meet to discuss their
problems. Frequently, the most effective work is done
in informal meetings, rather than in the formal public
meetings where members are often more inflexible.
The UN provides the only meeting place for some
rival hostile powers to attempt to solve their
disagreements.

The UN has been criticized for its failure to
prevent the outbreak of wars and the inability to
create an atmosphere of peace in the world. However,
until the intense hostilities which lead to war have
been reduced, the UN can only be a forum to reduce
the effects of those conflicts. In the late 1980s, the
nations of the world seemed to be tiring of the
constant threat of war. In this atmosphere, there
seemed to be renewed hope that the UN would again
play a significant role in preserving world peace.

The Cold War

Everything of importance that happens in the world is of interest to Canada — often of direct and immediate interest. For us there is no escape in isolation or indifference. Recent events have brought home to all of us the increasing threat to our democracy of the rising tide of communism.

Louis St. Laurent, 1948

What is a "Cold War"? It is not guns, bombs, tanks, and soldiers. It is a war of words, threats, spies, secrets, and fear. It is an arms race, in which each side strives to have more and better weapons than the other. The big powers now possess enough nuclear weapons to kill everyone in the world several times over. The world spends more on arms than it does on food, housing, or medicine.

When World War II came to an end, the Soviet Union met her western allies along a line through central Europe. That line was to become an "Iron Curtain" dividing the world into two rival camps. The Soviets did not withdraw from the lands they had occupied.

Soviet armed forces remained in Romania, Hungary, Bulgaria, Czechoslovakia, Poland, and East Germany. Under Soviet influence, rigged elections were held, in which only Soviet-sponsored candidates could run for office. All of these countries became Soviet dependencies (or satellites) within the Communist eastern Europe block. Western governments protested but, unless they were prepared to go to war, they could do nothing.

In the words of Winston Churchill, "From Danzig on the Baltic, to Trieste on the Adriatic, an Iron Curtain has descended on Europe." The Cold War had begun.

Fear and Suspicion

The Cold War overshadowed the peace and prosperity

The Hooded Spy

In September 1945 Igor Gouzenko left the Soviet Embassy in Ottawa with 109 top secret documents hidden under his shirt. They revealed the existence of a spy ring that had passed vital atomic secrets to the Soviet Union.

Canadian authorities believed Gouzenko had made the whole thing up until he was nearly kidnapped by Soviet agents. Then the RCMP put Gouzenko under their protection and began to hunt the spies down.

Thirteen spies were on the staff of the Soviet Embassy, but others were Canadian military officers, scientists, and one member of parliament.

The Gouzenko affair marked the beginning of the Cold War — a hostile and suspicious relationship between the western world and the U.S.S.R. Gouzenko died in 1982.

of the fifties. The climate of fear in the West was intensified when the Soviet Union exploded its first hydrogen bomb in 1953 just 7 months after the United States. It reached a peak in 1957 when the Soviets launched a space satellite, Sputnik, long before the American space program was ready to do so. Americans began to build nuclear fall-out shelters. Some expected nuclear war was very near.

In the decades that followed, the world learned to live with the Cold War. At times the Soviet Union and the United States seemed to come closer together. They have signed treaties limiting the size and type of weapons they will develop. At others it seemed a single spark might turn the Cold War into a "hot war." Certainly there have been numerous "brush-fire wars" over local issues in many parts of the world. The two super powers have often tried to increase their influence by supplying "military assistance" to one side or the other in local wars.

After examining the map on this page, explain why Canada has been deeply involved in the Cold War.
Do current events indicate the Cold War is getting "colder" or "thawing"?

1900 1910 1920 1930 1940 1950 1960 1970 1980 1990 2000

Canada and the Cold War

Canada lies directly between two giant war machines, the United States and the Soviet Union. Therefore, Canada has a special stake in maintaining world peace.

Canada is firmly on the side of the United States. She is a member of the American-led NATO alliance. She is a partner in NORAD, the North American defence system. At the same time Canada has tried to serve as a peace-maker. She has maintained friendly relations with communist countries like the Soviet Union, China, and Cuba at times when the United States would not do so. This has been useful in times of crisis, because both sides have been ready to respect Canadian diplomats.

Canadian troops were part of the United Nations forces that were involved in the Korean conflict, 1951-53.

The Cold War Wanes

The Cold War between the U.S. and the U.S.S.R. became much hotter during the presidency of President Reagan in the 1980s. The fundamental mistrust of the two nations was added to by the use of Soviet troops in Afghanistan, and the involvement of both the Soviet Union and the U.S. in supporting rival forces in Nicaragua. Any possibility of understanding was further destroyed as both sides engaged in an expensive arms race. The stakes were raised even higher as the United States pursued its "Starwars" technology.

By the late 1980s a new atmosphere emerged. The Soviet Union under Premier Gorbachev showed a desire for a peaceful world. President Reagan and Premier Gorbachev made many agreements for arms reduction, and the Cold War seemed to recede. The Soviet Union began to loosen its hold on Warsaw Pact countries and withdrew its armies from most of those countries. By 1991, the Soviet Union itself was dissolved into separate nations, effectively ending the Cold War.

Canada's Alliances

Several times a year, a Canadian Forces officer is found in charge of the largest, most sophisticated defence system in the world. This officer has the power to start a massive nuclear strike almost anywhere on the planet. Yet Canada has no nuclear weapons and limited armed forces. It is Canada's alliances that have gigantic military strength.

An alliance is formed when two or more nations agree to help each other. Most are military alliances for defence. Canada belongs to two major alliances — NATO and NORAD. Canada joined these alliances because of the threat of the Cold War, and the lessons learned from two world wars. It is a strange thought that in order to prevent another war, Canada is part of two massive military machines.

Canada and Europe

Canada was an active founding partner of the North Atlantic Treaty Organization (NATO) in 1949. This alliance includes the United States, Britain, and other European nations. The main purpose of this alliance is to protect western Europe. In response, the Soviet Union brought the Communist countries together in an alliance called the Warsaw Pact. Both alliances are ready to fight an all-out war.

All countries in NATO are pledged to support each other if attacked. They contribute to the defence of western Europe and the North Atlantic. Today Canadian ships patrol the ocean for NATO watching for submarines. Five thousand Canadian troops are stationed in Europe.

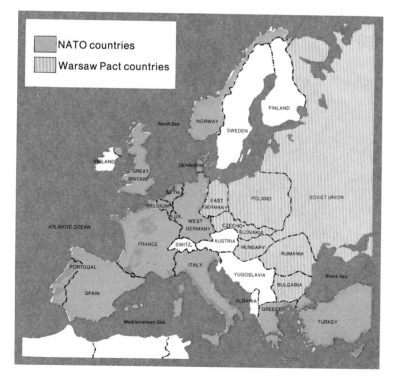

Canadian forces on NATO exercises in West Germany.

What is the purpose of NATO and NORAD?
Explain whether or not you think there should be any changes in
Canada's membership in NATO and NORAD.

1900 1910 1920 1930 1940 1950 1960 1970 1980 1990 2000

Canada in North America

In 1958 Canada and the United States entered an alliance for North American Air Defence (NORAD). NORAD is designed to protect North America from attack by the Soviet Union by detecting and intercepting manned bomber or missile attacks.

North America is defended by lines of radar stations and air bases in the North. Hundreds of missiles are aimed at targets in the Soviet Union. Bombers and fighters are in the air at all times ready for combat. It would take only few pushed buttons for destruction to be unleashed on the Soviet Union.

HMCS *Iroquois* tests a Sea Sparrow missile near Puerto Rico.

NORAD headquarters are located deep inside a granite mountain in Colorado. The commander of NORAD is always an American. The second-in-command is always a Canadian. When the American is absent, the Canadian officer is in charge of this huge military machine.

Recently, however, Canadians have raised serious questions about our alliances. Some of these questions concern costs. Others are about the basic nature of the alliances.

The F-18 A Hornet, Canada's new fighter aircraft.

The Alliances Today

Maintaining NATO and NORAD is extremely costly. Perhaps Canada should spend more on foreign aid or social programs at home. In a cost-cutting move, Canada reduced the size of her armed forces during the 1970s. This angered other members of the alliances.

Many Canadians feel it is dangerous that these alliances are so heavily dominated by the United States. They fear war may break out before Canada is properly consulted. They feel the alliances would be more useful if they were cultural and economic as well as military.

The world is once again in a period of tension and uncertainty. In times like these, there is little desire to pull out of NATO and NORAD. Rather than pull out, Canada is starting to re-equip her armed forces. Up-to-date weapons like the CF18 Hornet fighter have been ordered so Canada can better fulfil her commitments to these alliances.

Alliances would be no protection from the tragedy of a nuclear war. The only hope is that they may help to prevent it happening.

Commonwealth and Francophonie

Canada is a member of two multiracial and multicultur[al] associations: the Commonwealth and La Francophoni[e]. These two world-wide "clubs" have helped Canadians establish friendly ties with many nations.

The Commonwealth

The British Empire once controlled colonies all over the world. As these countries gained their independence, the Empire evolved into the Commonwealth. By the 1950s, many of the former colonies, such as India and Pakistan, had become independent republics. However, in 1951, it was agreed that the King or Queen of Britain would continue to be the symbolic head of the Commonwealth. Britain, as the former leader of the Empire, continues to play a leadership role. All members recognized the continuing British legacy of the English language, British common law, and the British parliamentary system.

The Commonwealth is a loose economic and cultural organization. Members assist one another by attempting to encourage mutual trade, although this has not proven to be too successful. The "have" members (Britain, Canada, Australia, and New Zealand) have attempted to assist the less-developed nations. In 1950, the Colombo Plan was organized to give aid and technology to underdeveloped members. Canada has made great contributions through the Colombo Plan to provide technical assistance, resources, financial assistance, and scholarships.

Commonwealth leaders meet regularly. Traditionally, Britain has been the leading member. Since the 1960s, the major issue facing the Commonwealth has been the racist policies followed by the government of South Africa. In 1961, South Africa was asked to leave the Commonwealth because of its policies of *apartheid* (forced racial segregation of blacks and whites). Throughout the 1970s and 1980s, the Commonwealth countries have tried to apply pressures on South Africa to force them to alter their harsh racial policies. This pressure has had little effect.

By the mid-1980s, Canada and other Commonwealth members were calling for economic sanctions (cutting off all trade and investments) with South Africa. The British government, led by Prime Minister Thatcher, refused to agree with this policy. As a result, Prime Minister Thatcher was bitterly criticized by many African Commonwealth members.

Gradually, Britain seemed to lose interest in her leadership role in the Commonwealth. As a result, in the Commonwealth meetings of 1986 and 1988, Prime Minister Mulroney emerged as one of the new leaders of the Commonwealth.

> "We (the Commonwealth) must stand for strong moral principles, which must rise above balance sheets and commercial trading patterns, and deal with a fundamental evil that exists in South Africa."
>
> *Prime Minister Mulroney at the opening of the Commonwealth Conference, London 1986.*

La Francophonie

After Paris, Montreal is the largest French-speaking city in the world. It is natural that Canada should be a member of La Francophonie, a voluntary association of French-speaking nations.

La Francophonie is a little like the Commonwealth. Most of the participating nations were once part of the French Empire. Canada has had no political links with France for over 200 years, but the ties of language and

What types of activity are promoted by the Commonwealth?
Why did *apartheid* become one of the major issues facing the
Commonwealth?
What is Canada's current attitude towards South Africa?

1900 1910 1920 1930 1940 1950 1960 1970 1980 1990 2000

culture remain deep. La Francophonie is less organized than the Commonwealth. The economic connection is less well developed. For example, a lot of Canadian aid goes to poorer countries in La Francophonie. However, it is given directly rather than through the association. On the other hand, cultural ties are probably stronger than they are in the Commonwealth.

Windows on the World

The Commonwealth and La Francophonie provide Canada with friendly contacts all over the world. Canada, with her two official languages, is a leading member of both associations. In the long run, such economic and cultural ties may prove more rewarding than military alliances.

Mulroney addresses delegates to the Commonwealth Conference, held in Vancouver, B.C., in 1987.

The Third World

Over half the world's population never has enough to eat. Home is often a shack, crowded with children and adults. Many people never have a chance to learn to read and write. If they get sick, medical aid is often non-existent. In times of war, floods, or earthquakes, there are no disaster funds for emergency relief. On top of this many nations are governed by ruthless power cliques. Citizens may have no civil rights.

Observers have divided the modern world into three communities:

The First World is made up of wealthy "democratic" countries with highly developed technological societies. Canada is part of this world.

The Second World is made up of the "communist" nations. The Soviet Union leads this world.

The Third World consists of most of the nations in Africa, Asia, and South America. These nations are generally poor. The bulk of their people are usually non-white. Many are former colonies of First World countries. Some of these countries have found oil and other valuable resources. They are using these resources to improve their position. Most Third World nations, however, are poor and getting poorer. Two-thirds of the world's people live in the Third World.

Why should Canada help the countries of the Third World? Besides humanitarian reasons, Canada has 3 major concerns.
Political: It is in our interest to help Third World countries. Great poverty can push them to try a communist system of government. They might become unfriendly towards us.
Economic: We can help ourselves by helping Third World countries. If countries become richer through Canadian aid programs, they may be able to buy Canadian products and Canadian technology.
Military: Poverty and hardship can lead to violence and war. If poor countries are not given help, they may use war as a tool to better themselves. First and Second World countries could also come to blows over their different hopes for Third World countries.

Yet these concerns are not uppermost in the hearts and minds of Canadians when they reach into their pockets or leave their homes to teach, nurse, or help feed the people of the Third World. Canadians care because fellow human beings suffer.

Left, in the west African country of Benin, learning farming methods is as important as math or shorthand. Below, in Colombia, South America, city children attend a "school of benches" in a neighbourhood backyard. UNICEF helps parents act as "teachers" and provides materials.

FOCUS

What is the Third World?
Give 4 reasons why Canadians should be concerned about conditions in the Third World.
Does aid to the Third World really help? Discuss.

Aid for the Third World

A great deal of assistance from the First and Second World is channelled through the United Nations and UN agencies. Canada contributes to many UN aid programs.

Canada also has her own program of foreign aid, run by the Canadian International Development Agency. Canadian money and expert advice are used in many Third World countries to find wells, build dams, teach good nutrition, or develop farms, fisheries, or factories.

Volunteer groups like the Red Cross, the Save the Children Fund, and the Foster Parents Plan also do their part. Money comes from Canadians in all walks of life. Young people collect money on Hallowe'en for UNICEF or undertake special projects to aid the Third World.

Yet the problems remain severe. The money spent on foreign aid is a small fraction of what the world spends on weapons. Often aid never reaches the people it is intended for because of inefficiency or dishonesty.

Cardinal Léger enjoys a game played by some patients at his Rehabilitation Centre in Cameroon.

Some projects have been poorly thought out and are massive failures. Others have been wiped out by floods or wars.

Is it worth it? International aid seems to be a losing battle. But Canadians must remain hopeful and have faith in humanity's future. They must be prepared to be even more generous. The pinch of inflation does not change the fact that Canada is a rich country. It can afford to help. The alternative is to give up on half the world's people. The future is with the children. Can Canadians turn their backs on them?

Paul-Emile Cardinal Léger
"The bishop who serves"

1904 — born in Valleyfield, Que.
1923 — felt called to priesthood.
1929 — made a priest. Went to France to study and teach.
1933 — sent to Japan to open seminary for priests.
1939 — recalled to teach in Montreal.
1940 — returned to work in Valleyfield.
1947 — rector of Canadian Pontifical College in Rome. Raised money in Canada for poor in the war-torn city.
1950 — made Archbishop of Montreal. "The little ones, the humble, the poor, the sick, and the workers will be the chosen portion of our fold."
1953 — made a cardinal, a prince of the R.C. church.
1962-65 — at 2nd Vatican Council argued for reform of church to make it more relevant to modern world.
1963 — visited Africa. Set up *Fame Pereo* (I am dying of hunger). Organization has aided 82 leprosy colonies in 20 African countries.
1967 — "retired" from high post in Montreal to serve as missionary in Africa. Set up Centre for the Rehabilitation of the Handicapped in Cameroon.
1970 — set up organization to administer and raise money for his many projects.
1979 — appointed with Roland Michener to head special fund to help Vietnamese boat people. Officiated at funeral of brother, Jules (governor general, 1973-79).

Hotspot: The Middle East

World War I started in Europe. World War II had its roots in Europe and East Asia. If there is to be a third world war, many observers expect it will flare up in the Middle East.

The Middle East has huge oil reserves. For that reason alone, the super powers each want to dominate the region. They try to influence the internal politics of Middle Eastern countries and their relationships with the rest of the world.

The Suez Crisis

1956 was probably the first time many Canadians were aware that the Middle East was an unstable trouble spot. Four years before, the Egyptians had overthrown their ruler, King Farouk. The new leader, Colonel Nasser, was determined Egypt should be strong. Britain and France had controlled the country when the hated Farouk was king. Therefore, Nasser turned to the Soviet Union for military and economic aid. This made Israel nervous of the power of her Arab neighbour.

In 1956, Nasser nationalized the Suez Canal, taking it from its French and British owners. Israel invaded Egyptian territory. France and Britain bombed Egypt and captured the canal. The Soviet Union threatened to send troops to help Egypt. The United States announced she was against the use of force. Yet she did little to discourage France and Britain.

The United Nations feared this would mean another world war. Canada worked hard through the UN to end the crisis. Lester Pearson developed a plan to end the fighting. All forces withdrew from the combat zone. They were replaced by a UN peace-keeping force. The force contained 1000 Canadian troops as well as soldiers from other nations. It was led by Canada's General Burns. Although trouble remained, the crisis was over. Pearson received the Nobel Peace Prize for his efforts.

Tensions in the Middle East

The Middle East has been a centre of conflict since the creation of Israel in 1948. Following World War Two, the State of Israel was created as a home for the Jews, in their traditional homeland in Palestine. However, most of the Arab states opposed the new state, claiming that it was created out of the Arab territory in Palestine. The tensions, acts of terrorism, and wars have continued ever since.

Israel-Palestine conflict

Following the 1967 Arab-Israeli War, the Israelis also occupied the area west of the river Jordan (west bank area). Their intention was to provide a more defensible border. The result was to include 1.5 million Palestinian Arabs within Israel. These Palestinians have demanded the right of self-government. They claim as their leader Yasser Arafat, the leader of the Palestinian Liberation Organization (PLO). The Israelis consider the PLO to be too dangerous a group to take over as a neighbouring state. This issue and the resulting conflict will continue until a workable compromise is arranged.

Iran-Iraq War, 1980-1988

The Arab nations cannot be regarded as one group. They also have serious differences among themselves. In 1980, a war broke out between Iran and Iraq. The war lasted for eight years and resulted in approximately 2 000 000 soldiers and civilians being killed. It was a barbaric war; for instance, Iraq used

Give 3 reasons why the Middle East is important to Canada.
How did Canada help end the Suez crisis?
Collect information on the present relationship of the Palestinians
and the Arabs.

1900 1910 1920 1930 1940 1950 1960 1970 1980 1990 2000

Palestinian residents arguing with Israeli soldiers in the occupied Gaza Strip.

banned poison and nerve gases on Iranian soldiers and civilians. By 1988, both sides grew tired of the useless slaughter and a peace treaty was signed. Canadian troops were used as part of the United Nations peace-keeping forces.

A Canadian Position

For a country like Canada, maintaining good relations in the Middle East is like walking a tightrope. On the one hand, Canadians wish to respect and help the Israelis in their right to independence and freedom from terrorist attacks or invasion. On the other hand, most Canadians wish Palestinians to have the right to self-determination also. As well, Canadians are dependent on imports of Middle Eastern oil, and wish to have peaceful relations with the Arab states.

The Middle East is one of the world's hot spots. The issues are not likely to go away in the near future. Canada will have to continue pursuing policies to reduce the tensions in this area for the benefit of the countries involved. Also, we must aim to reduce the possibilities of an incident which could lead to an even wider war.

In Pursuit of Peace, 1988

Following the peace settlement in 1945 after the end of World War Two, the world quickly moved into the era of the Cold War. Although a hot war of fighting had not broken out between the superpowers, the U.S.A. and the U.S.S.R., for over 40 years the world was divided into two hostile rival alliances. This atmosphere of conflict, rivalry, and suspicion was characterized as the Cold War. The superpowers were involved as rivals in conflicts around the world, such as in Korea, the Middle East, Vietnam, and Central America. Through the 1980s, a condition of real peace seemed distant and elusive.

In 1988, however, hopes for a more realistic peace appeared in a number of areas:

U.S.A.-U.S.S.R. relations

Premier Gorbachev of the U.S.S.R. and President Reagan of the United States negotiated a treaty which reduced the number of missiles for the first time. In addition, Gorbachev announced a unilateral reduction of 10% of the Soviet armed forces.

Iran-Iraq War

An armistice was arranged to end the bitter eight-year war between Iran and Iraq.

Afghanistan

The U.S.S.R. withdrew its armed forces from Afghanistan after a military occupation which had lasted for five years.

Nicaragua

A truce was arranged between rebel and government forces to temporarily end the civil war which had disrupted Central America for several years.

Angola and Namibia (southern Africa)

Cuban forces agreed to withdraw from Angola; in return South African forces withdrew from the occupation of Namibia, ending a rebel war which had lasted for several years.

Arab-Palestinian conflict

Yasser Arafat, the leader of the Palestinian Liberation Organization (the PLO), publicly agreed to recognize the boundaries and existence of the State of Israel. He also called for an end to terrorism, and an opportunity to sit down with Israeli representatives to negotiate a peaceful solution to the problems dividing the Israelis and the Palestinians.

India-Pakistan

The Premier of Pakistan Benazir Bhutto and Indian Prime Minister Rajiv Gandhi signed agreements to promote military and cultural co-operation between their two nations. India and Pakistan had lived in an atmosphere of conflict and tension since the creation of Pakistan and India in 1947.

Problems and issues remained in various parts of the world. The Middle East remained a tinderbox ready to ignite a wider war. Problems remained in parts of Africa and Central America. Terrorist attacks against civilian aircraft and innocent civilians continued. The endless struggle in Northern Ireland defied all efforts to find a solution. Yet no year since 1945 offered so much hope and optimism as the year 1988.

The Thaw

What had caused this great change which raised the world's hopes for peace?

Undoubtedly the major change came from the new leadership and directions in the Soviet Union. Premier Gorbachev seemed to be sincerely interested in changing the atmosphere of East-West relations. The economy of the Soviet Union had experienced severe problems; its industrial development was falling behind all of the industrial nations of the West and Japan. To stimulate economic growth, Gorbachev had introduced a policy of ''perestroika'' (reducing structure and controls) within the Soviet Union. This had been followed by a policy of ''glasnost'' (openness and friendly co-operation) both within the Soviet Union and with foreign nations. The result was an open invitation to get along with other nations, particularly the United States, and to reduce armaments and international conflict. U.S. President Reagan responded to these initiatives, and, together, the two leaders created an atmosphere of co-operation which spread to their allies around the world.

There also seemed at last to be a greater recognition of the spirit of international co-operation. Not since the 1950s had the United Nations been recognized as a possible solution to the threats of international war. It was also recognized that many of the world's problems — pollution and environmental concerns, disarmament, starvation, and poverty in the Third World — were international problems and could not be solved by national rivalries.

In 1988, the world appeared to have moved several steps away from nuclear conflict and towards an atmosphere of international agreement. Whether this was a more permanent trend or merely a temporary ''blip'' in international relations, remained to be seen. Undoubtedly new conflicts will emerge, or old ones revive. Yet the year 1988 seemed to offer some hope to a world longing for a change from constant tension.

The pursuit of peace would remain one of the major challenges facing Canada and other nations of the world in the 1990s.

YOUR TASK

Focus — Examine areas of international conflict in the world today. Select one problem area for further research and study.

Organize — Select several headings or topics to examine the area of research. You might concentrate on the causes of the conflict and some possible solutions or consequences.

Locate — Collect further information on your topic from newspapers and magazines, and from the vertical file in your library.

Record — Record your data in point form, to develop an outline.

Assess — Go over your report with a fellow student. Have your partner question your interpretation, and require you to prove your idea (or hypothesis).

Communicate — Write your ideas in first-draft form for a five-paragraph report. Have your partner edit your material.

Present — Present your report to your teacher in proper essay form, or present it to the class in the form of an oral report.

The American Connection

In the past Canadians and Americans have shot and killed each other. They have also fought and died side by side against a common enemy. Canadians and Americans have invaded each other's territory. Yet today they share the world's longest undefended border.

Canadian governments have made laws designed to keep American money and influence out of Canada. However, they have also co-operated with Americans and jointly spent billions on vast projects that benefit both countries.

Relations with the U.S. are the most important Canada has with any foreign country. These relations will continue to play a central part in the lives of both peoples. Both hope that in the future they will be partners rather than rivals.

Yet how well do Americans know Canadians? How well do Canadians know Americans? Might their views of each other stand in the way of understanding?

Canadians Talk of Americans

Everyone in the U.S. owns a gun, or would like to.

Americans all live in cities in big apartment buildings. They have to breathe their air through filters so they won't die of smog and pollution.

Americans just think about money and big business. They either have big houses or fast cars.

Americans show their feelings more than we do. They might be the first to get angry, but they're the first to help you out of a tight spot, too.

Americans get their foreign policy from those John Wayne movies — "Shoot first and ask questions later."

The major threat to Canadian survival today is American control of the Canadian economy.
The Waffle Manifesto

American Woman — stay away from me!
The Guess Who

Americans Talk of Canadians

Mountains. I think of mountains, and people singing.

Canadians are healthier than we are because they have to fight the elements to survive. Also probably because they're mostly descended from Eskimos, Indians, and Mounties.

The one thing I remember about Toronto is that you can read the map on the subway. In New York I never know where I'll end up, but Toronto's such a neat, itty-bitty place you can't get lost.

Canadians are nice and polite, not rude and noisy like some Americans you see. 'Course, I've only met but two Canadians I know of.

You're the ones who gave India the bomb, aren't you?

Canada will always be remembered by my generation as the nation that stood for peace, whether in the Middle East or Vietnam or Cyprus. If I were a Canadian, I'd rather have that said about me than anything else.

Short and fat and dark mostly and some of them speak French.

Why is Canada's "American connection" important?
How well do you think Canadians and Americans know each other?
In your opinion, what has been the most important event
in Canadian-American relations? Why?

Partners or Rivals?

1775 — Americans invade Canada during the American Revolution.

1783 — British loyalists leave the U.S. to settle in Canada under the British flag.

1812-14 — War of 1812. Americans and Canadians invade each other's territory from the Atlantic to the Great Lakes.

1866 — Irish-American Fenians invade Canada.

1867 — Nova Scotia, New Brunswick, Quebec, and Ontario unite to form Canada partly in defence against the U.S.

1871 — Treaty of Washington — Canada, Britain, and U.S. settle long-standing differences peacefully.

1878 — John A. Macdonald's National Policy tries to defend Canadian economy from American economy.

1903 — Alaska boundary dispute. Americans gain territory at expense of Canada.

1911 — Election on reciprocity. Canadians reject idea of free trade with U.S.

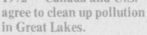

1939-45 — In 1940 Canada and U.S. create a permanent Joint Board of Defence. From 1941 they fight side by side in the battles of World War II.

1949 — NATO is formed. Canada and U.S. are among founding members.

1951 — Massey Report warns of American cultural influence in Canada.

1954 — St. Lawrence Seaway project started. In 1959 Seaway is opened by Queen Elizabeth II and President Eisenhower.

1958 — NORAD is formed for defence of North America.

1961 — Columbia River Treaty. Gigantic joint power project on West Coast.

1962 — Cuban missile crisis. Canadian and American leaders disagree over action to be taken.

1963 — Canadians divided over issue of nuclear warheads for Bomarc missiles from U.S.

1965 — Auto Pact brings free trade and better job security for large segments of the auto industry.

1965 — Pearson criticizes U.S. role in Vietnam War.

1968 — Watkins Report warns of American domination of Canadian economy.

1969 — U.S. oil tanker *Manhattan* voyages through Arctic waters against wishes of Canadian government.

1972 — Canada and U.S. agree to clean up pollution in Great Lakes.

1974 — FIRA (Foreign Investment Review Agency) created to screen foreign take-overs of Canadian businesses.

1977 — Canada and U.S. agree to recognize 200 mile fishery limits.

1980 — Canadian government aids escape of American diplomats from Iran after U.S. embassy take-over.

1981 — Canadians and Americans debate who is to blame for acid rain pollution killing northeastern lakes.

1984 — Mulroney government ends FIRA and invites Americans to invest in Canada — "Canada is open for business."

1986 — negotiations begin for a free trade agreement between Canada and the United States.

1989 — free trade agreements approved by Canadian Parliament.

The Political Connection

Canada and the United States share a vast continent. Relations between the two countries are usually warm and friendly. Sometimes there are moments of tension and concern. The prime minister of Canada and the president of the United States share the job of guiding the course of Canadian-American relations. The management of this intricate process is a true test of political leadership.

Prime Minister Trudeau and President Ford at the White House.

Foreign Affairs

Most of the time Canada and the United States agree about relations with other countries. They share many interests, have the same "friends," and belong to the same military alliances (NATO and NORAD). Occasionally the two countries disagree about how a situation should be handled.

One area where Canada and the United States have common interests is in the Middle East. Both want political stability in the Middle East. For example, they worked together to end the Suez crisis in 1956. Both want to ensure a secure supply of oil from the region.

On the other hand Canada did not approve of American involvement in the war in Vietnam. When

Pearson and Johnson.

Prime Minister Lester Pearson criticized the war to President Johnson, the president reacted in rage. A Canadian aide said he almost hit Pearson. In international affairs an "incident" like that might have been serious.

The United States has not approved when Canada established "diplomatic relations" with communist governments in Cuba and China. On the other hand, American leaders have later used Canada's stand as a stepping stone to creating better relations with these countries themselves.

American laws forbid American companies to sell goods to "enemy" countries. The United States government claims these laws extend to Canadian branches of American companies. Canadians have protested the loss of jobs when a Canadian branch is forced to cancel a sale by its parent company.

The Canadian Caper

Canada showed her friendship for the United States when the staff of the United States embassy were taken hostage in Iran in 1979. Six American diplomats who escaped found refuge in the homes of Canadian embassy officials. Over two months later in January 1980, they left Iran using fake Canadian passports. The Royal Canadian Mounted Police and the American Central Intelligence Agency had co-operated in preparing the passports and smuggling them into Iran. Overnight the Canadian ambassador, Ken Taylor, became an American hero. Perhaps, though, the greatest courage was shown by the wives of the Canadian officials. Night and day they lived in fear that the Iranians would discover the presence of their "house guests." It was up to these women to act at all times as if everything was completely natural in their homes.

Ken Taylor.

FOCUS

Note 3 areas of agreement and 3 areas of disagreement between Canada and the United States.
Do you agree or disagree with Prime Minister Mulroney's closer relations with the United States? Explain your opinion.

Art Gallery page 29

Mulroney and Reagan

Continental Affairs

Just as important as foreign affairs are direct relations between the two countries. Over the years Canada and the United States have co-operated on a wide range of projects. For example the St. Lawrence Seaway was started as a joint project in 1954. In 1961 a treaty was signed to dam the Columbia River to provide electricity for British Columbia and the State of Washington. The nations also have agreements to build several pipelines in the West. For various reasons these projects have not always run smoothly.

In the 1970s the environment became a matter of increasing concern. For example, the Canada-United States border runs through the Great Lakes. However, the water and the pollution in it flow freely from one

> **Geography has made us neighbours. History has made us friends. Economics made us partners and necessity has made us allies. Those whom nature hath so joined together, let no man put asunder.**
>
> *President John F. Kennedy to the Canadian Parliament, 1961*

side to the other. In 1972 a joint project was undertaken to clean up the Great Lakes.

Canadians are now worried about the effects of acid rain. The industry of central Canada and the northern United States creates air pollution. This is absorbed into the rain that falls on eastern North America. The most noticeable effect is that the rain kills plant and animal life in lakes. Canadians are trying to work out a treaty like the one that started the Great Lakes clean-up. As yet, American leaders have shown little interest in the idea.

Improved Canadian-American relations

While Trudeau was Prime Minister, relations with the United States remained cordial but cool. Trudeau had very little use for President Richard Nixon. He had very little in common with President Reagan's militant anti-communism or his business-oriented policies.

With the election of Brian Mulroney in 1984, the atmosphere changed. Mulroney was determined to have a more open and friendly Canada-U.S. relationship. In March 1985, Mulroney and Reagan met in Quebec to discuss common issues. The leaders got on together very well personally, and moved towards common approaches to common policies. Because the conference extended over March 17, St. Patrick's Day, and the two "Irishmen" got along so well, the conference was called the "Shamrock Conference". "Shamrock" diplomacy lasted for the remainder of their terms.

Many welcomed this new positive relationship between the two neighbours. Others were concerned that by too closely embracing American policies, Canadians might be in danger of losing their national and cultural identity.

The Cultural Connection

Many people claim that Canadians and Americans share much of the same culture. Culture means lifestyle. This includes beliefs, customs, attitudes, language, ways of working and relaxing. Is there any difference between Americans and Canadians?

The United States is a dynamic world power. The effects of Americanization are all over the world. You can sit down to a Big Mac in Europe or sip a Coke in China. Canada, for reasons of geography, numbers, and language, is the country most open to American influence.

Canada and the United States share a border 9000 km long. They have a similar history of settlement, immigration patterns, attitudes and approaches to the rest of the world. Canada's population is only one tenth the size of the United States'. Most people in the two countries speak the same language.

American radio, TV, movies pour across the border. Canadian artists, writers, actors, and musicians have found it hard to earn a living in their own country. Many talented Canadians have had to "make it in the U.S." before their work was accepted in Canada. They claim Canadians suffer from an inferiority complex when it comes to enjoying their own culture. They assume that "If it's Canadian, it can't be any good."

> A Canadian is someone who drinks Brazilian coffee from an English teacup and munches a French pastry while sitting on his Danish furniture having just come home from an Italian movie in his German car. He picks up his Japanese pen and writes to his Member of Parliament to complain about the American take-over of the Canadian publishing business.
>
> *Campbell Hughes, publishing executive, 1953.*

In the 1970s changes in the tax laws made it more expensive for foreign magazines to publish in Canada. Today Canada has a booming "homegrown" magazine industry.

Some Canadians automatically read *Time* magazine rather than *Maclean's*. Their TVs are always on American channels. They listen to American pop songs and go to American movies. Their attitude seems to indicate they would really prefer to be American all the way.

Why is Canadian culture so open to American influence?
Why do Canadian stars often find they must "make it in the U.S."?
Does being Canadian mean something special to you?
Debate: "Resolved that we are more North American than Canadian."

1900 1910 1920 1930 1940 1950 1960 1970 1980 1990 2000

"International" Canadian stars: Anne Murray, Bryan Adams, Brian Orser, Donald Sutherland, Karen Kain.

A Canadian Identity?

Yet when these same people go to Europe or Asia, a strange thing happens! If they are taken for Americans they become very indignant. "No, we are Canadians," they say. They paste maple leaves on their bags, so people will not make the same mistake again. Suddenly they are proud of their country and their heritage.

Which is the real Canada? Is is just the United States moved north? Or is there something about Canadian culture that is special and different?

The federal and provincial governments believe most Canadians want to retain an identity that is different from their neighbours to the south. Therefore they have looked for a number of ways to support the arts. The CBC, the National Film Board, the Canada Council, the Canadian Radio and Television Commission and the Canadian Film Development Corporation have all sprung from the federal government's concern. Many provinces have provincial arts councils which try to support local and regional cultural activities as well as the arts in general. Business, too, realizes the benefits of a strong cultural life. Many companies give generously to sponsor concerts, theatre and dance companies or art shows.

All this helps to give Canadian artists the opportunity to be appreciated in their own country.

However, the real decision about the future of Canadian culture lies with average Canadians. Only Canadians can decide if they want to be different from Americans. Only Canadians can develop their own dancers, novelists, sculptors, jazz musicians and architects. If it means something special to be Canadian, Canadians must work to discover their national identity.

The rock group, The Box, record and perform in both French and English.

The Economic Connection

Canada lives next door to a giant. The American economy produces over a trillion dollars worth of wealth a year. Canadians both share and contribute to this wealth.

> No matter where they locate in relation to where we reside, we're always delighted to hear of branch factories being established in Canada because of the employment they create for Canadian labour, the market they provide for Canadian farmers and merchants, and the business activity they stimulate in countless ways and in countless quarters.
> *H.H. Stevens, Minister of Trade and Commerce, 1930*

Canadians and Americans are the closest trading and business partners in the world. Each year, billions of dollars worth of goods and services flow across the border. Americans invest and vacation in Canada. Canadians invest and vacation in the U.S. Many foreigners see Canada and the United States as a single economic unit.

> Our problem is not to divorce the United States but how to live with it
> *John Holmes, former Canadian diplomat*

However, Canada and the U.S. are not *equal* economic partners. The Canadian economy is much smaller than the American economy. The interests of Canadians and Americans are not always the same. The close relationship does present some problems.

> The multinational corporation is like the man who came to dinner. You welcome him as a guest and then find that he's making the rules and giving the orders for the household.
> *from* Gordon to Watkins to You: The Battle for Control of our Economy, *published in 1970*

Dependence

Many Canadians feel that Canada is too closely tied to the American economy. Since Canada is so much smaller, this makes Canadians dependent on Americans for our prosperity. This makes it difficult for Canada to act independently of the U.S. Often the economic well-being of Canadians rises and falls with decisions made "south of the border."

> The United States is a good neighbour that never forgets self interest.
> *Harry J. Boyle, author and former head of the CRTC*

The Question of Ownership

Foreigners own 275 of the 500 largest corporations in Canada. It has been said that Canadians are tenants rather than landlords in their own country. Millions of dollars worth of profits and resources leave Canada for the United States each year.

On the other hand, economists point out that American money has helped Canada grow strong and wealthy. Canadians have benefited from American technology and know-how. American investment has created millions of jobs in Canada. The close economic link has helped create friendly political and military relations.

FOCUS
What are some of the positive results of Canada's close economic relationship with the U.S.?
What are some of the negative results of this relationship?

1900 1910 1920 1930 1940 1950 1960 1970 1980 1990 2000

> It is because of American capital investment and the technology that comes with it, that we enjoy one of the highest standards of living in the world.
> *Pierre Elliott Trudeau*

Canada must always make sure that economic ties with the U.S. are in the best interest of Canadians. The Canadian government has taken steps to exercise some control over the relationship.

American Investment in Canada

In the 1970s, Trudeau and the Liberals were concerned about the growing U.S. investment in Canada. They introduced FIRA (Foreign Investment Review Agency) to investigate the purchase of Canadian companies by foreign companies. The intent was to slow down the increasing U.S. control of Canadian industries and resources. The result was to slow down U.S. investment, and to irritate some Canadian business people. They felt it was an unnecessary intrusion of government into business affairs. It was also perceived by some Americans as an unfriendly action towards American business.

Shortly after taking office, Prime Minister Mulroney repealed FIRA, replacing it with "Investment Canada". "Canada is open for business," stated Mulroney to an American audience. The Mulroney government has been more concerned about increasing prosperity and jobs by industrial expansion, and less concerned with the source of investment. They expressed a confidence in Canadians to survive in spite of increasing American business in Canada.

> If we continue the same way it will not be possible by the end of the 1980s for Canada to retain control over its economy.
> *Mel Hurtig, Alberta publisher*

Petro-Canada

Up until the 1970s, the petroleum industry in Canada was almost entirely controlled by multinational corporations, most of which were American-controlled. The energy crisis of 1973 brought rapid increases in oil prices. Many Canadians immediately sought to bring part of the oil industry under Canadian control. They hoped to be able to increase Canadian production of oil and to move Canada closer to energy self-sufficiency. They also hoped to be able to establish a Canadian price for oil, independent of spiralling world prices.

In 1975, the Liberal government, under the urging of the NDP, created Petro-Canada, a government-owned oil company. The move was popular among many Canadians. However, it was strongly opposed by many Albertans and by some members of the business community. By 1989, over 50% of the petroleum industry was Canadian-owned.

By the 1980s, for many, the key question was no longer "ownership". In those years, there were several key questions:
— How can we best guarantee markets for our resources and industrial exports?
— How can we best guarantee more jobs for Canadians?

To try to answer these questions, the Conservative government turned to consider free trade with the United States.

> The day is going to come when people are going to say, "Why were you so stupid? Why did you give it all away?"
> *Eric Kierans, Canadian economist and former Quebec cabinet minister and head of the Montreal Stock Exchange*

Questions and Activities

Word Scramble

Unscramble the letters to form terms introduced in this chapter.
1. INTUDE STONIAN
2. DHIRT RODWL
3. LCMTENOMAHWM
4. ZSEU RSCISI
5. LDCO RWA
6. 002 LEMI TLIMI

Test Yourself

Match the words in column A with the descriptions in column B.

A	B
1. Lester Pearson	a) person responsible for day-to-day activities of UN
2. NATO	b) Canadian-American alliance
3. Security Council	c) informer who helped break Soviet spy ring
4. NORAD	d) winner of Nobel Peace Prize
5. FIRA	e) leader in aid for Third World, especially to the handicapped
6. Secretary General	f) agency to screen foreign take-overs
7. La Francophonie	g) alliance to defend western Europe
8. CDC	h) body of UN responsible for maintaining peace
9. UNICEF	i) UN agency for children's welfare
10. Cardinal Léger	j) agency to promote Canadian ownership
11. Igor Gouzenko	k) association of French-speaking nations

Ideas for Discussion

1. Assume you have been elected Secretary General of the United Nations. Prepare a speech to be delivered to the representatives of the world in the General Assembly. Your working title might be "What We Must Do to Survive."
2. Between 1947 and 1989, Canada participated in every UN peace-keeping mission. Do you think Canada should continue to volunteer for these activities? Why or why not?
3. There are now over 100 000 nuclear weapons in the world. This is enough to kill everyone on the planet several times over. With a small group of other students, discuss the chances of nuclear disarmament.
4. Working in teams, draw up lists outlining the good points and the bad points of Canada's membership in NATO and NORAD. Using ideas from all teams, draw up a master list on the board. Take a vote on whether Canada should continue as a member of these two alliances.

5. You can never really come to terms with the idea of nuclear war. You just put it out of your mind, get on with your work, and hope it never happens. But if it does, you do your duty. I don't think it would worry me, because by the time we're fighting back, I know my family and most everyone else on the outside would no longer exist.

Canadian Forces Officer with NORAD

6. Hold a debate on the topic: "Canadians are Americans in everything but name."
Draw up two lists showing the positive and negative results of Canada's close relationship with the United States. Which list is longer? Is the longer necessarily the more important.

Do Some Research

1. Find out more about the Nobel Peace Prize. Your report might answer the following questions:
   a) What are the origins of the prize?
   b) Besides Lester Pearson, who are some of the other winners of the prize?
   c) Why were they awarded it?
   d) Is there anyone you think should be awarded the prize? Why do you think so?
   e) There are Nobel prizes for other achievements as well as peace. What other Canadians have won a Nobel prize? In what field?
2. Since 1945 there have been over one hundred wars involving over eighty countries, and 25 million people have been injured or killed. Examine the causes, events, and results of one of these wars.
3. Find out about an agency that tries to help people in the Third World. By telephone and letter, gather as much information as you can about the projects this agency is concerned with. Some agencies you might study are:
   a) Canadian Save the Children Fund
   b) Red Cross
   c) Oxfam
   d) UNICEF
   Report your findings to the rest of the class.
4. Do further research on a Third World country which has recently been in the news. Use some of the following headings as organizers for your report: POPULATION; TYPE OF GOVERNMENT; RESOURCES; INDUSTRIES; PER CAPITA INCOME; TRADE; NATIONAL DEBT; OBSTACLES TO DEVELOPMENT.

5. Keep a record of the TV programs you watch for a week. How many hours did you spend watching:
   a) American programs?
   b) Canadian programs?
   c) programs from other countries?

Be Creative

1. **The last century made the world a neighbourhood; this century must make it a brotherhood.**
   J.S. Woodsworth

   Write your own short punchy sentence with the same general message.
2. Organize a fund-raising activity to support an aid project in the Third World.
3. Exchange letters and a "school capsule" with a school in another part of the Commonwealth.
4. Brainstorm to find as many endings as possible to a sentence beginning "Peace is...." Use your sentences as captions for posters.
5. Listen to the song "Imagine" by John Lennon. Write additional lyrics of your own. Collect a peace songbook. Can songs affect peace and/or war?

You Are There

You are the members of the newly appointed cabinet in the federal parliament. Your party has won the recent election, and you are eager to begin the task of leading Canada into the next decade.

One issue you wish to discuss is Canada's relationship with the United States. Your Prime Minister has promised that there would be a review of existing policies, and that this would lead to a statement of party policy.

Three experts have been brought in to give their opinions. With which do you most agree? What will be the cabinet's decision? After listening to the three positions, you must convince your colleagues to agree with your opinion.

Good luck Mr. Prime Minister!
Gook luck cabinet members!

Dear Mr. Prime Minister:

After much research, I suggest that the following action be taken by your government:
— the free trade deal is working so well, we should have complete economic union
— we should pool all North American energy resources
— we should remove all restrictions against American television or broadcasting
— we should begin discussions to permit Canada to join the U.S.

I have suggested this closer relationship with the U.S. because it is our ultimate destiny. Our peoples and culture are basically the same. We should seek our chance to join with the U.S., the greatest and most powerful nation on earth. Only then, can our economy truly prosper. Remember, united we stand; divided we fall.

Sam Union
Continental Consultants

Dear Mr. Prime Minister

Time is very short. The greatest crisis in Canadian history now faces us. We have become almost a colony of the United States.
Since the free trade agreement went into effect, the U.S. dominates nearly every aspect of Canadian life. Americans own most of Canadian resources; our economy is linked to theirs. Canadian culture is being submerged in American television. Our foreign policy is just a reflection of U.S. policy. To save Canada's future, I recommend the following:
— revise our involvement in free trade to reduce our ties to the American economy
— reclaim control over our energy resources to create a Canadian energy policy
— encourage investment and trade with the Pacific Rim countries (Japan, China, Korea, Taiwan)
— improve policies to protect Canadian culture
— place our defence emphasis on Canadian protection of the Arctic area
Act now, or Canada is lost.

Jane Canuck
Maple Leaf Enterprises

Dear Mr. Prime Minister:

I have made a thorough analysis of all aspects of Canadian-American relations. Quite frankly, things have never been better. I cannot see why there is a need for a review.

I would suggest that we continue our present policies:
— let the free trade agreement develop; it is bound to improve our economy
— maintain friendly relations with American presidents; the U.S. is our best friend and greatest ally
— continue to work to resolve environmental issues. The problems took years to develop; we cannot expect rapid action to solve the problems
— emphasize how much we have in common with Americans, rather than publicizing issues and problems.

Remember we are all North Americans, two great nations sharing the longest undefended border in the world. Let's keep it that way.

Stan Pat
Status Quo Enterprises

Research

No textbook can provide all of the information required for the study of history. To have a complete understanding of any topic, it will be necessary to do further research in other texts, encyclopedias and other sources. The following suggestions are offered to assist you in your research:

1. Read your textbook coverage of the subject to gain general background on the topic. This will also help you to begin to *focus* on the questions that you want to pursue in your research.
2. Consult further information sources in your library.
   a) Use the *card catalogue* to help you find other specific books.
   b) Many topics which you wish to research will be only *chapters or sections* of books on a larger topic. Consult your teacher or librarian for assistance in locating these other reference books.
3. Use the *Table of Contents* and *Index:*
   a) When you examine a book, look over the Table of Contents at the beginning. You may determine which chapters are most useful for your further research.
   b) The Index at the back of the book is the most effective way of seeing whether or not the book has information specifically related to your topic.
4. *Recording Information*
   When you find information that you think is worthwhile, record it in point form on your note paper or on 7.5 cm × 12.5 cm research cards:
   — use only *one side* of the page;
   — record information in *point form,* under appropriate headings;
   — record each topic on a separate piece of paper or cards.

As you record separate topics on separate pieces of paper, it will help you in *organizing* your report when you start to write it.

5. *Bibliography*
   When you complete your written report, you will have to indicate the *sources* of your information. For each book you consult and find useful, record the information in the following way:

Author (last name first)	Title (under-lined)	City of Publication	Publisher	Year

McFadden, F.C. *Canada in the Twentieth Century,* Toronto, Fitzhenry & Whiteside Ltd., 1989.

6. When you have collected all of your data or information, you should *organize* your material into an acceptable order. It will help your organization if you have recorded different information on separate pages or cards.

YOUR TASK

Select any topic from this chapter of study, and do further research in the library, using at least two other sources of information.

After completing your research, write a report approximately two pages long.
(See suggestions for writing a Five-Paragraph Report on page 251.)

Writing a Five-Paragraph Research Report or Essay

Two Forms of Reports

1. *Descriptive* Report
   Some historical reports simply describe events:

   Social Conditions in the 1920s
   Immigration into the West in the 1900s
   The Schlieffen Plan
   Trench Warfare in World War I
   The Baby Boom of the 1950s

   These reports merely *describe* in a narrative form what happened at a period in time.
2. *Explanatory* (or expository) Essay
   Writing an explanatory (or expository) essay is more complex and difficult. It involves *more varied research, selection* of material, and *organization.*

   You use this form when you are trying *to explain* an *issue,* or consider a viewpoint (or even an hypothesis) rather than just describe what happened. While your research is being completed, you must form an *opinion, take a point of view,* and try to *prove* your position.

Organization before writing

1. *Research* to collect data on your topic
2. Select one or two questions to *focus* your research on the topic.
3. *Organize* your supporting information or evidence in an appropriate order or sequence.
4. Think of an appropriate *conclusion* or consequence to explain why your topic is important or significant.
5. *Record* your — introduction — supporting information — conclusion in a *rough outline.*
6. Your outline should be in point form, and should not be more than one page long.

Writing Your Report or Essay

Writing a five-paragraph report is an expansion of how you write a five-sentence paragraph.

WRITING A PARAGRAPH	WRITING A FIVE-PARAGRAPH REPORT
1. *Introductory sentence* explains main idea of paragraph.	1. *Introductory paragraph* explains main idea of report.
2. *Contents* — 3 (or 4) sentences support the introductory sentence.	2. *3 (or 4) supporting paragraphs* — Each paragraph explains one idea supporting the introductory paragraph.
3. *Concluding sentence* summarizes or gives the importance of the paragraph.	3. *Concluding paragraph* gives conclusion or significance of the topic.

YOUR TASK

Write a *five-paragraph report* on *one* of the following topics:

— French-Canadian attitudes towards conscription
— The Quiet Revolution
— The War Measures Act, 1970
— The Rise of the Parti Québécois
— The Leadership of René Lévesque
— The Referendum of 1980
— Bill 101
— The Language Issue in Quebec in the 1980s
— Topic of your choice

Chapter Eight

One Nation or Two?
ADVANCE ORGANIZER

1 French Canadians can trace their roots on this continent back over 400 years. Their culture stems from the period when New France was a French colony. They lost most contacts with France after Quebec fell to Britain in 1759. Today 5 million French Canadians call Quebec home.

3 By 1960 a new generation of Quebeckers wanted more than just survival. They demanded equality. The "Quiet Revolution," a period of modernization, was underway. Vast natural resource projects led to economic expansion. The province took a fresh look at education and social policies. In the new political atmosphere, some Quebeckers claimed that independence was the only way to gain real equality with other Canadians.

2 After the conquest the *Canadiens'* goal was survival. They were granted the right to use their own language, laws, and religion. Yet they felt threatened by the growing numbers of English-speaking people in the colony. Confederation in 1867 created special guarantees for the French culture in Quebec. However, in the years that followed there were clashes between French and English over a number of issues. Quebeckers reacted by turning inward to their own society.

Word List

biculturalism	national anthem	sovereignty-association
bilingualism	Quiet Revolution	terrorism
extremist	referendum	War Measures Act
liberation	separatism	Yvette movement

4

In October 1970 headlines all over the world announced that James Cross, a British diplomat, had been kidnapped by the FLQ, a Quebec terrorist group. Pierre Laporte, a Quebec cabinet minister, was also kidnapped and later murdered. In response to the crisis, the federal government proclaimed the War Measures Act. This act gave police special powers. Hundreds of suspected separatists were arrested without charge. Many Canadians objected furiously to the loss of civil rights. However, the crisis convinced Quebeckers that change should only come through peaceful means.

5

In 1976, René Lévesque, the Parti Québécois leader, was elected Premier. He promised to lead Quebec to independence as a separate state. However, on 20 May 1980, the people of Quebec voted on a referendum. They were asked whether or not Quebec should negotiate a new relationship with Canada — "sovereignty-association". Nearly 60% voted against the plan. The defeat of the referendum led to the decline of separatist support.

6

Robert Bourassa returned as the Liberal Premier in 1985. He promised to work more closely with the federal government if Quebec's rights were protected and it was recognized as a "distinct society" within Canada. Prime Minister Mulroney negotiated the Meech Lake agreement, to recognize Quebec's distinctive conditions.

If the Meech Lake Accord was passed by all provinces, it would return Quebec to full participation in Canada. However, there were difficulties in getting support of all the provinces. Also, the language rights of English Canadians in Quebec remained an issue.

The French in New France

A modern replica of Jacques Cartier's ship in a park in Quebec City.

Most Canadians recognize names like Guy LaFleur, Pierre Trudeau, Genevieve Bujold, and Gilles Villeneuve. These famous Canadians are the descendants of a French-speaking society that settled in North America nearly 400 years ago.

In the 1530s Jacques Cartier sailed deep into North America up the mighty St. Lawrence River. His stories of rich furs, teeming fish, and gold lured other explorers to North America. In 1604 Samuel de Champlain brought a group of French settlers to the Bay of Fundy. In 1608 he brought another group to Quebec.

The government of France wanted to make money out of New France. They thought of the colony in terms of the furs, timber, and fish it could send back to France. However they soon realized that New France could not survive if it could not grow its own food. Soon farms dotted the shores of the St. Lawrence River. The colony began to have an independent existence. Champlain and other early leaders of the colony had another burning ambition. They wanted to convert the native people to Christianity. They encouraged missionary priests to come to New France. Nuns came as well, bringing with them nursing and teaching skills.

The harsh climate, isolation, and constant warfare with the Iroquois and the English colonies to the south kept the population of New France small. Men and women who prospered created a self-reliant, religious, hard-working society. Yet slowly the villages grew larger and stronger. By 1759 the population was 60 000.

New France continued to look beyond the settled area of farms and towns. The coureurs-de-bois, eager for riches, got their name from "roaming the woods" in search of furs. Champlain himself mapped much of what is now eastern Canada and the northeastern United States. French explorers reached the Gulf of Mexico, the shores of Hudson Bay, and the foothills of the Rockies. Traders established posts at points that later became the cities of Kingston, Toronto, and Winnipeg. By the 1750s the French had made their mark in every future province of Canada east of the Rockies.

By this time many people in New France thought of themselves as "Canadiens" rather than "Français."

Give 2 reasons why France set up a colony in North America.
Why did the population of New France grow only slowly?
How would average Canadiens have felt after the British conquest?
Why do Acadians today feel different from Quebeckers?

They would have felt like foreigners in France. Most had been born in North America and had developed a unique lifestyle suited to their environment. Some had intermarried with the native people, bringing the best of two ways of life together. They had built schools, a university, churches, hospitals, missions, factories, forges, even breweries. They had their own set of heroes like Madeleine de Verchères and Dollard des Ormeaux, coureurs-de-bois like Jean Nicolet and Pierre Radisson, soldiers like Frontenac and Le Moyne d'Iberville, missionaries like Jean de Brébeuf and Jeanne Mance.

The times had not been peaceful. The relentless search for furs brought New France into constant conflict with the English and their Indian allies. In 1756 a war began which was to change New France forever.

Traditional crafts are demonstrated at the Acadian Historical Village in New Brunswick.

The Conquest of New France

The empires of Britain and France were spread all over the globe. In 1756 war broke out between the two rival nations. The colonies were the pawns in this struggle.

France decided it was too difficult to defend the vast and distant colony of New France properly. Outnumbered and outgunned, French forces surrendered their outposts one by one. In 1759 the city of Quebec fell to the British at the battle of the Plains of Abraham. A year later Montreal fell. The Canadiens were under British military rule. In 1763 the British took formal control of the entire colony.

Much of New France lay in ruins. Farms and villages had been burned to the ground. Many of those who had ruled New France returned to their homes and families in France. The Canadiens, born and raised in the new world, remained in the land they knew and loved. They were isolated and under the rule of strangers.

Acadia

France's other colony in North America was Acadia (modern-day Nova Scotia). Acadia was the result of Champlain's first settlement in the Bay of Fundy. Often ignored by France, the Acadians became an agricultural community. They dyked and improved the rich farmlands around the bay. They traded with the English colonies to the south for the things they could not grow.

Acadia was soon caught up in the strife between Britain and France. After 1713, much of Acadia was under British rule. The Acadians tried to remain neutral, but the British never trusted them. In 1755 as tensions grew, the British decided to get rid of the Acadians. They rounded them up, herded them onto British ships, and sent them to the English colonies further south.

Some Acadians escaped this deportation. Others slowly made their way back to their homeland. Eventually many settled in what is now northern New Brunswick.

The French Canadians of the Maritimes have a proud heritage. They feel they are a different people from their neighbours in Quebec. They have a different history, different memories, a different culture. At the same time they look to the larger French-speaking population of Quebec as their allies in the struggle to maintain their identity in the often alien English-speaking culture of North America.

The French in British North America

Many French Canadians probably found their daily lives changed little after the British conquest. The new rulers wanted to win the respect and perhaps even the loyalty of the people. The way to do this was offer respect in return — respect for a language, system of laws, religion, and way of life. In 1774 the British parliament passed the Quebec Act. The Quebec Act was based on these principles.

Yet the colony could never be the same again. English-speaking settlers, some from Britain, some from the south after the American Revolution, were pouring in. These people did not like the French laws and customs they found in Quebec. The relationship between French and English became strained.

The history of the next hundred years shows various attempts to deal with the strain. In 1791 the colony was divided into "Upper Canada" (later Ontario and mostly English) and "Lower Canada" (later Quebec and mostly French).

Rebellions in 1837 in both colonies showed people were unhappy with the system of government. Lord Durham in a report to the British parliament recommended more self-government. However he also suggested that the colonies should be united again. This way the French Canadians would be outnumbered by the English. He hoped they would soon give up their language and way of life.

In 1841 the colonies were united according to Lord Durham's plan. But the arrangement did not work. By the 1860s the government was in a stalemate. English and French were too evenly balanced for either to take a firm lead. Both began to feel they would be better off handling local affairs on their own. A central government could run services both needed.

George Etienne Cartier joined with John A. Macdonald in proposing this "federal" form of

Quebec had to be rebuilt after the British siege in 1759, but today it still retains its character as a French city.

government. By 1867 their efforts had led to a confederation of four provinces — Nova Scotia, New Brunswick, Quebec, and Ontario. All expected other provinces would eventually become part of this new country called Canada.

French Canada after Confederation

Many French Canadians saw Confederation as a bargain with English Canada. In return for French participation in the new nation, Quebec was guaranteed control over religion and education. This ensured the survival of French and English in the new nation.

The partnership was not an easy one. In 1870 Manitoba joined Confederation as a bilingual province. The protection of the French language was largely the result of the armed resistance and negotiations of a fiery young Manitoban called Louis Riel. Fifteen years later

FOCUS

What did the Quebec Act guarantee to French Canadians?
Give 3 examples that show that Confederation was an uneasy
partnership between French and English.
How did the Union Nationale influence life in Quebec?

1900 1910 1920 1930 1940 1950 1960 1970 1980 1990 2000

Riel led another rebellion in the West against the new
Canadian government. He was captured, tried, and
executed. The execution pleased English Canadians, who
thought Riel was a tiresome rabble-rouser. French
Canadians were enraged because Riel had been trying to
protect the French-speaking people who had first settled
western Canada.

In 1890 the English-speaking majority in Manitoba
abolished French language rights. In 1912 Ontario did
the same. The conscription crises in the two world wars
divided English and French Canadians even more
deeply. Canada was in danger of becoming "two
solitudes." French Canadians felt their culture was
only safe in Quebec.

Church and Homeland

The Depression emphasized the fears and insecurities of
the French in Canada. It was easy to believe that Quebec's
economic problems were caused by "foreign" control.
The Union Nationale, a new political party, swept to
power in 1936. Their leader, Maurice Duplessis, promised
that decisions about Quebec's industry and resources
would be made in Quebec.

The Union Nationale wanted to preserve the French
language, religion, and culture. To do this, they worked
closely with the Roman Catholic Church. The church
controlled the schools and colleges. Young people were
taught to respect traditional values. Modern influences
were discouraged. As a result, a generation of French
Canadians grew up with very little background in
business, science, and technology.

Outside investment actually increased under
Duplessis. Large companies liked the Union Nationale
government. They gave the party money. In return the
church, the government, and the companies worked
together to keep trade unions weak in Quebec. They

Maurice Duplessis (Le Chef)

"I have no family. My only
responsibility is the welfare of
the province. I belong to
Quebec."

1890 — born in Yamachiche,
Que., near Trois Rivières.
1900 — at age 10 spoke at
political meetings.
1913 — graduated as lawyer
from Laval University.
1923 — narrowly defeated in provincial election.
1927 — elected. Announced: "Before you stands the
future premier of Quebec."
1933 — elected leader of Quebec Conservatives.
1935 — with his supporters, joined with rebel Liberals
to form Union Nationale.
1936 — Duplessis swept to power (UN 76, Liberals 14).
1937 — "Padlock Law" passed, giving police power to
close offices of "subversive" groups.
1939 — UN defeated in election called over Canada's
role in World War II.
1944 — re-elected, partly because of conscription issue.
1948 — Fleur-de-lis made Quebec's official flag.
1949 — used force to try to break a strike at Asbestos,
Que. Many Quebec figures (Léger, Trudeau) supported
the strikers.
1953 — appointed Tremblay commission to investigate
Quebec society and its place in Canada. Report "woke"
Quebec to desire for change.
1959 — died of heart attack at Schefferville, Que.
1960 — UN defeated in provincial election, though
returned to power in 1966.

thought unions were communist inspired. With weak
unions, the companies did not have to improve wages
or working conditions.

Except for a four-year period during World War II,
Duplessis remained in power in Quebec until his death
in 1959. By that time the people of Quebec were
becoming restless.

The Quiet Revolution

On 7 September 1959, "le Chef," Maurice Duplessis, died of heart failure. With him died the old Quebec.

Under Duplessis' rule, politics in Quebec had become very corrupt. The rural regions had far more power than the bustling cities. Areas that voted Union Nationale got new roads. Those that voted Liberal did not. The Roman Catholic Church had tremendous influence. English-Canadian, British, and American corporations soon discovered the way to do business in Quebec was to support Duplessis.

The effects were felt in all aspects of life. Labour unions were ruthlessly restricted. The church did not want French Canadians to mix with the English. The church-controlled education system did not prepare students for the modern business world. Furthermore, English was the language of big business. Corporations promoted English speakers rather than French speakers. Quebec was ripe for change.

The death of Duplessis left the Union Nationale in a state of collapse. In 1960 the Liberals under Jean Lesage won their first Quebec election since World War II. The people of Quebec were ready to look at their province and its place in their country and the world in a new way. The Quiet Revolution, a period of wholesale, dramatic change in Quebec society, had begun.

Quebec Seeks a New Identity

The goals of the Quiet Revolution were several. Quebec was to be speedily modernized. The survival of the French language and culture was to be guaranteed. The economy of Quebec was to be in the hands of the citizens of Quebec. French Canadians wanted to feel fully equal in Canada.

The government of Quebec made great changes during the 1960s and 70s. Education and medical services were brought under government rather than church

Quebec has vast energy resources. These lie not in oil or coal or uranium but in water power. Many fast-flowing rivers run into James Bay at the southern tip of Hudson Bay. The James Bay power project has flown thousands of workers and millions of tonnes of supplies and equipment to this isolated part of northern Quebec. There one of the world's largest hydro-electric complexes is being built.

control. Modern schools and hospitals were built for the Quebec people. Laws were passed to protect the use of the French language and to ensure the survival of French-Canadian culture. Other laws guaranteed the rights of labour unions and provided social benefits. In some cases,

List 3 goals of the Quiet Revolution.
What do you think were the most important achievements of this period in Quebec's history?
List 3 groups that developed different approaches to the future.

1900 1910 1920 1930 1940 1950 1960 1970 1980 1990 2000

such as in consumer rights, these laws were stronger than those in other parts of Canada. The government took more active part in developing provincial resources. In 1963 Quebec bought out all hydro-electric companies in the province. In the seventies the province undertook to build the world's biggest hydro power project in the James Bay region.

Quebec was becoming an active society with increasing self-confidence. This could be clearly seen in the arts. Hundreds of new musicians, writers, painters, and film-makers began to use their talents to portray the new Quebec. In politics, provincial leaders were ready to defend Quebec's interests capably and intelligently. People were gaining a new pride in their province. They began to call themselves Québécois (Quebeckers) rather than French Canadians.

Nearly all Quebeckers agreed with the goals of the Quiet Revolution. They had different ideas on the best way to achieve these goals. One group wanted Quebec to have more influence on the federal government in Ottawa. This group was led by people like Jean Marchand, Pierre Trudeau, and Jean Chrétien. Another group felt Quebec would be better off with far fewer ties to the rest of Canada. They saw Quebec's culture and interests as apart from those of other Canadians. They thought Quebec should be politically independent. René Lévesque, a former Liberal, united many people who felt this way in a new political party called the Parti Québécois.

Vive la France! Vive le Québec! Vive le Québec *libre!* President de Gaulle's words from the balcony of Montreal city hall were greeted with a roar of cheers. He had appealed to the deepest feelings of many Quebeckers. In Ottawa, the reaction was very different. By encouraging the Quebec independence movement in this way, the French president had "interfered" in Canada's internal affairs.

A far smaller group believed Quebec could only be free through violent revolution. They called themselves the Front de Libération du Québec (FLQ). They pledged themselves to a war of liberation. The first stage in this war was terrorism.

THE QUIET REVOLUTION 261

The October Crisis

On the morning of 5 October 1970 James Cross, a British diplomat, was kidnapped at gunpoint from his Montreal home. The kidnappers soon identified themselves as members of the FLQ terrorist organization. They demanded a ransom of half a million dollars. They also wanted free TV and radio time to broadcast their views to the Quebec people. FLQ members in prison for terrorist activities were to be released and given free passage out of Canada along with the kidnappers. They warned that Cross would be executed if their demands were not met. The FLQ hoped the kidnapping would spark a wave of violence that would result in the separation of Quebec from Canada.

Canadians were numb with shock. Terrorism could be expected on the other side of the world, not in nice, safe Canada. Police seemed to be able to find no clues to the Cross kidnapping. Then, five days later, the terrorists struck again.

On Saturday 10 October Pierre Laporte, the Quebec minister of labour was playing football with his son outside his suburban home. Armed men seized him and dragged him into a car. This second kidnapping drove many people in Quebec into a state of near panic.

For two months James Cross sat facing the wall in a room in the terrorists' hideout. He never saw his kidnappers except with masks over their heads. When he was taken to the bathroom he was always blindfolded so he would not be able to recognize his surroundings. He passed the time by playing solitaire. Sometimes he was allowed to watch TV. This picture, as it appeared in newspapers around the world, was taken by the FLQ to prove he was still alive.

The War Measures Act

The federal and provincial governments acted together in the face of crisis. The police seemed to be getting nowhere. They did not know where the next move might come from. They feared the FLQ might go even further. Finally Premier Bourassa of Quebec asked the federal government to proclaim the War Measures Act. This gave the police special powers to search, question, and arrest suspects.

Soldiers cordon off the street while police negotiate with the kidnappers of James Cross.

FOCUS

What demands were made by the kidnappers of James Cross?
Why did the government proclaim the War Measures Act? How did it use the powers the act gave it?
What were the results of the October Crisis?

Under the War Measures Act 497 people were arrested and held for up to three weeks. Most of them were later released without charge. They had been imprisoned merely "on suspicion." The army was called in to assist the police. Soldiers in full battle dress bearing machine guns patrolled the streets of Montreal, Quebec, and Ottawa.

On 17 October, police were tipped off about an abandoned car. When the bomb squad unlocked the trunk they found the lifeless body of Pierre Laporte. He had been strangled with the chain of his own religious medal.

It was ordinary police work, not the War Measures Act, that finally found James Cross. On 3 December, police and soldiers surrounded the house where Cross had been held for nearly 9 weeks. All Canada watched as the

An armed soldier mounts guard over the funeral of Pierre Laporte.

deal for his release was negotiated. Television crews in helicopters followed the kidnappers' car as it raced at 80 km/h through downtown streets to Man and His World, the site of Expo 67. There Cross was released into the custody of the Cuban consul while the kidnappers were flown to Cuba.

On 6 November one of the kidnappers of Pierre Laporte had been found in a closet during a search of a Montreal apartment. Police did not realize till later the others were hiding behind a partition in the closet. It was not until 28 December that they were found in a secret underground tunnel in an abandoned farmhouse 30 km southeast of Montreal.

After the Crisis

The results of the October Crisis were far-reaching. The FLQ was in ruins. Any sympathy Quebeckers had for the organization was wiped out. Those who believed in separatism for Quebec were now firmly convinced it would have to come by peaceful means. Other Canadians, both English and French, became truly aware of the feelings dividing the country for the first time. They resolved to work even harder at co-operation and understanding.

Canadians had learned a bitter lesson. Their country was not immune to violence and terror. How could they prevent similar occurrences in the future?

The funeral of Pierre Laporte.

René Lévesque and the Parti Québécois

For many English Canadians, separatism means René Lévesque. He, more than anyone else, represents the separatist movement. Lévesque led the first government in the history of Quebec that avowed the intention of taking the province out of Confederation. In 1980 his government asked the people of Quebec to vote on the question of the political independence of Quebec.

René Lévesque was born in 1922 in New Carlisle, Quebec. He grew up in a town where both English and French were spoken. As a boy, Lévesque often fought and traded insults with English kids.

Lévesque was a bright but restless student. He intended to become a lawyer, but dropped out of law school. He turned to journalism instead. Lévesque's skilled reports on the news soon made him one of the most popular radio and television personalities in Quebec.

After the death of Duplessis, the Liberals were looking for good political candidates in order to win the 1960 provincial election. They recruited the popular Lévesque. The Liberals won the election and Lévesque became a member of Jean Lesage's cabinet. He was one of the leading figures of the Quiet Revolution.

A Liberal Cabinet Minister

"Maîtres chez nous," or "Masters in our own house," became the Liberal slogan. Lévesque believed strongly that Quebec should control its own economy. The provincial government bought out the last privately owned hydro-electric companies in Quebec to make them part of the vast corporation of Hydro-Québec.

During this period of the Quiet Revolution, it seemed that the aims of Quebec often conflicted with the aims of the federal government and of the other provinces. Some Quebeckers became more and more

René Lévesque in the Quebec National Assembly.

frustrated with Quebec's role in Canada, extremists and terrorists were beginning to fight for the "liberation" of Quebec. The rise of the FLQ was marked by riots and bombings in the 1960s. Other French Canadians were divided and confused as to the future of their province and their country.

Lévesque was frustrated too, but violence was not his answer. He was looking for a political solution to Quebec's problems. In 1967, while the majority of Canadians were celebrating the Centennial of Confederation, René Lévesque came to the conclusion that only an independent Quebec could protect the language, culture, and economy of Quebec. The Liberal party was firmly committed to the federal system. As Lévesque could no longer support this, he left the party.

Lévesque's views on the FLQ kidnappers of October 1970:

If they really thought they had a cause, they killed it along with Pierre Laporte. By shaming themselves, they have given a bad name to the entire separatist movement.

Their act was not only criminal but senseless. One can only hope that they live long enough to see that they stand for nothing and represent no one who matters. That would be the worst punishment they could have.

FOCUS

What was Lévesque's career before he entered politics?
Why did Lévesque leave the Liberal party?
Other than political independence for Quebec, what are some of the policies of the Parti Québécois?

The Democratic Approach

In 1968, Lévesque was elected as leader of a new political party, the Parti Québécois. This new separatist party attracted a wide range of Quebeckers. Among its strongest supporters were many of the young and well educated. They looked forward to an exciting future in a new, independent country. However, party members believed in democracy. A free and democratic vote was the only road to the political independence of Quebec.

The PQ pledged to end corruption in Quebec politics, protect the French language and aid the weaker groups in society. To ease fears that independence might bring a loss of money and jobs, Lévesque stressed that an independent Quebec would have close economic ties with Canada.

The PQ had many supporters. Yet in the provincial election of 1970 and 1973 they were unable to turn votes into seats in the legislature. In 1976 there came a dramatic turnaround. Quebec voters were tired of what they saw as mismanagement by the Liberals under Bourassa. Lévesque led the PQ to a huge victory over the Liberals.

Many Canadians in other provinces thought that the election of a PQ government meant the end of Confederation.

Jacques Parizeau, leader of the Parti Québécois

Many Canadians were stunned. It took several months before English Canadians recovered from the shock of having a separatist government in power in Quebec.

Lévesque knew much of his support had come from people who were not really in favour of separatism. Quebeckers had just wanted to get rid of the Liberals. The Parti Québécois had promised that a vote for their party did not automatically mean separatism. That question was to be voted on at a later date. The PQ set to work to persuade the people that independence was the best answer to Quebec's problems. Across the country, Canadians waited anxiously as Quebeckers prepared to vote for or against Canada.

The Referendum

The Parti Québécois had promised to give Quebeckers a chance to vote on their future. Late in 1979 they announced that chance would come on 20 May 1980. For the first time in the history of Canada an entire province would vote on the idea of leaving Confederation.

PQ leaders laboured for years over the exact wording of the question they would put to the voters. They knew many people were afraid of separatism. They wanted to persuade them the idea was not really dangerous. They finally asked the Quebeckers to vote *oui* (yes) or *non* (no) to giving the Quebec government "a mandate to negotiate sovereignty-association with Canada."

What the Referendum Question Meant

By *sovereignty* the question meant that Quebec would be politically independent. Only the Quebec government could collect taxes. Quebec would run its own foreign affairs. No law passed in Ottawa would have any effect in Quebec. By *association* the question meant that Quebec would still be tied to Canada economically. The two "countries" would use the same money. They would have the same tariffs on imports. By *mandate to negotiate* the question meant that a *oui* vote would not necessarily mean Quebec would leave Canada. It only meant the government would try to work out a deal with the rest of the country. The government also promised Quebeckers they would get another chance to vote on any agreement reached.

Oui or *Non*

People for and against the political independence of Quebec feverishly prepared to win over the hearts and minds of the voters. They bombarded the province with rallies, speeches, pamphlets, and radio and TV ads.

Lévesque and his followers launched a passionate campaign. They claimed a *oui* vote was needed to protect the French language and culture of Quebec. Even if a *oui* vote did not lead to sovereignty-association, it would give Quebec the power to negotiate a better deal from the federal government. Lévesque urged his fellow citizens to remember their history and their pride in their homeland when they went to vote.

Leading the *non* side against the idea of sovereignty-association was Claude Ryan. Ryan had been the editor of *Le Devoir,* the influential Quebec newspaper started by Henri Bourassa in 1910. Even though he had no experience in politics Ryan had been chosen as the new leader of the Liberal party. This was his first real political campaign. Many people regarded this as a test of his leadership ability.

Ryan started the campaign by attacking the wording of the question. He stressed that the PQ was trying to disguise separatism by calling it sovereignty-association. Many thought Ryan's approach was too dry. They said he should appeal to people's feelings, not just to their minds. However, as the campaign progressed, Ryan's speeches became more passionate. He began to impress the voters as a sincere and dedicated man.

Members of all three federal parties threw their support to the *non* side. Pierre Trudeau used his personal popularity in Quebec to persuade people of the advantages of staying in Canada. Conservative leader Joe Clark and NDP leader Ed Broadbent put aside party differences to work for the unity of their country. One million Canadians signed a petition to tell the people of Quebec they wanted them in Canada. A group of Ontario high school students made their statement by travelling to Quebec to work for the *non* side on the day of the vote. One man flew a plane over Quebec towing a banner saying "Canada loves you!"

What does the term "sovereignty-association" mean?
How did some non-Quebeckers get involved in the campaign?
How did the "Yvettes" affect the referendum results?
Do you think the idea of separatism is finished in Quebec?

20 May 1980

On referendum day Quebeckers streamed to the polls. People waited in long lines as 85% of the 4 362 588 eligible voters cast their ballots. When the polls closed people across the nation waited in hushed suspense as the first results trickled in. Within an hour the outcome was clear. Lévesque and the PQ had been dealt a considerable defeat. Only 40% had voted *oui*. Almost

60% of Quebeckers had voted *non*. They did not want even to negotiate an independent Quebec. They wanted to stay in Canada.

The defeat of the referendum doomed Lévesque's dream of independence for Quebec. Shortly after, in 1985, he resigned as premier. In 1987, he died, and his funeral attracted large crowds. Though most Quebeckers could not accept his ideas of separatism, they loved the man with the giant heart who had given so much of his life for the people of Quebec.

After the departure of Lévesque, support for the Parti Québécois declined to about 20% — the same percentage of the population which had supported separatism in the early 1960s. For the present, the separatist movement has lost the support of the vast majority of the people of Quebec.

The Yvette Movement

The turning point in the referendum debate came with the Yvette campaign.

Lise Payette, a PQ cabinet minister, made a speech in which she called Claude Ryan's wife an "Yvette." She even went on to accuse all women who voted against the PQ of being "Yvettes." Yvette was the name of a girl in a grade two reader used in Quebec. The reader showed Yvette staying home to cook and sew while her brother had exciting adventures. Payette was implying that women who were against sovereignty-association were submissive to men and unable to think for themselves. Payette soon regretted her careless remark.

Enraged women in Quebec started an Yvette movement. Within a week of Payette's comment, the "Yvettes" held a mass rally of 15 000 women. They showed their love of Canada and their anger at being insulted. One of the speakers proudly said, "We are mothers who have inherited this great country of Canada from our ancestors. We want to hand it on to our children intact."

The Yvette rally was the first serious setback for the PQ. Payette's apology came too late to make any difference. From this point on, the federalist campaign gathered momentum. A large majority of Quebec women voted *non* in the referendum. One PQ organizer commented, "The Yvettes killed us."

A Distinct Society

"I know that in the Province of Quebec, there are wounds to be healed, worries to be calmed, enthusiasms to be rekindled, and bonds of trust to be established...
"We will have to make commitments and take concrete steps to reach the objective... to convince the Quebec National Assembly to give its consent to the new Canadian Constitution with honour and enthusiasm."
Brian Mulroney, Sept Îles, August 1984

The Constitutional Act of 1982 was popular everywhere in Canada, except in Quebec. Although the constitutional agreement was legally binding on Quebec, it was unacceptable that it had not been agreed to by the government of Quebec.

Mulroney's vision

Prime Minister Mulroney was determined to resolve the issue as soon as he took office. Meetings were held with various provincial leaders, including Robert Bourassa, the new premier of Quebec.

Because of its distinctive features, most Quebec leaders have always regarded Quebec as being more than just another province in Canada. Other Canadian leaders opposed granting special status to Quebec, as being disruptive, and potentially weakening the powers of the federal government. While Prime Minister, Trudeau had fought for equal rights for French- and English-speaking Canadians in all parts of Canada, but he was strongly opposed to special rights for Quebec.

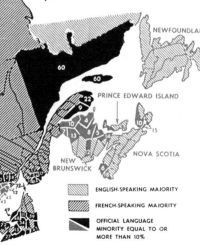

CANADA
Census Divisions where the Official Language Minority is equal to or more than 10% of the Population

Source: Census of Canada, 1961
Drawn by McGill Geography Department, 1967

ENGLISH-SPEAKING MAJORITY
FRENCH-SPEAKING MAJORITY
OFFICIAL LANGUAGE MINORITY EQUAL TO OR MORE THAN 10%

In 1963 Prime Minister Pearson asked Davidson Dunton and André Laurendeau to lead a Royal Commission on Bilingualism and Biculturalism. The "Bi and Bi" commission report was a thoughtful analysis of French-English relations in Canada. However, it did not ignore the presence and needs of other cultural groups in Canada, such as the Chinese, the Italians, and the Ukrainians. Many of the commission's ideas have become government policy.

Jean-Luc Pépin and John Robarts led a similar commission in the 1970s to study the issue of national unity.

This map of Canada was published by the Bi and Bi commission in its report in 1967. It shows areas of Quebec where English-speaking Canadians make up more than 10% of the population in solid black. It shows areas of the rest of Canada where French-speaking people make up more than 10% of the population in solid colour. The commission recommended that these areas be made "bilingual districts." The federal government provides services to these districts in both languages.

How did Trudeau and Mulroney differ in their views of special rights for Quebec?
What were the key ideas of the Meech Lake Accord?
What is the current status of the Meech Lake Accord?

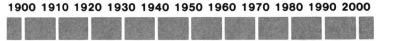

1900 1910 1920 1930 1940 1950 1960 1970 1980 1990 2000

Meech Lake Accord

Mulroney believed that recognition of Quebec's special status would be necessary in order to bring Quebec back into the constitutional agreement. A conference was held at Meech Lake, the Prime Minister's summer residence in Quebec, on April 30, 1987. The principles that were agreed upon there have since been known as the Meech Lake Accord:
— Quebec is recognized as a "distinct society" within Canada;
— provinces have the right to recommend the appointment of Supreme Court judges and senators from their province;
— future changes to federal institutions (such as numbers of members of the House of Commons, Senate, and Supreme Court) and changes from territories to provinces would require agreement by *all* provinces as well as the Canadian parliament;
— provinces could opt out of new national social programs, and receive revenue from Ottawa for their own programs, if they met "national objectives".

The Meech Lake Accord was to go into effect when it had been approved by the Canadian government and *all* provinces.

The accord was popular in most parts of Canada. It had the approval of all three federal parties; it was quickly approved by 8 of the 10 provinces. Opponents felt that the price paid to bring Quebec into the constitution had been too great. They felt that the agreement weakened the powers of the federal government too much. Many also felt that the phrase "distinct society" had no precise legal meaning, and would undoubtedly cause legal and constitutional problems in the future.

Prime Minister Mulroney did not in fact succeed in his major objectives: to return Quebec to the constitution, end the era of conflict and crisis, and to replace it with a period of co-operation. It remains to be seen what the price of compromise for unity will be.

The Meech Lake Accord was not approved by Manitoba and Newfoundland, but in the summer of 1992, all provinces and national leaders agreed to a new constitutional proposal to present for their constituents' approval.

In 1880 the song that would become Canada's national anthem was written by Adolphe-Basile Routhier and Calixa Lavallée to help celebrate French Canada's national day, St. Jean Baptiste Day. It was an instant hit.

In 1908, to celebrate the 300th anniversary of the founding of Quebec, Stanley Weir wrote English words to Lavallée's famous tune. His version became popular in English Canada.

However, it was not until 1980 that parliament gave full recognition to *O Canada* as the national anthem. Minor changes were made in the English words, but the French version is as Routhier wrote it.

The National Anthem

Ô Canada! terre de nos aïeux,
Ton front est ceint de fleurons glorieux!
Car ton bras sait porter l'épée,
Il sait porter la croix!
Ton histoire est une épopée
Des plus brillants exploits.
Et ta valeur, de foi trempée,
Protégera nos foyers et nos droits.
Protégera nos foyers et nos droits.

O Canada! Our home and native land!
True patriot love in all thy sons command.
With glowing hearts we see thee rise,
The True North strong and free!
From far and wide, O Canada,
We stand on guard for thee.
God keep our land glorious and free!
O Canada, we stand on guard for thee!
O Canada, we stand on guard for thee.

A DISTINCT SOCIETY 269

The Return of Robert Bourassa

In 1985 the Parti Québécois was defeated by the Liberal Party, and Robert Bourassa returned as Premier. After a decade of controversial government by the Parti Québécois, the people of Quebec seemed ready for a period of more stable government and economic growth.

Bourassa's first years in office were both popular and successful. His demand that Quebec be recognized as a "distinct society" was accepted in the Meech Lake Accord; once again Quebec was a part of the Canadian constitution. The Quebec economy was helped by the federal government which granted federal contracts for airplane, shipping, and other industries. Phase 2 of the James Bay project was to begin in 1988, with the promise of vastly increasing hydro-electric resources for use in Quebec and for export to the United States. The Quebec economy prospered, unemployment decreased, and once again Montreal became a dynamic and prosperous city. It appeared that Quebec was headed towards economic growth and harmonious relations with the rest of Canada.

Bill 101 — The Language Issue Again

In 1977, the Parti Québécois government had passed Bill 101, a bill to entrench French as the official language and the language of use in the workplace and throughout Quebec society. The bill was supported by most francophones. Many anglophones were opposed to some parts of the bill restricting the use of the English language.

Ten years of Bill 101

1977 — Parti Québécois introduces Bill 101, as a charter to protect the French language in Quebec:
— French was to be the official language in Quebec;
— all signs and billboards were to be in French only;
— the language of instruction in schools was to be French for all children except for children of parents who previously lived in Quebec and spoke English.

1982 — the Quebec Supreme Court ruled that signs must be in French, but could also include other languages (e.g., English)

1984 — the Supreme Court of Canada upheld the right of parents of immigrant children to have instruction in English if preferred

1988 — the Supreme Court of Canada heard an appeal on the right to have signs in English. The Supreme Court ruled that:
— the government of Quebec had the right to require that all signs be in French;
— the government of Quebec did *not* have the right to forbid the additional use of other languages on the signs;

1988 — Premier Bourassa's government passed legislation:
— requiring *French only* signs on the outside of buildings;
— permitting *bilingual* signs on the *inside* of buildings;
— used Clause 33 of the Charter of Rights (the notwithstanding clause) to prevent the courts from over-ruling this legislation.

1989 — the government of Manitoba announced that because of these policies of the government of Quebec, it would not support the Meech Lake Accord.

Once again the language-issue controversy divided Canadians in Quebec and across Canada. The "notwithstanding" clause had been introduced into the Charter of Rights as a compromise to gain the acceptance of some of the Western provinces who feared placing too much power in the Supreme Court of Canada. However, its use in Quebec to violate the basic language rights of the anglophone minority in Quebec caused an immediate crisis all across Canada. Many wondered what other rights within Quebec might be modified within the concept of Quebec as a "distinct society" as described in the Meech Lake Accord.

The language issue once more threatened to disrupt the precarious harmony of francophones and anglophones in Quebec. Others, including the governments of Manitoba and New Brunswick, began to wonder about the possible consequences of the Meech Lake Accord and the use of the notwithstanding clause by *other* provinces in the future.

The Notwithstanding Clause (Clause 33 of the Charter of Rights)

Parliament, or the legislature of a province, may expressly declare an Act of Parliament or the legislature, as the case may be, that the Act or a provision thereof shall operate *notwithstanding* provision included in... this charter.

The clause was included in the Charter as a compromise to gain the agreement of several of the Western provinces. They feared the Charter might have given too much power to the courts, and taken too much power away from the local legislature.

Reactions to the Bourassa legislation
"All of us are human beings first, with rights, and I'll fight to my last breath for that....Rights are rights are rights; there is no such thing as inside rights and outside rights. No such thing as rights for the tall and rights for the short. No such thing as rights for the front and rights for the back or rights for the East and rights for the West."

Clifford Lincoln, Minister of the Environment, Quebec, 1989

Questions and Activities

Test Yourself

Match the people in Column A with the descriptions in Column B.

A	B
1. Samuel de Champlain	a) leader of the Union Nationale
2. Maurice Duplessis	b) a Father of Confederation
3. James Cross	c) founder of Quebec in 1608
4. Claude Ryan	d) first leader of Parti Québécois
5. George Etienne Cartier	e) leader of the *non* forces in the 1980 referendum
6. René Lévesque	f) kidnap victim of the FLQ

Quick Recall

Identify the following in a few sentences:
1. FLQ
2. Yvette Campaign
3. Quiet Revolution
4. Quebec Referendum
5. Acadia
6. War Measures Act

Instant Analysis

Some statements can be labelled true or false. Others may depend on a variety of facts, opinions, and special situations. Place these statements in three categories: True, False, or It Depends. Explain your answer.
1. Quebec wants to separate from Canada.
2. English and French Canadians rarely co-operate.
3. Like other provincial governments, governments of Quebec are usually prepared to defend their provincial rights and responsibilities.
4. The Quiet Revolution was a period of tremendous change for Quebec.
5. Confederation has generally been a bad deal for French Canadians.
6. Language rights will always be an issue in Quebec and in Canada.

Do Some Research

1. Find out more about the expulsion of the Acadians. Why did the British government decide the Acadians had to go? How many were forcibly removed from their homes and lands? Where were they sent? How many ever returned to their homeland? Where are there pockets of their descendants in North America today?
2. Select a newspaper item about an issue involving French Canadians or Quebec.
   Write a news report to accompany the news clipping, including a paragraph on each of the following:
   a) the issue or problem
   b) The Quebec or francophone position
   c) The anglophone or other viewpoint
   d) *your opinion* as to how the issue should be resolved
3. Most Canadians do not realize that O Canada was originally a French Canadian song. The lyrics in French are quite different from the lyrics in English. Find or make an accurate translation of the French lyrics and compare the two. What conclusions can you draw about the ways the two versions reflect the country?
4. The War Measures Act has been used at two other periods in Canadian history. Investigate these periods and compare and contrast the actions taken under this law.

Ideas for Discussion

1. Assume that you are a Canadian living in New France during the British Conquest. Write a letter to the new British governor outlining both your fears and your hopes for the future.
2. What do you think would have happened if René Lévesque and the *Oui* forces had won the Quebec Referendum in 1980? Write a brief summary of the possible events. Present your ideas to the rest of the class.
3. Organize a class debate on the use of the War Measures Act during the October Crisis. The motion you debate might be: Resolved that the War Measures Act was an unnecessary threat to civil liberties and should not have been used.
4. What does the term "official bilingualism" mean? Do you support the policy? Take a vote to find out the opinion of your class on official bilingualism.
5. Examine the pictures on the next page. What do they tell you about the Quebec people and Quebec culture? Do you think that they give an accurate picture of life in the province? Using these pictures, and your other knowledge of Quebec, write a report on "The People of Quebec Today".

Be Creative

1. **Exchange letters, tapes, photos, and information packages with a francophone school in Quebec or elsewhere in Canada. Perhaps you can even organize visits between your two schools.**
2. **Listen to some of the music of French Canada. Perhaps your French teacher could help you translate some of the lyrics.**
3. **Make a bilingual poster advertising the benefits of living in a nation with two official languages.**

You Are There

It is May 1980. In a few days, you, the people of Quebec, will be voting in the referendum on sovereignty-association. A Quebec television network has brought people together from across the province for a live debate. Some are prominent people in the news. Others are ordinary Quebeckers. You are among them, and tonight your opinion will be heard.

Those present include:

René Lévesque
Claude Ryan
Pierre Trudeau
A young student
A single mother
An English-speaking Montrealer
A dairy farmer from the Eastern Townships
A fishing boat captain from Gaspé
A member of the Yvette movement
A former member of the FLQ
A hotel owner from a Laurentian resort
Reporters from small-town French and English newspapers
Reporters from three Montreal daily newspapers

As special guests, the network has also invited:

An Acadian teacher from Moncton, New Brunswick
A worker for Newfoundland Light and Power at Churchill Falls, Labrador
A French-Canadian miner from Sudbury, Ontario
A member of the Alberta cabinet
The mayor of a mainly French-speaking town in Manitoba
A Ukrainian-speaking political scientist from Alberta.

The debate is chaired by a diplomat from Belgium, a country that also has two official languages.

Are you planning to vote *oui* or *non*? Might this debate change your mind? It's time to find out. The lights are on. The cameras are rolling. The meeting is open.

Chapter Nine

Regional Report
ADVANCE ORGANIZER

1

Yukon
Capital: Whitehorse
Area: 483 000 km²
Population: 23 500
Origins: 46% British, 5% French, 15% Native People, 8% German, 26% other
Industries: mining (lead, zinc, oil and gas production and exploration), fishing, trapping, hunting
Energy sources: thermal and hydro-electricity, oil, gas

Northwest Territories
Capital: Yellowknife
Area: 3 380 000 km²
Population: 52 200
Origins: 25% British, 6% French, 33% Inuit, 21% Indian, 15% other
Industries: mining (gold, lead, zinc, copper, oil and gas production and exploration), fishing, trapping, hunting
Energy sources: thermal electricity, oil, gas

2

British Columbia
Capital: Victoria
Area: 949 000 km²
Population: 2 900 000
Origins: 58% British, 4% French, 2% Native Peoples, 9% German, 6% Scandinavian, 3% Italian, 3% Dutch, 3% Oriental, 12% other
Industries: lumbering, pulp and paper, wood products, mining (coal, copper, lead, zinc, gas), tourism, farming, fishing
Energy sources: hydro-electricity, coal, gas

3

Alberta
Capital: Edmonton
Area: 661 000 km²
Population: 2 380 000
Origins: 47% British, 6% French, 2% Native Peoples, 12% German, 8% Ukrainian, 4% Scandinavian, 21% other
Industries: mining (oil, gas, coal), farming, petro-chemical industries, meat packing, food processing
Energy sources: oil, gas, coal

Saskatchewan
Capital: Regina
Area: 652 000 km²
Population: 1 014 000
Origins: 42% British, 6% French, 4% Native Peoples, 20% German, 9% Ukrainian, 5% Scandinavian, 14% other
Industries: farming, mining (potash, oil, gas), meat packing, petroleum products
Energy sources: oil, gas, hydro-electricity

Manitoba
Capital: Winnipeg
Area: 640 000 km²
Population: 1 082 000
Origins: 42% British, 9% French, 4% Native Peoples, 12% German, 11% Ukrainian, 22% other
Industries: machinery and metal products, agricultural implements, meat packing, dairy products, farming, mining (nickel, copper, zinc), lumbering
Energy sources: hydro-electricity

Word List
compromise
decentralized
diversity
freight rates
industrial waste
isolationist
natural resources
regionalism
renewable resources
resource industry
secondary industry
taxation

4

Ontario
Capital: Toronto
Area: 1 069 000 km²
Population: 9 400 000
Origins: 59% British, 10% French, 6% German, 6% Italian, 3% Dutch, 2% Portuguese, 2% West Indian, 12% other
Industries: automobiles, machinery and metal products, food processing, electronics, farming, mining (nickel, zinc, gold, silver, uranium), lumbering, pulp and paper
Energy sources: nuclear and hydro-electricity

5

Quebec
Capital: Quebec City
Area: 1 541 000 km²
Population: 6 530 000
Origins: 79% French, 11% British, 10% other
Industries: lumbering, pulp and paper, mining (iron ore, copper, asbestos, aluminum and other metal processing, gold, silver), farming, electrical and transportation equipment, textiles, clothing
Energy sources: hydro-electricity

6

New Brunswick
Capital: Fredericton
Area: 73 000 km²
Population: 723 000
Origins: 58% British, 37% French, 5% other
Industries: Farming, food processing, fishing, mining (zinc, copper, lead), lumbering and pulp and paper
Energy sources: thermal and hydro-electricity, nuclear electricity (potential)

Nova Scotia
Capital: Halifax
Area: 55 000 km²
Population: 873 000
Catch: Origins: 77% British, 10% French, 5% German, 8% other
Industries: mining (coal), steel, farming, fishing, food processing, tourism
Energy sources: thermal electricity, oil (potential)

Prince Edward Island
Capital: Charlottetown
Area: 5657 km²
Population: 127 000
Origins: 85% British, 12% French, 3% other
Industries: farming, fishing, food processing, tourism
Energy sources: thermal electricity

Newfoundland and Labrador
Capital: St. John's
Area: 405 000 km²
Population: 568 000
Origins: 94% British, 3% French, 3% other
Industries: mining (iron ore), fishing, fish processing, lumbering, pulp and paper, oil exploration
Energy sources: hydro-electricity, oil (potential)

The Challenge of Regionalism

A typical Prairie landscape with grain fields and grain elevators.

There are three main themes in Canadian history. The first is the drive to build a strong country separate from the United States. The second is the struggle to accommodate the rights of two founding peoples, the French and the English. The third is regionalism — the recognition of the very different histories, geographies, cultures, and economic strengths and weaknesses of the various regions of Canada.

Canada is the second largest country in the world. Its territory covers about 10 million km². Despite this vastness, less than one-tenth of its area is occupied by cities, towns, or farmland. The rest is wilderness, mountains, or the biting cold of the North. The regions of Canada are kept apart by geography. British Columbia is separated from the prairies by the Rockies. Dividing the prairies from central Canada are rocky woodlands of northern Ontario. The mountains of Maine cut the Maritimes off from Quebec, and Newfoundland is kept from the mainland by the sea. The North is isolated by its own geography — the lonely expanse of the Canadian shield and Arctic tundra.

Balancing Powers

Today, many of the provinces want to see a more decentralized system of government. They want to have more say in matters that directly concern them. They seek greater control in many areas of government: cultural affairs, natural resources, taxation, distribution of goods and services, and their general economy. Finding the best balance between federal and provincial powers is an essential task for Canada.

Each region of Canada has been subject to its own forces — history, geography, politics, culture, language, traditions, and economics. Some of these forces help keep the Confederation together; others hold it apart. Are we Canadians, or are we Albertans,

What have been three main themes of Canadian history?
What are the six regions of Canada?
What factors have contributed to the growth of "regionalism" in Canada?
Why does regionalism conflict with centralism? Give examples.

Québécois, Ontarians, and Newfoundlanders? Prime Minister Trudeau once said, "My name is Québécois and my name is Canadian too." What did he mean?

What are the backgrounds of the people of the regions of Canada? What sort of jobs do they have? What are their problems? What are their similarities and their differences?

What do they contribute to Confederation, and what do they expect in return?

In each region, the physical elements helped to shape the attitudes and livelihoods of the people. Natural forces influenced not only regional economics, but social patterns as well. In Newfoundland the sea encouraged tiny, isolated fishing settlements. This in turn bred a relatively slow-paced, "small-town" way of life. Similarly, the harsh living conditions of the Prairies forced the settlers to adopt a communal, "co-operative" lifestyle. This approach to problem-solving eventually led to many government policies that affected all Canadians.

The isolation of one region from another had a significant effect on Canada's development. Each region had risen from its own cultural roots. It was with some reluctance that they followed one another into Confederation. Local concerns remained more important than national issues. Strong regional loyalty still is a part of the Canadian character.

The idea of Canada was born principally in the areas that are now Ontario and Quebec. They were the largest of the original provinces. They were further strengthened by the policies of the new federal government. As other provinces entered Confederation, they often felt neglected in favour of Quebec and Ontario.

Quebec sculptor
J.J. Bourgault of
St-Jean-Port Joli

The North

In the past, residents of the North used local materials for buildings. Today, in Tuktuk, N.W.T., most buildings have been prefabricated elsewhere and put together here.

Yellowknife, N.W.T., in the late 1940s was a remote community. Even today the usual way in and out is by airplane.

Musk oxen are hardy enough to survive harsh Northern winters. In summer, their fur helps them ignore the blackflies.

CBC Inuvik announcer/operators who covered the Northern Games at Inuvik in 1979 in English, Loucheux, Slavey, and Eskimo.

Nature and Technology

When Canadians refer to the North they generally mean the Yukon and the Northwest Territories. This immense region occupies 40% of Canada's total land area. Yet less than 1% of the population lives there. Labrador and Northern Quebec should probably also be considered as part of the North. However, Canadians usually reserve the term for the territories.

The population of the North divides roughly into two groups. Immigrants to the North, often from southern Canada or the United States, usually live in the larger communities such as Whitehorse and Yellowknife. Some of these people are permanent residents. Others come to take a job for a few years and then move back south. The other group is the native people of the North. They are over 50% of the population. This is by far the largest proportion of native people in all the Canadian regions.

The native people belong to two main cultures — the Dene (pronounced *Den-nay*) and the Inuit. The Dene live south of the "tree-line," the northernmost point at which trees grow. Traditionally they depended on the vast herds of caribou that once grazed the land. The Inuit live north of the tree-line — mainly where the northern rivers meet the Arctic Ocean. These people lived by fishing and hunting bear, caribou, and seal.

The traditional way of life in the North was first disrupted by Hudson's Bay Company fur traders. They traded modern conveniences for furs, which were greatly valued in Europe and the South. Gradually the people of the North began to depend on the traders. They became used to things like tobacco, tea, and cooking pots, which had previously been unknown. They began to use guns and ammunition to hunt game.

The next major change occurred when mining and oil companies started to explore the North. The mines, transportation routes, and settlements upset the delicate northern balance of nature. In particular, the migration routes of the caribou were disturbed and the herds grew smaller. A fear of pollution of the Arctic Ocean began to develop. Gradually the natural economy of the North was disappearing.

Caught Between Old and New

The federal government wanted to help the native people of the North prepare for a new way of life. In the early years of the twentieth century they felt the best way to achieve this was through education.

Because the native communities were so small, native children were brought to boarding schools. Here, they were completely cut off from their families for periods of several years. They were often punished if they spoke their native language. They were taught by southern teachers from books meant for southern children. The Inuit and Dene students did not understand these books because nothing in them related to their way of life. These children returned to their families as strangers. They had

The old ways.

Describe the characteristics of the three main Northern groups:
a) "southern" immigrants, b) Dene, c) Inuit.
How have the immigrants disrupted traditional Northern ways of
life? Why do so many people of the North want provincial status?

lost important years of training in hunting, fishing and other life skills. Yet they had not really adapted to the "modern" world.

By midcentury the government thought the native people would be better off in permanent settlements. Southern-style housing was erected in a few "central" locations. The people were encouraged to move to these new homes. Here they could be near stores, schools, medical centres, and other government services. However, moving to these permanent settlements meant the people could no longer follow the migrating caribou or choose the best fishing grounds. Their way of life was killed by the combination of the move and the impact of technology.

The government expected new jobs would soon be available for the native people. The South wanted to exploit the North's natural resources — minerals and oil. However, native people don't generally possess the skills needed to work in mines or on oil rigs. The companies

bring in workers from the South. These people come north for a few years. They make a good deal of money, which they take with them when they go home. The native people often get neither jobs nor profit from this invasion of their land.

The change from the traditional, nomadic way of life has given the native people little. Too often it has meant they are no longer dependent on their own wisdom and the skills of their own hands but on a government welfare cheque.

By the 1960s and 70s the native people of the North began to realize that the government's attempts to help them did not meet native people's needs. They decided to take more responsibility for their own future.

Controlling the Future

The people of the North are striving to gain more control over their own land, its resources, and its economy. The North is the only region which is still more or less a colony. The Northwest Territories and the Yukon are administered by the federal government from Ottawa. Before 1905 Saskatchewan and Alberta were part of the Northwest Territories. In that year their population and development had reached the point where they could manage their own affairs as provinces. The newer inhabitants of the North, as well as the natives, feel the northern territories too are now ready for provincial status.

Canada's native people are the true "founding nation" of Canada. They are demanding that this fact be recognized, as they struggle to regain their way of life within the confines of Confederation. To make their voices heard more clearly, the Inuit and Dene are joining forces with the native peoples of southern Canada. Together they hope to achieve direct participation for native people in federal policy making.

The new ways.

British Columbia

Today, water transport is as important to British Columbia as it was in the past. Steamers chugged into Yale during the Cariboo gold rush, and ferries now ply the waters under the Lion's Gate Bridge in Vancouver.

R.O'Brien

Carving a Kwakiutl totem pole in Thunderbird
Park, Victoria B.C.

Percussion drilling to prospect for copper and
molybdenum.

Skiers on Whistler Mountain.

Butchart Gardens, near Victoria,
were created in an old gravel pit.

Mountains and Seacoast

Canada's westernmost province is British Columbia. The area was settled largely by people who arrived by sea rather than overland from eastern Canada. With the Rocky Mountains on one side of them and the sea on the other, the people of British Columbia have always felt somewhat shut off from the rest of the nation. British Columbia is probably the most "isolationist" of Canada's English-speaking provinces.

This trend reached its peak between 1953 and the early 1970s. During this period, Social Credit Premier W.A.C. Bennett tried to keep the province out of national affairs. As much as possible he wanted British Columbia to function independently from the rest of Canada.

British Columbia

The Social Credit Party has remained in power in British Columbia throughout the 1980s. At first, the premier was Bill Bennett, son of W.A.C. Bennett. He was succeeded by Bill Vander Zalm. Both have fought for the rights of their province against the federal government.

The Vancouver waterfront in the 1980s.

Felling a cedar tree, near Bella Coola.

Bennett said that his province had been a victim in some of the federal government's policies. Ottawa tried to protect Canadian manufacturing industries by placing high tariffs on incoming foreign goods. Most manufacturing in Canada is centred in Ontario and Quebec. Other regions of Canada, like British Columbia, have protested that the tariff policy does nothing for them. Their economies are based on resource industries like lumbering, mining, or farming. These industries depend largely on selling their products abroad. In the past the Ottawa government has done little to help resource industries get good prices. Regions like British Columbia feel it is unfair that Quebec and Ontario are protected by tariffs which all Canadians have to pay. Many business people in British Columbia welcomed the new free trade agreement. It would reduce their dependence on obtaining manufactured goods from central Canada. Opportunities for exchange of goods with the adjacent market in the western United States would be greater.

FOCUS

Can you explain the "isolationist" feelings of many British Columbians?
Why are many British Columbians opposed to Canada's tariff policies?

British Columbians would like to insure that their interests are better protected by the federal government. To this end they would like to receive increased representation in Ottawa. B.C. wants to be sure it has a real voice in the making of government policies.

Not for Sale

At the same time British Columbians wish to be firmly in control of their own economy. In 1979, Canadian Pacific Investments, a subsidiary of the CPR, tried to buy British Columbia's largest resource business, the Macmillan Bloedel paper company. The head office of CPI is in Montreal. Premier Bill Bennett saw the take-over bid as an attempt by central Canadian interests to extend their control of British Columbia's economy.

He firmly stated that British Columbia was "not for sale" and successfully stopped this take-over. The paper company has since been bought by other "outside" interests, but Bennett was expressing an attitude held by many people in the province.

British Columbians often have different attitudes one from another. The people of the fertile fruit-growing valley of the Okanagan do not have the same outlook on life as the Indian fishermen of the Queen Charlotte Islands. Neither do the people of Victoria and the cowboys of the Cariboo. Yet they are all conscious of their identity as westerners.

British Columbia's demands on the federal government are echoed by many other provinces. But with the isolation already created by geography, British Columbians perhaps feel these issues more keenly.

A ranch in Deadman Valley, west of Kamloops.

The Changing Prairies

Some things change, but cattle herding is the same operation today as it was a hundred years ago.

The city of Winnipeg.

Chuckwagon races at the Calgary Stampede.

Sunset on a northern lake, Saskatchewan.

Oil refinery.

The New West

When Canadians talk of the "New West," they usually mean all the provinces west of Ontario. These provinces are united by the common goal of greater political and economic freedom. These are the Prairie provinces — Manitoba, Saskatchewan, and Alberta — and British Columbia, which lies on the Pacific coast. Because of its geography and individual character, British Columbia is often thought of separately from the other western provinces.

The Prairies were settled more rapidly than any other region. Until the 1880s the area was the territory of Indians and Métis who followed the great herds of buffalo. Then the newly built Canadian Pacific Railway brought in would-be farmers. Until the first World War, immigrants flooded into the Canadian West. The first settlers came from eastern Canada, the United States, and the British Isles. From the 1890s on they were joined by people from Poland, Hungary, the Ukraine, and other countries of eastern Europe. As the railways expanded, wheat farms and cattle ranches gradually filled the land.

A Land of Hardship

Living conditions on the Prairies were harsh. The vast remoteness of the region and its severe weather, created a particularly hostile environment. Farming families had to endure dry, searing heat in summer and intense cold in winter. They lived with the knowledge that a storm could level a year's crop in seconds.

These conditions deeply affected the people's attitudes. In the end they helped shape the society. The Prairies forced people to band together if they were to survive. Families helped one another to gather the harvests and raise barns and homesteads. Their co-operation served them well when bad weather or poor

Today, a troop of harvesters goes through a grain field almost as fast as an army of grasshoppers during the Dustbowl years.

economic conditions brought hard times. This spirit of solidarity led to a number of new ideas in Canadian politics. Women first got the right to vote in Manitoba in 1916. In the 1920s and 30s the first large-scale co-operatives were set up on the Prairies. Saskatchewan started the first government hospital plan in 1944.

The western provinces have long felt that central Canada has treated them as an outpost. They have had to cope with tariff policies that favour the central provinces, Ontario and Quebec. In early years they resented the monopoly the CPR was given on the shipment of grain. They had to deal with banks that were based in Montreal or Toronto and did not understand western farmers' problems. Western Canadians feel they have been ignored by the federal government. They have protested this state of affairs since the days of Louis Riel. Resentment reached its peak with the Depression. Economic hard times lingered over the region for more than thirty years. They ended dramatically with the development of the region's major oil and gas reserves.

Energy Resources

In 1973, the world price of energy, especially oil products, shot up dramatically. The economy of Alberta began to boom as oil revenues poured into the province. In spite of a recession in oil prices in the early 1980s, the future of the Western economies seemed bright.

Saskatchewan and Manitoba have not experienced the prosperity of Alberta. Both have suffered through declining grain prices. But in Saskatchewan, they have high hopes for a more diversified economy. And Manitoba has been harnessing its extensive hydro-electric resources to fuel its own industries; it plans to sell electricity to Saskatchewan and Alberta. Manitoba hopes to profit from the oil boom as well.

The West no longer depends entirely upon agriculture. Though the price of wheat and freight rates are still major issues, the chief concern of the typical prairie dweller today is the demand for western oil. Oil has given the western provinces new economic power. They hope to use this power to get political changes that will benefit themselves as well as the rest of Canada. The New West is rising to take its place as an equal partner in Confederation.

Part of the high cost of searching for oil and gas reserves is the expense of operating a drilling rig.

The Price of Energy

An oil drilling rig on farmland in the Peace River district between Fort St. John and Dawson Creek, B.C.

A study of the regions of Canada is not complete without a close look at how the problem of energy supply is affecting the country now and how it will affect us in the future. In many ways the New West is the product of the energy crisis.

Alberta is the centre of Canada's oil boom. The province has more than half of the country's known oil deposits. In 1980 geologists estimated these reserves at a minimum of one trillion barrels. This is 16 times more oil than Saudi Arabia is believed to have.

The Pricing Debate

Since world oil prices shot up in 1973, the government of Alberta has been involved in a number of disputes with the federal government. Other energy-rich provinces have been watching these disputes with interest and concern. The issues centre on the price of oil and how the revenues should be shared. Prime Minister Trudeau maintained that the rise in oil prices within Canada was a major issue for all Canadians. His government insisted that Alberta sell its oil within Canada at below world price.

Describe the position of a) the federal government, b) the Alberta government in the energy debate of the early 1980s. How successful have the Western provinces been in diversifying their economies?

At the same time he placed a tax on oil exported to the United States. Eastern Canada could not use the cheap oil from Alberta because the oil pipeline did not reach that far. The eastern provinces had to pay the world price for imported oil. Therefore the federal government gave some of the export tax money to help offset these higher costs.

Trudeau's oil policies angered many Albertans. To them they were yet another example of how the federal government protected central Canadian interests at the expense of the West. Alberta premier Peter Lougheed produced figures in 1979 that showed Alberta had lost almost $20 billion because the province had sold its oil at below the world price. Lougheed believed Albertans were being denied a rightful source of revenue. They felt entitled to their wealth, as central Canadians had been entitled to theirs.

The Heritage Fund

In 1976, the government of Alberta established the Heritage Fund. The intention was to create a reserve fund from the profits of the oil-and-gas industry, which would be used to develop other industries within Alberta. The Alberta economy was heavily dependent on the oil industry, based on a non-renewable resource. The intention was to develop related industries, such as plastics, petro-chemicals, textiles, and fertilizers. The Fund would also help to create other industries to diversify the economy and to provide jobs for Albertans.

During the prosperous period of the booming oil industry in the 1970s, 30% of all of the provincial revenues were placed in the Heritage Fund, which grew to over $10 billion. However, by the early 1980s, the National Energy Policy had caused a decrease in Revenues in the petroleum industry. From 1983 to 1987, the Heritage Fund received only 15% of oil revenues. By 1986, with the drop in world oil prices, the Alberta economy moved from expansion to recession. There were *no* surplus revenues for the Heritage Fund.

By the late 1980s, the Heritage Fund remained at about $15 billion. This is a significant fund meant to provide investment for the future growth of Alberta. However, it is far below the optimistic dreams of the early 1980s and it has not yet been possible to diversify the Alberta economy. For the immediate future, it appears that Albertans will continue to depend on their oil and agricultural resources.

Non-renewable Resources

Another concern is shared by all the oil-producing provinces. Fossil fuels like oil and gas are non-renewable resources. By the 1990s, supplies may begin to run low, unless new sources are discovered. Then electricity generated from water power and nuclear energy will become the new main sources of energy. In 1980, electricity accounted for about one third of all energy use. This proportion will grow to about one half before the end of the century. Therefore, the importance of Alberta, Newfoundland, and other oil-rich areas is likely to fade somewhat. In the meantime, they naturally wish to sell their resources at the best possible price.

Throughout the 1980s, the Alberta economy fluctuated from boom to recession. Albertans believed that federal government policies were discouraging further exploration for oil. Also, by the late 1980s, the price of oil, which had reached $40 a barrel, had dropped to under $15 a barrel.

In the midst of this uncertainty, Westerners still feel confident, as they have always felt, that the best times are yet to come.

Ontario

The frontier communities of early Upper Canada have become the bustling cities of modern day Ontario.

Iron ore open-pit mining at Atikokan, in northwestern Ontario.

Ontario Place, an entertainment centre on islands specially built in the waters of Lake Ontario. The lighted dome is a movie theatre.

Niagara Falls attracts many tourists and is an important source of electricity.

Moosonee is a favourite tourist centre for "southerners."

The Industrial Heartland

Since the first days of Confederation, Ontario has had the largest population of all the provinces. Today Ontario is home to over a third of all Canadians. Half the nation's manufacturing industries are based in the province.

In recent years most immigrants to Canada have been city dwellers who wish to seek jobs in industry. Therefore they tend to head for the cities of the "golden horseshoe," Canada's industrial centre around the west end of Lake Ontario. As a result, Ontario receives more than half of all immigrants to the country. Ontario has changed from being the most "Anglo-Saxon" province at the turn of the century to being the most "multicultural" one.

Industrial Expansion

Ontario's industries started to grow toward the end of the nineteenth century. The province's forests, farms, and mines supplied the new factories with raw materials. Ontario's natural richness, size, and central situation helped guarantee its success as an industrial region.

Ontario's large population gave the province more seats than any other in the federal House of Commons. This fact, plus its economic importance, helped the province to dominate most national issues.

The development of Canadian industry has been a main concern of this country's economic policies since John A. Macdonald introduced the "national" policy in 1878. The federal government has protected industry by imposing high tariffs on foreign imports. All Canadians had to pay these tariffs. However, a study has shown that over 85% of the jobs protected by tariffs were located in Ontario and its neighbouring province Quebec. Eastern and western Canada have provided, at low prices, the resources that help the industries of Ontario to prosper.

This situation has created much friction over the

The control room in a steel mill in Hamilton.

years between Ontario and the other provinces. By the 1980s the balance of power was shifting. The energy-producing regions of Canada were gaining new economic power. Ontario relied on these regions for much of its fuel. And so Alberta, Saskatchewan, and even Newfoundland were adding a new dimension to the question of economic policy.

This changing balance created new resentments. Many Canadians living in other provinces wanted political power to equal their new economic power. However, Ontario still had the largest population and therefore the most seats in parliament. With support from Quebec, whose economy was also based on industry, Ontario could control political decisions of the federal government.

People tend to think of Ontario's economy as based entirely on industry. Yet many fertile farms still dot the province. Some of Canada's finest vegetables are grown here. Some parts of the Niagara Peninsula are as far south as northern California. In this mild climate and rich soil, vineyards and orchards yield excellent produce.

What natural advantages make Ontario the "industrial heartland?"
How has the tariff, since 1878, encouraged Ontario industries?
Why has northern Ontario not prospered as has southern Ontario?

Northern Ontario

Ontario's industrial growth has occurred in the south of
the province. Northern Ontario is a sparsely settled area
rich in mining and timber resources. However, the region
has never developed a stable economy of its own. The
north has always been dependent on the richer south. The
people of northern Ontario are now demanding that the
provincial government encourage more industrial growth
in the area. This would greatly improve the employment
opportunities in the north.

The Industrial Heartland

For most of the twentieth century, Ontario has been
the richest province in Canada. Taxes paid by Ontario
citizens and businesses have gone in equalization
payments to poorer provinces. As with other
provinces, the Ontario economy has experienced ups
and downs in recent years. The economic slump of the
late 1970s and early 1980s was followed by boom
conditions in the late 1980s. As industry expanded,
employment increased; Ontario again became a
magnet for unemployed people from all across
Canada. Investment capital from Hong Kong, Japan,
and Europe poured into new industries. Large
numbers of immigrants were attracted to settle
particularly around the "golden horseshoe" and
Toronto.

As the heart of the Canadian industrial economy,
the people of Ontario looked forward to the results of
free trade — with hope and some anxiety. The large
population of nearby American states offered great
potential for Canadian industry. It also created some
concern about the potential return flow of American
goods and culture. Ontario has the most to gain
economically, and the most to lose culturally through
closer relations with the United States.

A Sense of Identity

Most people in Canada have a dual sense of identity. They are both
Canadians and Nova Scotians, Canadians and Quebeckers, or
Canadians and Manitobans. In Ontario this sense of a provincial
identity as distinct from the national one is not as strong.

Since 1867 Ontario has been the province with the largest
population. As Canada grew, the province's central location
increased its importance. The nation's capital is situated there.
Perhaps these facts make it harder for the people of Ontario to
distinguish in their hearts between their province and their country.
Certainly they are often surprised at other Canadians' strong
feelings about their own regions.

A pulp and paper mill in northern Ontario.

Quebec

Montreal, seen from Mount Royal a hundred years ago, and from an island in the St. Lawrence River today.

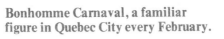

Bonhomme Carnaval, a familiar figure in Quebec City every February.

The Montréal Canadiens and the Québec Nordiques play hockey.

Alcan's aluminium smelter at Jonquière, Quebec, in the Canadian shield.

A coastal village in the Gaspé Peninsula.

La Belle Province

Quebec has always been different from the other provinces of Canada. Many of the provisions of Confederation were designed to protect these differences.

Quebec was settled by the French before the British took over what is now Canada. All other provinces developed under British influence. Quebec was an established community following its own laws, customs, and language. Quebeckers seldom felt welcome in other parts of Canada. This encouraged a tendency for French Canadians to look to their own province for support.

For nearly 200 years Montreal was the business centre of Canada. It was closest to the bustling cities of Boston and New York. Ocean-going ships dropped and picked up cargo there because they could get no further up the St. Lawrence River. Businesses set up their head offices in Montreal. Industry grew up around the city. It was not until the twentieth century that the focus of business activity moved west to Ontario. It was not until the midcentury that Toronto surpassed Montreal in population.

The Economy of Quebec

The Quiet Revolution of the 1960s and 1970s asserted Quebec's cultural and political differences from the rest of Canada. Perhaps the most powerful symbol of the new restless energy of the province is the mammoth James Bay hydro-electric project. Since 1972, 20,000 workers have been carving one of the world's largest energy projects out of the rugged northern wilderness. By 1990 the gigantic dams and generating stations of James Bay will provide Quebec with 40% of its energy needs. Unlike oil and gas, hydro power is a renewable resource. Quebec will be able to prosper because it has a reliable energy supply.

Quebec is also rich in minerals. Asbestos, iron, zinc, and copper are abundant. The rising price of gold in the early 1980s meant a boom for Quebec's gold mines. The province's vast electricity supplies are harnessed to produce aluminum.

The Daniel Johnson Dam (Manic V), finished in 1969, holds back a reservoir of 140 billion m³ and produces over 7 billion kwh each year.

What is meant by the "Quiet Revolution?"
Why was a referendum held in Quebec in 1980? What was the result?
Do any issues currently divide French Canadians and English Canadians?

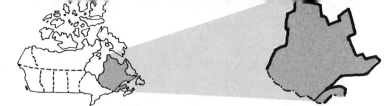

Olympic stadium, Montreal.

La Belle Province

Yet the Quebec economy continued to have its problems. Unemployment continued to run above the national average. The St. Lawrence Seaway and the growth of air travel meant that Montreal was no longer the nation's leading port and financial capital. The fear of separatism in the 1970s caused many companies to move their head offices out of Montreal. Over 100 000 anglophones moved out of Montreal to re-settle in Toronto. Investment from outside the province dried up in the unstable political conditions.

By the mid-1980s, conditions began to improve. Co-operation between Prime Minister Mulroney and Premier Bourassa restored good relations between Quebec and the rest of Canada. The federal government provided large contracts for aircraft and shipbuilding. Montreal is again booming with increased investment and industrial development.

Quebeckers again have a new sense of faith and optimism. Bill 101 has guaranteed French as the language of business and the workplace. Young Quebeckers are now taking over business positions previously held by anglophones.

The free trade agreements may adversely affect important Quebec industries, such as textile, shoe manufacture, and food-processing. Nevertheless, many Quebeckers look forward in the 1990s with some hope, seeing the language conflict modified, the constitutional problem being resolved, free trade holding promise in investment and industry, and the development of new hydro-electric power helping at home and abroad.

Horsepower is still often the most efficient way to gather maple sap.

The Atlantic Region

There are still villages like Grand Pré, Nova Scotia, in Atlantic Canada, but cities like Saint John, New Brunswick, with its port facilities, railways and superhighways, are also part of the present-day scene.

Fish are diverted into a fishing weir where they can be netted easily.

The people of Grand Manan Island in the Bay of Fundy make their living from fishing, lumbering, and tourism.

Prince Edward Island, better known for its potatoes, also grows fine tobacco.

The Maritimes

Sharing the southern shores of the Gulf of St. Lawrence are the Maritime provinces — Nova Scotia, Prince Edward Island, and New Brunswick. French settlers arrived here before the founding of Quebec. They were later joined by English, Scottish, and Irish immigrants. The American Revolution sent north large numbers of Americans loyal to Britain.

Wind and sail power dominated the nineteenth century. This was the golden age of the Maritimes. Situated on the sea, the Maritimes had an ideal vantage point for world trade.

With Confederation a new era arrived. The Maritimes had once profited from their location on the sea. Confederation made them a less significant area on the edge of a much larger territory.

A Canadian Outpost

The main goal of Confederation became developing the country's interior. This involved a new mode of transportation, the railway. To encourage manufacturing industries, a new import tariff was imposed on all the provinces and territories. The Maritimes could no longer trade freely with other ports. The end of free trade and the introduction of the railway meant the age of sail and Maritime prosperity was over. It had been replaced by the new age of steel, coal, and steam.

The Maritimes fell into a period of decline. They were labelled the "weak sisters" of Confederation. They suffered from heavy unemployment and slow economic growth. Unable to find work at home, Maritimers began to move to other parts of Canada.

Many people of the Maritimes blamed their difficulties on the federal government. They had been hurt by the high freight rates and tariff policies that favoured the industrial regions of Quebec and Ontario. Instead of being a centre of commerce and trade, they

were now a Canadian outpost. This, combined with the change from wooden sailing vessels to steel-hulled steamships, had deprived them of their shipping and shipbuilding industries.

The next blow to Maritime fortunes came as homes and industry moved from coal to cleaner oil-based fuels. Even the railways switched — the last coal-burning steam engines in Canada were retired in the midfifties. Production in the coal mines of Cape Breton and mainland Nova Scotia slowed. Miners were laid off. Whole communities almost died.

The New Value of Resources

A turnaround began in the 1970s. The region's natural resources became of increasing value. Industry began to look once again to coal as oil prices shot up. Coal mines expanded or re-opened. Miners went back to work. The price of other minerals rose as well. Lead and zinc mines in northern New Brunswick also prospered. New potash mines have recently been opened.

Hay harvesting in the Saint John River Valley.

OCUS

Why did the Maritimes enter an economic decline in the years after 1867? Why are there new reasons for optimism in the 1980s? Why do many Maritimers resent the federal government, yet feel the need for federal support?

Farming is also important to the Maritime economy: Prince Edward Island has become world-renowned for its fine potatoes. The orchards of the Annapolis Valley in Nova Scotia produce excellent apples. Dairy farming is good business.

In 1977 the federal government declared a 200-mile fishing limit. This benefited all the Maritime provinces. The new limit gives Canadians first rights at fishing in all waters as far as 200 nautical miles (370 km) from the Canadian shoreline. This gives Canadian fishing boats a new advantage over their competitors from Norway and the Soviet Union. The federal government has recently given financial aid to the Maritime fishing industry. Canada is resuming its role as one of the world's leading fish suppliers.

The city of Halifax is a bustling centre of the Maritime region. Its modern container port allows goods to be shipped in enormous containers without being repacked at any stage. Plans are underway for a new marine industrial park. Here marine equipment such as mini-submarines, fishing gear, and underwater sonar devices will be produced. Projects like these combine the economic benefits of manufacturing with Nova Scotia's location on the sea.

Most Maritimers want a share in the new industrialized society. Yet they want to avoid some of the harsher effects of industry. People in the Maritimes still live differently from people in other parts of Canada. Fewer goods and services are available in this region, and there is less money to buy them with. The pace of life is slower. Maritimers value this. So do the many tourists who visit the region each year. They come not only for the breathtaking scenery but also for the atmosphere. They say visiting the Maritimes is like walking back to a gentler time.

Many Maritimers feel their place in Canada is a frustrating one. They resent the federal government for the policies that made their region so dependent on central Canada. Yet they need federal funding to help them establish independent secondary industries. It is this revitalization of Maritime resources that is giving the region a renewed opportunity for strength and prosperity.

Oyster farming on Prince Edward Island. Malpeque oysters are enjoyed in many areas around the world.

Newfoundland and Labrador

Newfoundland was Britain's oldest colony. In 1949 it became Canada's newest province. For centuries French, English, Irish, and Portuguese fishermen competed for fishing rights in the island's waters. The unique mixture of these founding people has given Newfoundlanders a rich folk culture and a special sense of humour. The province retains its distinct character to this day.

The early settlers lived from fishing out of necessity. Newfoundland's infertile soil yielded only small quantities of potatoes and vegetables. There were few animals to hunt. Most Newfoundlanders lived in isolated fishing villages called "outports." St. John's was the only town to grow to any size.

It is easy to see Newfoundland's economic heritage isn't nearly as great as its cultural one. Historically Newfoundland has been Canada's poorest province. It has always had the highest rate of unemployment.

Despite these bleak statistics, Newfoundland is making great strides in a number of economic areas. The island's fishing and fish-processing industries, are being modernized. Inland, the same is happening to mining and forestry.

Labrador

Labrador is the rocky eastern coast of the Canadian mainland north of the Gulf of St. Lawrence. At the turn of the century, Wilfred Grenfell became concerned about conditions in the tiny Labrador fishing villages. His Grenfell Mission established hospitals, nursing stations, orphanages, schools and centres for small industry all along the coast. Since that time Newfoundlanders have begun to exploit Labrador's rich resources of lumber, iron ore, and hydro-electric power.

For many years Quebec and Newfoundland both claimed Labrador as part of their territory. This dispute was settled when an international commission established

Gaining riches from the sea: the fishery . . .

the border in 1927. However, Quebec has never accepted the decision of the commission.

It is partly because of this that the two provinces cannot agree about hydro-electric power from Labrador. Quebec refuses to allow Newfoundland electricity to pass over its borders for sale to other provinces or the United States. It will buy the power for use in Quebec — at a price that was established over 20 years ago when no one expected the tremendous rise in the cost of energy. Newfoundland has been trying to renegotiate the deal but so far· without success. Quebec has offered to exchange free flow of Newfoundland's hydro-electric power in trade for Labrador. Newfoundland has refused.

FOCUS

What does it mean to say "Newfoundland has a rich cultural heritage yet a weak economic heritage?"
Labrador's sale of electricity to Quebec has caused friction. How?
Why are some Newfoundlanders concerned about offshore oil?

A New Resource from the Sea

Newfoundland may yet become a wealthy province. Offshore oil reserves valued at $15 billion have been discovered. Already a new dispute has arisen. This one is between the federal and the provincial governments. As with Alberta, the dispute centres on taxation and revenue rights to the oil. Newfoundland's Premier Brian Peckford argued that Newfoundland should decide how much oil revenue it will share with the federal government. Like Alberta's Premier Peter Lougheed and other provincial leaders, Peckford was fighting to gain more financial control over the province's own resources. However, Canada's oceans are a federal responsibility.

Finally, in 1988, Prime Minister Mulroney and Premier Peckford signed an agreement to permit the shared development of the Hibernia oil fields. Newfoundland's hopes of increased prosperity, based upon its oil, had been achieved.

No matter how this is resolved, Newfoundland faces a difficult and challenging period of transition. Those in the fishing industry are concerned for the delicate balance of life in the sea. They fear industrial wastes may poison prime fishing grounds. If the fishing resource is looked after properly it will always be there. They argue, "If you kill the fish, what happens when the oil and gas run out?" Employers in the fishing industry fear they may lose many young workers to the oil business where there is big money to be made.

Another concern is the effect that big industry is likely to have on the general way of life. The residents want time to adapt to the influx of new people and technology. Big business isn't likely to make it a gradual process. Many Newfoundlanders feel they are being forced to adapt not only to central Canadian economics, but also to central Canadian values. Says one Newfoundlander, "With oil and all these mainlanders flooding in, who knows? In fifty years we could be just as bland as someone from southern Ontario."

Newfoundlanders are wary of sacrificing their traditions to this new source of income. The new oil revenue, they argue, will be only a temporary one. Their heritage goes back several hundred years! Newfoundlanders have a two-fold challenge. They want to preserve their way of life. At the same time they want to use the oil boom to fuel their economy.

. . . and the petroleum industry.

A Pattern of Regions

The falling tide, Nootka Sound, Vancouver Island.

April on the Prairies.

Lake Louise, Banff National Park, Alberta.

Large countries have a problem that small ones don't: their diversity. There are two ways of handling the situation. One way is to force the entire country to share the same cultural and economic structure. The other is to accept this diversity and to make it work for the country. This is the way Canada has chosen. Making it work is one of Canada's main challenges.

The problem of diversity is perhaps greater in Canada than in any other country. Most, if not all, of the larger countries — including the United States, Russia, China, Japan — have chosen the other path. Their people are encouraged to subdue their individual traditions to unite their countries. Canadians are encouraged to remain unified but maintain their own cultural individuality. This makes the task of governing much more difficult. National leaders must try to avoid their own traditions and prejudices. Only in this way can they respond fairly to the needs of each region or group.

Debate: Resolved that only by increasing provincial powers can Canada become a true federal state; **or** Resolved that reducing federal economic, financial, and political powers would lead to disintegration of Canada into separate regions.

Art Gallery pages 22 and 24

Skating on the Rideau Canal at Ottawa.

Notre-Dame-des-Victoires, the oldest church in Quebec City.

Many of the differences between the federal and provincial governments are reactions to unresolved historical problems that have gone unsolved for many years. Others are due to new situations that have arisen out of Canada's development as an industrial power. Such differences are probably unavoidable in any democracy, especially in one that encourages cultural diversity.

The regions of Canada are all seeking greater power and autonomy. The eastern and western provinces in particular want to have a larger say in setting government policies. Each region or province is also prepared to speak up for its own needs. Only in coming to terms with its diversity will Canada become more unified. At that point, the possibilities of a Canada based upon its regional differences may be fully explored.

Cleaning the catch, Peggy's Cove, Nova Scotia.

Questions and Activities

Test Yourself

1. Make a chart for the 6 regions of Canada. For each region list
   a) three main economic features (resources, industries, etc.)
   a) one idea of *agreement* with the federal government
   c) one idea of *disagreement* with the federal government
2. Which region has the highest per capita income? If the region or province is considered poor, what does the federal government do to help?

Ideas for Discussion

1. a) Examine the three themes in Canadian history referred to on page 248 (The Challenge of Regionalism). List the three in order of importance to your region today. Explain your reasons.
   b) How might the order of importance be different in other regions of Canada today?
2. Discuss or debate the topic: "That Canada would be better off with a free trade policy, than with retaining the protective tariff."
3. Hold a debate on the topic: "That separatism will always be an attractive option for many Quebeckers."
4. Discuss the future of the manufacturing industry in Canada. Make all kinds of suggestions — sane or crazy — you can do research later to pick out workable ideas.
   a) Should the federal government continue to support older industries (automobile, farm-equipment, etc.) by tariffs and subsidies?
   b) Should the government shift support to newer high technology industries (computers, electronic equipment, etc.)? Why? How would your suggestions affect the different regions in Canada?
5. Looking at pages 246 - 247, study the "Industries" and "Resources" and discuss the possibility of developing new industries in each region. What might those industries be? Does geography always dictate settlement and industry decisions?

Do Some Research

1. Write a brief research report on the following people from one region.
   a) a premier or political leader
   b) a business person or labour leader
   c) a sports or entertainment personality

2. Find out to what extent the economy of British Columbia is related to the Pacific Rim countries, rather than to the rest of Canada.
3. How much money is currently in the Alberta Heritage Fund? How is the money being used? Find out if any other provinces have similar funds.
4. Do some research on a recent (or upcoming) first Ministers' conference. (The Prime Minister of Canada and the 10 provincial premiers). What are the key issues in the conference? What were the viewpoints of your provincial premier? How were they similar or different from the federal position?
5. Report on the effect that energy resources development has on the economy and on the way of life of the people in Alberta and Saskatchewan.

Be Creative

1. Form a group to prepare a *folder* on *one* region of Canada. In your folder include:
   a) a *map* of your region, showing the key economic resources.
   b) a *poster* for the region, inviting tourists and/or immigrants.
   c) a *written description* of the region, describing the factors that would attract a new wave of immigrants.
   d) a *written statement* of your region's opinions about the current federal government economic policies (i.e., energy prices, manufacturing, unemployment, transportation).
   e) a biography of *one* person from the region.
2. Write a letter to the editor of your local newspaper on one of the following topics:
   a) a statement of *someone from your province,* giving a viewpoint to another province or the federal government.
   b) a criticism of *your* provincial policy from the viewpoint of another region.
   c) a suggestion of the advantages of cooperation by all regions.
3. Prepare a *collage* for one of the regions of Canada from newspaper and magazine materials. Your collage might include industries, tourist attractions, people, sports and entertainment, controversial issues, etc.
4. Prepare a radio or TV program on a recent or future First Ministers' Conference. Focus on the key issues and present regional attitudes likely to be expressed by the different ministers. Include information on such extras as language facilities, dinners featuring regional specialties, and security provided by the conference organizers.

You Are There

The Regional Conference

The prime minister has convened a conference of regional representatives. The objective is to provide recommendations for the federal government to help in deciding on policies to satisfy the different needs of different regions of the country, and to meet the needs of Canada as a whole.

Procedure

1. Elect a prime minister from your class.
2. Each member of the class should become a representative of one region of Canada. A recommended split for representatives:

Atlantic provinces	— 4	Prairies	— 6
Quebec	— 8	British Columbia	— 4
Ontario	— 8	North	— 1

3. The regional conference is to consider several proposals submitted by the federal government.
4. After re-examining the information about each region in this chapter, and other resources, each region is to select the proposals which they would support. It is agreed that all representatives of each region must support their own region's proposals.
5. Representatives from each region should meet with other regions in order to gain support for their proposals.
6. Any region may submit *additional proposals* if the representatives can gain the support of other regions.
7. The prime minister has stated:
   a) The total revenues available to the federal government are $1 500 000 000.
   b) Any proposal to be accepted must have the support of 2/3 of the total number of representatives.
8. The prime minister, in carrying out discussions with regional groups, is concerned about:
   a) the welfare of the whole country.
   b) the need of the government to be re-elected in the next election.
9. Break the conference into five sessions:
   Session 1 — Introduction of topic, explanation of rules, selection of regional representatives
   Session 2 — Development of regional viewpoints, consideration of regional policy on different proposals.
   Session 3 — Negotiations with other regions to try to gain support.
   Session 4 — Formal conference; presentation of viewpoints; final voting on proposals.
   Session 5 — Debriefing — analysis of what happened and why.

List of proposals for discussion

The federal government has submitted the following proposals after consultation with the premiers. Remember, the maximum amount of money available is $1 500 000 000.

A. *Increased industrial subsidy to the Atlantic Provinces*
Money is required to subsidize a steel mill in Nova Scotia, a pulp mill in New Brunswick, a potato-processing plant in PEI, and a fish-processing plant in Newfoundland. These new industries would provide employment for over 3000 people in the Atlantic Provinces. COST: $400 000 000

B. *Additional grain subsidy to Western farmers*
Because of a recent drought and the fluctuating prices of grain, a further subsidy is needed to guarantee income to western farmers. COST: $100 000 000

C. *Modernization of Canadian armed forces*
As part of our NATO responsibilities, we wish to build 3 new military bases in British Columbia, Saskatchewan, and Newfoundland, and to purchase 50 new fighter planes. Parts of these aircraft will be built in Ontario and Quebec. COST: $1 000 000 000

D. *New oil pipeline to Eastern Canada*
A new oil pipeline is to be built through Quebec to the Maritimes. This will increase the sale of western oil, will reduce energy costs in the Maritimes, and help move Canada towards energy self-sufficiency. COST: $800 000 000

E. *Additional CBC network*
In order to counteract the influence of American television, and to provide more opportunities for Canadian musicians and entertainers, additional funds are needed to expand the CBC network and Canadian programs. COST: $100 000 000

F. *Unemployment insurance*
Because of increased unemployment in some areas, and inflation, more funds are required for longer periods of unemployment, and for higher payments. COST: $300 000 000

G. *Increased day-care programs*
Because of the rising costs due to inflation, more women have to go out to work. Therefore the federal government is proposing greater subsidies to the provinces to support day-care centres for working mothers. COST: $20 000 000.

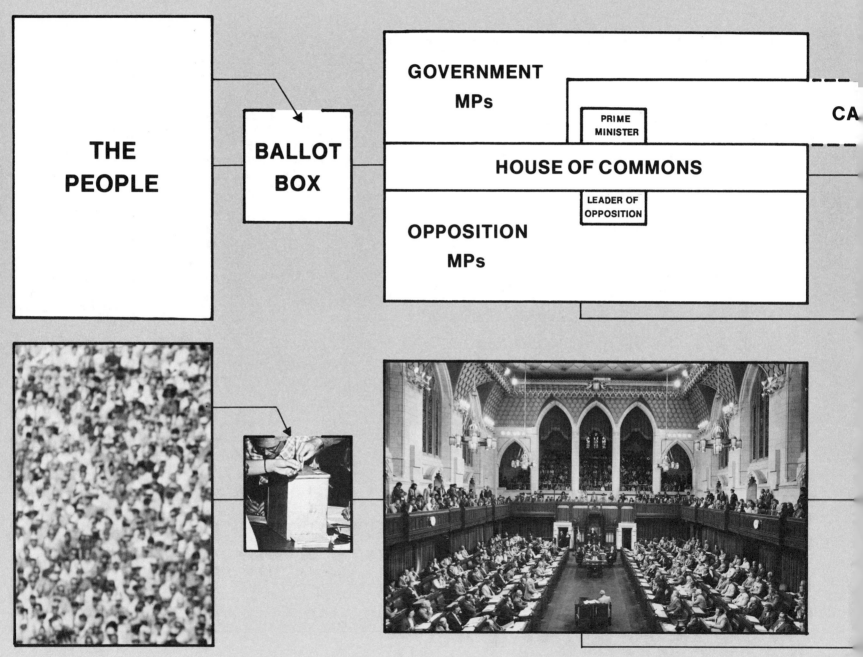

Chapter Ten

Government in Canada
ADVANCE ORGANIZER

THE PEOPLE

BALLOT BOX

GOVERNMENT MPs

PRIME MINISTER

CA

HOUSE OF COMMONS

LEADER OF OPPOSITION

OPPOSITION MPs

Word List

ballot
bill/act/law
campaign
candidate

Charter of Rights
constituency
constitution
federalism

municipality
political platform
province
reading

SENATE

GOVERNOR GENERAL

LAW AND THE COURTS

PUBLIC SERVICE

THE PEOPLE

Why Do We Have Government?

Spaceship *Aurora*

Imagine that your class has been selected to join a spaceship, the *Aurora*, on an exploratory trip to a distant corner of the galaxy.

You and your classmates are assigned a central cabin with individual survival chambers. Travelling swiftly through space, you are soon many light-years from earth.

Suddenly the pilot speaks from the control room. The ship has passed through a mysterious cosmic storm that has damaged it and robbed it of most of its power. There is just enough fuel left to land on a nearby planet. A scan of the surface shows that the atmosphere is breathable and there is enough water and vegetation to support human life. However, the pilot does not know the state of the reverse thrust landing gear. She asks all passengers to return to their cabins and prepare for an emergency landing.

Touchdown is violent. In your padded chamber you are safe, but others may not have been so lucky. Cautiously, you emerge to take stock.

All adults, whose cabins were near the outer walls of the ship, have been killed. Only your classmates, in their individual chambers, have survived. No older people are around to give orders or impose rules. You are "free" to do whatever you want.

But what *should* you do?

At the moment, you have no supplies of food or water. You have no place to sleep and no way to keep warm. It is obvious that you will be on this planet for several weeks, months, or even years.

At first, no one seems to know what to do. People make various suggestions. There is much shouting and arguing, but no useful plan of action emerges. Gradually you realize that you can only solve your problems by working together as a group.

You gather in small groups to discuss and answer the following questions:

1. How will you make your decisions?
2. Who will be your leaders, and how will they be selected?
3. What kinds of people do you want as leaders? What characteristics do you think that they should have?
4. What kind of rules will you make? Who will make these rules?
5. What will you do if some person or group refuses to abide by the rules?

As you examine these questions, you are considering the same problems that are faced by any group of people trying to work together. All societies and nations have faced these problems. Different groups arrive at different solutions, but all must meet the same basic needs. They must establish rules, make decisions, and select people to run the organization. In other words, they must set up a system of government.

Canada has a democratic system of government. Leaders are chosen in elections. Canadian citizens 18 years of age and over vote for the candidate of their choice. The candidate with the most votes wins. This candidate is a representative of the people, who have chosen him or her to make decisions on their behalf.

All groups or societies establish certain basic rules or laws. Imagine a hockey game with no rules, or no referee to enforce them. It would be chaos, just as society would be without laws.

Canada's laws are made either by the federal parliament, or by provincial legislatures, or by town governments. It is the duty of law courts to see that the laws are applied fairly, and to pass judgement on people who break the law.

The basic framework of laws and conventions that a society develops is called the constitution. For example, the NHL rules are hockey's constitution. Canada's constitution is based on the British North America Act of 1867 (now called the Constitution Act, 1867), which sets out Canada's system of government. In 1982, the act was amended to include a Charter of Rights, which adds to the basic framework of rules that Canadians have agreed are important.

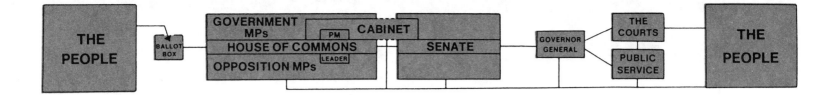

Governments in democracies are elected by the passengers to steer the ship of the nation. They are expected to hold it on course, to arrange for a prosperous voyage and to be prepared to be thrown overboard if they fail in either duty.

Senator Eugene Forsey

What Government Does

Government often seems to be something that happens a long way away. Few people think of government as something that affects their daily lives. Yet most Canadians cannot make it through a single day without coming into contact with government.

Consider a typical day in your life. You wake up, turn on the electric light, and take a shower. The chances are that both electricity and water are public utilities, which means that they are run by the government and supported by taxes. The waste from your bathroom is carried away by the public sewage system. The sidewalks you walk on and the bus you take to school are both likely to be provided by the government.

School teachers, fire fighters, street cleaners, and police officers are all paid with money raised through taxes. The food sold in stores is inspected by government officials to make sure it is fresh and clean. Every time you listen to a weather forecast (supplied by government experts) on the radio (all stations must have licences from the government), visit a public library, or go skating at a public arena, you are coming into contact with some form of government.

Testing a lake for the effects of acid rain.

Checking weather data.

Keeping the city clean.

Governments have a lot of power over you. Give an example of how the government can help you in each of the following ways:

1. Provide financial assistance if you are out of work
2. Pay medical bills
3. Help you find a job
4. Support you if you are too old or too sick to work
5. Protect you from robbery or unfair treatment
6. Teach you useful skills
7. Pick up your food waste and other unwanted possessions

Governments can also force you, as a citizen, to do certain things. Give examples of how governments can do each of the following:

1. Send you to jail
2. Require you to risk your life
3. Regulate the movies you watch
4. Control the music you listen to on the radio
5. Demand that you give them some of your money
6. Force you to do things "for your own good," such as wearing safety clothing at work, using seat belts in cars, or avoiding drugs
7. Limit your right to make statements harmful or insulting to others without evidence to support them

Look at the picture of an imaginary Canadian community. Find examples of things that governments do.

In groups of three or four students, make a list of these examples.

Compare your list with other groups' lists. Make a total class list. Save this to refer to later in this chapter.

Choose what you think are the five most important things that governments do. In a class discussion, give reasons for your choice.

All's Well that Amends Well

The "constitution" has been much discussed throughout Canada's history. But can you say what it is? Is it some sort of document, rather like the Official Rule Book of the NHL, that sets out rules and regulations for the government of Canada? Or is it a more vague and abstract thing, a mass of unwritten rules and traditions?

In Canada, the answer is that it is both.

The written part of the constitution consists mainly of the Constitution Act. This used to be called the British North America Act, which was passed by the British parliament in London, England, in 1867. The BNA Act set out most of the rules for the working of the Canadian government. At that time, the newly confederated Dominion of Canada was still part of the British Empire, which is why the British parliament had to pass the law that created Canada.

Canada's parliamentary system of government is very closely modelled on the British system. The Fathers of Confederation took this for granted, so they didn't think it was necessary to include in the BNA Act obvious things like "Canada will have a prime minister" or "The governor general will always act on the advice of the prime minister and cabinet." As a result, many very important parts of Canada's system of government have never been written down. The rules of this "unwritten" constitution are called constitutional customs or conventions. Although they are not laws, conventions are very powerful. If officials disobeyed them, they would probably be removed from office very quickly.

An Obstacle to Independence?

In the years following 1867 the relationship between Canada and Britain changed, and various laws were passed making the changes official. For example, in 1949 the Supreme Court of Canada was made Canada's highest court. Until then, lawyers had been able to appeal to a committee in Britain (the Privy Council) for rulings on Canadian cases.

By the 1980s, Canada was functioning as a completely independent nation. There were still many cultural and trade links between Canada and Britain. But as far as Canada's system of government was concerned, there were only two remaining ties. One was that both countries recognize the queen as head of state. The other lay in the constitution.

For although Canadians had been running their own government for many years according to the rules

It should be borne in mind that there is nothing more difficult to arrange, more doubtful of success, and more dangerous to carry through than trying to change a nation's constitution.
Niccolo Machiavelli, Italian political scientist, 1469-1527

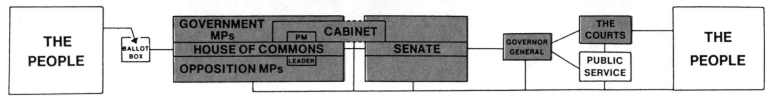

of the BNA Act, the act itself could only be changed, or "amended," by the British Parliament. That is to say, Canadian government could work independently *within* the system; but in order to change the *system* itself, it was necessary to go through the British government. And though a law (the Statute of Westminster) prevented Britain from changing the Canadian constitution except at Canada's request, many Canadians found the situation unacceptable. They felt it prevented Canada from being a truly independent nation.

Patriating the Constitution

What was the problem? The British didn't want to keep the power to change Canada's constitution. For more than fifty years they waited for Canadians to decide on a way to change it themselves. The problem was that the federal government and the provincial governments couldn't work out how to balance their interests. From time to time Canadian politicians came together to look for a suitable "amending formula." Twice they came close, but on each occasion Quebec felt unable to join the agreement, and the idea was dropped.
By 1981, Canadians were beginning to lose patience.

At last, on 5 November 1981 the federal and nine provincial governments reached a three-point agreement:
1. The power to amend the constitution would be brought from Britain to Canada.
2. Thereafter, changes could be made to the constitution if the federal government and seven or more provinces, representing 50% of the population, agreed. Provinces that did not agree to the changes would be allowed to "opt out."
3. A "Charter of Rights and Freedoms" would be added to the written constitution to protect human rights in Canada.

Apart from the amending formula and the Charter of Rights, the substance of the constitution remained almost unchanged by the historic agreement of 1981.

All's well that Amends well

Earlier, Quebec had agreed with seven other provinces on some points that they wanted to see in the agreement. But Premier Lévesque of Quebec could not agree with the final form of the Constitution. As a result, Quebec did not accept the 1982 Constitution.

In 1987, Quebec agreed to the principles of the Meech Lake Accord. This had satisfied Quebec's demands to have a veto on any future changes in Quebec's representation in the federal House of Commons, Senate, or Supreme court. It also confirmed that Quebec would be viewed as a "distinct society".

It remains to be seen how well the amended constitution stands up to the needs of a developing Canada.

Discuss the reactions of these provincial premiers to the constitutional agreement of 5 November 1981.

William Davis, **Premier of Ontario: It represents a feeling around this table that there is something to this nation, that there is something to being a Canadian.**

René Lévesque, **Premier of Quebec: It is an insult done to Quebeckers by English Canada.**

Brian Peckford, **Premier of Newfoundland: I feel more fully a Canadian today than I have ever felt since I have been old enough to think, to know, to understand.**

If you had been premier of your province, what would your reaction have been?

The Canada Act

On 2 December 1981 the House of Commons passed a constitutional resolution to be presented to the queen. The resolution requested her to have an act called the Canada Act passed by the British parliament. Members of all parties supported the resolution, and it passed by 246 votes to 24. One MP left a hospital bed where he was recovering from open-heart surgery in order to be on hand for the historic occasion. After the vote was taken, the rafters shook as the members joined in a rousing chorus of O Canada in both English and French.

Within days the Senate also passed the resolution, and the governor general had agreed to have it presented to the queen. The stage was set for the British parliament to pass the Canada Act as contained in the Canadian resolution. This would be the last time Canadians called on the British parliament to approve changes in Canada's constitution. The Canada Act would end all legal authority that Britain held over Canada. It would remove one of the last symbols of Canada's former colonial status.

Now Canadians were faced with understanding the new law. It was long and detailed. Its words and phrases seemed complicated, but this was not to make things difficult for ordinary citizens. It was the only way of making sure it said precisely what it meant. Canadians, including politicians, lawyers, teachers, and students, all worked hard to grasp the full meaning of the new constitution.

Queen Elizabeth signs the proclamation of Canada's constitution

The Canada Act contains the Constitution Act, 1982. On the opposite page is a summary of some of the major provisions. Remember that it is *only* a summary. To understand the act fully, you would have to read the complete version.

What do you think is the most important provision of the act? Be prepared to explain your choice.

Not all Canadians were happy about the passage of the Canada Act. Some groups were upset at what the act left out, such as protection of the rights of the unborn, or recognition of "all" not just "existing" native rights. Civil rights workers felt the provinces should not have been allowed to "opt out" or override the Charter of Rights. The Quebec government felt the act did not agree with its hopes for the people of Quebec.

Still, it was a giant step forward in Canadian nationhood. Canadians from coast to coast knew that their nation was ready to face the future on its own feet and its own responsibility.

Part I
Canadian Charter of Rights and Freedoms

Fundamental Freedoms
Freedom of conscience and religion
Freedom of thought, and expression, including freedom of the press and other media of communication
Freedom of peaceful assembly
Freedom of association

Democratic Rights
The right to vote
The right to run for election

Mobility Rights
The right to enter, remain in, or leave Canada
The right to move to, live in, and work in any province of Canada

Legal Rights
The right to "life, liberty, and security of the person"
Security from unreasonable search or seizure
Security from arbitrary arrest or detention
When arrested, the right to be told why and to hire a lawyer
When accused of a crime, the right to a fair bail hearing, to a quick trial, and to be assumed innocent until proven guilty
The right not to be subjected to cruel and unusual punishment

Equality Rights
Equality before the law regardless of race, national or ethnic origin, colour, religion, sex, age, or mental or physical disability (however, programs may be introduced to help "disadvantaged" groups)

Official Languages of Canada
Equal status for the use of English and French in the government and courts of Canada and of New Brunswick

Minority Language Education Rights
The right to education in English or French wherever there are reasonable numbers of Anglophone or Francophone students (not to come into effect immediately in Quebec)

These rights and freedoms are to be enforced by the courts.

All provisions apply to men and women equally.

Certain sections of the charter may be "over-ridden" for periods of up to five years by the provincial legislature (or the federal parliament in matters under its control, including the Yukon and the Northwest Territories).

Part II
Rights of the Aboriginal Peoples of Canada

"Existing aboriginal and treaty rights" of the native peoples (Indians, Inuit, and Métis) are recognized.

Part III
Equalization and Regional Disparities

The federal and provincial governments are committed to promote equal opportunities for the well-being of Canadians. They also agree to make equalization payments to poorer provinces.

Part IV
Constitutional Conference

A special first ministers conference is to be called within one year of the proclamation of the act. It is to define and identify the aboriginal rights of native peoples. Representatives from the Yukon and Northwest Territories are to be invited to take part in discussions of items that affect the territories.

Part V
Procedure for Amending the Constitution of Canada

Amendments to the constitution require the approval of the parliament of Canada and of the legislatures of at least seven provinces representing at least 50% of the population. (Proposed changes will need a great deal of support before they become law. On the other hand, no one province can permanently stall a change wanted by the rest.) Provinces that do not approve the amendment may "opt out" if they wish.

Part VI
Amendment to the Constitution Act, 1867

The Constitution Act, 1867 (the BNA Act) is amended by adding important new provincial powers to section 92. These powers relate to the development and management of non-renewable natural resources, forestry resources, and electrical energy.

Part VII
General

The Constitution of Canada is recognized as the supreme law. No laws that are inconsistent with it are valid. English and French versions of the Act have equal force.

Federalism: the Division of Powers

Agreements are as necessary between Ottawa and the provinces of Canada as they are between Canada and other countries.
From Government and You *by Charles Kahn and Richard Howard, McClelland and Stewart, 1979.*

When Canada's system of government was being worked out between 1864 and 1867, two of the most important things to be considered were the size of the country, and the fact that it was made up of several distinct regions. Each of these regions had its own history, its own type of terrain and resources, and its own culture. It would be difficult to govern such a country from a single, central capital.

Instead, a *federal* system of government was established. Power was divided between the central government in Ottawa, often called the federal government, and several provincial governments.

At Confederation, powers were divided up very carefully between the two levels of government. The division of powers was set out in Sections 91, 92, and 93 of the British North America Act (now the Constitution Act, 1867).

The Fathers of Confederation chose to give Canada a strong central and weaker provincial governments. A number of very important powers, such as taxation and defence, were therefore given to the federal government. The federal government was also given any powers which were not specifically assigned to the provinces in Sections 92 and 93.

Canada also has a third level of government: local government. The governments of towns and cities are called municipal governments, and they are responsible for purely local matters. It is up to the provincial governments to see that municipal governments work fairly and legally.

Partners in Government

Canada's provincial governments play a large and increasingly important role in the lives of the people of Canada. As their powers and responsibilities have grown, so has the need to communicate and plan with each other and the federal government. Therefore, they have set up a system of federal-provincial conferences to co-ordinate their activities. At these conferences civil servants and ministers meet regularly to plan policies for all Canada.

First Ministers' Conferences

The conferences that receive the most attention in the news are usually first ministers' conferences. These are often televised. The prime minister and the provincial premiers meet to discuss matters of the greatest concern, such as the economy or amendments to the constitution.

These conferences are often the scene of sharp disagreement and intense political battles — under the full glare of television cameras. They also often result in compromise and co-operation. Whatever the outcome, the cameras give Canadians a chance to view their political leaders at work.

Some commentators have accused first ministers of "showing off" to the cameras to impress people back home. They suggest this makes it harder for the ministers to solve their joint problems.

Some Municipal Powers and Responsibilities

local roads
garbage disposal
public transit
maintenance of schools
police and fire protection
libraries
sewage disposal

matters of purely local concern

Some Provincial Powers and Responsibilities
(Sections 92 and 93):

direct taxation (for example, sales taxes)
setting up and supervising municipal governments
management and sale of public lands, and
    supervision of forests
        development and management of non-renewable
          natural resources, forestry resources, and
          electrical energy (added in 1982)
    administration of justice and the courts
public and reformatory prisons in the province
        hospitals and asylums
        shop, saloon, and other licences, in order to
          raise money for local and provincial purposes
            property and civil rights
            provincial highways
            education

              all matters of "a merely local or
              private nature in the province"

Some Federal Powers and Responsibilities (Section 91):

postal services
armed forces and defence
currency and coinage
    banking and the issuing of paper money
    regulation of trade and commerce
    seacoast and inland fisheries
    any form of taxation except provincial sales tax
        matters relating to Indians and land
          reserved for Indians
        the census
        management of penitentiaries
        criminal justice

        all matters not assigned exclusively to the
        provinces

---

1. Do you think it is better for political leaders to meet "in the public eye" or "behind closed doors"? What are the advantages or disadvantages of each method?

2. Make three headings: Federal Responsibility, Provincial Responsibility, and Municipal Responsibility. Put each item in the list below under the appropriate heading.

a) Canadian airforce   g) skating arena
b) new sidewalks   h) automobile licences
c) importing oil from Saudi Arabia   i) post office
d) fire department   j) issuing of gold coins
e) regulations about forests and parks   k) sales tax on gasoline
f) sewers   l) highways

3. Refer to the list of things government does that you made from the picture on page 287. Divide the list into federal, provincial, and municipal responsibilities.

4. The government workers in the photographs on page 286 are all concerned with some aspect of the environment. Can you work out whether they are federal, provincial, or municipal employees?

The Provinces

YUKON
• Whitehorse

NORTHWEST TERRITORIES

Yellowknife •

BRITISH COLUMBIA

ALBERTA
Edmonton

SASKATCHEWAN

Regina •

MANITOBA

Winnipeg •

• Victoria

ONTARIO

QUEBEC

Quebec •

Ottawa •

Toronto •

NEWFOUNDLAND

• St. John's

PRINCE EDWARD ISLAND

Charlottetown
Fredericton   Halifax

NEW BRUNSWICK

NOVA SCOTIA

CANADA

> Examine the coats of arms of Canada, the provinces and territories. Choose one and try to identify the various symbols it contains. What do these symbols reveal about the history, geography, and people of the area? Does the coat of arms include a motto? If so, what does it mean?

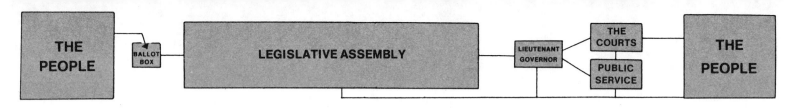

THE PEOPLE → BALLOT BOX → LEGISLATIVE ASSEMBLY → LIEUTENANT GOVERNOR → THE COURTS / PUBLIC SERVICE → THE PEOPLE

1. Who is premier of your province?
2. What political party is in power in your province?
3. What political party forms the opposition in your province?
4. What are the most important political concerns in your province?
5. Perhaps you do not live in a province, but in one of Canada's northern territories. What is the form of your territorial government?

The structure of government in the provinces is very similar to that of the federal government. Elections are fought in much the same way. Elected candidates represent the voters of the province in the Legislative Assembly. In some provinces the legislature goes by a slightly different name. For example, in Newfoundland and Nova Scotia it is called the House of Assembly. In Quebec it is the National Assembly. Bills are debated and passed in the legislature as in the federal House of Commons. (However, they do not have to be debated again in an upper house: the provinces have no Senate.) The premier selects a cabinet and leads the government as the prime minister does.

As the queen's representative, the lieutenant governor of the province signs provincial bills into law. The lieutenant governor is appointed by the governor general on the advice of the prime minister and has similar duties. These are largely ceremonial — opening new hospitals, greeting important visitors, giving the speech from the throne at the beginning of a session of the legislature.

It is in areas of responsibility that provincial governments are different from the federal government. For example, the provinces cannot make laws about the size of Canada's armed forces. The federal government cannot decide how much time grade 3 students should spend on physical education each week, or what rules should control lumbering operations in the province's forests.

Each province is different from every other. Each has its own history, its own heroes, its own strengths, its own weaknesses. The *structure* of government is similar across the land. However, the experience of each province leads to varied political views, attitudes, and leaders. These provide a healthy dynamism to Canadian political life.

The Territories

We tend to speak of the provinces as "Canada." Yet 39% of our land area is not part of any province. The vast regions of the Yukon and the Northwest "Territories" are still largely administered by the federal government.

These territories contain only 0.3% of Canada's population. This is considered too small for them to undertake all the responsibilities of provincial government. However, both territories elect territorial councils that have some limited powers and duties.

In 1982 the people of the Northwest Territories voted in a referendum to divide the vast area in two. This proposal was made because the Inuit in the east live quite differently from the Métis, Dene, and others of the western territories. Some feel that this proposal could lead to the creation of two new provinces in the future.

The call for new provinces in Canada's North will get louder and more forceful in the years to come. The people of the territories point to the rapid development of the oil and gas reserves expected in the near future. This may soon drastically change their way of life. If the territories were provinces, they would have more control over development and the changes it will bring.

The Indian, Inuit, and Métis argue that with full provincial status they could better protect the interests of their people.

Political Parties

It is very difficult for one person alone to bring about change in government. But a large group of people working together can make an impact on the government, change policies, and affect decisions. In your local community, people probably have different opinions about where a new road should be built or whether or not a dump for chemical waste should be set up nearby. On a larger scale, in a country as large and diverse as Canada, people will have very different ideas about how things should be run.

A political party is a group of people who share similar ideas about how the government should work, and who band together to put their ideas into effect.

What Political Parties Do

A political party organizes its opinions on various issues into a statement called a political platform. This summarizes the attitudes shared by members of the party, and sets out the way the party would run the government. The platform tells the public about the party's policies. Voters sometimes discover that they support some ''planks'' in the platform but do not agree with others. However, most voters find that political platforms make it easier to decide which party they want to support.

The Parties in Canada

Canada has three main political parties: the Liberals, the Progressive Conservatives, and the New Democratic Party.

Political parties know that they need a broad range of support in order to be elected. They therefore try to attract voters from all walks of life — farmers and factory workers, executives and clerks, homemakers and storekeepers, recent immigrants and Canadian-born citizens, students and old-age pensioners, loggers in British Columbia as well as bankers in Newfoundland.

To appeal to so many different groups, political parties must compromise. Often a political platform is a compromise between what members really believe is best and what they think will appeal to most voters.

The Liberals and Conservatives are known as middle-of-the-road parties. They have always attempted to attract support from all groups. NDP leader Tommy Douglas once called them ''Tweedledum and Tweedledee,'' poking fun at the fact that there sometimes seems little to choose between them.

The CCF started out in 1933 as a socialist party. It appealed to workers and farmers, and did not attempt to attract support from other groups. By the forties and fifties, however, the CCF was winning less and less support in federal elections. In 1961 it became the New Democratic Party. The NDP presented a more moderate program in order to attract a wider range of voters.

At the same time both the Liberals and the Conservatives began to adopt some of the CCF's popular social policies such as unemployment insurance and medicare. When these policies were first suggested, they seemed outlandish to the middle-of-the-road parties.

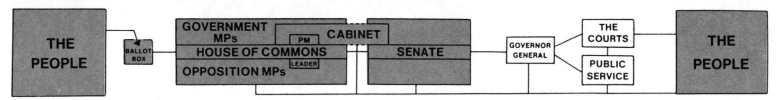

It is difficult to imagine what federal and provincial elections would be like without political parties. Almost all candidates belong to one of the major political parties. When you vote for Mr. X or Ms. Y, you are also voting for a political party. The party with the most supporters elected forms the government.

Each party chooses its leader at a leadership convention. Leadership conventions are among the most colourful and exciting events in Canadian political life. Delegates from local party associations across the country converge on the convention site.

In groups, choose a political party and collect information about it. You can do this by:
a) visiting the local party committee office
b) reading party campaign literature
c) reading newspaper accounts
d) interviewing a member of the party
e) watching television reports
   Summarize your chosen party's viewpoints on the following issues:
a) employment   c) energy
b) inflation   d) one other policy of your choice
   Compile a scrapbook, and prepare your own summary of your party's platform for presentation to the class.

The first days of the convention are spent in speeches, social events, and discussion as candidates try to win support among the delegates. Songs, hats, buttons, banners, and pamphlets describing the candidate and outlining policies, are all part of the campaign. After a succession of votes, the name of the new party leader is announced. This is the person who will become prime minister or premier if the party is elected to power.

Political parties also organize election campaigns. They select and advise candidates, raise funds, prepare advertising campaigns, and provide information to the media and the public. On election day, each party tries to make sure that as many of its supporters as possible get to the polls to cast their votes.

In most countries today, political parties are a vital part of the government. It is important that voters always have a choice between two or more parties, so that no one party can ever put all of its policies into effect without opposition.

Everything a political party does is geared towards the next election. The election is the key. Only if elected, will the party have the power to start putting its ideas into effect.

Liberal Party

Progressive Conservative Party

New Democratic Party

Federal Elections

Politics is a strange game. You *stand* for nomination, so you can *run* for election, to *sit* in parliament.

The scene is set:

The election machinery: The country is divided into electoral districts called *constituencies* or ridings.

The candidates: In each constituency the local branches of political parties are at work. They *nominate* candidates for the next election. Some candidates do not have the support of any political party but run as *independents*.

The voters: During the government's term of office, voters watch the words and actions of both government and opposition parties. They develop opinions about who would be best to govern after the next election.

An election is called:

The election campaign swings into action. The candidates are out to persuade the voters of the constituency to support them. They make speeches, hold meetings, shake hands at bus stops and supermarkets, visit the voters in their homes. Eager campaign workers run the campaign headquarters, canvass from door to door, and give out pamphlets and buttons. A special squad erects posters wherever friendly voters will allow them. Teenagers too young to vote may have strong political opinions. They are often among the most active volunteers.

Many voters feel the real campaign is being waged in their newspapers and on their television screens. They watch the leaders of the major parties as they swing across the country trying to make the headlines. The parties spend millions of dollars on paid political announcements. They make every effort to reach into people's homes to win the voters' support for the party platform, the party leader, and the local party candidate. Many voters find the bombardment of information confusing. But in the end most come to a decision on the way they will vote.

Meanwhile, a list of eligible voters is compiled by *enumerators*. In federal elections all Canadian citizens 18 years of age and over may vote. (The rules vary slightly in provincial and municipal elections.) The *district returning officer* has ballots prepared and hires people to run each *polling station* on election day.

On election day:

Polling or voting stations open up throughout the constituency. Each station is run by a *deputy returning officer* and a *poll clerk*. They work under the watchful eyes of *scrutineers* representing the various candidates. This is only one of many precautions to ensure there is no cheating or sloppiness in the election.

Survey results are based on 811 interviews

Results from today's poll for The Globe and Mail by Environics Research Group Ltd are based on interviews with a total of 811 eligible voters: 210 French-speaking voters interviewed on Tuesday and Wednesday and 601 English-speaking voters interviewed on Wednesday

Interviewing was conducted over the period to provide enough time after the two leaders' debates to obtain a representative nation-wide sample and to allow enough time to gauge public reaction to media coverage of the debates.

The margin of error for — or minus 3.4 p— samp—

the margin for the French-speaking voters is plus of minus 6.8

Interviewing was conducted by telephone from Toronto

All respondents in the post-debate poll were originally interviewed as part of the Globe-Environics Poll completed in early September and reported in The Globe and Mail on Sept 10. By returning to this panel of voters, the pollsters were able to track changes in voting intentions over the past seven weeks and to determine the effect of the debate on party preference

Respondents were asked

● Did you watch any of the live television broa— —the deb— —three n—

Tories keep big lead, Gallup says

By Alan Christie Toronto Star

The Progressive Conservatives are heading toward another huge majority government with four weeks to go until election day, according to a Gallup— released

On eve of vote, Conservatives lead in 3 polls

A third national public opinion ll gives the Progressive Conserv-re party a comfortable lead in —r support h—

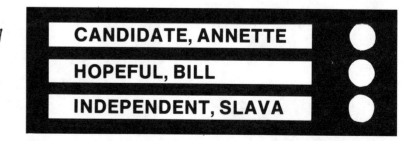

CANDIDATE, ANNETTE	○
HOPEFUL, BILL	○
INDEPENDENT, SLAVA	○

The voters mark their ballots in private. The ballot is secret: no one but you knows how you have voted.

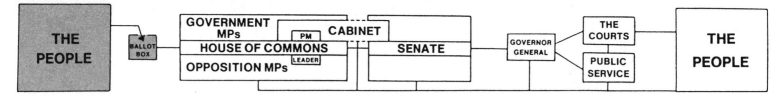

THE PEOPLE	→ BALLOT BOX →	GOVERNMENT MPs	PM CABINET	SENATE	GOVERNOR GENERAL	THE COURTS	THE PEOPLE
		HOUSE OF COMMONS				PUBLIC SERVICE	
		OPPOSITION MPs LEADER					

Today the candidates' campaign headquarters are scenes of frantic activity. The aim is to "bring out the vote." Workers want to make sure every possible supporter casts a ballot. The phone lines hum as scrutineers call in to report on activity in their polls. Canvassers call to find out who has not yet voted in their area. The office co-ordinates a babysitting service for homemakers with young children and free drives to the polls for the elderly and disabled.

The polls close:

The ballot box is opened. The returning officer counts the ballots while the scrutineers check to make sure the count is accurate. When all polling stations have reported to the district returning officer, the final figures are announced and the candidate with the most votes is named member of parliament.

Tension is mounting at campaign headquarters. During the day workers put up wall charts to list the results from each poll as they come in. Canvassers, drivers, and scrutineers join the office staff to watch the vote totals mount. Has their candidate won? Will they have a victory party tonight?

Before election day, the candidates actively campaign in their ridings. Often he or she will recruit other influential members of their party to work with them to bring in the vote.

People want to know more than the result in their own constituency. They want to know the result of the *general election* — the election in every constituency across the country. Most turn on their TVs to find out.

Depending on where a person lives in Canada, the wait for the election results could be long or short. Coverage in the Atlantic provinces starts as soon as the polls close in the Maritimes. By then, the first results are trickling in from Newfoundland, where counting started half an hour earlier. An hour later, the polls close in central Canada, and Quebeckers and Ontarians turn on their sets to see what trends are developing in the Atlantic region. No election results may be broadcast in a region of the country until the polls are closed in that time zone. This means, however, that by the time people in B.C. and the Yukon join the network most of the results from the east are known. This has made some westerners feel that their votes have little influence on the election results, particularly if one party has already gained enough seats to form a government. Actually, of course, their votes are just as important as everyone else's — it is only the timing that causes bad feelings. In the early 1980s a plan was developed to avoid this problem by having the same voting period right across the country, even if the local time is different in each zone. However, it was rejected by Parliament.

Each vote affects the result in one particular constituency. The candidate with the most votes will "sit" in parliament as the member for that constituency. Depending on the number of "seats" won by his or her political party, the elected member will sit on the government or opposition side of the House of Commons.

Hold an election:
- Divide the class into three groups (L, PC, NDP) and let each nominate a member as candidate.
- Make buttons and posters; write pamphlets.
- Select *one* problem as the election issue; decide your party's attitude; and present the candidate to the class. Have each make a short speech giving the party's point of view and its promise to the electors.
- Select a Returning Officer and a Polling Clerk. Have them prepare ballots and a ballot box. After you hold your election, have them count the vote and report the results to the class.

Member of Parliament

Who is your member of parliament? Which political party does your MP belong to? What is the name of the riding or constituency in which you live?

If you are like most Canadians, you probably were unable to answer these questions correctly. That's a pity, because members of parliament make the laws that rule much of our lives. They also represent us in the parliament of Canada.

The MP's Job

Once in parliament, the new MP usually faces a wide range of responsibilities. Members of parliament are expected to perform well in three main areas: in parliament, in the constituency, and as a member of a political party.

During their term in office, when Parliament is not in session, MPs spend part of their time in their constituency.

The House of Commons has a "seat" for the member of parliament from each constituency in Canada. After the election of 1980, there were 282 seats, for 282 MPs.

Although MPs are paid good salaries and receive free air and rail passes, the workload can be crushing. The MP must spend a great deal of time in Ottawa, often far away from family and friends.

In Parliament

An MP is required to play an important and demanding role in the business of parliament. An MP must:
- attend debates in the House of Commons
- make speeches in the House of Commons, especially on issues that affect his or her constituency
- vote on bills presented to the House of Commons
- work on special committees preparing laws
- maintain a parliamentary office to help constituents (people who live in the MP's constituency) with their problems

In the Constituency

The people back home in the local constituency or riding expect their MP to act on their behalf. A good MP must:
- be available through his or her riding office
- deal personally with constituents' problems, such as old age pensions or local pollution
- attend social and political functions in the riding to meet people and keep abreast of local issues

In the Political Party

Members of parliament are also members of political parties. They must work for the party they represent. These duties can include:
- speech making
- television and radio interviews
- visits to other parts of Canada
- helping make party policy
- attending "caucus" (meetings of all MPs belonging to the same party)
- attending party conventions
- working on election committees, fund-raising, membership drives

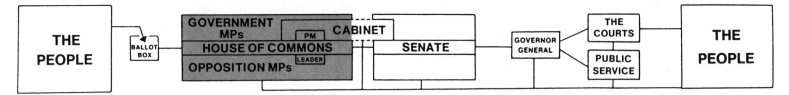

Politics involves considerable tension which can affect the health of members of parliament. MPs can never be sure whether they will be "out of a job" after the next election.

One of an MP's most important duties is voting on bills in the House of Commons. A bill is a proposed law. No proposal can become law without the support of a majority of MPs. When MPs vote for or against a bill, they are making decisions that affect the way the country is run. Thus each member's vote is very important.

In making their decisions, MPs must consider their own consciences, the interests of their constituents, and the views of their political parties. It is the duty of the "party whip" to make sure MPs support the party in important votes.

Some MPs

Sheila Copps (L): born 1952, Hamilton, Ontario. *Education:* University of Western Ontario, University of Rouen (France), McMaster University. *Career:* Journalist, MPP for Hamilton Centre. *Parliament:* Elected 1984, re-elected 1988. Opposition critic for Housing and Labour, National Health and Welfare, and Environment.
Riding: Hamilton East, Ontario

Jeanne Sauvé (L): born 1922, Prud'homme, Sask. *Education:* Universities of Ottawa, Paris, London. *Career:* Catholic youth organizations, journalist, CBC broadcaster, lecturer on art, director of media firms. *Parliament:* Elected 1972, Liberal cabinet (Science & Technology, Communications & Environment), 1980 Speaker. *Riding:* Laval des Rapides (Que.).

Nelson Riis (NDP): born 1942, High River, Alberta. *Education*: Degrees in education and geography. *Career:* teacher, professor, municipal politician, trustee. *Parliament:* Elected 1980, re-elected twice. Critic for regional expansion, finance, Parliamentary House Leader for the Federal caucus, serves on various Parliamentary associations.
Riding: Kamloops, British Columbia

The Decision

Perhaps the most difficult moments for members of parliament occur when their personal views clash with the views of their party or their constituents. Read the following fictional account and decide how you think Albert Martin should vote.

Albert Martin, MP, has only two hours left in which to make the most difficult political decision of his life. The young man has spent a week agonizing over his decision. After talking with friends, reporters, and political opponents, he still isn't sure how he will vote on the government plan to increase the size of the armed forces by 10%.

His party is proposing to expand the armed forces because of increased world tension and the urging of Canada's allies. Albert is being pressured by the party whip to support the prime minister or risk losing the help of the party in the next election.

The voters in his riding seem to be split on the issue. Many feel the expansion is necessary because Canada's armed forces seem too small to defend Canadian interests adequately. Other voters feel the expansion will be too costly, and only add to world tension.

Albert himself is a firm believer in non-violence. He is a deeply religious person who is convinced military might can only lead to more wars.

How should he vote?

He owes the party and prime minister his loyalty. He wants to represent the feelings of the voters in his riding fairly. He also has to listen to his own conscience. Time is running out.... He has to decide.

The Prime Minister

Canadians often say they wish they had the chance to run the government, if only for a day. Have you ever wished that you were prime minister of Canada? What would it be like? What does being prime minister involve? What kind of people would seriously want the job? Would you?

The prime minister is usually the leader of the party with the largest number of seats in the House of Commons. The job lasts until the prime minister's party is defeated in a general election, though prime ministers sometimes resign to let new leaders take over between elections. Being prime minister means being the first minister and the most powerful member of the cabinet.

The Prime Minister's Job

The prime minister earns a good salary, lives in a large house with a butler, housekeeper, cook, and other servants, and is treated with great respect. At first glance this seems a very comfortable way of living. Yet the job involves some very serious responsibilities. The prime minister must:

- select and lead members of the cabinet
- appoint senators, justices of the Supreme Court, and many other officials
- lead the government party in the House of Commons
- recommend to the governor general the times for summoning parliament and for calling elections
- keep the party popular with the voters
- work with the provincial premiers
- speak for Canada to other world leaders

Being a leader requires special qualities. Many people are worried that the demands and difficulties of being prime minister scare away some of our brightest potential leaders. Few people want to take on these pressures and responsibilities. The work is difficult, the hours are long. Being prime minister can be very hard on family life. When times are tough, the criticism can be difficult to take. During times of crisis, the prime minister can be a lonely figure.

All things considered, do you have what it takes to be prime minister? Would you really want the job?

Leadership requires special characteristics. Few people have all the qualities necessary to be successful leaders. Here are some descriptive terms that people often associate with leadership. Which do you feel are the most important? Which apply to you?

intelligent	determined	imaginative
bilingual	outgoing	careful
attractive	flexible	financially secure
cool under pressure	well-educated	middle aged
self-confident	power hungry	exciting
decisive	organized	

Write a letter to the present prime minister of Canada. Explain your views or ask for information on an issue that is important to you. Wait for the reply and share it with your classmates.

Remember that when parliament is in session, it is not necessary to place a stamp on the envelope when writing to a member of the House of Commons.

Pierre Trudeau (L): born 1919, Montreal, Que. *Education:* Law, politics, and economics. *Career:* World traveller 1948-49, federal government adviser 1949-52, founded reformist magazine *Cité Libre,* opposed Quebec separatism. *Parliament:* Elected 1965, Minister of Justice 1967, party leader 1968, PM 1968-79, re-elected PM 1980, oversaw patriation of Constitution with Charter of Rights.

Brian Mulroney (PC): born 1939, Baie Comeau, Quebec. *Education:* St. Francis Xavier University (Antigonish, N.S.), Laval University (Quebec) Law School. *Career:* Specialized as a labour relations lawyer; 1984, defeated Joe Clark, to become PC leader; elected Prime Minister in landslide PC victory; 1988, elected as Prime Minister for second term.

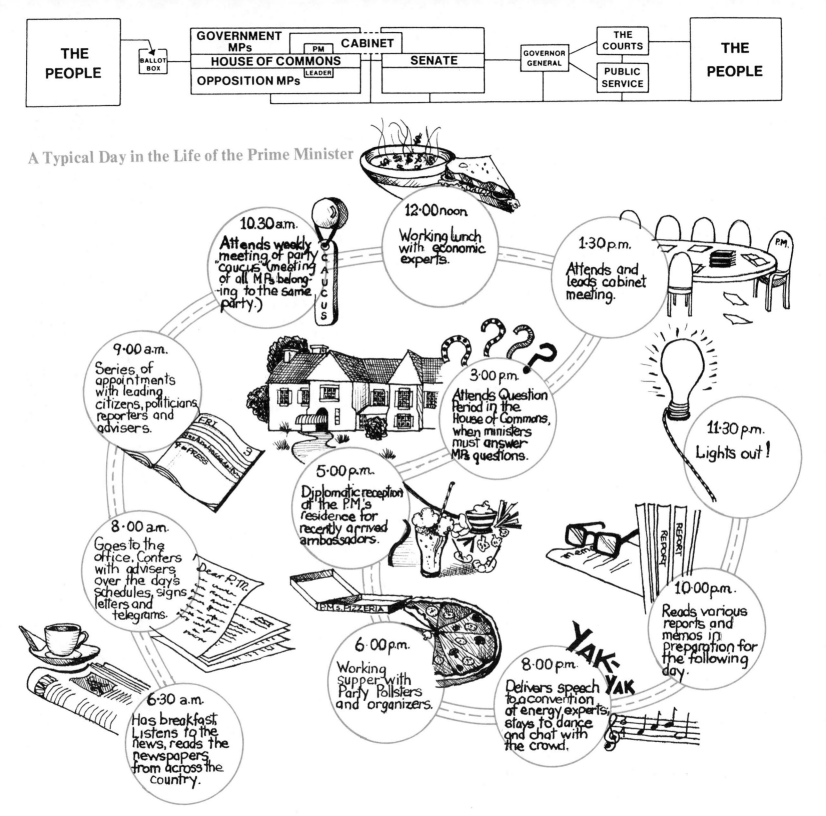

THE PEOPLE

GOVERNMENT MPs

BALLOT BOX

PM

CABINET

HOUSE OF COMMONS

LEADER

OPPOSITION MPs

SENATE

GOVERNOR GENERAL

THE COURTS

PUBLIC SERVICE

THE PEOPLE

A Typical Day in the Life of the Prime Minister

10.30 a.m. Attends weekly meeting of party "caucus" (meeting of all MPs belonging to the same party.)

CAUCUS

12.00 noon Working lunch with economic experts.

1.30 p.m. Attends and leads cabinet meeting.

P.M.

9.00 a.m. Series of appointments with leading citizens, politicians, reporters and advisers.

FRI

3.00 p.m. Attends Question Period in the House of Commons, when ministers must answer MPs questions.

11.30 p.m. Lights out!

5.00 p.m. Diplomatic reception at the P.M.'s residence for recently arrived ambassadors.

8.00 a.m. Goes to the office. Confers with advisers over the day's schedules, signs letters and telegrams.

Dear P.M.

10.00 p.m. Reads various reports and memos in preparation for the following day.

REPORT

memo

P.M.'s PIZZERIA

6.00 p.m. Working supper with Party Pollsters and organizers.

YAK-YAK

8.00 p.m. Delivers speech to a convention of energy experts; stays to dance and chat with the crowd.

6.30 a.m. Has breakfast. Listens to the news, reads the newspapers from across the country.

The Cabinet

The prime minister chooses about 30 other ministers to help govern the country. Together these people form a group called the cabinet. Most of the ministers are given "portfolios," which means they are put in charge of particular departments, such as external affairs or finance. A minister "without portfolio" has no department to run but may be given special responsibilities. Sometimes the cabinet is divided into an inner and an outer cabinet. The inner cabinet is more powerful, and meets more often with the prime minister.

A Cabinet Minister's Job

Being a cabinet minister usually brings prestige and increased political power. It also means a great deal of work. A cabinet minister has to acquire a detailed knowledge of his or her department. He or she must also:
- oversee the running of the department
- speak for the department in parliament and to the press
- present to parliament new laws that will affect the operations or duties of the department
- advise the prime minister on policy concerning the department
- help the prime minister and the cabinet make other political decisions
- explain the government's policies to the public
- help set up the party's election strategy

Choosing the Cabinet

An outsider might think that choosing a cabinet meant simply picking the best person for each job. It is actually a complicated juggling act. The prime minister has to consider the skills, experience, and personalities of potential ministers. He or she must also guarantee that the various regional, religious, and ethnic groups of Canada will be fairly represented. For instance, cabinets usually contain an equal number of representatives from Ontario and Quebec. The minister of agriculture is often a farmer from the West.

Some Recent Cabinet Ministers

Monique Begin (L): born 1936, Rome, Italy. *Education:* McGill University, University of Montreal. *Parliament*: Elected 1972, re-elected 1974, 1979, 1980 (did not run again in 1984 election). Minister of National Revenue 1976-77, Minister of National Health and Welfare 1977-84.
Riding: St. Leonard-Anjou, Quebec

Joe Clark (PC): born 1939, High River, Alta. *Education:* Degrees in history and political science. *Career:* Lecturer in political science, University of Alberta, journalist for CBC, *Calgary Herald* and *Edmonton Journal* 1965-67, special assistant to senior PC's 1967-70.
Parliament: Elected 1972, PC leader 1976, defeated Liberal government 1979, re-elected 1980. *Riding:* Yellowhead, Alberta.

John Crosbie (PC): born 1931, St. John's, Nfld. *Education:* Degrees in political science, economics, and law. *Career:* Lawyer, municipal politician, Liberal MLA and Cabinet member 1971-1976. *Parliament:* Elected 1976, re-elected four times. Minister of Finance, Minister of Justice and Attorney-General of Canada, Minister for International Trade. *Riding:* St. John's West, Newfoundland.

Barbara McDougall (PC): born in 1937, Toronto, Ontario. *Education:* University of Toronto, degree in political science and economics. *Career:* investment analyst, columnist, financial consultant. *Parliament:* Elected 1984, re-elected 1988. Minister of State for Finance, Minister of State for Privatization, Minister Responsible for the Status of Women, Minister Responsible for Regulatory Affairs, Minister for Employment and Immigration. *Riding:* St. Paul's, Toronto, Ontario.

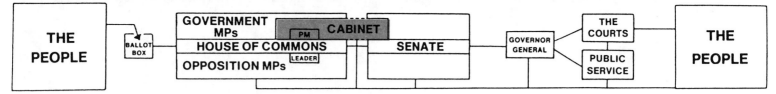

The minister of fisheries usually comes from the Atlantic region or British Columbia. Today care is also taken to include members from groups such as women or minority groups that have not always been represented in the past.

Sometimes it is not possible to meet all these needs from members of the House of Commons belonging to the governing party. For instance, during much of Brian Mulroney's time as prime minister, the minister responsible for the Wheat Board was Senator Lowell Murray, later Secretary of State.

The prime minister must also keep party considerations in mind. Powerful and popular members of the party must be included even if they are rivals of the prime minister. Otherwise the prime minister may lose the loyalty of the party.

Cabinet Solidarity

The cabinet meets regularly to discuss important issues. These meetings are often stormy and full of harsh words. However, once a decision has been reached, *all ministers are expected to support it in public.* If a minister finds it impossible to support the prime minister or fellow cabinet members, that minister usually resigns. For example in 1963 Douglas Harkness resigned as minister of defence in John Diefenbaker's cabinet when the cabinet refused to arm Canadian Bomarc missiles with nuclear warheads.

A prime minister must balance several factors when choosing a cabinet minister. Ability, experience, ethnic or religious background, popularity, and regional origins are some important points to be considered.

Assume you are the prime minister. Choose one of the three candidates described here to be your **Minister of Finance**. Be prepared to explain your choice.

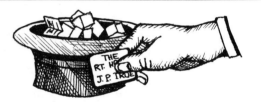

Eileen Dewar, 42, MP from Toronto.
Religion: Protestant(United).
Marital Status: Married with three children. Husband a financial adviser for several big corporations.
Education: degree from McGill University(Montreal) in business finance.
Work Experience: served as financial expert for corporations and government agencies.
Finances: worth several million dollars in stocks and bonds.
Standing in Party: little known; a relatively new MP; popular with female members of the party who are keen to see a woman in charge of such an important department.
Personality: quiet but firm; poor speaker but in private has a dry and witty sense of humour; well organized and excellent with statistics.

Armand Bolduc, 37, MP from Moncton.
Religion: Roman Catholic.
Marital Status: single; a swinging bachelor with many glamorous friends.
Education: Ph.D in Economics; studied at universities in Canada, England and the United States.
Work Experience: has done research for major corporations and labour unions; has taught economics at several universities across Canada.
Finances: only income is salary as an MP.
Standing in Party: seen as a leader by younger members; perceived as a bit "radical" by older members; MP for two years.
Personality: sincere, dedicated, witty; tends to be emotional; a free-thinking, independent type.

George Homeniuk, 51, MP from Calgary.
Religion: Eastern Orthodox.
Marital Status: separated; has four children who live with their mother.
Education: left high school after Grade 10 to support parents.
Work Experience: worked his way up from the bottom in the petroleum industry; built a giant oil company from scratch.
Finances: multi-millionaire.
Standing in Party: several years' experience as MP; liked by press but feared by some party members; controversial and outspoken about party policy.
Personality: tough, hardworking, energetic; excellent speaker but sometimes gets carried away; cares more for exciting ideas than dull statistics.

The Opposition

We tend to think of elections in terms of winners and losers. The "winners" are the members of the party with the largest number of seats in the House of Commons. They run the country. Their leader becomes prime minister, their leading members are appointed to the cabinet.

But what about members of the other parties? They are "losers" in the sense that they do not control the government. They are winners too, though, because each of them has won the election in his or her constituency and has a seat in the House of Commons.

MPs who belong to parties that came second or third in elections continue to play an important and effective role in our government. They form the opposition. In effect, they earn their salaries by criticizing the party in power.

The leader of the party with the second largest number of seats in the House of Commons becomes "the Leader of Her Majesty's Loyal Opposition". This honour and responsibility brings an extra salary and an official residence (Stornoway) in Ottawa.

The Leader of the Opposition's Job

The leader of the opposition must make sure that opposition members provide intelligent, effective criticism of government policy. Opposition MPs must be kept informed of what the government is doing, and they must decide how to respond. In some ways organizing the opposition can be nearly as hard as running the government. The leader must:

- appoint leading party members to monitor, or "shadow" specific government departments. Together, these opposition MPs form the "shadow cabinet"
- decide which questions should be asked, and by whom, during Question Period
- appoint members to the committees that examine proposed laws
- speak across the country at party rallies and conventions, and appear on TV to promote party policy
- keep the party machinery across the country rolling smoothly, encourage membership drives and fund-raising campaigns.

The Opposition is allowed to raise its own concerns and criticisms during Question Period, a time set aside each day Parliament is in session. The proceedings are televised.

Members of other parties are also part of the opposition. Their power and importance depends on the number of seats they hold in the House of Commons.

Members of the opposition sit facing the government, on the other side of the House of Commons. The prime minister and the leader of the opposition sit directly opposite one another.

The Importance of the Opposition

The opposition plays a vital role in Canadian government. Without a spirited and well-informed opposition, the party in power would be free to make whatever laws it wanted. The opposition keeps the government party on its toes, presents alternative viewpoints, and sometimes forces changes in government policy. Occasionally an alert opposition will expose government errors, waste, or corruption.

When the opposition is at its best, it provides informed and intelligent criticism. It offers voters and

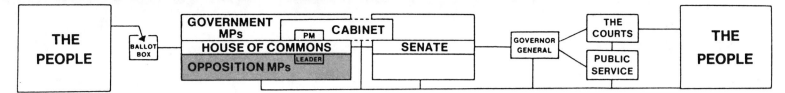

the media an alternative to the party in power. Sensible criticism can bring about needed changes in proposed laws, or prevent the introduction of bad laws. Parliament can become the centre of reasoned and intelligent debate that is a credit to all Canadians.

When the opposition is weak or divided, it may criticize blindly. Opposition members may try to harrass and embarrass the governing party. There are times when debates in the House of Commons become trivial, bitter, and petty.

Sometimes it seems that the opposition is simply out to attack all government policies, good or bad. We should remember that members of the opposition do not have access to all the facts and ideas that lead the government to set these policies. Even so, insults are not valid substitutes for intelligent criticism.

A Motion of Non-Confidence

When the opposition wishes to highlight its criticism of the government, it proposes a motion of non-confidence. In effect, this means that the House of Commons must vote on whether the party in power should continue to govern. Opposition MPs usually support non-confidence motions; government MPs, who want to stay in power, usually vote against it. If a majority of MPs show that they no longer have confidence in the government, then the government must resign.

In a majority government, non-confidence motions can usually be easily outvoted. But non-confidence motions are very dangerous for minority governments. If the opposition parties unite, the government can be defeated, and forced to resign. This happened in 1979, when Joe Clark's minority government was brought down by a non-confidence motion supported by Liberals and New Democrats.

Leading the Opposition

Jean Chrétien (L): First elected in 1963. MP for St. Maurice. Served as Minister of National Revenue, Indian Affairs, Treasury Board, Industry, Finance, Justice, Energy, and External Affairs. In 1990 he was elected Leader of the Liberal Party of Canada, and became Leader of the Opposition.

Audrey McLaughlin (NDP): First elected in 1987. MP for Yukon. Appointed to the Privy Council, January 1991. In December 1989 she was elected Leader of the New Democratic Party of Canada. She has been NDP critic on the Constitution, Northern Development, Tourism, and Revenue Canada.

1. Name the present leader of the opposition in the federal government and your provincial government. Write to them both, asking for information on their careers. Find a newspaper or magazine article on each of them.
2. Examine recent statements by members of the opposition. Try to decide whether the statements are:
a) constructive suggestions to improve government policy
b) opposition for the sake of opposition
c) an alternative to the government's policy
3. Watch question period on your local television station. How would you describe the words and behaviour of the opposition? How did the government respond in your opinion?

The Senate

Not all members of the Parliament of Canada are elected. Members of the Canadian Senate are appointed. The Senate and the House of Commons are the two houses of Canada's Parliament. The Senate is sometimes called the Upper House.

The Senate shares power with the House of Commons. For example, all bills must be debated and passed in both houses before becoming law. But the House of Commons holds more power than the Senate because it is elected by the people of Canada.

Senators are appointed by the governor-general, who follows the advice of the prime minister and cabinet. Once appointed, senators hold office until the age of 75, when they must retire.

To be eligible for a seat in the Senate, you must be a Canadian citizen between 30 and 75 years of age, and own property worth at least $4000. In addition, you must reside in the province you are appointed to represent. These are the technical requirements. Theoretically, you must also have shown the prime minister that you will be able to play a useful role in helping to run the government.

In practice senators are often appointed for being loyal "party warhorses." This type of purely political appointment weakens the prestige of the Senate.

A Senator's Job

As a member of Canada's Upper House, it is the senator's duty to:
- represent the interests of his or her province in the federal Parliament
- give "sober second thought" to bills passed by the House of Commons
- delay, amend, or stop unwise and careless bills which are passed by the House of Commons
- introduce bills (Senators may not introduce bills that involve the raising of money. Only MPs, because they are the elected representatives of the Canadian people, have that power. Since most laws require the raising and spending of money, this greatly reduces the Senate's power).

Some Recent Senators

Thérèse Casgrain (NDP, Que.): born 1896, died 1981. *Career:* Early supporter of women's rights and civil liberties. Led the CCF in Quebec but failed to get a House of Commons seat. During WW II she opposed conscription and the internment of Japanese Canadians. *Senate:* appointed at 74, forced to retire at 75. One of few NDP members appointed to Senate. After retirement she actively continued to oppose the Quebec separatists to the end of her life.

Duff Roblin (PC, Manitoba): born 1917, in Winnipeg, Manitoba. *Career:* served for four years with the RCAF in World War II, was elected as an MPP in Manitoba Legislature in 1949, re-elected five times. Premier of Manitoba 1957-1968. *Senate:* appointed 1978, served as leader of the Government in Senate 1984-1986.

Lorna Marsden (L, Ontario): born 1942, in Sidney, British Columbia. *Education:* University of Toronto and Princeton University (U.S.). *Career:* professor, vice-provost, president of the National Action Committee on the Status of Women, vice-president Liberal Party. *Senate:* appointed 1984.

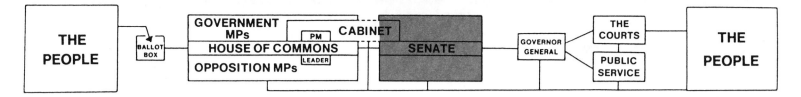

Should the Senate be changed?

Not everyone is convinced that the Senate is a useful and necessary part of Canadian government.
It has altered little since it was created in 1867.

The Senate should be elected

a) We need a more efficient Senate, a TRIPLE E Senate - elected; effective; with equal representation.

b) Election is the only democratic way, so that Senators truly represent the wishes of the people.

c) Once elected, Senators should have the same powers as the House of Commons.

d) Representation in the Senate should be balanced to give equal representation to all the provinces, to balance the power of the larger provinces of Ontario and Quebec.

e) The Senate should be as important in Canada, as the Senate is in the United States.

Reform of the Senate

1) Do further research on the Senate. Consult your library, newspaper, and magazines. Contact your local MP and a Senator from your province if possible.

2) Join one of four groups, representing your opinion:
   a) to abolish the Senate
   b) to elect the Senate
   c) to leave the Senate as it is
   d) to reform the Senate in some other way

3) Prepare your arguments to join in a class debate: "Resolved that the Senate should be left as it is."

The Crown

God save our gracious queen,
Long live our noble queen,
God save the queen.

Your Majesty

It often surprises Canadians to learn that the official head of state for Canada is not the prime minister. It is someone who does not even live in Canada: the king or queen of Britain. This is a reminder of the fact that Canada was once part of the far-flung British Empire. Although Canada is now an independent country, the monarch in England is still recognized as Canada's head of state.

Canada's form of government is known as a constitutional monarchy. This means that the monarch's power is limited by a series of laws and customs. The monarch has little power in Canada, or in Britain.

The monarch's role in Canadian government is said to be "symbolic." A symbol is something which stands for something else. For example, the Canadian flag is a symbol of Canada. The monarch, as head of state, is a personal symbol of the system of government that Canadians have chosen.

Symbols are more important for what they stand for than for what they are. So rather than talking about actual kings or queens, we use the term "the crown" to refer to the symbolic role of the monarch. In court cases, the crown attorneys represent the people of Canada as a whole. Publicly owned lands are known as crown lands. A crown appears on many government documents as a symbol of government authority.

The Crown is an idea more than a person and I want the Crown in Canada to represent everything that is best and most admired in the Canadian ideal.

Governor General Edward Schreyer

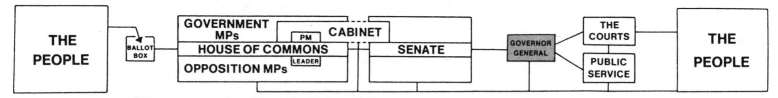

THE PEOPLE → BALLOT BOX → GOVERNMENT MPs / HOUSE OF COMMONS / OPPOSITION MPs / PM CABINET LEADER → SENATE → GOVERNOR GENERAL → THE COURTS / PUBLIC SERVICE → THE PEOPLE

Governor General Jeanne Sauvé and Maurice Sauvé

Your Excellency

The monarch is represented in Canada by the governor general. When Canada was still a group of British colonies, the governors actually ran the government. Today the governor general advises, but it is the prime minister who actually leads the nation.

The governor general is appointed by the king or queen on the advice of the Canadian prime minister. A great deal of care goes into the selection. Governors general usually serve terms of five to seven years.

In 1952 a Canadian-born governor general, Vincent Massey, was chosen for the first time. Until then governors general were sent by the monarch from Britain. After 1952 there was a pattern of alternating French and English Canadians in the post. Edward Schreyer from Manitoba was the first governor general of neither French nor English ancestry.

The Governor General's Job

The duties of the governor general are largely ceremonial. As head of state, the governor general:
- represents the crown in Canada
- is the symbol of national unity
- is the ceremonial and social leader of Canada
- is the official host for visiting heads of state from other countries
- acts as an impartial adviser to the prime minister, who must keep the governor general informed of political decisions
- signs all acts of parliament before they become law
- awards honours and medals such as the Order of Canada
- summons and dissolves parliament on the advice of the prime minister
- makes the "speech from the throne" which outlines government policy at the beginning of each session of parliament
- may travel abroad as an official representative of Canada

The governor general lives at Government House (also called Rideau Hall), in Ottawa, and has a summer residence in the citadel in Quebec City. Being governor general means long hours of work and travel, days and nights of receptions, tours of schools, hospitals, and factories, formal dinners, balls, and many thousands of handshakes. The governor general does not have the most powerful position in the country, but has the top ceremonial post. Officially, he or she is the most honoured person in Canada.

1. In August 1980 a nation-wide Gallup Poll found that 47% of Canadians approved of having the queen as Canada's head of state. 43% did not approve. 10% were undecided. What do you think? Take a poll in your class or school to find out what other students think.
2. What do you think are the important things to consider in choosing a governor general? If you had to choose a prominent Canadian to be governor general, how would you decide? Who would you choose?

Making a Law

There ought to be a law.

popular complaint

All laws start with ideas about solving problems. Adults complain about the use of drugs by teenagers. Minorities demand an end to discrimination. Couples want fair family laws. City residents complain about high levels of noise and pollution. Military specialists want better equipment for the armed forces. Manufacturers want protection from foreign competition. Government workers want to change the way their departments operate. We all have problems, complaints, and issues that we want solved.

When we demand action from the government, we are asking for laws. Laws to prevent or stop this. Laws to provide the money to do that. Laws! Laws! Laws! Some people feel there are too many laws and want laws to end laws.

Laws are made at all three levels of government in Canada. At the federal level, law-making is the chief responsibility of Parliament.

Where do Laws Come From?

Pressure for new laws, or changes in existing laws, may come from newspaper editorials, opinion poll results, election promises, public demonstrations, the advice of respected experts, or the government's own policies. As the pressure builds for action, the law-making process begins.

When the prime minister and cabinet have decided a new law is required, public servants, lawyers, and other experts get to work on the exact details. The cabinet will look it over and perhaps make some changes. The minister whose department is most concerned will introduce the proposed law to parliament.

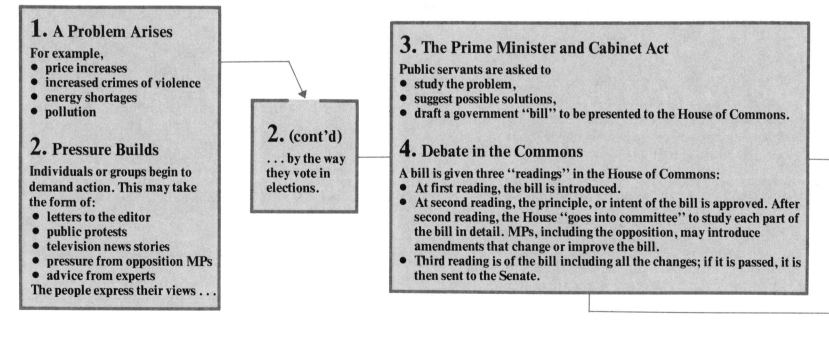

1. A Problem Arises

For example,
- price increases
- increased crimes of violence
- energy shortages
- pollution

2. Pressure Builds

Individuals or groups begin to demand action. This may take the form of:
- letters to the editor
- public protests
- television news stories
- pressure from opposition MPs
- advice from experts

The people express their views . . .

2. (cont'd)

. . . by the way they vote in elections.

3. The Prime Minister and Cabinet Act

Public servants are asked to
- study the problem,
- suggest possible solutions,
- draft a government "bill" to be presented to the House of Commons.

4. Debate in the Commons

A bill is given three "readings" in the House of Commons:
- At first reading, the bill is introduced.
- At second reading, the principle, or intent of the bill is approved. After second reading, the House "goes into committee" to study each part of the bill in detail. MPs, including the opposition, may introduce amendments that change or improve the bill.
- Third reading is of the bill including all the changes; if it is passed, it is then sent to the Senate.

At this stage the proposed law is called a *bill*. When it has been approved by all three divisions of parliament — the House of Commons, the Senate, and the Crown — it will become an *act of parliament*. Its provisions will then be *law* and binding on all Canadians and other people in the country.

Together we are Parliament
Queen Elizabeth II in the speech from the throne to the Senate and Commons of Canada, 1967

What would you like to pass a law about? Write your ideas down as a "bill." Read your bill to your classmates so that they know what it is about. Then read it again so that they can discuss it in detail.

Some students may be able to suggest improvements. On the other hand, others may completely disagree with your ideas. What are their criticisms? Are they valid? If so, should you scrap your bill, modify it, or start all over again?

Read your bill again, complete with any changes you have made. Then put it to a vote.

If you really feel strongly about your ideas, who should you approach? Do they come under federal, provincial, or municipal responsibilities?

Think hard: Is your law really workable in Canada today?

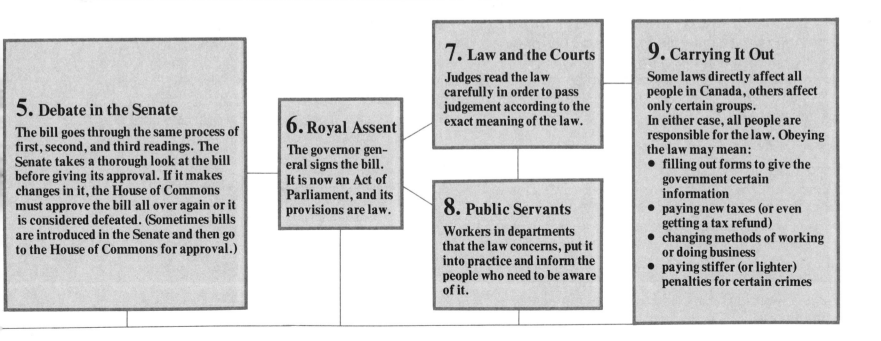

5. Debate in the Senate

The bill goes through the same process of first, second, and third readings. The Senate takes a thorough look at the bill before giving its approval. If it makes changes in it, the House of Commons must approve the bill all over again or it is considered defeated. (Sometimes bills are introduced in the Senate and then go to the House of Commons for approval.)

6. Royal Assent

The governor general signs the bill. It is now an Act of Parliament, and its provisions are law.

7. Law and the Courts

Judges read the law carefully in order to pass judgement according to the exact meaning of the law.

8. Public Servants

Workers in departments that the law concerns, put it into practice and inform the people who need to be aware of it.

9. Carrying It Out

Some laws directly affect all people in Canada, others affect only certain groups.
In either case, all people are responsible for the law. Obeying the law may mean:
- filling out forms to give the government certain information
- paying new taxes (or even getting a tax refund)
- changing methods of working or doing business
- paying stiffer (or lighter) penalties for certain crimes

Why We Need Laws

As part of our everyday life, we follow many rules: most of them are unwritten; some are written. Most of our contact with other people is on a casual, *informal* basis. Sometimes, often with people we don't know, our contact is *formal* and a strict set of rules applies. The difference between these two types of contact is discovered by a group of hockey players.

An Informal Game

Early on a crisp Saturday morning, Brad and his friends meet at the neighbourhood rink for their weekly game of shinny. The players wear a variety of uniforms. Some have helmets and protective equipment. They rely on Chris to bring the nets. The players allow Jean and Glen to divide the groups into teams. The puck is casually pushed up the ice by Brad, and the game begins. No whistles are blown, no body checks are given, and no gloves are dropped to the ice, which would signify a fight. The players have never even considered having a referee. Some players leave for their Saturday jobs and are readily replaced by newcomers. After the game, the remaining group goes for hamburgers and sits around to relive the game in excited chatter.

A Formal Game

Brad also plays on a team in the City Hockey League. The organization and atmosphere are very different from those of the Saturday morning group. Here the players must sign a contract before joining a team. The dates of the games are printed on a schedule at the first of the season. The rules are printed and agreed upon by all teams before the start of the season. Players wear uniforms, and proper equipment is compulsory.

The games are exciting and teams are very competitive. There must be a referee to control the game and to enforce the rules.

A Rough Evening

One night the referee did not show up; the coaches agreed to allow a player from each team to wear the striped jersey and to do the referee's job. Within a few minutes the game became "chippy" and soon several fights broke out. The game had to be cancelled. After such a game, players from opposing teams did not get together as friends would to discuss the game.

Why was this type of hockey game so different from the informal game of shinny?

Why We Have Rules

In many ways, our society is like an organized game, such as hockey. If our society consisted of a small community of friends, like the shinny game, we would not need rules and organization. However, society involves large groups of people, most of whom we do not know. Therefore, we require a society controlled by rules or **laws.**

Focus Question
What roles do the following play in organized hockey?
— scheduled games
— printed rules (agreed upon in advance)
— a referee
— a penalty box
— an official scorekeeper

Organizer

Construct a chart using some of the headings from your focus question. Compare the organization of a hockey game and the need for rules and organization in society.

Hockey Game	Society
Printed rules agreed upon in advance	
Schedule	
Coach	
Referee	
Penalty box	
Scorekeeper	

When you have completed your chart, consider ways in which the organization of sports and society are **different.** Hold a class discussion about the differences.

1. List written and unwritten laws observed
   a) at home and
   b) in school.
2. Why do we obey the unwritten rules?
3. Which written laws are commonly disobeyed? Why?
4. Brad's exhibition game ended in an uproar. Do we only need rules and referees when we don't know our opponent?

A City Without the Rule of Law

How would Canadians behave if the police suddenly stopped enforcing rules and protecting the public? In the town of Bathurst, New Brunswick, citizens found out.

Society Without Laws: What Would Life Be Like?

Read and discuss the following quote.
What do you think?

"In a time of warre, where every man is Enemy to every man; In such condition, there no place for Industry,...no Culture of the Earth, no Navigation...no Building...no Knowledge of the face of the Earth...no Society...continual feare, and danger of violent death; And the life of man, solitary, poore, nasty, brutish, and short." — Thomas Hobbes

Write a diary entry for a typical day in your life. Pretend that you could not trust anyone you met during that day. Is your description similar to that of Hobbes?

Clean-up after another night of near-riots. When the municipal police force went on strike in Bathurst, crowds gathered downtown for a few nights in a row, looting, vandalizing, and generally making a nuisance.

Police and Citizens

In an earlier section, we discussed the importance of a referee. The referee must enforce the rules, so that all can play fairly. The referee also catches those who break the rules, and gives them an appropriate penalty or punishment.

In society, the police play part of the role performed by the referee. They are responsible for securing and protecting the community. This means that they must catch people who violate the laws and bring them to the courts for trial.

Our laws state that the police have the power to

- search and arrest with a warrant or without a warrant if they suspect an indictable crime has taken place;
- search and arrest without a warrant if they suspect that narcotics are present;
- ask a driver to produce a driver's licence, ownership, and insurance papers.

Suspects are escorted into court in handcuffs.

Canadian law also states that the police are not allowed to
- arrest or take to the police station a person who is not charged with a crime;
- question an individual against his or her will;
- search without a warrant without a reasonable belief that an indictable crime has taken place;
- break the law.

The **rule of law** in Canada allows us to live safely and happily. Every Canadian is protected by the law and every Canadian must obey the law. Canadians have a history of respect for our police forces. Part of that respect is due to the fact that the police must obey the law, including our most important law: the Charter of Rights and Freedoms. Because Canadians gave the police the power to enforce the law, we act as careful watchdogs, making sure that our police operate within the rules of the Charter of Rights and Freedoms.

Read the following headlines. Which section of the Charter of Rights and Freedoms is the headline concerned with?
- "Blacks Complain Police Harassment in Drug Sweeps"
- "Man Kept Overnight in Jail Cell Without Charges"
- "RCMP Sends Multiracial Team Looking for Recruits"
- "Indian Stopped and Searched at Roadside — Non-Indians Allowed to Pass"

Plan a publicity campaign to improve police-community relations.
1. Collect news clippings about police activities: heroism, arrests, crimestoppers...
2. Interview police and the public. Visit the courts.
3. Arrange for a police officer to visit your class to discuss the role of the police.

Residents furious over police drug raid

By Phinjo Gombu

Residents of an apartment building in Flemingdon Park are furious at a large-scale police drug raid in which three units were ransacked to find what police call "small quantity of drugs."

"The police ...

hastily scrawled note stuck to her fridge door from the police saying they had been there.

Yesterday th...

All police forces urged to videotape interrogations

project by Halton police.
From July 1, 1985, to June 30, 1987, 901 suspects at three Burlington police stations consented to having their statements videotaped while 45 refused.

Police board backs minority hiring policy

By Royson James
Star

officer can use a firearm.
"You don't shoot people first and ask questions later," Eng said. Task force members had recommended because they felt ...

Criminal law in dire need of revision judges agree

By Rick Haliechuk

The time for piecemeal reform of Canada's criminal law is over and a major overhaul is needed now, says the president of the Law Reform Commission of Canada.

Making incremental improvements to the Criminal Code is "like tinkering with the sparkplugs when what we need is a whole new engine," Mr. Justice Allen Linden told delegates to the biennial Criminal Justice Congress in Toronto yesterday.

Linden, a judge of the Supreme Court of Ontario, said the public is becoming increasingly concerned about the welfare of the country's criminal justice system.

"To keep the law bright and shiny, we need to have machinery that's bright and shiny and not rusty," Linden said.

...ent years, Linden said, law ...rs have moved to simplify ...rovisions of the Criminal ...hile strengthening others, ...while working to have it ...rm with the Charter of

'Out of touch'

...ting that the Criminal Code ...nacted in 1892, Linden said it ...dly out of touch ...th 20th cen-

Charter of Rights and Freedoms

Guarantee of Rights and Freedoms
The Canadian Charter of Rights and Freedoms guarantees the rights and freedoms set out in it subject only to such reasonable limits prescribed by law as can be demonstrably justified in a free and democratic society. (Section 1)

Fundamental Freedoms
Everyone has ... freedom of conscience and religion. (Section 2 a)
Everyone has ... freedom of thought, belief, opinion and expression, including freedom of the press and other media of communication. (Section 2 b)
Everyone has ... freedom of peaceful assembly. (Section 2 c)
Everyone has ... freedom of association. (Section 2 d)

Equality Rights
Every individual is equal before and under the law and has the right to the equal protection and equal benefit of the law without discrimination and, in particular, without discrimination based on race, national or ethnic origin, colour, religion, sex, age, or mental or physical ability. (Section 15 (1))

In 1981, the Canadian government made the Charter of Rights and Freedoms a part of the Canadian Constitution. Before this, Canadians assumed that many of the Rights and Freedoms now enshrined in the Constitution were protected. However, since they were not part of the Constitution, this was not always so. The Judicial Branch's duty to protect laws and Rights and Freedoms has never been more important. Sometimes in protecting these Rights and Freedoms the courts are asked to decide whether a law imposed on Canadians might violate the Charter. These decisions are called **interpretations** and the law in question is said to be **challenged** by a member of the public.

Challenging the Laws

Examine the following Canadian laws and the view of the Charter of Rights.

The law says:	The Charter says:
Police have the right to "spotcheck" cars looking for impaired drivers.	Everyone has the right not to be arbitrarily detained or imprisoned. (Section 9)
Publishing false information about the Holocaust is wrong.	Everyone has ... freedom of thought belief, opinion, and expression, including freedom of the press and other media of communication. (Section 2 b)
Retirement in many jobs is mandatory at age 65.	Every individual is equal before and under the law and has the right to ... equal benefit of the law without discrimination ... based on ... age.

If you were a judge, would you allow those laws to remain, in view of the Charter of Rights?

The courts must carefully examine such challenges and decide whether the existing law should remain in light of the Rights and Freedoms outlined in the Charter. The Charter of Rights and Freedoms is superior to all other laws in the country.

The Courts Decide

How do the courts decide whether the law imposed on an individual violates the Charter? There is often a conflict between what is good for the individual and what is good for the community. A neo-Nazi group might want to parade and feel that their freedom to "assemble" and to have "free speech" entitles them to do so. However, this parade might offend many more people in the community.

The courts must decide whether the rights and freedoms claimed are subject to "... reasonable limits prescribed by law". The way a law restricts one's rights and freedoms must be proven to be reasonable. Laws which prohibit under-age drinking may discriminate by age, but it is considered reasonable that this law is necessary to protect young people and all of society. All laws take away some of our rights and freedoms, but most of the time we accept them as reasonable in our democratic society.

CANADIAN CHARTER OF RIGHTS AND FREEDOMS

The Charter of Rights and Our Daily Lives
a)   A man boards a crowded bus carrying a portable radio. He sits at the back of the bus and turns up the volume.
b)   It is a cold January day. A group of commuters is huddled in a bus shelter. A woman enters and lights a cigarette.

In both cases, several members of the group object to the actions. Both the man and the woman claim that the Charter allows them to have "freedom of expression".

Choose one of the situations and conduct a debate. Three members of the class will argue that the **individual** has the right to "freedom of expression", and three will argue that the **group's** rights are more important.

Research Activity
Many organizations are involved in examining the rights of the individual in our society.
1. Contact *one* of the organizations related to one of the following issues!
   • drinking, drugs, and driving
   • rights of the handicapped
   • political freedom
2. Communicate your results in one of the following ways:
   • a poster campaign
   • a play
   • a letter-writing campaign
   • a taped interview

Criminal and Civil Law

Criminal Law

Canadian **criminal law** prohibits specific behaviours which harm individuals and groups. It also states punishments for those acting in the prohibited way.

A Case Study

Gwen Lee was thrilled with her promotion to the position of sales manager and invited several of her co-workers to celebrate with her at *"Arnold's"*. After two hours, several of the group left and urged Gwen and the others to do the same. Instead, Gwen accepted the offer of her boss to stay for another round of drinks. "Arnold's" was across the city from Gwen's home, there was no public transit available, and Gwen's husband was not available to pick her up. Feeling fine, Gwen said good-night and drove away, wondering why the brightly lit tow truck seemed to be following her. She was overtaken and the "tow truck" turned out to be a police car. Gwen produced her licence, ownership, and insurance. Her heart was pounding.

"Ms. Lee, have you had anything to drink this evening?"

"Yes, a couple of glasses of wine after work."

"Ms. Lee, I observed you failing to stop for a red light. I'd like you to provide a breath sample. Please breathe into this approved screening device."

Unfortunately for Gwen, her breath sample lit the Alert's red light, indicating that she was driving with more than 0.08% of alcohol in her blood. Gwen was arrested and taken to the police station where a further breathalizer test confirmed the bad news. Gwen Lee was charged under the Criminal Code of Canada with driving with more than 80 mg of alcohol in her blood.

Gwen's actions are considered to be a **crime** because *two important elements* are present.
- her drinking and driving was *harmful to society as a whole;*
- *her action of drinking and driving was* **intentional.**

Gwen's crime as all other offences in the Criminal Code will fall into a category of seriousness:
- A **summary** offence is the least serious of offences. Some examples of this are: causing a disturbance, making an indecent phone call, and soliciting for the purposes of prostitution. Trials for summary offences are held in Provincial Court and the top punishment is usually a $2000 fine or six months in prison or both.

- An **indictable** offence is serious and the category includes drug trafficking, sexual assault, theft over $1000, breaking and entering, and murder. Trials may be held in Provincial Court or, in the case of murder, in a Supreme Court before judge and jury. The penalties may be severe, including life imprisonment. Had Gwen caused the death of another while impaired, she would face a maximum of 14 years in prison.
- A **hybrid** offence may be treated as either a *summary* or an *indictable* offence: the Crown attorney decides.

Gwen's impaired driving charge is a hybrid offence, and, because she has had a clean record, the Crown attorney decided to hold her trial in a Provincial Court. If convicted, she will be fined $300 and will be suspended from driving for three months.

Research Activity

1. Examine your local newspaper. Find at least one example of a *summary* offence and an *indictable* offence.
2. Bring your cases to class, and share them with others in the room.
3. Create a chart for summary and indictable offences. Include the following as your organizers:
   NATURE OF OFFENCE; DESCRIPTION OF WHAT HAPPENED; VERDICT; PUNISHMENT

RIDE

REDUCE IMPAIRED DRIVING EVERYWHERE

THE METROPOLITAN
TO POLICE

METRO SAFETY
COUNCIL

Play It Smart

Impaired Driving: A Continuing Problem

Civil Law

Canadian **civil law** involves lawsuits between individuals who feel that they have suffered an injury because of another's actions.

A Case Study

Senator Rawlski, dressed for a committee meeting on Parliament Hill, smiled at his wife and two children, absent-mindedly picked up the *Ottawa Tattler,* thinking it was his financial newspaper, and sat down to coffee and toast. The quiet of the home was soon shattered. Senator Rawlski sputtered, fumed, turned red, and pointed to the headline: "Senator Rawlski Discovered in Gambling Den!" Under the headline was a story with quotes from a Miss Dollars and a picture of her and a much thinner man with the Senator's head neatly pasted on. Instantly, Senator Rawlski arranged a meeting with Mr. Lawson, an expert civil lawyer whose specialty was libel. The Senator's good reputation was ruined in print!

Civil lawsuits are started by an individual or by a group of individuals who feel that they have *suffered an injury because of another's actions.* The injury may be personal: falling down a neighbour's rotting steps; it may be because of wrongful dismissal from a job; or it may be an injury to your good name — as was suffered by the Senator.

Many well-publicized civil lawsuits show that the **claimant,** or person starting the lawsuit, won millions of dollars in settlement for the injury. However, this is not always the case. Lawyer's fees may take a bite out of the settlement won by the claimant. There is also a chance that the claimant will lose the case. Senator Rawlski, however, decided that his suit was worth the risk and that he would sue the *Ottawa Tattler.*

Senator Rawlski hired *Mr. Lawson* as his lawyer. Mr. Lawson wrote a **Statement of Claim** and presented it to the newspaper. Within a short period of time the *Ottawa Tattler* delivered a **Statement of Defence.** Mr. Lawson spent a great deal of time gathering evidence proving the Senator's fine reputation. At a **discovery** meeting, the lawyers for both sides examined each other's clients, trying to weaken their stories. As with many civil lawsuits, this libel action was settled out of court. Senator Rawlski received less compensation than he expected, but he avoided an upsetting trial, covered his costs, and was given a public apology by the *Ottawa Tattler.*

Small Claims Court — Civil Law Available to All

Rita Givens, a plumber, was becoming exasperated with Steve Popoulis. She had completed his downstairs bathroom five months earlier and still hadn't received payment. Rita depended on her customers' prompt payments to keep her small business afloat. She had no choice but to fill out a claim for settlement in Small Claims Court. The bill for her services was $2300, below the Small Claims Court limit of $3000. Steve Popoulis, the defendant, was notified and given 30 days to file a defence.

Small Claims Court is informal, inexpensive, with no lawyers. Rita represented herself as did Mr. Popoulis. Both came prepared with contracts and any notes they had kept. The judge made a decision immediately and explained his reasons to the plaintiff and the defendant. Mr. Popoulis was ordered to pay the $2300 owed.

The Court System

Court cases heard by each level of the Canadian court system

CRIMINAL COURT

Provincial Court
- *summary* offences
- 90% of cases heard here
- preliminary hearings to see if there is enough evidence to hold trial

Family Court and Youth Court
- family disputes, such as failure to pay support to ex-spouse or ex-mate and children
- truancy and other charges under the Young Offenders Act

County Court
- all *indictable* crimes, such as drug offences, except murder, treason, and piracy
- other offences concerning business — false advertising, income tax fraud, etc.

CIVIL COURT

Small Claims Court
- claims for under $3000

County Court
- claims up to $25 000

CRIMINAL COURT

Provincial Supreme Court
- all *indictable* crimes — the Crown Attorney will ask that a case be tried in Provincial Supreme Court, rather than County Court, if the Crown feels it is important that the trial get publicity
- appeals of lower court decisions

Supreme Court of Canada
- court of last resort — apeals are final here
- Charter of Rights decisions

CIVIL COURT

Provincial Supreme Court
- claims for unlimited amounts as in personal injury cases
- divorce cases

Work in groups of three
1. Write a small claims court case study (remember the steps outlined above);
2. Switch the case studies and role-play: the plaintiff, the defendant, and the judge.

Working With the Law
1. Follow the progress of a Canadian
   - civil trial; and/or
   - criminal trial;
2. Collect newspaper articles and write brief reports of TV coverage;
3. Post these on a bulletin board under these headings: Pre-Trial, Trial, Verdict, Sentencing or Payment

CRIMINAL AND CIVIL LAW   351

Arrest and Trial

The Arrest

Police Constables Grégoire and Singh had an ordinary night on patrol. They had recovered a lost wallet intact, returned it to its grateful owner; resolved a parking dispute between two neighbours; and had given directions to a family visiting the city. On Simcoe Street they noticed a white van with a missing headlight. They circled, stopped the car, and checked the police computer for unpaid traffic tickets against the car's owner. The computer revealed that the van was wanted in a "hit and run" accident which tragically had killed a young schoolgirl three days earlier.

Constable Grégoire informed the driver, Lucille Green, that he had **reasonable** and **probable grounds** to believe that she had committed an *indictable offence*. Ms. Green was charged under the **Criminal Code** with leaving the scene of an accident. — *Everyone has the right on arrest or detention to be informed promptly of the reasons therefor (section 10 (a)).* Constable Grégoire told the **accused** of her right to speak to a lawyer. — *Everyone has the right on arrest or detention ... to retain counsel without delay and to be informed of that right (section 10 (b)).*

Ms. Green was taken to the police station for questioning. Because she couldn't afford a lawyer, Ms. Green qualified for **Legal Aid** which provided a lawyer free of charge. After questioning, with her lawyer present, Ms. Green was fingerprinted and photographed. Following this, she appeared before a judge who set bail. This meant that she agreed to appear in court and guaranteed this by putting up a sum of money. — *Any person charged with an offence has the right not to be denied reasonable bail without just cause (section 11 (e)).* Ms. Green's case

was **remanded** or put off to a later date allowing her and her **defence lawyer** to prepare a case for her **defence.** — *Any person charged with an offence has the right to be tried within a reasonable time (section 11 (b)).*

PCs Grégoire and Singh went to a judge for a **search warrant** which allowed them to search Ms. Green's apartment for evidence, such as the clothes eyewitnesses reported her wearing. — *Everyone has the right to be secure against unreasonable search and seizure (section 8).*

Preparing for the Trial

Ms. Green and Mr. Tannate, a lawyer appointed for her through Legal Aid, considered the possibility of **plea bargaining** or agreeing to plead guilty before the trial. Either action would avoid a long and costly court case and possibly result in a lighter sentence for Ms. Green. However, Ms. Green insisted that she wished to plead not guilty.

The next decision faced by the defence was whether or not to ask for **trial by jury.** Mr. Tannate explained to Ms. Green her choices: the advantages and disadvantages of trial by jury, or of a trial by judge.

Trial by Jury

Advantages for Defendant

- a unanimous decision is needed — this is difficult to obtain;
- the jury might feel sorry for you;
- a good defence might affect them emotionally;
- the jury is picked by the Crown and the Defence and won't be biased.

Disadvantages for Defendant

- the jury might not understand the law;
- a good prosecution might affect the jury emotionally;
- the jury might be biased.

Trial by Judge

The main reason for choosing trial by judge is that the judge does not bring personal prejudices to the procedure, whereas a jury might do so. Members of the jury might be influenced by the accused's clothing or nationality. The judge will have a better understanding of legal points than would a jury. The judge also is less likely to be influenced by the rhetoric of Defence or Crown attorney. The judge's knowledge and experience lead to a decision based on law and the facts. Except for jury selection, the trial will proceed in the way of trial by jury.

Mr. Tannate and Ms. Green chose **trial by jury.** The jury of twelve was chosen from a group of Canadian citizens whose names were taken from the voter's list. The jurors came from all walks of life (except police, lawyers, doctors, and some convicted criminals) and were thought to be Ms. Green's equals or peers.

THE COURT ROOM

The Trial

The trial opened with the black-robed judge entering the court. The charge was read to Ms. Green and she pleaded "not guilty".

The Crown

The Crown Attorney, representing the public, had to prove to the jury that Ms. Green was guilty beyond a reasonable doubt. This placed a great burden on the Crown or **Prosecution.** Guilt had to be established without question. The Crown prepared to produce **witnesses** and **evidence** which would prove beyond a **reasonable doubt** that Ms. Green did hit the young girl and leave the scene.

The Crown Prosecutor gave an opening statement to the jury outlining how she was going to prove Ms. Green guilty. **Crown witnesses,** sworn to tell the truth, testified to: seeing a van identified as Ms. Green's leaving the scene; seeing a woman getting out of the van and looking at the girl; and matching the paint and debris found at the accident scene to Ms. Green's van. After each Crown witness was called, the Defence had the opportunity to cross-examine that witness. The Defence hoped to discredit the Crown witness's story and create a doubt in the jury's minds.

The Defence

Mr. Tannate believed in his client's innocence. His job was to defend her against the charge, using his knowledge of law. Above all, he knew that his client was to be treated by the judge and jury as innocent until proven guilty, and he reminded them of this throughout the trial. — *Any person charged with an offence has the right to be presumed innocent until proven guilty according to law in a fair and public hearing by an independent and impartial tribunal (section 11 (d)).*

When the Crown finished examining witnesses, the Defence presented witnesses and evidence which tried to prove the accused's innocence. The Defence set out to show that Ms. Green did not commit the **act** of "hit and run" nor did she have the **intention** to do so. Mr. Tannate produced evidence that Ms. Green was at a meeting at the time of the accident, and that she had left her car keys at work the morning of the accident and did not regain possession of them until five hours after the accident. He also produced witnesses who testified that Ms. Green was a kind woman who loved children. Ms. Green agreed to act as a witness. However, the accused is not required to give evidence in a case. — *Any person charged with an offence has the right not to be compelled to be a witness in proceedings against that person in respect of the offence (section 11 (c)).* (Remember it is the responsibility of the Crown to prove that the accused is guilty, not the responsibility of the accused to prove his or her innocence.) The Crown was then allowed to cross-examine each witness with the goal of showing that the witness and evidence was not believable. After all the witnesses were examined and cross-examined, the Defence Attorney gave a speech summarizing his reasons why his client should be found "not guilty" or **acquitted.** The Crown Attorney closed the trial with a summary of points indicating why Ms. Green should be found guilty.

The Judge

The Crown and the Defence presented arguments as **adversaries** or opponents. The **judge** did not take a side. The judge interpreted the law and kept order in the court. If the jury presented a guilty **verdict** he would sentence the defendant. In the examination of witnesses, the judge did not allow **questions** which **led** or put words into their mouths. The only testimony from witnesses which was allowed was what they saw, heard, or experienced themselves. **Hearsay** or second-hand information was not allowed. If an attorney felt that an adversary's question was not correct, he or she would object to the judge who then decided whether or not to allow the question. The judge warned that **perjury** or lying while under oath is a serious offence and is punishable by a jail sentence. Saying "I don't remember" when you really do is considered to be perjury.

The Jury

Once the Crown and Defence finished their examination of witnesses, the judge addressed or **charged** the jury. The jury was reminded that the accused must be declared innocent unless they found her guilty beyond any reasonable doubt. The jury adjourned to a special room, guarded by the **sheriff** and away from the public. Sometimes, in a highly publicized trial, the jury is **sequestered** or not allowed to leave their rooms. One of the jurors was elected **foreman.** The foreman's first job was to take a vote and ask for an explanation of each juror's opinion. The jurors knew that there had to be a **unanimous** decision in order for them to return to the court and deliver their **verdict.** If they weren't able to decide, a **hung jury** would be declared and a new trial would be ordered. The jury asked for help in understanding legal points, and in going over the evidence again.

After three hours the court was called back and the foreman gave the **court clerk** the jury's decision. The court clerk read the decision and in Ms. Green's case it was: Guilty. The judge's final role was to sentence Ms. Green; that was to be at a later date.

The Sentence

The judge sentenced Ms. Green to six months in prison for the offence of "leaving the scene of an accident". The judge explained that this crime is a serious one, and that the act of leaving a dying girl was considered disgraceful and callous by the public. However, this was weighed against Ms. Green's lack of a criminal and driving record and the good character witnesses who spoke highly of her. The judge hoped that others would hear about Ms. Green's sentence and would think twice about committing the same crime.

Sentencing — The Judges' Decision

Sentencing

When an accused person has been convicted, it is the responsibility of the judge to determine the sentence. The Criminal Code states the minimum and maximum sentence. The judge decides the length of the sentence after considering the nature and seriousness of the crime, and the convicted person's past behaviour.

The Purposes of Sentencing

1. Deterrence

Sometimes a severe sentence is given to deter (or discourage) the individual from committing the crime again, and to deter others from committing such a crime.

2. Segregation

Sometimes a criminal is guilty of such serious crimes, that the only apparent solution is to segregate that person from others, by placing the person in a prison. This solution provides immediate protection for society.

3. Rehabilitation

The most important aspect of punishment is the rehabilitation of the convicted person. The purpose of the prisons is to help the individual to learn life skills and to learn positive attitudes during the stay in prison. It is hoped that the convicted person can thus become a successful citizen on release from prison. Therefore, prisons should provide educational, vocational, and psychological assistance to prepare their inmates for their return to normal life in society.

4. Punishment

Some people believe that an individual who commits a crime should be punished to a degree similar to what the victim experienced. Some supporters of the death penalty believe that, because one person has killed another, that person should be killed also.

Selection of Sentence

Some choices open to a judge are:

a) Imprisonment
  - a term under two years to be served in a provincial jail
  - a term of over two years to be served in a federal jail
  - an "intermittent" sentence to be served on weekends or nights

b) Fine
  - a fine which may or may not accompany a jail sentence

c) Compensation or Restitution
  The court may order the convicted person to compensate the victim for financial loss. For example, if the convicted person had vandalized or destroyed a house or school, the convicted person could be required to pay all or some of the costs of repairs. He or she might also be required to do community work to help to pay for the crime.

d) Suspended Sentence
  If the court believed that the convicted person is unlikely to commit any more crime, it can suspend the sentence. This means that he or she is released without serving the sentence.

e) Probation

The person given a suspended sentence is usually placed on probation. This means that he or she must lead a clean and law-abiding life, and must report regularly to a probation officer. If the person violates the terms of probation, he or she may be returned to the courts for further sentencing.

Dangerous Offender

Sometimes a person who has been convicted of a serious offence (murder, serious personal injury, sexual assault) appears unlikely to be reformed during a term in prison. Therefore, that individual may be judged a dangerous offender. Under these conditions, the convict may be sentenced to an indefinite term in prison. That person is kept until he or she can be proven ready to be returned to normal life outside the prison.

"Everyone has the right not to be subjected to any cruel or unusual treatment or punishment." (section 12)

1. Does a judge have the right to declare a person a "Dangerous Offender"?
2. Does a prison have the right to put a misbehaving prisoner in "solitary confinement"?
3. Is **capital punishment** "cruel and unusual" punishment?

Prisons and Punishment

From Revenge to Rehabilitation

For many centuries the penalty for most crimes was death. By 1700, there were 200 kinds of crime considered to be capital crimes in England. **Corporal punishment,** such as whipping and public humiliation in the stocks, was reserved for less serious crimes. As America and Australia were being settled, convicts were "transported" to serve as cheap labour in these growing colonies. Prisons were filthy, brutal places. Some humane people were able to convince the government to change the purpose of prisons. Rather than simply punishing those imprisoned, the prisons would **reform** them: training prisoners for their successful return to society. Prisoners were required to be silent, to perform hard labour, and to spend their time in solitary confinement as part of their reform.

Now prisons try to **rehabilitate** their prisoners, giving them help with social or psychological problems. Prisons want ex-prisoners to live normally in society. **Half-way** houses provide a home for the ex-prisoner when he or she is released into the community.

The judicial system realizes that it is difficult for prisoners to adjust to life outside of prison. It is feared that ex-prisoners could fall back into criminal behaviour. The **Temporary Absence Program** eases prisoners back into society. This program allows prisoners to spend time at home with their families during the latter part of imprisonment. This program also serves as an **incentive** for good behaviour in prison.

Emily Murphy conducting juvenile court, 1918. Murphy was appointed a judge in 1916 and came up with the idea of womens' court. She was also a writer and her exposé of the drug trade led to new laws governing narcotics.

Parole

Inmates apply for **parole** or **early release** after serving one-third of their sentences. The Parole Board members meet to hear the application. They consider the following before making a decision:

- the prisoner's behaviour in prison and prior to being imprisoned
- the seriousness of the crime
- the prisoner's attempts to rehabilitate himself or herself
- the amount of support waiting for the prisoner in society

Parole Problems

The public becomes aware of problems with the parole system when a released prisoner commits a crime. This shows a failure of rehabilitation and of the Parole Board System.

Read this quote from a well-known Canadian criminal lawyer:

"Something is wrong with the parole system. It is simply that it fosters the wrong values. In prison, instead of helping to bring about actual rehabilitation, it puts a premium on "playing the game". Essentially, the game consists of convincing the Parole Board that one has become "rehabilitated". Whether shrewd and experienced parole officers can see through it or not (they all claim they can, of course), the fact remains that prisoners concentrate harder on trying to con the Parole Board than on virtually anything else. Who can blame them when two-thirds or more of their time inside depends on whether they succeed or not.... Why not, I suggest, sentence people to the actual terms we expect them to serve in jail?"

Edward L. Greenspan and George Jonas.
Greenspan: The Case For the Defence,
Don Mills: Collins Paperbacks, 1988, pp. 358-359.

- Research the purposes of parole.
- Think about the question: Should the parole system be abolished?

Research and Organize

Collect at least 10 newspaper articles on criminal trials and sentences handed down by judges. Summarize the data from each article using these headings:

- Charge
- Court Type
- Sentence
- Chance of Parole

Analyze your results: Do judges differ in sentencing for similar offences?

Questions and Activities

Famous Pairs

Explain the connection between each pair:
1. Defence attorney and the jury
2. Criminal act and criminal intent
3. A Young Offender and the Press
4. The Police and the Charter of Rights
5. A witness and perjury

Ideas for Discussion

1. Imagine that the Charter of Rights and Freedoms could be applied to other laws and events in Canadian history. Research the following events, then explain what you think the Supreme Court would have decided.
   - the internment of Japanese Canadians as "Enemy Aliens" during World War II, while other Canadians whose heritage could be traced to other "enemy" countries could live freely;
   - the imposition of the War Measures Act in Quebec in 1970. This was the first peacetime use of the Act which has the power to severely limit civil rights;
   - the placing of a "head tax" on Chinese immigrants to Canada at the turn of the century. The Chinese were the only immigrant group to pay such a tax;
   - the Doukhobors, a religious group which feels that the law of God is superior to that of governments, were imprisoned for keeping their children out of school.

2. "I haven't the slightest moral conflict defending people accused of homicide, sexual assault, business fraud, environmental offences, or even crimes against humanity. I don't "draw the line" at anything. If I defended crimes; maybe I would — but I don't defend crimes. I only defend innocent people. Until they are found guilty there are no other kinds of people for me to defend, and what difference does it make what an innocent person is accused of?" (Greenspan, op. cit., pp. 264-265)
   - Write down your reaction to this statement. Compare your reaction with others.
   - Look through the newspaper. Is there any person you would not want to defend? Why?

3. Examine the following laws which have been challenged under the Charter of Rights:
   - seat belt laws
   - motorcycle helmet laws
   - laws prohibiting the use of English on signs in Quebec

   For each case, state
   a) reasons for supporting the law;
   b) reasons for opposing the law;
   c) consideration of the law in relationship to the Charter of Rights.

4. Do Some Research
   Prepare a **glossary** of new legal terms and their definitions which you learned in this chapter.

The Young Offenders Act

Case Study

You are 16 years old and are at the mall with some friends. In a sporting goods store, your friends divert the store clerk while you try on ski sweaters. You conceal the sweater under your jacket, and you and your friends leave the store. Immediately, a hand is placed on your shoulder and you are asked to return. The police are called, and they inform you of your right to a lawyer. You gather your courage and phone your mother. She insists that you remain silent until the family lawyer arrives. The police take you to the station where you are charged with theft, fingerprinted, and photographed.

Your lawyer questions you about the incident, beginning to prepare your defence. Finally, your mother arrives and you are released in her custody.

Your trial in Youth Court will be a private matter. The **Young Offenders Act** forbids the publication of your identity. You are grateful for this — this is the community where you and your parents and younger sister live and where you hope to have a successful future.

Your Defence Attorney has explained to you the judge's options.
a) She can *have you declare yourself* "not guilty".
b) If you plead guilty or are found guilty, she can
- place you on probation for up to two years;
- order you to pay restitution to your victim;
- order you to perform community work;
- fine you up to $2000;
- grant you an absolute discharge;
- sentence you to up to three-years open custody in a group home or closed custody in a training school.

Before sentencing you, the judge will prepare a **predisposition report.** This will give the judge an opportunity to find out about you. You, your parents, teachers, friends, and employers will be interviewed. Your trial day arrives. You hope that your clean record, good school and employment reports, and lawyer's skill will see you through.

Role - Play

Select five people to role-play the above case: The accused, the Defence Lawyer, the Judge, the Crown attorney, the store security officer.

After you have completed the role play, members of the class should form small groups, and decide which optional sentence the judge should award.

Young Offenders Act

The Young Offenders Act was introduced in 1981. It is based on the assumption that young people make mistakes and, although responsible for their actions, should not bear the same consequences as adults. Therefore, the Act established a separate system of justice for young offenders and adults.

Several years ago, before the Young Offenders Act become law, the Juvenile Delinquents Act oversaw children and the law. The legal minimum age for offenders was 7 years while the new Act considers that 14 is the age at which children can be held responsible.

Parents took responsibility for their children's actions. Today, parents cannot be required to answer for something their child has done. The greatest change in the Act is the treatment of children accused of serious indictable offences. The Juvenile Delinquents Act allowed children over the age of 14 to be tried in adult court. The Young Offenders Act does not allow children to be tried in adult court, with the exception that serious crimes can be tried in adult court if the Crown or the youth asks for it.

Special Features of the Young Offenders Act

The Young Offenders Act in some ways treats young people in a fairer, more adult manner. The law understands that young people make mistakes and that young people should be rehabilitated, not punished for their crimes. Youthful offenders, not their parents, are expected to take the blame for their actions. Youthful crimes are not held permanently against offenders, as records for summary offences are destroyed after two years and records for indictable offences are destroyed after five years.

The Young Offenders Act Under Fire

Since the Young Offenders Act became law, many Canadians have voiced their objections to it:
- three years imprisonment is the greatest sentence that can be given, no matter what the crime;
- children of 10 who commit crimes are protected from prosecution;
- young offenders' identities are protected, putting the community at risk.

Case Study

In 1985, a young offender shot a man, his wife and their daughter in a suburban Toronto home. The case was treated under the Young Offenders Act. Because of the severity of the crime, the case *could* have been transferred to adult court. However, both the Defence Attorney and the Crown Attorney chose to have the case tried according to the Young Offenders Act. Both believed that the judge would rule that the person was insane at the time of the crime, and would sentence the offender to an indefinite term, with psychological counselling. However, the judge ruled that the juvenile was sane. Upon conviction, the juvenile received the maximum term of three years. After three years in a provincial institution, the young offender was released.

1. List the advantages and disadvantages of the Young Offenders Act.
   a) Which parts of the Act would you keep?
   b) Which parts of the Act would you change?
2. Design a new Young Offenders Act.
3. Create a list of questions suitable for a questionnaire on the Young Offenders Act.
   - survey a wide range of people: students, parents, police;
   - compile your results;
   - illustrate your results on a graph.

Culminating Activity

Studying history and contemporary issues is like being a detective:

- you are confronted with a *mass of facts and events,* which are often like a puzzle;
- you seek to find a *pattern* to the mystery;
- you raise questions in your mind to *focus* your thoughts;
- you *organize* your information to tentatively answer your questions;
- if necessary, you seek *more information* to answer your questions;
- you draw tentative *conclusions* to answer your questions;
- you *assess* your conclusions to see if they are the best answer to the mystery;
- you *communicate* your conclusions to others in oral or written form.

When you study history, you go through a process similar to a detective investigating a crime. No doubt there have been other "detectives" (historians) who have previously examined your historical question. But there is no guarantee that they have solved the case.

History, then, is in part a story. But it is also a series of "cases" still waiting to be examined. Good luck on applying your skills as a detective in studying history.

YOUR TASK

To select a topic for a two-page research report from your history course. (Some suggestions for topics are included.)
You may choose your own topic, or your teacher may provide a list of possible topics.
Use your skills as a *detective* to examine your chosen topic or question.

Check List for Your Research Report

Have I:	Yes	No
• defined my topic?		
• completed general reading in my text or other references to clarify the topic?		
• raised questions to *focus* my thinking and research?		
• *organized* my thoughts in chart or point form?		
• completed *further research* to locate more information to answer my focus questions?		
• formed a *tentative conclusion* (or thesis) to explain the issue or topic?		
• assessed my ideas and information for completness, and taken into account different viewpoints?		
• prepared a *first draft* or *rough outline,* in point form for the introductory paragraph, supporting paragraphs, and conclusion?		
• edited my rough draft for corrections and clarity?		
• prepared my *final draft* to communicate to the teacher or other members of the class?		

Some Possible Topics for Your Research Report

— The Changing Role of Women, 1900 to 1920s
— The Treaty of Versailles: Cause of World War II?
— The Dieppe Raid: Triumph or Tragedy?
— The Treatment of Japanese Canadians in World War II
— The Case for (or against) Using the Atomic Bomb in 1945
— Immigration to Canada, 1945 to 1960s
— Immigration to Canada, 1970s and 1980s
— The Need for Changes in Canadian Immigration Policy Today
— The Achievements and Importance of (choose *one*)
  — Mackenzie King
  — John Diefenbaker
  — Lester Pearson
  — Pierre Trudeau
  — Brian Mulroney
— The Need for Changes in the Role of Women in Canada Today
— Canadian Culture: Worth Preserving?
— The Changing Role of Canada in the UN
— Western Canadian Discontent Today
— The Case for Senate Reform
— What We Should Do About Our Fragile Environment
— Wanted: A New Foreign Policy For Canada

Recruiting effort in World War I — an opportunity for travel and adventure.

Recruiting effort in World War II — most of the Reserve Army was eventually sent overseas.

Chapter Eleven

Towards the Next Century
ADVANCE ORGANIZER

1

Canadians live in a world of continuous change. Every aspect of our lives is changing faster than at any other time in history. What the future will bring, we cannot know for sure. However, with our knowledge of the past as a guide we can at least try to make reasonable guesses, and consider some of the key issues that may face Canadians as they approach the twenty-first century.

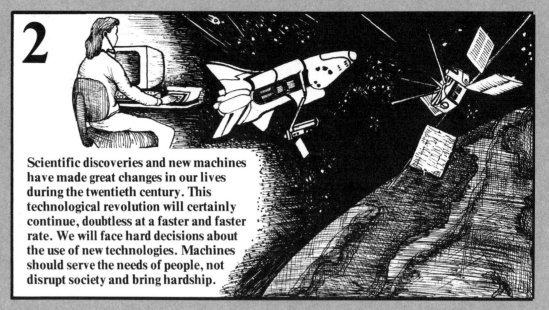

2

Scientific discoveries and new machines have made great changes in our lives during the twentieth century. This technological revolution will certainly continue, doubtless at a faster and faster rate. We will face hard decisions about the use of new technologies. Machines should serve the needs of people, not disrupt society and bring hardship.

3

A growing technological society like Canada uses energy — lots of energy. As oil becomes more expensive and supplies are used up the search for other kinds of energy will become more important. The hunt for oil and gas will continue, but other forms of energy will be studied. The challenge will be to develop cheap, safe, reliable energy sources without poisoning the environment and bringing disruption to particular regions or groups of people.

Word List

Candu	identity	society
fibre optics	pluralistic	technology
gross national product	silicon chip	Telidon

4

Our national identity is still evolving to reflect our changing society. Canadians of native ancestry are speaking out for their rights and traditions. English-speaking Canadians are becoming more aware of the concerns and aspirations of French Canadians. And Canadians of French and British ancestry have been joined over the years by people from many other lands. The contribution of all Canadians, new and old, will influence the kind of society that we know in future.

6

History is like an unfinished journey leading from the past into the future. Canadians will face great challenges in a changing and uncertain world. The way ahead, however, is based on past events. Perhaps we can be inspired by the examples of Canadians who, through courage and determination in the face of adversity, have overcome great difficulties. With a reasoned pride in our past we can face the challenge of the twenty-first century.

5

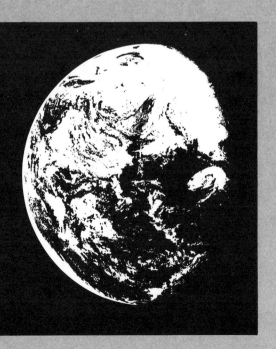

More and more, we live in an interdependent world. In an age of jet travel, intercontinental missiles and space satellites the safety and well being of Canadians is linked to that of all other people. War and peace, poverty and development, human rights, international trade, the uses of outer space, the fate of the world's oceans, these and many other questions will concern Canadians in the world community of the future.

The High Tech Revolution

High technology means many things — jet planes, space satellites, atomic reactors, lasers, and much more. Perhaps most of all in the future it will mean computers. Computers have already brought incredible changes to our lives but, according to many experts, "You ain't seen nothin' yet!" The real computer revolution is still to come.

The Computer Age

The first electronic computer, called ENIAC, began operating in 1945. It cost $13 million, weighed 30 t, covered 150 m² of floorspace, needed 19 000 vacuum tubes, and used as much energy as a railway locomotive. By the 1980s you could go to your nearest electronics store and buy a computer that cost less than $200, could be held in your hand, used the energy of a light bulb, and could perform more functions, faster and more accurately, than ENIAC.

This progress was made possible by improvements in the electronic components that are used to build computers. The heart of today's computer is the chip, a paper-thin slice of silicon, smaller than your fingernail, printed with hundreds of microscopic circuits and capable of performing thousands of complex operations in microseconds.

Applications for computer technology have

A computer chip can fit in the eye of a needle.

grown rapidly over the years. Early computers did just that — they made mathematical computations and recorded the results. As they improved, computers came to do many other things. Now, computer chips operate your pocket calculator, digital watch, clock radio, self-focusing camera, electronic games, and many household utensils. Combinations of chips are being used to make sophisticated office and industrial machines. Without them, the space program, with its many complex calculations, would be impossible.

Computers and Canada

Canada has been a leader in some areas of computer technology, such as fibre optics, communications satellites, the Telidon two-way television system, and digital communications. Many new industries have grown up.

The "Canadarm" on the U.S. space shuttle. As high technology gets more expensive and more complicated, companies in many countries may work together on projects like the shuttle.

In the Ottawa area by the 1980s there were over 200 Canadian-owned high-technology companies. By 1990, these numbers had increased in Ottawa, Toronto, Montreal, Vancouver, and other Canadian cities. But there are areas in which Canada is still

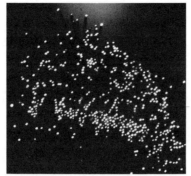

Optical fibres made of glass use pulses of light instead of electricity to transmit data.

dependent on foreign imports. Canadians annually spend billions of dollars importing computers and parts. The free trade deal may create problems in parts of the industry. Many working in the computer industry welcome the opportunity to expand their markets. Others fear that the competition from the United States and Asia will wipe out the smaller Canadian companies. As with so many other parts of the Canadian economy, no one knows for sure what the impact of free trade will be.

The Information Revolution

What will happen in the field of high technology is anybody's guess. The trends to smaller, faster, and cheaper computers will doubtless continue. Chips may soon be made of a new material, gallium, which has been found to transmit electrical impulses two to five times faster than silicon. Engineers are exploring ways to make circuits even smaller and more compact — perhaps only a few molecules thick. Scientists keep looking for materials that will transmit signals even faster — perhaps at the speed of light.

Some people have predicted that the future will be known as the Information Age, when control of computers and the information that they can store, will be the key to power and progress. Already computers are being linked in networks that pass vast amounts of information back and forth between continents and across international boundaries. Computers will also affect our working lives. Computerized machines, such as word processors in offices and "robots" in factories, will take over many routine jobs now done by humans. This will create new jobs in the computer industries, and will help keep Canadian companies efficient in world markets, but some people are afraid that many jobs will be lost as people are replaced by computers.

This kind of assembly line may soon be obsolete. In the future, these snowmobiles may be made entirely by computerized "robots," without need for human workers.

No one can predict the future of the high technology revolution, but one thing seems certain — computers and related technology will affect virtually every aspect of our daily lives, and will be of vital importance to the security and prosperity of the country.

Our Fragile Environment

Dinosaurs

Dinosaurs ruled the world for 150 000 000 years, only to disappear in the blink of an eye 65 000 000 years ago. Their fate remains a mystery. Was the earth struck by an asteroid filling the earth's atmosphere with noxious gases? Or was there a change of climate that gradually killed off the vegetation on which many of the magnificent creatures fed?

One thing is certain, whatever the trigger, an environmental catastrophe ultimately ended their reign.

Today signs increasingly warn that the earth is again being rendered unfit, but this time the catastrophe is being caused by people.

Craig McInnes, Environmental Writer
Toronto *Globe and Mail*

Since the end of World War Two, the world's greatest fear has been the possibility of a nuclear war. By the end of the 1980s, such fears were receding, as the spirit of "glasnost" spread around the world. However, a potentially even greater crisis was emerging — the crisis of our fragile environment.

The problem was illustrated by a series of events in the late 1980s:

— Diseased mussels were discovered in some of the fishing areas off the Martime Provinces. The suspicion was that this condition was caused by industrial pollution in the offshore fishing areas.

— In 1988, fire in an industrial-waste warehouse in St. Basile-le-Grande (near Montreal) released poisonous fumes forcing over 3500 people to leave their homes.

— The St. Lawrence River had become an "open sewer" due to the dumping of untreated sewage and chemicals into the river.

— Much of the forests of Ontario, Quebec, and the Maritimes was threatened by acid rain. Maple sugar, lumbering, fishing, and tourist industries were threatened. The source of this pollution was the hydro-generating plants and industries of the northeastern United States and Canada.

— Lake Ontario had the highest concentration of toxic chemicals of any of the Great Lakes. Over 500 pollutants have been detected, including DDT, arsenic, lead, and dioxin, one of the deadliest pollutants known. The source was suspected to be the untreated pollutants poured into the Great Lakes from Canadian and American industries.

— In the 1980s, the Prairie Provinces experienced several seasons of higher-than-normal temperatures and drought, reducing crop growth. Some scientists wondered if this was an early stage of the "greenhouse effect", the gradual heating of the earth's surface brought on by excessive carbon in the atmosphere.

— Whales living in the coastal waters of British Columbia have been found to have high levels of mercury poison in their bodies. It is suspected that this is due to untreated industrial pollutants from the pulp-and-paper and other industries on the British Columbia coast.

What do these events indicate?

Until recent years, we have assumed that the earth's atmosphere and oceans were so vast that they could absorb an infinite amount of the pollutants created by mankind. However, since Rachel Carson wrote *Silent Spring* in the 1960s, environmentalists

How can we balance the benefits of our industrial society with the growing dangers to our environment and quality of life?

have warned that the neglect of our environment would eventually threaten the existence of all life upon this earth. The environmental crises of the 1980s indicate that this warning was not exaggerated nor alarmist; the environmental crisis is here.

Greenhouse effect

Are we entering the greenhouse effect already?....There are trends which indicate that the earth is already starting to warm....The global temperature has increased about one half degree in the past 150 years....But the five warmest years have occurred since 1980, and seven of the ten warmest years occurred since 1973, so something is happening.

Craig McInness, Environmental Writer,
Toronto *Globe and Mail*

"Throughout human history, the boast of our species has been that we love our children and hope that they have a richer, fuller life than we did. Yet now, for the first time, we know with absolute certainty that our children's lives will be immeasurably poorer in bio-diversity and filled with massive problems that we have foisted on them in our shortsighted pursuit of immediate profit and power."

David Suzuki

"For the first time in history, millions of people all over the world are not just worried about their own and their children's future; they are deeply anxious about the future of this planet."

Gro Harlem Brundtland, Prime Minister of Norway, 1989

Public Opinion concerning Environmental Pollution (based on 1987 survey of Canadian opinion)
— 87% believe a clean environment is within our technical know-how
— 87% are upset by the lack of action by governments to regulate the environment;
— 66% believe that government spending to clean up the environment will aid the economy;
— 78% are willing to pay higher taxes to improve environmental protection;
— 92% believe that corporate executives should be held personally accountable if their companies pollute the environment;
— 80% are concerned about the effects of pollution on their health;
— the world's greatest litterbugs are from the richest countries;
— the average Canadian citydweller produces between 1.4 and 1.8 kg of garbage every day;

The Oceans

For several hundred years, the nations of the world have used the ocean as a dump for untreated sewage, hazardous chemicals, used marine oil, and industrial pollutants. In addition, prevailing winds have moved acid rain from industrial areas and deposited it in the oceans. The deaths of marine life in various parts of the ocean warn us that the oceans are reaching their saturation point in their ability to absorb these toxic materials.

Vessels cut through oil-slicked water on their way to an oil tanker that ran aground near Valdez, Alaska, resulting in the worst oil spill ever seen in North America.

Atmospheric Pollution

We now realize that the atmosphere is no longer capable of absorbing the amount of toxic gases that the industrial nations of the world deposit in the air. Automobiles, industries, and coal-burning hydro-generating stations produce carbon dioxide and sulphur which combine to produce a noxious chemical which eventually is brought back to the earth in the form of acid rain and snow. It has now been confirmed that acid rain destroys the normal lifecycle of fish, and slows down the growth of certain broad-leafed trees or destroys them. As a result, in Canada, the fishing, forestry, and maple syrup industries are suffering severely from this problem. There are fears that acid rain might prove to be a health hazard for humans, but as yet this has not been proven.

Most of our large industrial cities suffer from air pollution, brought on by the excessive production of industrial noxious gases. Scientists have also recognized that by the 1980s the ozone layer of the atmosphere had been damaged. Ozone in the atmosphere protects us from the ultra-violet rays of the sun. The reduction of the ozone layer permits greater amounts of the sun's ultra-violet rays to enter the earth's atmosphere, greatly increasing the danger of skin cancer for humans and some animals.

Industrial Pollution

The industrial and technological developments of the 20th century have greatly improved the lifestyle and standard of living of people all over the industrialized world. At the same time, these changes have threatened our environment and introduced life-threatening health hazards. Whether it is in the polluted air we breathe, or in the infected water we drink, or in the increasing amount of untreated industrial pollutants poured into our lakes and rivers, or in the massive amounts of non-degradable garbage deposited near our cities, we are paying the price. The history of technology shows that every technological improvement has costs.

Nuclear Power

When nuclear power was introduced in the 1960s, it was perceived as a clean and inexpensive source of power. Since then we have discovered some of the problems of disposing of nuclear waste which will remain dangerously radio-active for hundreds of years.

In 1986, when the Chernobyl nuclear plant in the U.S.S.R. exploded, it created a cloud of nuclear fallout which killed several hundred people immediately. The fallout threatened the lives of thousands for years, and poisoned animals and agricultural produce in over 25 countries. Accidents of this type are fortunately rare, but the fear of nuclear plant breakdowns alarmed citizens of the world.

The Canary's warning

In World War One, soldiers carried canaries in cages up to the front lines, as an advance-warning device for poisonous gases released by the enemy. The fragile canaries would breathe small particles of the gas and die, giving a warning to the soldiers, who might then have time to put on their gas masks.

In the 1980s, environmentalists have been concerned about the frequent episodes of mass deaths of seals, whales, and other sea creatures. Some of these deaths may be caused by poisonous chemicals deposited in the sea, as yet not harmful to people.

Some environmentalists ask "Are these advance warnings, as were the deaths of canaries in World War One?"

As we look forward to the 21st century, citizens all over the industrial world are concerned about the danger to our fragile environment. We have begun to realize that there is no guarantee to human survival in the face of human policies which ignore the frailty of the planet. The problem in this new crisis is entirely made by human beings. Similarly, the solutions will have to be made consciously by human beings.

When the astronauts were on the moon looking toward the earth, they were impressed by the beauty of the globe — a globe without nations and boundaries. They returned to earth with a sense of oneness about the earth and its peoples, a sense of national pride in their achievements, but a sense of common humanity with all others. Most had a willingness to work in co-operation with other nations and peoples to overcome common problems.

It will require the application of this attitude to face the environmental challenges of the years ahead.

The Canadian Identity

Skaters enjoying a winter outing on the Rideau Canal in Ottawa — what could be more typically Canadian? But if these are typical Canadians, what would we expect them to be like? Blond hair or brown? Tall or short? White skin, black, yellow, or brown? As you can see, any attempt to choose one physical description for a typical Canadian would be difficult and misleading. Canadians come in all shapes, sizes, and colours.

To describe the culture and beliefs of a typical Canadian would be just as difficult. Most of these people probably speak English. But if they are representative of the country as a whole, every third person would speak French as his or her usual language. It is also possible that a few of our skaters speak other languages, such as Italian, Vietnamese, Arabic, or many others from around the world. In religion, most of these Canadians would be nominally Christian, but some would be Jewish, Muslim, Buddhist, Hindu, or other. Even among the Christians there would likely be a wide variety of Protestant, Catholic, and Orthodox believers.

A Multicultural Experiment

Canadians have not one identity, but many. Canada is already a mixed, pluralistic society. Our future lies in a country where people speak different languages, follow different religions, and come from many racial

Some people, such as these Mennonites in Kitchener, Ontario, have come to Canada to preserve their beliefs and way of life.

and cultural backgrounds. Most Canadians accept this and enjoy the chance to meet people of different cultures and languages. Some, however, do not.

In the past there has been prejudice against people of different races, languages, and cultures. French-speaking Canadians were sometimes denied the right to schooling in their own language. Japanese Canadians were unfairly treated during the Second World War. And the history of other countries has shown that it is not always easy for people of different races to live together peacefully.

With the change in immigration policies in the 1970s and 1980s, the number of immigrants into Canada from Asia and the Caribbean has greatly increased. If immigrants come from Europe, they usually become "invisible" as part of Canadian society. However, people with a different skin colour remain part of a "visible" minority. Unfortunately, the record of Canadians and other peoples in dealing with visible minorities has often not been good.

Some minorities perceive that they receive unfair treatment in obtaining housing and employment. Some have said that schools have not encouraged some visible minorities to pursue post-secondary education. In times of economic recession, racist incidents seem to increase. Is it because more people are competing for fewer jobs?

Canadian society and its economy will require increased immigration in the future. It is likely that large numbers of these immigrants will be from visible minorities. Canadians will face a great challenge to see if we can develop a mixed society, which will welcome all, in spite of race, colour, or religion. The great experiment is to see if Canadians can welcome new citizens with our traditional attitudes of humanity and caring, rather than the dangerous attitudes of racism and discrimination.

Canada's Native Peoples face special difficulties and have concerns about preserving their traditions and way of life. Many native groups have land claims against Canada. How should these be settled? Should native people have special rights and privileges? Should economic development be slowed or stopped in the north to protect the traditional way of life of the Dene and Inuit?

Native workers in an oil company cafeteria at Norman Wells, N.W.T. Canada's native peoples face difficult choices as they try to adjust to modern conditions while preserving their separate identity.

Canada and the World Community

Whether we like it or not, Canada's future will be influenced by the rest of the world. Our planet is one interdependent whole; problems in one country may affect any other. More than ever, Canadians will have to be aware of, and take part in, the affairs of the global community.

War and Peace

Perhaps the deadliest threat is nuclear war. In a full nuclear exchange between the U.S. and the U.S.S.R. it is estimated that 200 to 300 million people would die — and Canada would be right in the middle. Should Canada acquire nuclear weapons of its own? Should we encourage efforts to reduce or even ban them?

A more basic question is "What is Canada's defence role in the changing world of East-West relations?" Events of the late 1980s moved the world closer towards an atmosphere of détente, or reduced tensions, between the U.S.S.R. and the Western world. Should Canada continue to play its traditional role in NATO and NORAD, or should we be seeking a new role to help reduce international conflict? Should we be spending money to defend the Arctic region, or seeking to neutralize the entire region? Or should we Canadians be turning our attention to development and aid instead of military preparedness?

Canadians are committed to being a part of the Western Alliance in the Cold War. Because Canada is not a nuclear power, our efforts are focussed on conventional forces (the regular army, navy, and air force, using non-nuclear weapons). The emphasis has shifted to modernization of our forces, so that the armed forces have been provided with the latest military equipment — Leopard tanks for the Army, F-16s for the Air Force, new frigates for the Navy,

and proposed nuclear-powered submarines for the Arctic Patrol. However, the issue remains as to whether the money being spent on arms in Canada and around the world is bringing security, or increasing the chances of war. Does the cost threaten the world economy and needlessly use up scarce resources? Would it be better to spend this money on economic development and social services where perhaps 1000 million people do not know how to read and write, 500 million do not have enough food to eat, and half a million children die each month from infectious diseases?

Stephen Lewis addressing the United Nations assembly. Lewis taught English in Africa before becoming a prominent organiser and later, leader, of the Ontario NDP Party. In 1984, Conservative Party Prime Minister Mulroney appointed Lewis as ambassador to the UN. He now lectures at university.

Which role should Canada play in world affairs — armed defender, peacemaker, or helper to the underdeveloped nations of the world?

In the future, food may become the most precious resource in an overpopulated world.

Population, Development, and Trade

World population continues to grow. Every day there are 200 000 more people on Earth, over 700 million new people every year. Many of these people live in the developing countries in conditions of poverty, disease, and hunger. These nations will continue to fall behind the developed countries. Canada has a good record of assistance to developing countries, but we still spend less than 1% of our gross national product on aid. Should Canada spend more, or should we encourage businesses to build up these countries through private investment?

Some people feel that in the 21st century, we must reduce our concern and investment on the "East-West split". We must put greater emphasis on overcoming the "North-South split" — the division between the industrialized, developed, and prosperous nations of the northern hemisphere, and the underdeveloped, poorer nations of the southern hemisphere.

Many of the nations of the southern hemisphere (Latin America, Africa, Asia) and underdeveloped countries, with a relatively low standard of living. Their economies are usually based upon trading raw materials in exchange for necessary and expensive manufactured goods. Many of these countries, such as Brazil and Mexico, have huge national debts owed to banks in the richer northern countries. In many cases, the repayment of these debts is crushing the economy of the already struggling nations.

Some Canadians feel that the Canadian role in world affairs should change, to emphasize helping the people of these nations to have a basic standard of living. What should Canada's role be in helping these nations? Should we increase our aid? Should we help to reduce the payments on their national debts? Should we change our trade policies to help their struggling economies?

Or are these issues really their own problems? Should we concentrate our energies on helping other Canadians solve their problems?

This question of Canada's role in international affairs, as participant in military alliances or helper to underdeveloped nations may replace the Cold War as the major issue in future Canadian foreign policy.

The Unfinished Journey

When we think about the future, it is easy to get discouraged. The problems and dangers are all too obvious. Will there be war? Inflation? Pollution? Overpopulation? Separatism? Unemployment?

We should not forget, however, that Canadians have faced problems before. We have made mistakes. We have sometimes lost chances through timidity and hesitation. We have had our share of failures. But over all, Canadians have faced up to the challenges of the twentieth century with energy, courage and imagination.

When we think about the future we can look with pride to the achievements of the past. From a country of less than five and a half million in 1900, Canada has grown to a population of over 24 million. Working together, native-born Canadians and immigrants have built an open, democratic society with a high level of health care, education, economic opportunity and social justice for most people. From a land of fishermen, lumberjacks, small farmers, and shopkeepers, we have become the seventh largest industrial nation in the Western world. From a sheltered position in the British Empire, Canada has moved onto the world stage as a fully independent member of the international community.

Following the tragic death of Terry Fox, others have picked up the challenge. Steve Fonyo, another one-legged runner from British Columbia, in 1985 completed the journey begun by Terry Fox by running across Canada, from Newfoundland to the Pacific Coast. Rick Hansen, a friend of Terry's, completed a journey around the world in a wheelchair in 1987.

These courageous exploits have shown what exceptional Canadians can do when facing difficulty. Their efforts can be an inspiration for all Canadians as we continue our unfinished journey into the future.

Terry Fox

1958 — born in Winnipeg. Family moves to Port Coquitlam, B.C. where Terry grows up. Shows strong interest in athletics, works hard to excel.

1976 — enters Simon Fraser University, makes the Junior basketball squad.

1977 — right knee begins to hurt. Despite drugs, the pain continues. Cancer is diagnosed.

9 March 1977 — right leg amputated above knee. During recovery, must take drugs that make his hair fall out. "I got more upset over the loss of my hair than of my leg." Receives artificial leg after a few weeks, learns to walk, jog, play golf, drive a car. Returns to university, begins to run regularly, builds up physical and emotional strength.

1979 — has idea of running across Canada to raise money for cancer research. Cancer Society gives support.

12 April 1980 — dips artificial leg into the Atlantic Ocean at St. John's, Newfoundland and sets out for Victoria, B.C. on Marathon of Hope.

1 July 1980 — reaches Ottawa for Canada Day celebrations.

28 July 1980 — celebrates 22nd birthday at Gravenhurst, Ontario.

3 August 1980 — passes halfway mark at French River, Ontario.

29 August 1980 — approaching Thunder Bay, feels pain in chest.

30 August 1980 — chest pains increase. Runs for most of the day but finally collapses in exhaustion. Has reached 5340 km mark. Taken to Port Arthur General Hospital. Cancer of the lungs is diagnosed.

2 September 1980 — returns home for treatment.

19 September 1980 — invested as youngest Companion of the Order of Canada. Receives many other awards. Millions of dollars from across Canada pour into the Terry Fox Fund for cancer research.

February 1981 — cancer continues to spread. Doctors announce his condition is getting worse. Despite pain, continues to try to live as normal a life as possible.

June 1981 — enters hospital on the 19th and dies ten days later.

April 1982 — commemorative stamp issued in honour of Terry Fox and the Marathon of Hope.

Glossary

abolish do away with.

abortion an early end to pregnancy, usually caused intentionally.

accord agreement

ace a war pilot who has destroyed five or more enemy aircraft.

acid rain rain that has become an acid because it has absorbed chemicals in polluted air.

acquit declare that someone accused of a crime is innocent.

act a bill that has passed through both houses of parliament and become law; compare with *bill* and *law*.

agitators people who try to excite others into action over social or political issues.

air raid bombing attack by enemy planes; **air raid warden** someone who organizes and protects people during air raids.

alcholholism disease resulting from drinking too much alcohol over a long period.

aliens people from other countries.

ally friend or helper; **Allies** nations that helped one another fight Germany and her supporters during the two world wars.

ambassador representative of a country's government in a foreign country.

amend change, improve.

amplification in radio, a device for increasing the volume of sound.

Anglophone an English-speaking person

annexation joining or adding one thing (land or country) to another by force or agreement.

anti-Semitism a hatred or dislike for Jews or other Middle East people.

appeal to ask a higher court to reconsider a decision made by a lower court.

appeasement giving in to some of an enemy's demands in the hopes of keeping peace.

apprentice a worker who learns a trade or business on the job.

armaments weapons and military equipment.

armistice truce, the agreement to end a war.

artillery large guns; also army units who use them.

assassinate murder someone (usually a public figure) in a surprise attack.

assembly line a way of organizing workers so that each person does the same job over and over as the product moves through the factory.

astronaut space traveller.

atomic bomb a bomb that uses energy from the splitting of atoms to cause an explosion of tremendous force

atrocities terrible or cruel actions.

backlog a build-up which overloads the system and causes delay.

bail out to jump out of a plane with a parachute.

ballot voting paper showing the names of election candidates. The voter marks the ballot to indicate the choice of candidate.

ballot box sealed box in which voting papers are placed in elections.

bankrupt to have lost one's money in business; being unable to pay one's debts.

barbarous crude, savage-like.

benzene chemical that burns easily.

big business term used to describe the group of large companies that have a lot of power.

bilingual able to speak one's own language and another equally or almost equally well.

bill a proposal for a law; compare with *act*.

binder farm machine that cuts and ties grain.

biography the written story of a person's life.

biplane plane with two sets of wings, one above the other.

birth control use of methods or devices to prevent pregnancy.

black market unofficial (often illegal) system of buying and selling goods.

blockade using force to cut off supplies to an enemy.

boat people refugees who set out for other countries with very few possessions and no proper documents to allow them to enter those countries.

bolsheviks communists who took part in the Russian revolution.

bombardment an attack with heavy fire of shot and shell, or with bombs.

bond a certificate which you buy, and can later cash at a profit.

boom grow rapidly, do well;

boomtown fast-growing town.

bootlegging making and selling something (often liquor) illegally.

boycott avoid, refuse to deal with.

branch plant local factory owned by a company with its head office in another place or country.

bribery use of gifts or money to buy favours.

budget an estimate of the amount of money that can be spent, and the amounts to be spent for various purposes, in a given time (e.g. a year).

bush pilot pilot who flies light planes to remote areas.

buggy light carriage.

bully beef canned beef.

by-election special vote called in a constituency between general elections to replace a representative who has resigned or died.

cabinet group of government members which advises the prime minister.

campaign presentation throughout the constituency, province, or country to convince electors to vote for a political party or its candidate.

Canadian shield vast rocky area in northeastern Canada that is rich in minerals.

Candu a special type of atomic reactor developed in Canada and used since 1962 to produce nuclear energy.

canvass door-to-door or telephone approach to voters to get their support for a party or a candidate.

capitalism economic system in which most businesses are owned by private individuals, not the government, and run to make a profit for their owners; compare with *communism*.

capital punishment punishment inflicted on the body; in law it includes imprisonment and death.

cash crop crop grown for sale rather than for use on the farm.

casualties soldiers who have been killed, injured, or taken prisoner.

centennial 100th anniversary celebration.

citizen a person who by birth or acceptance by the government has full rights and responsibilities in a country.

civilian a person who is not in the armed forces.

civil law laws about the property, rights, duties and responsibilities of individual citizens.

civil rights freedoms and privileges of citizens guaranteed by a country's constitution or charter of rights.

clique a group that sticks together and keeps outsiders out.

closure a rule in parliament that lets the government cut off debate and bring about a vote on a bill.

colony a territory under the political control of another country; **colonial** someone from a colony.

combat fight, battle.

commerce buying and selling, especially between countries.

commonwealth a political association of a group of independent nations (including Canada) that used to be part of the British Empire.

communism economic and political system in which the state as a whole owns all property and runs business and industry for the common good, rather than for private profit. No opposition to the government is permitted; compare with *capitalism*.

compensation something given to make up for a loss, injury, etc.

competition contest; two or more businesses trying to sell the same things to the same people.

compromise splitting the difference; an agreement in which neither side gets everything it wants.

concentration camp prison camps to hold large numbers of political enemies or unwanted people.

confederation the joining together of several political units into one large unit or country; especially the Canadian Confederation.

conscription a system to make people join the armed forces.

conservation protecting, saving, and using wisely natural resources such as trees, wildlife, etc.

conspiracy a plot to do something evil.

constituency the parliamentary representative's home district, or the group of people in that district.

constitution the framework of rules and traditions which set out how something (such as a country) is run.

consumers people who buy things.

contract formal agreement covering the purchase of goods or services or any other business deal.

convention 1) a meeting or conference; 2) accepted customs, rules, etc.

convict in a trial, declare someone guilty of a crime.

convoy a group (of ships) travelling with a protective escort.

corner the market to buy all supplies of something, so that you can sell it at a high price without competition.

corporation business, company.

coureur de bois "runner of the woods"; independent fur trader.

court of appeal a higher court that reconsiders the decisions made in trials.

Créditiste a member of the Quebec

wing of the Social Credit Party.

criminal law laws about major crimes such as murder, robbery, arson and other dangerous actions.

crown (the) the symbol of the authority of the monarch.

crude oil oil before it has been refined

culture *1)* way of life; *2)* the learning and arts (including painting, music, literature, drama) of a nation.

Czar emperor of Russia.

dairy farm farm that keeps cattle to produce milk, not meat.

debt something (usually money) owed to someone else.

decentralize reorganize so that things are run in local districts rather than from one central place.

deficit the amount of shortage of income needed to cover a budget.

delegate representative, someone who attends a meeting on other people's behalf; **delegation** a team of delegates.

demand how much people want something, combined with how much they can pay for it.

demilitarized area area that armed forces are not allowed to enter.

democracy system of government by the people or by representatives elected by the people.

demonstrate *1)* show; *2)* make a public protest (by marching, gathering with signs, etc.)

Dene "the people"; group of native Indian tribes now living in the Northwest Territories that is working to maintain their people's hunting and fishing areas and other traditional rights.

depression a period when business drops and there are few jobs.

deputy returning officer (DRO) person responsible on election day for operating a polling station, counting the ballots, and sending results to the district returning officer.

descendants your children, their children, their children, and so on.

détente the easing of tensions, especially between nations or political groups.

diabetes disease caused when the body fails to produce enough insulin to control blood sugar levels.

dictator single ruler who holds all power and usually uses force to stay in power.

diplomat civil servant who looks after dealings between countries.

diplomatic relations official dealings between the governments of countries.

discrimination treating people differently on the basis of their sex, skin-colour, background, etc.

distribution of wealth the way money, property, and goods are divided up among people, called *unequal* when some people are much richer than others.

diversified having a variety of parts

dividend a payment that is a share of profit.

dock place where ships can load and unload cargoes.

documentary presenting or recording factual information in an artistic fashion, as in a film or book

drifter a person drifting from place to place, usually looking for work.

drudgery very hard, dull, badly-paid work.

dustbowl in Western Canada and U.S.A. where dust storms are frequent and violent.

economy all of the business, industry, trade, and financial affairs of a country.

editorial an article in a newspaper or magazine by or under the editor's direction, giving the opinion or attitude of the paper's owner(s) regarding some subject or issue.

elect choose someone by voting.

emigrate leave one country to live in another.

employee someone who works for someone else in return for pay.

employer someone who pays other people to work for her or him.

empire a group of countries under one government.

energy power to heat and light homes, run cars and factories, etc., such as oil, hydro-electricity, the sun's rays.

enumerators people who compile the list of eligible voters for municipal, provincial, and federal elections.

environment the natural world: the air, sea, countryside, lakes, rivers, etc.

equality the same rights and treatment for everybody.

equalization payments payments made by the federal government to the poorer provinces so that they can provide the same level of services to the people as the richer provinces.

era a certain period of time, for example, the rock'n roll era.

exploit (*n*)heroic act; (*v*)treat someone unfairly for your own gain; to put something to profitable use, e.g. iron ore.

explosive something which explodes powerfully and easily.

exposition (*Fr.*) exhibition, display; for example, Expo 67.

extremist someone who holds unreasonably strong views.

factory a centralized place where workers and machines make a product.

fallout radio-active dust that falls after a nuclear explosion.

family allowance "baby bonus"; money given by the government to help families support children under 16.

fascism a form of dictatorship backed up by secret police and the army based on nationalistic and racist theories.

federal national level of government in a country that has regional governments as well.

federalism a system of government in which some powers are held by the central government, while others are held by regional governments.

feminism a doctrine that favours increased rights and activities for women.

fibre optics a system using optical fibres — thin glass filaments that transmit impulses of light that are converted into computer code at the receiving end. More messages can be sent at one time by this method than can be sent over wires.

foreclosure take over mortgaged property when payments have fallen behind.

forge furnace where metal can be heated and shaped.

foreign affairs government relations with other countries.

fortify make stronger.

Francophone a French-speaking person.

free elections elections in which any candidate who wants may run and in which people are free to vote as they wish.

free trade buying and selling between countries without any tariffs or customs duties.

freight goods that are transported from one place to another.

front battleground; the line where opposing armies meet.

furrow groove dug by a plough as it is pulled through the ground.

fuse material that burns easily and is used to set off an explosion.

futuristic suggesting styles, inventions, changes that may occur in the future.

general election an election held in every constituency across the country or province. General elections must be held at least every five years but may be called sooner if the government resigns or is defeated. They give voters the opportunity to show approval or disapproval of the government and to elect new members to parliament or the provincial legislative assembly.

generating station place where electric power is produced.

generation gap lack of understanding between people of different age groups.

geologist a scientist who studies rocks and the structure of the earth.

ghetto a part of a city inhabited by a racial, national, or religious minority.

grain elevator a tall building where grain is stored.

graphic lifelike or vivid; of or about designs and their use; shown by a graph.

gross national product (GNP) the total market value put on goods and services produced in one country within one year.

guarantee be responsible for, promise to protect.

hardtack hard, dry biscuit, rather like a dog biscuit.

heckler someone who interrupts with jeers and annoying questions during a public speech.

heritage culture, traditions, and learning handed down from the past.

holocaust total destruction, especially the Nazis' mass killing of Jews, gypsies, homosexuals, and others in World War II.

horsepower a unit used to measure work based on the amount of work a horse can do.

humanitarian showing kindness and concern for human beings.

ideal the way a person or group think things should be if the world were perfect.

identity distinctive character of a person or group.

ideology a strongly held system of beliefs about how the world should be run.

immigrant someone who comes to live in a new country.

immune free from, protected from disease.

imperialist someone who supports an empire, such as the British Empire, or would like to set one up.

import (*v*) to bring things into a country; (*n*) something which is brought into a country.

independent managing by oneself; free; not under another's control.

indictable liable to be charged with an offence or crime; giving enough evidence against an accused person to justify a trial.

industrialization 1) the growth of factories; 2) the changes that occur when large factories take over from small workshops, stores, and farms.

industrial waste liquids and solids left over and usually thrown out when an industrial product is made.

industry business operation that makes a special product, whether it be cars and trucks or canned lobster.

inflation rise in prices.

inquiry a search for information, knowledge, or truth.

insulin hormone produced naturally in most people to control blood sugar levels. Diabetics do not produce insulin and must receive it through injections or pills.

insurance an agreement where you make small payments to a private company or government agency in return for protection in a big emergency (such as losing your job, a car accident, sickness, or a fire in your home).

interest the money someone has to pay to make use of someone else's money, usually calculated as a percentage of the loan. **Interests** a group of people with a special concern for something, for example, farming interests.

interior inland area, far from the coast.

internal affairs anything that goes on strictly within one country.

investor someone who puts money into a business in the hope of making a profit.

isolationism the political belief that the country should look after its own needs and not form ties with other countries.

issue a point to be debated; a problem.

job market the number and range of jobs available at any one time.

jockeying competing as in a horse race; trying to get into the best position.

journalism the work of writing for, editing, managing, or producing a newspaper or magazine.

judicial having to do with courts, judges, or the administration of justice.

jury a group of citizens chosen to hear evidence in a trial and to decide whether the accused person is innocent or guilty.

juvenile delinquency crimes and violence committed by people too young to be tried in a regular court.

Kaiser the emperor of Germany.

laissez faire economic theory that the government should not interfere with business or industry.

Legal Aid free service of a lawyer provided to an accused person who cannot afford to pay for his or her defence in a court trial.

legal system organization of laws, courts, and the law enforcement in a city, province, or the whole country.

legislature provincial parliament.

legitimate rightful or lawful; allowed, acceptable.

liberation setting free.

lice small insects that live on the skin or in the hair of people or animals.

lieutenant governor the representative of the Queen and the Governor general in each province.

life span the length of time someone can be expected to live.

lime a type of white clay used in making plaster and cement.

livelihood the way people make their living.

locomotive train engine.

lord chancellor a very high-ranking British government official with important legal duties.

loyalty faithful support, especially for the government.

lure (*n*) pull, attraction; (*v*) attract, tempt.

majority more than half a group, especially more than half the members of parliament, as in *majority government*.

malfunctioning not working properly.

mammoth huge.

management 1) planning and directing; 2) the people in a business whose job is to plan and direct the operation.

mania great enthusiasm.

manifesto a statement of beliefs and policies by a political group.

manpower human strength; the number of people available to work.

manufacturer a person or company that makes a product on a large scale, usually in a factory.

margin a part payment to buy shares, the stock broker lending the remainder.

market any area where buying and selling is done on a regular basis.

marquis wheat a type of wheat, developed in Canada to grow well in the weather and soil conditions of the prairies.

mechanize to bring in machines to do a job that used to be done by hand.

Medicare health care paid for by the government.

military machine whole system of armies, ships, supplies, weapons, etc.

militia ordinary citizens trained to act as soldiers in an emergency.

mill a place where grain, etc. is ground up; any place that processes raw materials, e.g. a pulp and paper mill.

mine a place where coal, minerals, or ores are extracted from the ground.

minimum wage the amount set by law that is the least an employer is allowed to pay a worker.

minister a cabinet member who is responsible for a department, e.g. fisheries.

minority less than half of a group, especially less than half the members of parliament, as in minority government.

missile a self-propelled bomb or rocket.

missionary someone who goes to a distant country to spread a religion.

mobilize set in motion; prepare for war.

morality ideas about right and wrong; standards of behaviour.

mortgage a contract in which money lent for the purchase of a house or other property on the understanding that the lender may take over the property if the loan is not repaid.

mosaic something that is made up of many separate, distinct pieces.

motto a special saying that goes with a coat of arms.

mower a machine for cutting hay, grass, etc.

multicultural including or representing many different cultures.

multiracial including or representing many different races.

municipal of a town or city.

munitions guns and ammunition.

nation a country or the people of a particular country; a group of people with a common origin and strong cultural ties, e.g. the Dene nation, the French-Canadian nation.

nationalism patriotic feelings or efforts; desire and plans for independence; the desire of a people to preserve its own language, religion, traditions, etc.

nationalize to place an industry or resource under government (as opposed to private) management by "buying it out" or, in some countries, simply taking it over.

Native Peoples the first inhabitants of a country — i.e., of Canada — the Indian and Inuit peoples.

Nazi (national socialist) supporter of an extreme type of fascism that dominated Germany from 1933 to 1945, under Adolf Hitler.

neutral not taking sides in a dispute or war.

nomadic leading a wandering life, with no fixed home.

no man's land the stretch of land between two opposing armies, which is controlled by neither.

nominate suggest a person to represent a political party in an election.

non-renewable resources natural materials, like oil and other minerals, that do not grow back after they have been used up.

non-white term used to refer to skin colour in mainly "white" societies.

nostalgia a longing for the past, often remembered as better or happier than it really was.

nuclear power energy created when the central "nucleus" of an atom is split, or when atoms are fused.

observers people who study and analyse various current events, usually political.

occupied Europe the part of Europe under the control of Germany and its allies during World War II.

offensive attack or movement toward a goal.

offset to balance or make up for weakness or strength.

oil refinery an industrial plant where crude oil is made into gasoline, heating oil, kerosene, solvents, etc.

opposition members of parliament who do not belong to the governing party.

optimism a hopeful outlook, expecting the best.

ore a rock or other natural substance that contains a metal.

output the amount of goods produced.

overproduce to produce more of something than you can sell.

pacifist someone who believes in solving all problems peacefully, and is especially opposed to war.

pancreas the gland in the body that produces insulin to control the blood sugar levels.

parachute a large, frameless umbrella used to slow the fall of a body through the air.

paratroopers soldiers brought in by aircraft who parachute into battle.

parliament the highest lawmaking body in certain countries.

parole a conditional release from prison or jail before the full term has been served.

partisans strong supporters; organized but unofficial army that fights to drive out a foreign invader who controls the country.

patriotism strong love and support for one's country.

patronage the power to give jobs or favours, especially political jobs for favours done to help the person(s) in power.

pavilion a large tent or other structure used for displays at fairs or exhibitions.

pawns people who are used by others for selfish purposes.

peasants farm workers or farming families without very much money. Also used to mean poor, uneducated country people.

pension money paid regularly to certain people, e.g. the elderly, the disabled, the retired.

pessimism a hopeless outlook, expecting the worst.

phenomenon a remarkable event, occurence, or object.

phonograph a record-player.

pick a pointed tool used for breaking rock or ground.

picric acid a chemical used in making explosives.

pioneer someone who settles in a new region, e.g. the prairies; someone who investigates a new field of research, e.g. nuclear medicine.

pith helmet a light fibre helmet worn for protection from the sun.

platform things that a political party or candidate promises to do when and if elected.

plead to argue a civil or criminal case in a court of law.

pledge a promise.

plough a tool for breaking up soil (so seeds can be planted).

pluralistic a society where various religions, ethnic, racial, and political groups live in the same community.

policy a plan of action, especially in government.

political concerned with ideas of government.

polling station temporary office set up for election day where people go to vote in municipal, provincial, or federal elections.

pollution the presence of damaging chemicals and other inpurities in the air, land, or water.

poverty the state of having very few of life's necessities (food, shelter, clothing).

prejudice an opinion (usually bad) formed before one has had time to judge someone or something fairly.

premier person who leads the government in any one of the Canadian provinces.

primary industries industries that harvest natural resources, e.g. mining, farming, fishing, lumbering; compare with *secondary industries*.

privy council a committee of high government officials appointed to advise the monarch or the governor general.

processing treatment that turns raw materials into finished products.

profiteers people who try to make unfair profits by taking advantage of others' needs in time of war and disaster.

prohibition a total ban on making and selling alcohol.

propaganda a systematic plan to persuade people that one political outlook is better than all others, using radio, T.V., the press, and other means.

propeller a set of rotating blades that moves a boat or plane through water or air.

property any possession, such as jewels, house, land, or money.

prosecute to take legal action against someone for a crime or other wrongdoing.

prospector someone who searches for valuable mineral deposits.

prosperity well-being, wealth.

public service workers for the Canadian government.

pulp a soggy mixture of wood fibres used to make paper.

quintuplets five babies born to one mother at one time.

rabble-rouser someone who excites crowds in order to cause a riot.

racial connected with race, colour, or nationality.

racism prejudice or hatred based on race, colour, or nationality.

radiation the energy released during a nuclear reaction or explosion that can harm or change living tissue.

ration (*v*) to divide something scarce (such as food or gas) into equal portions; (*n*) a portion or allowance.

raw materials the unprocessed materials used to make finished products, e.g. wood for paper or furniture.

rebellion an organized attempt to overthrow a government.

recession period of temporary business decline, shorter and less extreme than a depression.

reciprocity an agreement between two countries to allow imports and exports with few restrictions.

recreational facilities parks, swimming pools, community centres, etc. that are provided for pleasure and relaxation.

recruit (*v*) to enlist or hire people to join the army or navy; (*n*) a person who has just been hired in this way.

referendum a vote by all people to accept or reject a government proposal. Also called a *plebiscite*.

reformers people who want to change society or government for the better.

refugees people who have had to leave their countries to escape cruel treatment because of political disagreement with the government, other dangers, or war.

rehabilitation restoring a person to more acceptable behaviour and attitudes before that person leaves prison and returns to society.

relief money, food, or clothes provided to people in need. The modern equivalent of "relief" is "welfare."

renewable resources natural products, like lumber or fish, that can grow again as they are used.

representative someone chosen by a group of people to speak for them and make decisions on their behalf.

resistance organized secret groups working to throw out a foreign invader who controls the country, e.g. the French or Yugoslav resistance during World War II.

resource useful natural product such as oil, fish, iron ore, water, wood;

resource industry industry that uses and depends on natural resources.

revenue money collected by governments by taxation of the citizens of that country or state.

revitalization bringing back to live.

revolution the overthrow of a government by some of the people.

riding a political division (based on the number of residents) represented by a member of parliament or a member of the legislative assembly (see *constituency*).

rights the opportunities and standards of treatment that every human being should be able to claim.

riot wild, often violent outburst by a large group of people.

role a part someone plays and the duties it involves.

royal commission an investigative group set up to study some matter or problem on behalf of the government and to make a report recommending suitable action.

rural to do with the country, or farms; compare with *urban*.

sabotage deliberate damage, especially in war, to anything the enemy might use for military purposes.

sandbag a small sack filled with sand; used to build military defences or to hold back a flood.

sanction permission with authority, approval; an action against a country by other countries to force it to obey international law.

sanitation clean, healthy habits and facilities like running water and proper waste disposal.

satellite a small body that revolves around a larger one, e.g. the moon, or a space station around the Earth.

scapegoat someone who is made to bear the blame for another person's mistakes or crimes.

schooner a type of sailing ship with two or more masts and sets of sails.

scrutineer party member who attends at election polling stations to see that no irregularities happen.

secondary industries industries that use natural products to manufacture things, such as cars and radios. Compare with *primary industries*.

security safety; the safe-keeping of a nation's secrets about defence or other matters.

seeder a farm machine for sowing seed.

self-government government of a region by the people who live there.

self-sufficient able to live and function without help from others.

Senate the second or "upper" branch of many legislatures, such as the Canadian Parliament or the U.S. Congress.

separatism movement to separate Quebec from the rest of Canada and give it political independence.

sequence the order in which things occur, one after another.

services industries or businesses that supply service (rather than things) such as dry cleaning and education.

settlers people who go to a new area and make their homes there; pioneers; colonists.

shares equal parts of the ownership of a business; people who buy these shares are called *shareholders.*

shell ammunition fired from large guns containing explosives, etc.

shrapnel pieces of metal hurled out in all directions by a special type of shell that explodes in the air or on impact.

sickle a tool with a curved blade for cutting grass or grain.

significance importance, meaning.

silicon chip a tiny wafer with a greatly reduced photographic engraving of an electronic circuit on its surface. These chips are used to reduce the size and weight of the circuitry used in computers, thus increasing the variety and complexity of the jobs computers can do.

sit-in a lot of people sitting down in a public place to cause inconvenience, to demonstrate for a cause, such as civil rights, peace, etc.

skilled specially trained for certain types of work (plumbing, car maintenance, etc.)

slum area of a city where poor people live crowded together, often in unsanitary housing.

slump a period when business is poor and there are fewer jobs.

smelter a furnace in which metal ores are melted down to separate the metal from the rock, etc.

sniper someone who shoots from a hidden place.

social of or about human beings living together as a group.

socialism a political and economic system in which property and business are owned by the community rather than individuals, and all people share in both the work and the profits.

society *1)* all the people in a community or country; *2)* a group of people with similar interests, attitudes, or standards of living.

sodbuster settler on the Prairies who broke up the sod in order to prepare the land for raising crops.

solidarity standing together; loyalty among people who have common problems or goals.

soup kitchen a place where soup or other food is served to the poor or homeless.

sovereignty supreme power or authority; the quality of being sovereign over oneself.

spearhead to lead an attack.

spiral winding or twisting round and round, like a spring.

stalemate a stage in an argument, war, or discussion when neither side is willing or able to make a move.

standard of living the level at which a person (or the average person in a group or country) lives, with respect to food, shelter, and the variety and quality of goods and services that can be expected.

state a nation (e.g. the state of Japan) or a political unit within a nation (e.g. the state of Kansas); the government of a nation.

status rank or position.

stock market the buying and selling of stocks and shares; the stock exchange is where this takes place.

strike a refusal by the workers to continue working.

stumbling block an obstacle or problem in the way of getting things done.

subsidy a grant or contribution of money, expecially one made by government to support an industry or organization.

subsoil the layer of earth which lies just under the surface or topsoil.

suburbs the outskirts or outlying districts of a city.

supersonic faster than the speed of sound (some jet aircraft travel at supersonic speeds).

supertanker a huge ship designed to carry a large cargo of oil.

supply the money the government needs to run itself (run the Houses of Parliament, pay MPs salaries, and so on).

supreme court the highest, most authoritative law court in Canada; the "court of final appeal."

symbolic used as a symbol, representative.

synagogue a building for Jewish worship and instruction.

tank a huge armoured war vehicle designed to cross all sorts of rough territory.

tank traps obstacles (such as blocks of concrete placed close together) which tanks cannot pass.

tariff a special tax on imports and exports.

tax money paid to or collected by the government.

taxation the system of arranging and collecting taxes.

technology, technological use of up-to-date scientific know-how in industry and everyday life.

Telidon a two-way communication system developed in Canada using a combination of television and computers.

temperance *1)* refusal to use alcohol; *2)* use of moderation.

terrorism organized use of violence and illegal acts to create an atmosphere of great fear and to put pressure on the government.

thresher, threshing machine a machine for separating the edible part of a crop (the grain) from the plant stalks.

timber wood or trees.

TNT an explosive.

token something meaningless in itself which is meant to stand for something more important; a symbol.

totalitarian a dictatorial government that allows no competing political groups and that exercises rigid control of industry, the arts, etc.

traitor someone who does something to harm his or her own country, especially giving away its military or commercial secrets.

transcontinental spreading across a continent.

transistor a tiny device that controls electric current; used in many electric appliances, allowing them to be small.

transportation the means of moving lots of people or goods.

treadle a foot-operated lever that controls the part(s) of a machine that spins or turns.

treaty an agreement between two or more groups, which is supposed to solve their differences.

trench a long, narrow ditch dug in the ground.

trench warfare during World Wars I and II, soldiers dug trenches to camp in and walk along, so they couldn't be seen or shot at by the enemy.

trestles and ties the wood pieces that form the roadbed for a railway; ties lie crosswise under the steel track; trestles support bridges.

ultimatum a final statement of conditions, rejection of which may lead to breaking off of relations or sometimes to a declaration of war.

unemployment being out of work; a shortage of jobs.

unions organizations of workers in the same trade or working in the same industry.

united joined, sharing beliefs; sticking together.

unskilled with no special skill or job training.

urban in or relating to cities.

veto a legal and official refusal to allow a government bill or other proposal to take effect.

victim person harmed by a physical, economic, or political act.

violation the breaking of a law.

visible minority a group within a society that looks different because of skin colour, physical features, or clothing style.

voluntarily by one's own free choice; willingly.

volunteer one who offers to join the armed forces; one who works without pay for a service organization (Red Cross, political party, etc).

vote choose among political candidates in an election or between proposals in a meeting.

war effort the working together of armed forces, civilians, industry, and government when trying to win a war.

warrant a written order giving authority for doing something, such as arresting a suspect.

welfare state a state in which the government provides services for the people, such as health care, unemployment payment, old-age pensions.

will a legal declaration in which a person says what is to be done with his or her property after death.

witch-hunt an investigation of people, accusing them, with little evidence, of betraying the country; sometimes used to get rid of political opponents.

workforce all the workers of a nation.

zero hour the time set for an important event, such as an attack during war.

Index

Acknowledgements

Picture Credits: Illustrations are listed as they appear from top to bottom, in each column of the page. Unless otherwise identified, in the credits that follow, numbers preceded by C or PA refer to the National Archives of Canada (NAC) collection. Provincial Archives and Tourist Bureaus are identified by the initial(s) of the province followed by S and T respectively, e.g. AA, NBT. Other abbreviations used include: BQT — Bureau du Québec à Toronto: CN — Canadian National; DND — Department of National Defence; GA — Glenbow-Alberta Institute; IO — Imperial Oil; JCTA — James Collection, City of Toronto Archives; MTL, Metro Toronto Library Board; NFA — National Film Archives; OFL — Ontario Federation of Labour; PMO — Prime Minister's Office; SHF — Sports Hall of Fame; TY — Toronto Telegram Archives, York University.

Original Art: David Partington, pp 34-35, 92-93, 192-193, 254-255; Scott Caple, pp 64-65, 130-131; Dan Kewley, pp 164-165, 226-227, 315 (bottom); Penny Moir, 313, 315 (top), 316, 324, 331, 333.

Art Gallery: 4 Robert Stacey; 5 McMichael Canadian Collection; 6 Robarts Library; 7 Metro Toronto Library; 8 Glenbow-Alberta Institute, Robert Stacey; 9 Canadian War Museum; 10 Canadian War Museum, Robarts Library; 11 Canadian War Museum; 12 Robert Stacey; 13 Canadian Pacific; 14-15 Robarts Library; 16-17 Art Gallery of Ontario; 18 Hart House Permanent Collection, University of Toronto; 19 David Blackwood; 22-23 Wm. Kurelek Estate; 24 Western Producer Prairie Books; 25 Toronto-Dominion Bank Art Collection; 26 University of British Columbia; 27 Dr. Bernhard Cinader; 28 Arthur Horsfall; 30 Toronto-Dominion Bank Art Collection; 30 Radio Canada; 31 Toronto Dominion Bank Art Collection; 32 compiled by Robert Read.

Chapter 1, **A New Century 36** OA S 15070, C16378; **37** SA A6187, PAC 49972; **38** C681, NAC; **39** MA AA; **40** SA, PA88422, PAC 10400; **41** MA, PA41785; **42** GA NA1366-8, PA38590; **43** Eaton Archives, GA NA3403-13; **44** PA11566, PA42438; **45** PA61772, C56688; **46** United Church Archives, PA69966; **47** OA S2903, MA, PA60732; **50** MA, Ontario Hydro; **51** MTL, OA S13722; **52** PA38622; **53** C56695, General Motors, JCTA 42, PA37798; **54** Canadian War Museum J29642-2; **55** C2082, C5110; **56** JCTA; **57** JCTA 587, C17945; **59** Canadian Women's Movement Archives, C27674; **61** PA16831, OA 9066#14.

Chapter 2, **Canada Goes to War: 66** MTL, C89316; **68** PA4910, JCTA; **69** JCTA, PAC 2468; **70** PA683, PA648; **71** PA1398, PA1679, PA518, PA3737; **72** PA5001; **73** PA1879, PA1110, PA1332; **74** PA1654, PA25148; **75** GA NA1258-2; PA24363; **76-77** C19948; **77** JCTA 1782; **78** PA88504, PA42869; **79** JCTA, C95314, PA25180; **80** PA22784, PA156; **81** PA1368, PA4422; **82** C29484, C6859; **83** C12592, PA2318; **84** PA2946, JCTA, PA3270; **85** PA3842; **86** PA22997; **87** C24963; **89** JCTA 4007, PA74, Glenbow NA2001-14, PA83986; **91** PA3694.

Chapter 3, **Boom and Bust: 94** JCTA 906, PA33971; **95** JCTA, nk; **96** C37275, C39556; **97** nk, C66639; **98** C21569, Catherine Lyle Cleverdon; **99** MIL, C54523; **100** C56167, PA24412; **101** JCTA 1028, Eaton Archives; **102** PA30308, CN, CN, Grant McConachie; **103** Ontario Hydro, PACT, General Motors, CN, CN, CN; **104** Eaton Archives; **105** PA74716, PA86257, PA83988; **106** NFA, NFA; **107** NFA, NFA; **108** SHF, MTL, PAC 50440, SHF; **109** C4752, SHF, PA50338, SHF; **110** PA86236; **111** MTL; **112** GA ND3-6742; **115** GA 2496-1, MA; **116** C13236; **117** C24840; **118** C9064; **119** PA37922; **120** MTL; **121** C9339, C19518; **122** all NFA; **123** PA49651; MTL; **125** C29449; Air Canada 9944, University of Toronto.

Chapter 4, **The World at War: 132** C114781; **134** C16792, C16812; **135** C24954; **136** Roderick Stewart; **137** C24958; **138** DND/NAC PA 107907; **139** Bettman Archives/BBC Hulton V2394-M; **140** C29856; **141** C14160; **142** PA95708; **143** C33442, MTL; **144** C45026, C47402; **145** C46350, CBC; **146** MA; **147** DND/NAC PA107904; **148** PA108273, PA79525; **149** DND/NAC C107904, DND/PAC37479; **150** C92393; **151** C29452, C22001; **152** PA114482; **154** DND GM2243; **155** PA113697, DND ANP36701; **156** Yad Vashem; **158** TY; **159** TY, TY, C3570; **160** C25, MTL, MTL; **161** C29854, C29857, C29588; **162** C29866; **163** Vancouver Public Library #1384.

Chapter 5, **Midcentury: 166** TY; **167** C20049, C471; **168** C30760, C128080; **169** C17219; **170** AA P2733, TY; **171** C47009; **172** Ontario Hydro; **172-173** Map and graphs: St. Lawrence Seaway Authority: **173** JCTA 2140, **174-176** all TY; **177** TY, PA120148; C80883; **181** C15160, DND; **182** United Nations; **183** NAC; **184-185** all NDP Archives; **186** MA, MTL; **187** TY, TY; **188** PAC 26756, PAC 30084; **189** Expo 67, TY; **191** QT, MA.

Chapter 6, **Creative Tensions: 193** Darrell McCalla; **194** C27281; **195** C112579; **196** Canapress; **199** PA142625; **200** International Pipeline Ltd; **203** PMO; **204** DND; **207** David Smiley; **209** Employment and Immigration Canada; **210** Shing Wah Daily News, AT, Museum of Civilization, OT, MT; **210-211** QT; **211** OT, QT, NBT, Darrell McCalla; **212** Dept. of Indian Affairs and Northern Development, **214** IO, IO; **215** IO, West Baffin Eskimo Co-operative; **216** Canadian Women's Movement Archive; **218** Anthem Records Inc., Wally Ballach, MT, Graeme Gibson; **219** Stratford Festival; **220** Prudential Life; **221** Participaction, QT, D.J. Konihowski; **222** Petro-Canada; **225** JCTA.

Chapter 7, **Canada and the World: 228** United Nations Association of Canada; **229** UNICEF; **231** PA128825; **232** DND 12C75-365; **233** DND REC76-106, Lockheed; **235** Canapress; **236** both UNICEF; **237** Ken Bell, Torstar; **239** Canapress; **241** D. McCalla; **242** Torstar; **243** ROM, C6440, C DC8162-21, BCT, TY, Torstar, Time; **244** U.S. Consulate in Toronto, PA 117602, Dept. of External Affairs; **245** PMO, **247** Gord Marci, A & M Records, The Athletes Information Bureau, CBC, National Ballet of Canada, Alert Music; **248** Torstar.

Chapter 8, **One Nation or Two?: 256** QT; **257** NBT; **258** NAC: **259** MTL; **260** QT; **261** TY, PA 117531; **262-263** all TY; **264** BQT; **266** BQT, campaign buttons; **267** BQT, BQT: **268** TY; **269** MTL; **271** Valan Photos; **273** QT, QT, QT, Petro-Canada, Ville de Montréal, QT, QT, BQT.

Chapter 9, **Regional Report: 276** MA 73-5332; **277** QT; **278** MTL, Hudson's Bay Co.; **279** PA 116541, G.G. Graydon, Steven Bradley; **280** SA; **281** SA; **282** Picturesque Canada, BCT; **283** BCT, Rio Algom, BCT, BCT; **284-5** all BCT; **286** Picturesque Canada, AA; **287** AA, MT, SA R-A 9877 (5), AA; **288** SA; **289** IO; **290** BCT; **292** MTL, OT; **293** all OT; **294 SA; 289** IO; **290** BCT; **292** MTL, OT; **293** all OT; **294** Stelco; **295** OFL/Alan Pryde; **296** Picturesque Canada, Ville de Montréal; **297** QT, Denis Brodeur, Alcan, QT; **298** Techniques Audio-Visuelle; **299** QT, QT; **300** Picturesque Canada, NBT; **301** NBT, NBT, PEIT; **302** NBT; **303** PEIT; **304** George Draskoy; **305** Imperial Oil; **306** BCT, AT, ST; **307** QT, OT, NST.

Chapter 10, **Government in Canada: 310** SA 67-665-39, TY, WJL Gibbon; **311** Office of the Speaker of the Senate, Cavouk of the Colonnade, Cavouk, OFL/Alan Pryde, SA 67-665-39; **314** Environment Canada, Ontario Ministry of the Environment, Toronto Dept. of Public Works; **318** Canadian Press; **319** Canadian Unity Information Office; **327** Liberal Party; **328** Liberal Party; **329** Riding office, Liberal Party of Canada; **330** P.M.O.; **332** John Crosbie's office, Liberal Party, Dept. of Employment & Immigration, Dept of External Affairs; **334** Canapress; **335** John Turner's office, New Democratic Party; **336** Lorna Marsden's office, Harold Clark, Duff Roblin's office; **337** The Senate; **338** office of the Governor General; **339** Office of the Governor General; **341** Canadian Unity Information Office; **343** The Northern Light, Bathurst, N.B.; **344** Canapress; **348** Metro Toronto Police Dept.; **349** Metro Toronto Police Dept.; **352** R. English; **353** Darrell McCalla; **355** Darrell McCalla; **358** Metro Toronto Library Board; **363** PA61358.

Chapter 11, **Towards the Next Century: 367** NASA: **368** Northern Telecom 44633-2, NASA courtesy Spar Aerospace; **369** Northern Telecom, OT 6-J-0171; **370** Canapress, **372** OT7902001, MT OT77080518; **373** Ontario Hydro 7A19508, IO 80-1199; **374** United Nations; **375** AT, CN 69799-4; **376** MTL; **377** Oakville Journal Record/Pete Martin.

Text Credits: p 368, p 369 from articles by Craig McInness in the Globe and Mail.